CLASSICAL CONTRIBUTIONS

CLASSICAL CONTRIBUTIONS

Studies in honour of
Malcolm Francis McGregor

Edited by

GORDON SPENCER SHRIMPTON
and
DAVID JOSEPH McCARGAR †

J. J. AUGUSTIN · LOCUST VALLEY, NEW YORK
1981

CONTRIBUTORS

Mrs. Guy F. Atkinson
  (*in memoriam* D. J. McCargar)
Bishop's University
  (*in memoriam* D. J. McCargar)
C. G. Boulter
R. J. Buck
J. L. Caskey
J. A. Evans
Gary Ferngren
John Humphrey
Mrs. Z. Karapa-Molizani
Walter G. Koerner
The Koerner Foundation
D. R. Laing
R. J. Lenardon
H. Mattingly
H. McGregor Attwood
R. Rob McGregor
Benjamin D. Meritt
Lucy Shoe Meritt
Ruth Moorman

Ruth Pavlantos
A. J. Podlecki
A. E. and Isabella Raubitschek
James Russell
Joan Sandilands
R. Sealey
Brent Sinclair
Wesley Thompson
C. R. Trahman
John S. Traill
The University of British Columbia
The University of Cincinnati,
  Classics Department
The University of Victoria B.C.
Vancouver Community College (Langara)
Eugene Vanderpool
M. B. Walbank
M. B. Wallace
H. D. Westlake
A. G. Woodhead

TABLE OF CONTENTS

FOREWORD

Malcolm Francis McGregor B.A., M.A.,
Ph.D., D.Litt., D.C.L., F.R.S.C.,
Professor of Classics Emeritus,
University of British Columbia.

It is a pleasure and privilege to present to this man and to the scholarly world this superb collection of essays. It commemorates his seventieth birthday, May 19, 1980. If his next seventy years are as productive as his first, the scholarly world will be a richer place indeed. In blood a Scot, by birth a Londoner, and a Canadian by adoption he displays most of the best attributes we associate with these nations, and if he seems to have some of their bad ones it is more in the minds of people who do not understand his outspoken frankness than in reality.

From King George High School in Vancouver, B.C. he went to the University of British Columbia. There he became a Classicist under the gentle, guiding hand of H. T. Logan (there could have been no better), completing his B.A. in 1930 and his M.A. in 1931. McGregor began work on his Ph.D. at Michigan in 1931, but in 1933 he made the decisive move to Cincinnati. U.B.C. made him a Classicist, now emerges the epigraphist-historian, and, ultimately, the complete Malcolm McGregor. His work at Cincinnati culminated in the Ph.D. (1937), but it also involved him with A. B. West and thence with the production of B. D. Meritt's brainchild, *The Athenian Tribute Lists* (the story is told in the Preface to *ATL* 1). The year 1937–1938 saw McGregor closeted with the father of modern Greek epigraphy B. D. Meritt, and the brilliant historian H. T. Wade-Gery, as member of the Institute for Advanced Study, Princeton, for the production of *ATL* 1. His capacity for devoting huge amounts of energy to more than one task at a time was evident even then, for on 8 June 1938 he married his wife and life-long companion Marguerite. At the University of Cincinnati he began his distinguished teaching career in 1936 as Acting Instructor. In 1947 Wade-Gery, Meritt, and McGregor were together again for a year, preparing *ATL* 2 and 3. In 1954, he left for U.B.C., a full Professor of Classics and Ancient History, having served Cincinnati as Acting Dean of the Graduate School of Arts and Sciences (1941–1942). Here he became the man David and I were to meet. Head of the Department of Classics from 1954 until his retirement, and Assistant to the Dean of Arts and Science (1956–1964), then Director of Residences (1965–1968), and Director of Ceremonies (1968–1977). He was in Britain in 1961 as Visiting Professor of Classics at Oxford, Cambridge and London, invited by the British Council. Again in 1967/68, he was in Athens as Visiting Professor to the American School of Classical Studies studying Greek letter-forms with Donald W. Bradeen, his friend since 1939, and successor at the University of Cincinnati. This was a most fruitful collaboration. It gave the world *Studies in Fifth-Century Attic Epigraphy* (1974), and together they began editing Phoros, *Tribute to Benjamin Dean Meritt,* whose publication Bradeen did not live to see.

McGregor has served the cause of Classics in Canada exceptionally well. He is the tireless supporter of any and every Classical Association for which he is eligible. In 1969/70 he was President of the Classical Association of Canada (in the same year he presided over the American Philological Association and the Canadian Field Hockey Association). *Phoenix,* the journal of the Classical Association of Canada, is one of the world's finest. He has served often on the editorial board. He has done more.

From 1955 to 1960 McGregor served his community as member of the Board of Directors of the British Columbia Centennial Committee, and was called to the bar of the Provincial Legislature March 4, 1959. In 1967/68, he was Senior Fellow, Canada Council. In 1977/78 he was Chairman of the Joint Board of Teacher Education's Committee to study the "Education and Training of Teachers in British Columbia" (report submitted to the Minister of Education, June 8, 1978).

What has he been doing with his time? He has been an avid cricketer. He is Honorary Vice-President of the British Columbia Cricket Association and the British Columbia Mainland Cricket League. McGregor is not a man who experiences difficulty making up his mind. This quality has made all things possible for him, including his becoming one of the three Canadian, full members of the Association of Cricket Umpires. He is also a National Umpire in field hockey.

At present, McGregor is Honorary Professor of Humanities, University of Calgary (since 1978), Honorary President of the Classical Association of Canada (since 1977), Lecturer in History at Vancouver Community College, Langara, and member of the Managing Committee, American School of Classical Studies, Athens, but still an active scholar: for example, he is contributing (with B. D. Meritt) to the production of the third edition of *IG* 1. To date, this year he has delivered some thirty public lectures.

His energy has not gone unrecognized. He was John Simon Guggenheim Memorial Fellow in 1948, and received the Award of Merit from the American Philological Association in 1954. He won the Walter Koerner Master Teacher Award (1973), and the Queen's Jubilee Medal in 1977. Not surprisingly, the Hellenic community in Vancouver has honoured him, as has the Greek government, making him Commander, Order of the Phoenix (1979), the highest award it can offer a non-Greek.

All this is true. It is a life far larger then most, but the description still falls a good distance short of reality. Of these achievements he is justly proud, as he is of his impressive bibliography, but it may be a little surprising to know that he boasts of belonging to the oldest literary club in America (the Cincinnati Literary Club), and especially of having persuaded the American Philological Association to meet in Vancouver ("where it never snows") in 1978 after trying since 1959 (it was very cold, and it snowed).

I have experienced the warmth of his home, and the great-hearted hospitality of himself and his wife. His friends know that Marguerite has been an enormous help to him (no "flower in his lapel"), he alone knows how much. He is more: gentleman, father, the anachronism who still gives his clear and exciting college lectures in a chalky academic gown, lover of noisy (but friendly) arguments, and so on.

About the book that we are presenting to him a few brief remarks are appropriate. It was suggested to me by David McCargar about four years ago. David devoted much time and energy to it until sickness and death stopped him. I have tried to edit the book seeking to impose unobtrusively certain basic standards of format. These articles are, after all, gifts and I have felt it essential to do nothing to obliterate the characteristics, even idiosyncracies of each author. I have been helped. Audrey Hlady-Rousseau read much of the early typescript. Her professional methods of correcting copy became a model for my own. Individual papers were read for me at varying stages of preparation by Professors H. H. Huxley and Phillip Harding, and my friend, Jane Cobb. To these people I owe much gratitude. I must also thank the Department of Classics here at the University of Victoria for making things easier for me in so many ways, particularly our secretary, Mrs. Nasser. The publisher, J. J. Augustin, has been generous and helpful in every respect. May all good books find such publishers!

27 October 1980.   GORDON S. SHRIMPTON

BIBLIOGRAPHY
of
MALCOLM FRANCIS McGREGOR

1933

"Eponymous Priests under the Ptolemies," *CP* 28, p. 131

1934

Review of E. R. Hardy, *The Large Estates of Byzantine Egypt, CP* 29, pp. 360–361

1935

"Note on New Readings in the *Lapis Primus*," *BSA* 33, pp. 135–136
"Kleon, Nikias, and the Trebling of the Tribute," *TAPA* 66, pp. 146–164

1936

"Loan of Money," *Papyry in the University of Michigan Collection* (*Michigan Papyri,* III) 222–225
    (with V. B. Schuman)

1938

"The Last Campaign of Kleon and the Athenian Calendar in 422/1 B.C.," *AJP* 59, pp. 145–168

1939

The Athenian Tribute Lists, 1 (Cambridge, Mass.) (with B. D. Meritt and H. T. Wade-Gery)

1940

Review of W. B. Dinsmoor, *The Athenian Archon List in the Light of Recent Discoveries, Classical Weekly* 34, pp. 65–67

1941

"The Pro-Persian Party at Athens from 510 to 480 B.C.," *HSCP*, Supplementary Volume 1,
    pp. 71–95
"Cleisthenes of Sicyon and the Panhellenic Festivals," *TAPA* 72, pp. 266–287

1942

Review of P. Roussel, *Sparte, AJP* 63, pp. 121–122
Review of A. T. Murray (translator and editor), *Demosthenes, Private Orations* 2–3 (*Loeb Classical Library*), *AJP* 63, pp. 367–368

1943

Review of B. D. Meritt, *Epigraphica Attica*, *AJP* 64, pp. 244–246

1944

Review of D. W. Prakken, *Studies in Greek Genealogical Chronology*, *AJP* 65, pp. 290–291
Review of J. H. Finley, Jr, *Thucydides*, *AJP* 65, pp. 181–185

1946

Review of A. W. Gomme, *A Historical Commentary on Thucydides* 1, *AJP* 67, pp. 268–275
Review of C. Callmer, *Studien zur Geschichte Arkadiens*, *Class. Week.* 49, p. 38

1947

Review of J. Burnham, *The Struggle for the World*, *Cincinnati Enquirer*, September 19, p. 68
Review of *The American Speeches of the Earl of Halifax*, *Cincinnati Enquirer*, September 19, p. 68
Review of H. And H. A. Frankfort, J. A. Wilson, T. Jacobsen, W. A. Irwin, *The Intellectual Adventure of Ancient Man*, *Cincinnati Enquirer*, November 12, p. 7
Review of A. P. Dorjahn, *Political Forgiveness in Old Athens: The Political Amnesty of 403 B.C.*, *Class. Week.* 41, pp. 108–109

1948

Review of L. E. Lord, *Thucydides and the World War*, *Class. Week.* 41, pp. 139–141
Review of L. E. Lord, *Thucydides and the World War*, *AJP* 69, pp. 105–108
Review of H. D. Sedgwick, *Horace, A Biography*, *Cincinnati Enquirer*, March 9, p. 10
Review of F. Neilson, *Modern Man and the Liberal Arts*, *Cincinnati Enquirer*, July 8, p. 7
Review of S. Buchanan (editor), *The Portable Plato*, *Cincinnati Enquirer*, October 28, p. 7

1949

The Athenian Tribute Lists, 2 (Princeton, N.J.) (with B. D. Meritt and H. T. Wade-Gery)
Review of A.-J. Festugière, *Liberté et civilisation chez les Grecs*, *AJP* 70, pp. 332–334
Review of J. de Romilly, *Thucydide et l'impérialisme athenian*, *AJP* 70, pp. 105–107
Review of R. Allendy, *The Treason Complex*, *Cincinnati Enquirer*, February 12, p. 6
Review of F. R. Cowell, *Cicero and the Roman Republic*, *Cincinnati Enquirer*, March 5, p. 5
Review of M. Radin, *Epicurus My Master*, *Cincinnati Enquirer*, April 9, p. 5
Review of W. K. Pritchett and O. Neugebauer, *The Calendars of Athens*, *AJP* 70, pp. 422–425

1950

The Athenian Tribute Lists 3 (Princeton, N.J.) (with B. D. Meritt and H. T. Wade-Gery)
Review of P. Friedländer and H. B. Hoffleit, *Epigrammata*, *AJA* 54, pp. 151–152
Review of G. Boas, *The Hieroglyphics of Horapollo*, *Cincinnati Enquirer*, June 24, p. 5
Review of A. H. Chase and W. G. Perry (trans.), *The Iliad*, *Cincinnati Enquirer*, June 25, p. 5
Review of V. Martin, *La vie internationale dans la Grèce des cités (VIe–IVe s. av. J. C.)*, *AJP* 71, pp. 445–447

1951

Review of A. L. Whall (ed.), *The Greek Reader*, *Cincinnati Enquirer*, February 13
Review of T. J. Haarhoff, *The Stranger at the Gate*, *AJP* 72, pp. 206–208
Review of W. Schmid, *Geschichte der griechischen Literatur*, 1., 5 (2., 2), *AJP* 72, p. 451

1952

Review of A. E. Raubitschek, *Dedications from the Athenian Akropolis, CP* 47, pp. 32–35

Review of B. Davenport (ed.), *The Portable Roman Reader, Cincinnati Enquirer,* February 12, p. 7

Review of K. von Fritz and E. Kapp (trans. and eds), *Aristotle's Constitution of Athens and Related Texts, Class. Week.* 45, pp. 202–203

Review of G. E. Mylonas (ed.), *Studies Presented to David Moore Robinson, Classical Bulletin* 28, p. 70

Review of A. S. L. Farquharson, *Marcus Aurelius: His Life and His World, AHR* 57, pp. 721–722

Review of L. C. Stecchini, *Athenaion Politeia: The Constitution of the Athenians, Class. Week.* 45, p. 203

1953

The Athenian Tribute Lists 4 (Princeton, N.J.) (with B. D. Meritt and H. T. Wade-Gery)

Review of D. Grene, *Man in His Pride, AJP* 74, pp. 179–183

Review of H. T. Wade-Gery, *The Poet of the Iliad, Class. Week.* 46, p. 227

Review of G. Walter, *Caesar, Phoenix* 7, pp. 118–119

Review of H. Michell, *Sparta, Phoenix* 7, pp. 166–168

1954

Review of E. Delebecque, *Euripide et la guerre du péloponnèse, AJP* 75, pp. 218–219

Review of C. Hignett, *A History of the Athenian Constitution to the End of the Fifth Century* B.C., *Phoenix* 8, pp. 112–114

1955

Review of A. W. Gomme, *The Greek Attitude to Poetry and History, AJP* 76, pp. 329–330

1956

"The Politics of the Historian Thucydides," *Phoenix,* 10, pp. 93–102; reprinted in D. Kagan, *Problems in Ancient History* 1, *The Ancient Near East and Greece,* pp. 291–293; and J. N. Claster, *Athenian Democracy: Triumph or Travesty?,* 77–83

Review of A. D. Winspear (trans.), *Lucretius, the Roman Poet of Science, Vancouver Herald,* February 4, p. 16

Review of A. D. Winspear (trans.), *Lucretius, the Roman Poet of Science, Vancouver Province,* March 4, B.C. *Magazine,* p. 14

Review of O. Luschnat (ed.), *Thucydidis Historiae* 1 (*Bibliotheca Teubneriana*), *Phoenix* 10, pp. 37–38

Review of J. A. O. Larsen, *Representative Government in Greek and Roman History, Phoenix* 10, pp. 44–46

Review of B. Hemmerdinger, *Essai sur l'histoire du texte de Thucydide, AJP* 77, pp. 323–325

Review of C. Meyer, *Die Urkunden im Geschichtswerk des Thukydides, AJP* 77, pp. 442–443

Review of A. Andrewes, *The Greek Tyrants, Class. Week.* 50, p. 4

1957

Review of J. Bérard, *La colonisation grecque de l'Italie méridionale et de la Sicile dans l'antiquité: l'histoire et la légende, AHR* 63, pp. 90–91

1958

Review of A. W. Gomme, *A Historical Commentary on Thucydides* 2 & 3, *AJP* 79, pp. 416–423
Review of W. H. D. Rouse (trans.), *The March Up Country, A Translation of Xenophon's Anabasis, Vancouver Province,* May 3, p. 17

1959

"Thucydides and A. W. Gomme," *Phoenix* 13, pp. 58–68
Review of F. E. Adcock, *The Greek and Macedonian Art of War, Phoenix* 13, pp. 88–89
Review of A. H. M. Jones, *Athenian Democracy, AHR* 65, pp. 984–985

1960

"Kleisthenes: Eponymous Archon 525/4 B.C.," *Phoenix* 14, pp. 27–35 (with C. W. J. Eliot)
Review of A. G. Woodhead, *The Study of Greek Inscriptions, CJ* 55, pp. 285–286
Review of H. Lamb, *Cyrus the Great, Classical World* 54, pp. 60–61
Review of J. LaBarbe, *La loi navale de Thémistocle, AJP* 81, pp. 439–442
Review of N. G. L. Hammond, *A History of Greece to 322 B.C., Phoenix* 14, pp. 245–247

1961

Review of N. G. L. Hammond, *A History of Greece to 332 B.C., AHR* 67, pp. 420–421
Review of E. W. Bodnar, *Cyriacus of Ancona and Athens, CJ* 56, pp. 236–237
Review of *Harvard Studies in Classical Philology* 68 (1958), *CJ* 56, pp. 234–235

1962

"The Ninth Prescript of the Attic Quota-Lists," *Phoenix* 16, pp. 267–275
Review of B. D. Meritt, *The Athenian Year, AHR* 66, pp. 462–463
Review of S. Barr, *The Will of Zeus: a History of Greece from the Origins of Hellenic Culture to the Death of Alexander, CJ* 57, pp. 366–367
Review of S. Barr, *The Will of Zeus: a History of Greece from the Origins of Hellenic Culture to the Death of Alexander, Vancouver Sun,* March 7, p. 5
Review of A. Mannzmann, *Griechische Stiftungsurkunden: Studie zu Inhalt und Rechtsform, Class. World* 55, p. 257
Review of F. J. Stein, *Dexippus et Herodianus rerum scriptores quatenus Thucydidem secuti sunt, AJP* 83, p. 333

1963

Review of J. J. Buchanan, *Theorika: a Study of Monetary Distributions to the Athenian Citizenry during the Fifth and Fourth Centuries B.C., CJ* 58, pp. 228–229
Review of C. Hignett, *Xerxes' Invasion of Greece, Class. World* 56, pp. 288–289
Review of P. Sattler, *Studien aus dem Gebiet der alten Geschichte, Class. World* 57, pp. 24–28
Review of J. Day and M. Chambers, *Aristotle's History of Athenian Democracy, CJ* 59, pp. 79–80
Review of A. W. Gomme, *More Essays in Greek History and Literature, Phoenix* 17, pp. 310–311

1964

Review of J. A. Alexander, *Potidaea: Its History and Remains, Class. World* 57, pp. 254–255
Review of F. E. Adcock, *Thucydides and His History, AHR* 69, pp. 725–726
Review of J. L. Benson, *Ancient Leros, Class. World* 57, p. 351
Review of J. de Romilly, *Thucydides and Athenian Imperialism* (trans. P. Thody), *AHR* 70, pp. 104–105

Review of A. S. Graf von Stauffenberg, *Trinacria: Sizilien und Großgriechenland in archaischer und frühklassischer Zeit, Class. World* 58, p. 13

Review of J. de Romilly (trans. and ed.), *Thucydide: la guerre du Péloponnèse, livre II, AJP* 85, pp. 448–449

Review of R. M. Haywood, *Ancient Greece and the Near East, Class. World* 58, p. 47

Review of R. N. Frye, *The Heritage of Persia, CJ* 60, p. 88

1965

"The Genius of Alkibiades," *Phoenix* 19, pp. 27–46

Review of J. Boardman, *The Greeks Overseas, CJ* 60, pp. 280–282

Review of W. K. Pritchett, *Ancient Athenian Calendars on Stone, AHR* 71, p. 840

Review of A. J. Graham, *Colony and Mother City in Ancient Greece, Class. World* 58, pp. 240, 254

Review of F. E. Adcock, *Thucydides and His History, AJP* 86, pp. 326–328

Review of C. G. Starr, *A History of the Ancient World, Class. World* 59, p. 10

Review of M. Amit, *Athens and the Sea: A Study in Athenian Sea-Power, Phoenix* 19, pp. 251–252

Review of A. French, *The Growth of the Athenian Economy, Class. Journ.* 61, pp. 77–78

1966

"Methods and Manners in Greek Epigraphy," *Phoenix* 20, pp. 210–227

Review of M. C. Astour, *Hellenosemitica: An Ethnic and Cultural Study in West Semitic Impact on Mycenaean Greece, AHR* 72, pp. 521–522

Review of D. Kagan, *The Great Dialogue: History of Greek Political Thought from Homer to Polybius, CJ* 61, pp. 378–379

Review of K. J. Dover, *Thucydides, Book VI* and *Thucydides, Book VII, Phoenix* 20, p. 182

1967

Athenian Policy, at Home and Abroad (University of Cincinnati)

"The Postscript of the First Attic Quota-List," *GRBS* 8, pp. 103–112

"The Athenian Quota-List of 421/0 B.C.," *Phoenix* 21, pp. 85–91 (with B. D. Meritt)

Review of W. Culican, *The Medes and Persians, CJ* 62, pp. 182–183

Review of G. L. Huxley, *The Early Ionians, Class. World* 60, p. 255

Review of R. Carpenter, *Beyond the Pillars of Hercules: The Classical World Seen Through the Eyes of Its Discoverers, Class. World* 60, pp. 327, 347

Review of C. Roebuck, *The World of Ancient Times, CJ* 62, pp. 372–373

Review of P. J. Fliess, *Thucydides and the Politics of Bipolarity, Phoenix* 21, pp. 306–309

Review of W. H. McNeill, *A World History, Class. World* 61, pp. 8–9

Review of E. Badian (ed.), *Ancient Society and Institutions; Studies Presented to Victor Ehrenberg on His 75th Birthday, AHR* 73, pp. 110–111

1968

Review of E. Delebecque, *Thucydide et Alcibiade, AJP* 89, pp. 118–119

Review of S. Frere, *Britannia: A History of Roman Britain, AHR* 73, p. 782

1969

"The Two Rs: Role and Relevance," *Proceedings, Brock Latin Institute* (August, 1969), pp. 1–13

Review of H. Bengtson (*et alii*), *The Greeks and the Persians: From the Sixth to the Fourth Centuries, Class World* 72, p. 192

Review of H.-P. Drögemüller, *Syrakus: zur Topographie und Geschichte einer griechischen Stadt mit einem Anhang zur Thucydides 6, 96ff., und Livius 24.25, Class. World 63, p. 90*

Review of V. Ehrenberg, *From Solon to Socrates: Greek History and Civilization during the Sixth and Fifth Centuries B.C., Classical News and Views* 13, pp. 99–100

Review of H. D. Westlake, *Individuals in Thucydides, Phoenix* 23, pp. 395–397

1970

"Tribute Lists," in N. G. L. Hammond and H. H. Scullard (eds), *The Oxford Classical Dictionary*^{2}, p. 1093

Review of D. Kagan, *The Outbreak of the Peloponnesian War, Class. World* 63, pp. 201–202

Review of R. Meiggs and D. M. Lewis, *A Selection of Greek Historical Inscriptions to the End of the Fifth Century B.C., Phoenix* 124, pp. 176–282

Review of R. S. Stroud, *Drakon's Law on Homicide, Class. World* 64, p. 129

1971

"The Athenian Quota-List of 421/0 B.C.," *AJA* 75, pp. 91–92 (with B. D. Meritt)

"Democracy: Its Admirers and Its Critics," *Classical News and Views* 15, pp. 53–63

Review of A. G. Woodhead, *Thucydides on the Nature of Power, Phoenix* 25, pp. 76–78

Review of H.-P. Stahl, *Thukydides: die Stellung des Menschen im geschichtlichen Prozeß, AJP* 92, p. 757

Review of P. Green, *Xerxes at Salamis, American Classical Review* 1, p. 168

1972

Review of C. W. Fornara, *Herodotus: An Interpretative Essay, AHR* 77, pp. 1096–1097

Review of D. C. Kurtz and J. Boardman, *Greek Burial Customs, Class. World* 66, p. 188

Review of P. Deane, *Thucydides' Dates 465–431 B.C., Phoenix* 26, pp. 295–297

Review of P. Huart, *Le vocabulaire de l'analyse psychologique dans l'oeuvre de Thucydide, AJP* 93, pp. 641–642

Review of W. R. Connor, *The New Politicians of Fifth-Century Athens, American Classical Review* 2, pp. 148–149

Review of M. Miller, *The Thalassocracies: Studies in Chronography* 2, *American Classical Review* 2, p. 226

1973

Studies in Fifth-Century Attic Epigraphy (Norman, Oklahama) (With D. W. Bradeen)

"The Handmaiden of History," *Transactions of the Royal Society of Canada* 11, pp. 229–242

"Athenian Policy, at Home and Abroad," *Lectures in Memory of Louise Taft Semple*, Second Series, 1969–1970 (*University of Cincinnati Classical Studies* 2), pp. 51–84 (See under 1967)

Review of A. W. Gomme, K. J. Dover, A. Andrewes, *A Historical Commentary on Thucydides* 4, *Phoenix* 27, pp. 395–398

Review of R. A. Tomlinson, *Argos and the Argolid: From the End of the Bronze Age to the Roman Occupation, American Classical Review* 3, p. 101

1974

ΦΟΡΟΣ: *Tribute to Benjamin Dean Meritt* (Locust Valley, New York) (Edited, with D. W. Bradeen)

"The Join in IG I^2, 55," in D. W. Bradeen and M. F. McGregor (eds), ΦΟΡΟΣ: *Tribute to Benjamin Dean Meritt*, pp. 101–106 with Plate XV

"Phormion and Peisistratos," *Phoenix* 28, pp. 18–21

"Solon's Archonship: the Epigraphic Evidence," in J. A. S. Evans (ed.), *Polis and Imperium: Studies in Honour of Edward Togo Salmon*, pp. 31–34

Review of H. A. Thompson and R. E. Wycherley, *The Athenian Agora 14: The Agora of Athens, the History, Shape and Uses of an Ancient City Center*, *Phoenix* 28, pp. 254–256

1975

Review of W. B. Stanford and J. V. Luce, *The Quest for Ulysses*, *Vancouver Sun*, April 11, p. 33 A

Review of J. M. Scott, *Boadicea*, *Vancouver Sun*, June 27, p. 30

1976

"The New Fragment of the Fifteenth Quota-List," *Hesperia* 45, pp. 171–172 with Plates 27, 28

"The Attic Quota-List of 453/2 B.C.," *Hesperia* 45, pp. 280–282 with Plates 63–66

Review of D. Kagan, *The Archidamian War*, *Class. World* 70, p. 219

Review of J. D. Mikalson, *The Sacred and Civil Calendar of the Athenian Year*, *Classical News and Views* 20, pp. 107–108

Review of J. S. Traill, *The Political Organization of Attica: a Study of the Demes, Trittyes, and and Phylai, and their Representation in the Athenian Council*, *JHS* 96, p. 225

Review of B. D. Meritt and J. S. Traill, *The Athenian Councillors*, *JHS* 96, p. 264

Review of S. V. Tracy, *The Lettering of an Athenian Mason*, *JHS* 96, pp. 264–265

Review of W. K. Pritchett, *Dionysius of Halicarnassus: on Thucydides*, *Phoenix* 30, pp. 399–400

1977

Review of S. V. Tracy, *The Lettering of an Athenian Mason*, *Phoenix* 31, pp. 174–179

Review of Raphael Sealey, *A History of the Greek States 700–338 B.C.*, *Phoenix* 31, pp. 367–369

1978

"King Nestor's Surgeon," *Faculty Affairs* Vancouver Community College, Langara), 10. 7, pp. 11–12

1979

"The Flexible Mind," in John Woods and Harold G. Coward (eds), *Humanities in the Present Day*, 93–101

THE HOPLITE *KATALOGOS*

Aischines at 2.167–168 describes his military service, and begins with his two years among the *peripoloi;* πρώτην δ' ἐξελθὼν στρατείαν τὴν ἐν τοῖς μέρεσι καλουμένην, he was praised for his performance in a situation of some danger; καὶ τὰς ἄλλας τὰς ἐκ διαδοχῆς ἐξόδους τὰς ἐν τοῖς ἐπωνύμοις καὶ τοῖς μέρεσιν ἐξῆλθον, after which he turns to particular battles. He does not explain the distinction between these two forms of service, which we must presume was immediately intelligible to his audience.

For the second system, some explanation is provided in *Ath. Pol.* 53.4 and 7, cited by Harpokration s.v. στρατεία ἐν τοῖς ἐπωνύμοις to explain the passage from Aischines. Aristotle's mind was here principally on the *diaitetai,* men in their sixtieth year, and this leads him to explain the system of age-groups: ephebes were listed both under their tribal eponyms and under the archon in whose year they were enrolled, there were 42 years in the list, and the senior age-group of the current year passed on to become the *diaitetai* for the following year. Aristotle then adds that this list was also used for military expeditions, for which it was specified that the age-groups from a certain archon to another archon were to be called up. We have little further detail, but the outline of the system is clear enough.

The lexicographers did not take up ἐν τοῖς μέρεσι, except for a passage incongruously included in Suda s.v. τερθρεία, where it is stated that ephebes, after their service as *peripoloi,* could be called out in case of war, but served separately ἐν μέρεσι τοῖς ἀκινδύνοις τῆς μάχης, and this is the origin of the phrase. It is not explained what the danger-free areas of a battle may be, or how one might identify them beforehand. This satisfied *LSJ* (s.v. στρατεία 3);[1] but it looks to me more like an improvisation based on Aischines, neglecting the fact that he did run into danger on his first expedition, and that he served on other expeditions ἐν τοῖς μέρεσι besides his first.

More plausible is the view that ἐν τοῖς μέρεσι refers to a different and earlier general system for calling up soldiers for an expedition. Call-up by age-groups is not often attested at all, and never before the middle of the fourth century: Dem., 3.4, a call-up to the age of forty-five ordered in a momentary alarm in 352; Diod., 18.10.2, to the age of forty for the Lamian War. Age-groups are never mentioned in connection with a fifth-century expedition; instead we hear regularly, in Thucydides and elsewhere, of the call-up of a specified number of men. It is clear from Lysias and Aristophanes (below) that the system of the fifth and early fourth centuries involved the selection (καταλέγειν) of individuals by the military authorities. Some slight confusion is caused by the two uses of the word κατάλογος. The distinction is clearly set out by A. H. M. Jones, *Athenian Democracy* (Oxford 1957) 163: the basic list of all hoplites was ὁ κατάλογος, as e.g. Dem., 13.4 ὑπὲρ τὸν κατάλογον to mean over military age, but there were also κατάλογοι for particular expeditions listing the men who were to serve on that expedition, as e.g. Thuc., 6.26.2, 31.3. The actual work of enrolment was done by the taxiarchs, as we see from Ar., *Pax* 1180–1181 τοὺς μὲν ἐγράφοντες ἡμῶν τοὺς δ' ἄνω τε καὶ κάτω ἐξαλείφοντες δὶς ἢ τρίς; and it gave ground enough for

---

[1] F. W. Mitchel, *GRBS* 5 (1964) 102, note 3, prefers the solution given in *LSJ*. The special study there promised has not, to my knowledge, appeared.

complaint, e.g., *Eq.* 1369–1371. Lysias 9 shows that the ultimate responsibility lay with the generals: the speaker, recently returned from abroad, found himself enrolled and complained to the generals that he had already done service (4), and reminded them of their oath τοὺς ἀστρατεύτους καταλέξειν (15). The theory is evidently that each man on the basic *katalogos* must serve in turn, and that, presumably, is what ἐν τοῖς μέρεσι means. If this beautifully egalitarian procedure had been strictly followed, it would tend to the enrolment of a fair number of incompetent soldiers, and it is a reasonable guess that the generals in charge of a particular expedition would try, in spite of their oath, to collect the best men they could. Pressure would increase for an important expedition, and the prospect of rich booty would make conscription more attractive; on both counts this should produce a high-grade force for Sicily in 415, and the κατάλογοι χρηστοί of Thuc., 6.31.3 may have a more positive reference to the quality of the troops than we allowed in the note *ad loc.* in *HCT.*

The handbooks (e.g., Busolt-Swoboda, *Gr. Staatsr.* [Munich 1920–26] 1193) mostly accept that ἐν τοῖς μέρεσι refers to a system by which specified numbers of men were called up, but nevertheless add that there had to be an equitable distribution among the age-groups; for this there is no positive evidence, and Aristophanes and Lysias include no complaint on this score against the working of the system. Jones (*loc. cit.*), though he did not elaborate the point, appears to make a clear distinction between selective call-up and call-up by age-groups. This seems the more probable, and it implies a change of the basic system within the time of Aischines' military service. It perhaps accords with this that Aischines adds the qualification καλουμένην to service ἐν τοῖς μέρεσι, as if that were the system less familiar to his hearers. On the other hand, Harpokration (*loc. cit.*) tells us that στρατεία ἐν τοῖς ἐπωνύμοις was discussed by Philochoros in his fourth book, and the point of reference (see F. Jacoby, *FGrHist.* 328 F 38) was very probably the outbreak of the Peloponnesian War. This might suggest that the age-group system was already in operation in 431; but if Philochoros put in a digression on conscription at this point, his purpose was probably to warn his readers that the procedure of 431 was different from that in use in Athens in his own day, and discussion of the difference would involve saying something about the later procedure.

It is in any case beyond doubt that the fifth century practised a system of selective call-up, and that is of some help with two minor problems.

(a) Ar., *Av.* 1364–1369, where Pisthetairos arms the father-beater and tells him to go off and fight in Thrace, has long caused difficulty because the young man seems free to serve or not as he pleases: see especially H. D. Westlake, *CR* n.s. 4 (1954) 90–94, who glances at the view that men over 20 could volunteer under the fifth-century system, but for lack of evidence of volunteering opts instead for the alternative that the young man was under 20, when he could not be conscripted to fight abroad but might volunteer. There is no need for this complication; volunteering is easily compatible with selective enrolment, and it could be of help to generals trying to procure the fittest possible force. The anecdote in Plut., *Per.* 18.2, of the volunteers who went with Tolmides to Koroneia, both illustrates this point and indicates that the system known from the Peloponnesian War was already in operation soon after 450.

(b) Aristotle in *Pol.* 1303a 8–10 claims that the Athenian upper class was reduced in numbers διὰ τὸ ἐκ καταλόγου στρατεύεσθαι ὑπὸ τὸν Λακωνικὸν πόλεμον. *Ath. Pol.* 26.1 in a more complex sentence asserts that the ἐπιεικεῖς among both the people and the well-to-do were destroyed because service was at that time (the context vaguely suggests a period after Ephialtes' reform of the Areopagus) ἐκ καταλόγου and the generals were incompetent. There is some reprehensibly biased matter here, including a surprisingly exact echo from Isokrates (8.87), and the chronological indications, vague as they are, are not prima facie reconcilable; but the two passages share an assumption that at some specific period the system of service ἐκ καταλόγου produced differential casualties between the classes. Commentators have naturally been puzzled by this, since service must at all times have been based on the main hoplite *katalogos*, and conscription should mean that good and bad men had to serve alike. The standard, but incomplete, solution has been (Newman, Sandys, and others) a contrast between citizen service in the fifth century and reliance on mercenaries in Aristotle's time. That is to take Demosthenes' diatribes too literally—there were occasions enough when citizens fought, in Aristotle's time and even thereafter—and it can explain the differential casualties only on the assumption that all hoplites were in Aristotle's eyes ἐπιειϰεῖς; and even that (Busolt, *Gr. Gesch.* [Gotha 1904] 3.338, note 3) neglects the casualties among thetic oarsmen, substantial if not so easily counted. The passages become more intelligible if we can suppose that ἐϰ ϰαταλόγου refers not to the general list of all hoplites, but to the system by which generals made up their own ϰατάλογοι for particular expeditions.[2] To the extent that they succeeded in enrolling troops of good quality, they ensured that the wastage among these was disproportionately high; but the nonselective call-up of whole age-groups, as it was practised in Athens in Aristotle's time, would not weight the casualties in the same way.

This is not a very substantial point to put before my old friend Malcolm McGregor on this occasion. But, such as it is, I offer him the possibility that from a date around or before 450 the Athenians practised a system of selective enrolment of individuals, supervised by the generals and administered by the taxiarchs, in which theoretically every able-bodied man of the hoplite class served in his turn, though in practice the generals would try to obtain the best men they could; and that at some time in the second quarter of the fourth century they replaced this with a different system, the indiscriminate call-up of a specified number of age-groups.[3]

Oxford

A. ANDREWES

---

[2] Jones (*loc. cit.*) observes that the singular ϰατάλογος is always used for the main hoplite register, while the plural refers to selective call-up within this register. In the view I am putting forward, ἐϰ ϰαταλόγου could also refer to the system or process of selection, for which the verb is ϰαταλέγειν, as in the oath cited by Lys., 9.15. The reference may well be the same in Xen., *Mem.* 3.4.1 ἐϰ ϰαταλόγου στρατευόμενος; it is not here necessary, but Nikomachides' complaint is more forcible if he means that he had, as a competent soldier, been conscripted more often than others.

[3] I am grateful to D. M. Lewis for comments on an earlier draft of this paper.

EPIDAURIANS, AEGINETANS AND ATHENIANS

Aegina's early history is usually contemplated through its relations with Athens, particularly through the series of incidents termed the "Undeclared War." There has been much controversy in the past about the chronology, especially for that part of the war that was fought after the expulsion of the Athenian tyrants.[1] This paper, however, will look at earlier phases of the war, including its start; it will, with some diffidence, suggest a possible set of dates. It is offered in gratitude to a great teacher and scholar, and to a good friend.

Herodotus (5.82–88) is our main source for most of the events; he is supplemented by a few other references, notably in Pausanias and Strabo. Herodotus gives an extraordinary tale, full of miracles and quarrels over cult images, with aetiologies for various religious and social practices. The trouble all started, he tells us, with the revolt of Aegina from Epidaurus. The Aeginetans used their new, powerful fleet to ravage Epidaurus, and during one raid they carried off statues of Damia and Auxesia to a new shrine at Oea in Aegina. The Epidaurians had previously performed certain rites at Athens as a condition of having been permitted to make the cult images of Athenian olive wood. After they had lost the images, they refused to carry out these rites any longer. The Aeginetans also refused to do them. The Athenians then tried to get the images back and failed; in one version they were defeated with heavy loss at Oea by an Argive force. As a consequence of certain happenings ensuing from this defeat the Athenian women changed their style of clothing; the Argive and Aeginetan women changed the size of their brooch pins and dedicated these larger types to Damia and Auxesia; and Athenian products were embargoed at the shrine of the two goddesses.

This not-too-convincing story raises many questions. Why were the Aeginetans so very angry with the Athenians and the possessors of an ἔχϑρη προοφειλομένη? After all, the Aeginetans stole the statues and defeated the Athenians. Should it not be the other way around? Why were the cult images so important that the Athenians (not the Epidaurians) wanted them? Why did the Aeginetans simply not perform the rites at Athens and save a lot of feuding? Why was the Aeginetan fleet absent, so that the Athenians could land on Aegina unharmed?

The whole story is suspiciously aetiological. Damia and Auxesia were fertility divinities, as even their names make clear. They were widely worshipped in the Argolid, at Argos, Epidaurus, and Troezen, as well as in Aegina. Their cult resembles that of Demeter and Persephone in some of its ceremonies, including, it seems, the carrying on of a mock battle, a well-known fertility practice.[2] Perhaps the memory of a real battle nearby was thought of as the *aition* for this Aeginetan mock battle at Oea. The existence of the cult and the memory of the battle together provided *aitia* for other cult activities in Aegina and Argos, and the *aition* for an alleged change of costume among Athenian women. The invasion and the defeat are doubtless genuine memories,

---

[1] The bibliography to 1973 is conveniently summarized in Amit (1973), 20, note 37.

[2] Frazer, *Pausanias* 3. 266–268.

and the removal of the statues to Aegina from Epidaurus as booty sounds likely enough. What we have then is a tradition of an Athenian invasion associated, temporally, with a transferral of cult from Epidaurus to Aegina, and with the political separation of Epidaurus and Aegina. Beyond that we cannot go. The association with changes of ritual may or may not be associated temporally.

It is comparatively simple to construct a relative sequence of events on the basis of what Herodotus says, and to supplement it with material from other authors. This relative sequence will be laid out first, and then the dating will be offered later.

1. Dorian Epidaurians crossed over and settled Aegina, according to Pindar (F1 Bowra), Herodotus (8.46), and Pausanias (2.29.5).

2. Aegina continued for a long time to be so dominated by Epidaurus that the Aeginetans even went to Epidaurus for the trial of lawsuits among themselves, according to Herodotus (5.83.1). Clearly Aegina was regarded as an integral part of Epidaurus.

3. There was at an early stage a friendship, based on trade, between the Aeginetans and the Arcadians. Pausanias (8.5.8−9) has the Aeginetans sail to a harbour "below Cyllene," presumably by circumnavigating the Peloponnese, and bring their goods inland by pack train. Pompus, the king of Arcadia, named his son Aeginetes in honour of this friendship.

The story has been treated with scepticism, especially the landing below Cyllene, but Aeginetan trade with Arcadia is not in itself improbable. A shorter and easier land route runs west from Argos into northern Arcadia "below Cyllene."[3] A voyage around to Nauplia or Lerna and then inland to Orchomenus would be simple, as would an overland journey from Epidaurus to Argos, for that matter. Either would be practical for traders from Aegina who were under the protection of Epidaurus or Argos or both. The Epidaurians had close links with northern Arcadia that seem to have been long lasting. The tyrant Procles was married to an Orchomenian.[4] The story, corrected, would have to refer to happenings at an early date, since Pompus and Aeginetes are placed several generations before the Messenian Wars. The king list from Arcadia is clearly a late compilation, but the compiler had to work from some material, and we should have here a scrap of something early.[5]

4. At some point Aegina was attacked by and suffered great damage from the Samians, "when Amphicrates was king" (Hdt., 3.59.4). This attack must have been earlier than the overthrow of the last Samian king, at a time when the Samians had warships and the Aeginetans few or none. It should be remembered that Ameinocles of Corinth is supposed to have made the first warships, and for Samos.[6] Whatever the merits of the case for triremes, it is clear that a friendship was believed to exist between Corinth and Samos at an early date, somehow connected with warship construction. Aegina and Epidaurus were linked to Argos. Aegina was no doubt some sort of nuisance to be so treated by Samos, and the suggestion that Aegina was starting to compete on trade routes, especially those to the Near East, has some attraction.[7] But there is more than commercial rivalry behind an attack by an Epidaurian colony on a foundation and possession of the metropolis.

The Samian association with Corinth and the attack against an Argive ally speak for a time contemporaneous with or earlier than Pheidon, when Corinth was either free of Argive control, or resisting attempts to bring it back to the fold. It should not be later than Pheidon because the Aeginetan fighting fleet was then too formidable. Therefore the lack of Aeginetan warships, and the existence of trading voyages of a kind to annoy Samos, sound as if they should be prior to Pheidon.

---

[3] *Ibid.* 4. 195 f., describes this route.

[4] Diog. Laert., 1. 7. 1, 94.

[5] Miller (1970), 228 f.

[6] Thuc., 1. 13. 2−3, dated 704 B.C.

[7] Jeffery (1976), 151.

5. Pheidon of Argos is supposed to have controlled, *inter alia*, Epidaurus and Aegina.[8] If this is so, then his rule must precede the revolt of Aegina from Epidaurus, the independence of Epidaurus from Argos and the tyranny of Procles at Epidaurus, at least for economical reconstruction. He should, as noted above, be contemporary with or subsequent to the Samian raid on Aegina.

6. The revolt of Aegina from Epidaurus must have taken place after Pheidon's reign. According to Herodotus (5.83.1−2) it happened after Aegina had constructed a fleet and had become full of ἀγνωμοσύνη, pride, and after it had obtained control of the sea.[9] A Samian raid would not be appropriate at this time or later, but must have preceded this stage.

The revolt was against Epidaurus, but not Argos. In fact Argos and Aegina were on the best of terms, with Argive troops helping to defend Aegina against Athens, according to both Aeginetan and Argive tradition (Hdt., 5.87.1), and both observed the same anti-Athenian sanctions and the same mode of dedicating to Damia and Auxesia. Since they were so close, it follows that the separation of Epidaurus from Argos should precede the Aeginetan revolt, otherwise Aegina would be rebelling against Argos as well. Pheidon's reign, then, should precede the Epidaurian separation from Argos. This should mean, as we shall see below, that the accession of Procles should precede the Aeginetan revolt, but follow the reign of Pheidon.

7. In the course of Aeginetan raids during or after the rebellion the cult images of Damia and Auxesia were seized and carried off from Epidaurus to Aegina (Hdt., 5.83−84). We know that the tyrant Procles of Epidaurus was deposed by Periander, who then took control of the town (Hdt., 3.52.7). It is most improbable that the Aeginetans would attack and loot possessions of that redoubtable figure; therefore the action must either precede Procles' deposition or follow the death of Periander. Since Herodotus links the rebellion and the raids closely, the former is the more probable. This means that Procles was in power when Aegina revolted; in turn, then he must have seized power about when Epidaurus broke away from Argos, or shortly afterwards.

Athens was soon drawn into conflict over Damia and Auxesia, and Aegina appealed to Argos for help (Hdt., 5.86.4).

8. The Athenians were defeated with heavy loss in an attempt to land on Aegina and to recover the cult images. Herodotus (5.85−86) gives two versions of what happened, an Athenian one and an Aeginetan. The latter is backed up by Argive traditions. In the Athenian version, one ship came to Aegina and landed a small force. The Athenians, after an attempt to haul away the statues was interrupted by thunder and an earthquake, were driven mad and slew one another, so that only one survivor returned to Athens. In the Aeginetan, a large body of troops landed from a substantial Athenian fleet and was annihilated by an Argive force at Oea (a point confirmed from Argive sources), one survivor returning.

For one ship to make a sudden raid in an economical attempt to recover some cult images is *a priori* not an unlikely operation; but the madness and mutual massacre by an act of God struck Herodotus as not too convincing. He keys his narration to the acceptance, with reservations, of the Aeginetan-Argive version. The Aeginetan explanation of why the statues were kneeling he flatly rejects. He is curious about the absence of the Aeginetan fleet and suggests as alternatives either that the Aeginetans recognized that their fleet was inferior and so kept it out of the way, or, even if it was equal or superior, that they deliberately refused action. The Argive forces that wiped out the Athenians came to Aegina by way of Epidaurus, the city against which the Aeginetans revolted and from which the statues were stolen! The absence of the fleet and the arrival of the Argives via Epidaurus are two glaring improbabilities in the Aeginetan-Argive version. Most

[8] Str., 8. 3. 33 = Ephorus, Jacoby (1923−) 70 F 115; Str., 8. 6. 16 = Ephorus, F 116; Hdt., 6. 127 is little help; see below. Kelly (1976), 118 f. points out that the evidence for the rule of Argos over Epidaurus is weak.
[9] Cf. Paus., 2. 30. 4.

modern authorities, however, have followed Herodotus in accepting it in preference to the Athenian.

Acceptance requires the explaining away of the two improbabilities. For the first, either of Herodotus' explanations may be right, or perhaps the fleet was engaged in ferrying the Argives across to Aegina. If one wishes to follow this version, one cannot deny the existence of a fleet. For the second, if the Argives came the direct route from Argos to Aegina by way of Epidaurus, then it follows that Epidaurus was not independent when the Argives came. The idea that an independent Epidaurus would allow a force to pass through to aid a rebel who had done much raiding is highly unlikely.[10] If Epidaurus was not independent then the controlling state must have been either Argos or Corinth, both of which are remembered as having ruled it at one time or other. There is no evidence for an Argive domination of Epidaurus during or after the reign of Procles, nor after the reign of Pheidon. There is no warrant in our evidence for making this incident contemporary with Pheidon. Therefore, Argive rule at this stage may be rejected. On the other hand, Herodotus (3.52.7) makes it clear that there was a Corinthian domination of Epidaurus by Periander after the deposition of Procles. Therefore the controlling state should be Corinth under Periander. If this is so, then Periander must have been supporting an Aeginetan-Argive alliance, no doubt because it provided something for him, like a free hand in Epidaurus, or peace in the Nemea-Tegea area, or profitable trade contacts.

On the other hand it might be thought easier to reject the Aeginetan version and accept the Athenian, particularly if the supernatural elements can be ignored. The relative sequence would still be the same, with this incident following the seizure of Damia and Auxesia and so being subsequent to the accession of Procles. The link with Periander, however, disappears. Nonetheless, the Athenian attack must take place shortly after the seizure of the cult images, and this in turn must take place before Periander took Epidaurus.

The one-ship attack as a *casus belli* and a cause for the deep Aeginetan hostility to Athens sounds improbable; one cannot ignore the Athenian mutual massacre; the whole version seems like an Athenian whitewashing of a far more substantial and dangerous affair. The Aeginetan version as supported by the Argives is a little more credible, but not so much as to inspire overwhelming confidence.

9. According to Herodotus (5.88.2) there were four results of the raid: first, there was continuous hostility henceforth between Aegina and Athens, a hostility that manifested itself from time to time by raids; second, the Athenian women, after the murder of the sole survivor of the attack, were constrained to change from the Doric chiton, so as not to wear long pins; third, extra-long pins were used and dedicated to Damia and Auxesia by the Aeginetan and Argive women; fourth, there was an Aeginetan and Argive embargo on Athenian imports, at least to sanctuaries of Damia and Auxesia. The second and third are clearly aetiological and probably with no chronological significance here. The fourth may be chronologically significant, reflected in the archaeological evidence. If so, as will be seen below, the evidence has not yet been uncovered.

10. At some time the Aeginetans started minting some of the earliest coins in Greece. The link of coinage with Pheidon is now rejected,[11] and so the commencement of minting should be put when Aegina was independent and established enough to require coinage in its transactions.

11. Aegina as an important commercial power established a *temenos* in Egypt at Naucratis, according to Herodotus (2.178.2−3).

12. Smilis of Aegina, a sculptor, worked at Samos, making a statue of Hera. Pausanias (7.4.4.) says that he was a contemporary of Daedalus, no doubt assigning him to a place far back in early times. Clement of Alexandria (*Protrept.* 4.46) says that the aniconic statue of Hera was replaced by

---

[10] Jeffery (1976), 150 and How & Wells, 2. 148.
[11] Amit (1973), 13 f.

a female image "when Procles ruled." He is referring to Procles of Samos, the leader of the Ionian colonists, and is putting the incident roughly contemporary with Daedalus. It has been argued, however, that Clement or his source misunderstood the reference, and that the Procles is the tyrant of Epidaurus and that Smilis replaced the aniconic statue.[12] In this case Smilis should be assigned to a time before the Aeginetan revolt, but after the accession of Procles to power in Epidaurus. This is a possibility.

The friendship implied in the visit of an Aeginetan to Samos might fit better in proximity to the friendship alleged between Aegina and Polycrates, the tyrant who rebuilt the temple of Hera, at a time when Aegina had a flourishing school of sculpture.

13. Exiles who had fled from Polycrates were attacked by the Aeginetan fleet and enslaved.[13] This incident has been held to signify friendly relations between Aegina and Polycrates, although it need not necessarily do so. The resisters seem to have followed a well-known pattern, in which the search for resources to carry on the struggle ends up becoming banditry and piracy. Capture of exiles who have turned pirate need not imply friendship.

14. After the establishment of the Athenian democracy and the Athenian victory over the Boeotian and Chalcidian forces following the collapse of Cleomenes' invasion, the Boeotians and the Aeginetans made an alliance.

This relative sequence of fourteen items fits together reasonably enough, but the difficulty comes in trying to establish dates for those earlier than numbers 13 and 14. The embargo on Athenian imports πρὸς τὸν ἱρόν (sc. of Damia and Auxesia) by Aeginetans and Argives might give hope of getting definite limits. Any embargo should be reflected in the stratified layers at the sanctuaries. Unfortunately they have not been excavated. Some, however, have argued that the embargoes had a wider currency than simply the temples of Damia and Auxesia. An absence of Attic Late Geometric Ib material, datable 750–735, has been noted in the deposits on Aegina.[14] Imports of Late Geometric II pottery were resumed by 735. If this should reflect the embargo, then Pheidon, the revolt of Aegina, the ravaging of Epidaurus, and the fight with Athens would have to fall before 750. Although there is a tradition (for which see below) that puts Pheidon somewhere around 750, such a dating is not very satisfactory. The absence of Late Geometric Ib is not too compelling: there is a considerable diminution in the amount of this ware everywhere outside Attica, as if Athens did not export much of it.[15] Three hundred years is a long time for a short-lived and unsuccessful embargo to be remembered. Furthermore, the excavators of the Argive Heraeum noted a scarcity of Attic Orientalizing, black- and red-figured wares from that site in a span datable from 480 to earlier than 600.[16] Pheidon could then be set somewhere in the seventh century. The explanation, however, for the scarcity (not absence) of Athenian wares at the Heraeum is better considered as arising from other causes. Herodotus makes it plain that the embargo applied *only* to the sanctuaries of Damia and Auxesia, not to ordinary trade or other cults. The sanctuaries are unexcavated, and the validity of the embargo remains to be tested. The same applies to the presence or absence of extra-long pins; nothing convincing is known about the alleged change of fashion among Athenian women.

The date of Pheidon is not established. He is supposed to have presided over an Olympic festival at the acme of his career. Traditionally this is the eighth (748), as argued for by Ephorus.[17] But Ephorus is not overly reliable; the high dating creates difficulties with the relative chronology

---

[12] Frazer, *Pausanias* 4. 123; Jeffery (1976), 151.

[13] Hdt., 3. 59; How & Wells, 1. 272 f.

[14] Hopper (1976), 179; Jeffery (1976), 84; Coldstream (1977), 135.

[15] Jeffery (1976), 84, 106, note 1; Coldstream (1968), 360–62.

[16] How & Wells, 2. 44; Waldstein (1905), 2. 174 f. Waldstein (2. 173) also notes the extreme rarity of "Early Attic".

[17] F 115 and F 116. See also Paus., 6. 22. 2; cf. How & Wells, 2. 118 and Huxley (1958).

outlined previously, putting Pheidon at a considerable remove from the Cypselids and from Procles of Epidaurus.

Current opinion inclines towards a setting in the twenty-eighth Olympiad (668), an Anolympiad, on the basis of Strabo's remark (8.3.30) that after the twenty-sixth Olympiad the Pisatans instead of the Eleans celebrated the games a few times.[18] This brings Pheidon into association with the battle of Hysiae, the Second Messenian War, an alliance of Argos with Arcadian states, and with troubles between Corcyra and Corinth, not to mention feuds with the Bacchiads. None of these associations are found in our sources, except possibly the story of his death near Corinth may indicate some link with the Bacchiads. Therefore the links have been doubted by some.

Herodotus (6.127) sets Pheidon much later, apparently somewhere around the end of the seventh century, since he has his son as one of the suitors seeking the hand of Agariste at the court of Cleisthenes. The idea of a Dorian being allowed to be a suitor is improbable, but chronologically the Pheidon of Herodotus could be a grandson if Pheidon of Argos were set in the early seventh century, though Herodotus makes it clear that he thought of his Pheidon as *the* Pheidon. Attempts to put Pheidon at the end of the seventh century lead to an extensive redrawing of the portrait of Pheidon, and a considerable lowering of dates.[19]

Procles and his link with Cypselid chronology may help somewhat. Herodotus (5.92) says that Cypselus ruled for 30 years. Aristotle (*Pol.* 131b 22−27) that the dynasty ruled for $73^{1}/_{2}$ years; Cypselus for 30; Periander for 44 (corrected by most authorities to $40^{1}/_{2}$ for the arithmetic); Psammetichus for 3. Eusebius sets Cypselus' accession at 660, Periander's in 630 and Psammetichus' in 590. Apollodorus gives the dates 657, 627, 587. Most authorities tend to follow these.[20] At least four other sets of dates have been suggested in the past few years: 642, 612, 572; 626, 596, 556; 622, 592, 552; and 614, 584, 544.[21]

Procles has to be deposed after Periander's accession, presumably not too long after. Since the sons of Periander were about eighteen when they visited Procles shortly before his deposition, probably Periander married Procles' daughter Melissa at least twenty years previously. Melissa should have been of marriageable age then, at least fifteen or so. Procles would have been about twenty to twenty-five when he was married. The establishment of his tyranny would fall when he was approximately thirty-five. The tabulation of possible sets of dates is as follows:

	Eusebius	Apollodorus	I	II	III	IV
Accession of:						
Cypselus	660	657	642	626	622	614
Periander	630	627	612	596	592	584
Psammetichus	590	587	572	556	552	544
Marriage of Melissa	650	647	632	616	612	604
Birth of Melissa	665/60	662/55	647/42	631/25	627/22	619/14
Birth of Procles	680/75	677/72	662/57	646/41	641/37	634/29
Accession of Procles	645	642	627	611	607	599

Our phase 7 (the capture of Damia and Auxesia), 8 (the Athenian attack on Aegina), and 9 (the results) should lie in close juxtaposition and should not be too distant from 6 (the Aeginetan

---

[18] Amit (1973), 12; Andrewes (1956), 40 and (1949); Hopper (1976), 172; Jeffery (1976), 134−36; 143 note 63; How & Wells, 2. 117 f. Sealey (1976), 43 f. But cf. note 22 below.

[19] Cf. Kelly (1976), 94−129.

[20] Busolt, 1. 638 f.; How & Wells, 2. 54; Oost (1972), 10; Jeffery (1976), 147 f., 154 note 1; Hopper (1976), 133.

[21] Hopper (1976), 133; Miller (1970), 209−224; Ducat (1961), 418−25; Servais (1969), 28−81.

revolt). Phase 7 must be earlier than the Corinthian occupation of Epidaurus; phases 8 and 9, if the Aeginetan-Argive version is followed, must be later than Procles' deposition and Corinthian control of Epidaurus, so as to explain the passage of Argive troops through Epidaurus. Procles' deposition can be no earlier than Periander's accession.

There are a few considerations that might help to find out which of the six sets of dates is preferable. There has been a tendency to link Pheidon somehow with Cypselus, since he died at Corinth; to consider that in some way Pheidon paved the way for Cypselus' accession.[22] If this is so, then only the first two sets, Eusebius' and Apollodorus', need be considered, the rest falling far too low, unless massive revisions are applied to chronology. The same considerations apply to the Athenian defeat, which can be no earlier, though it may be later, than Periander's accession: variously 630, 627, 612, 596, 592, and 584. The last three fall close to the traditional dates of Solon and his reforms, not too likely a period, one may think, for stirring up the neighbours. The first two, however, fall close to a very lively period, when the *"prytaneis* of the naucraries" make their only appearance as important figures in Athenian history, when Cylon tried a coup.[23]

It is very likely that the discontent misread by Cylon and the temporary importance of the *prytaneis* of the naucraries both stem from the same cause: a sharp Athenian defeat and a consequent loss of ships and men. The naucraries were important in raising contingents for the army and ships for the navy. Their emphasis in Herodotus is not an error, though doubtless Megacles and the other archons were, as Thucydides says, ultimately in charge. Heavy losses at Aegina and great efforts to rebuild the forces would make the appropriate officials highly important and visible at the time. They would be the ones turned to by the archons to get troops to Athens. It was they who rallied to the archons and crushed the coup.[24] Cylon is dated to an Olympic victory between 636/5 and 628/7, on grounds completely independent of those dealing with the other dates.[25] The convergence on 630 is significant.

The first two sets, Eusebius' and Apollodorus', appear to be preferable. Phase 6 (the Aeginetan revolt) should be set after Procles' accession, but before his deposition, say about 640. Phase 7 (the raids) may have continued for some time, with the seizure of Damia and Auxesia close to the deposition of Procles, somewhere around 630, but before 628/7, the latest date for Cylon's Olympic victory. Phase 8 (the Athenian raid), if we follow the Aeginetan-Argive version, must come after the fall of Procles, and the loss of Epidaurian independence, so that the Argive troops can pass through Epidaurus, even though it must be linked causally with phase 7 and closely with the capture of Damia and Auxesia. Herodotus implies a duration of less than a year between phases 7 and 8, but a few years and various delays could well be telescoped together. I should place phase 8 in 629 or 628, just before Cylon's attempted coup.

The chronological scheme could be developed as follows on the basis of Eusebius:

Ca. 695: birth of Cypselus.
Ca. 680/75: birth of Procles.
      668: Pheidon presides over 28th Olympiad; birth of Periander.
Ca. 665: death of Pheidon at Corinth.
      660: Cypselus tyrant of Corinth.

---

[22] Jeffery (1976), 136, 143, note 3, 147; Hopper (1976), 130, 133; Sealey (1976), 47 f.; Andrewes (1949); but see Huxley (1958) and Coldstream (1977), 154–56 for a dating of 748 for Pheidon. For Pheidon ca. 600 see Kelly (1976), 94–111. Kelly relies excessively on the story of Agariste.

[23] Hdt., 5. 71; Thuc., 1. 126; Gomme, *Commentary* 1. 426; How & Wells, 2. 37 f.; for naucraries see also Arist., *Ath.Pol.* 21.

[24] This is not to deny that a change of emphasis, a "cover-up," may have been attempted on behalf of Megacles. This seems to be the point of Thucydides' re-telling of the incident, and his emphasis on the role of the archons, not the *prytaneis.*

[25] Jeffery (1976), 87; Miller (1970), 97.

Ca. 650/45: Procles tyrant of Epidaurus; marriage of Periander to Melissa; separation of
      Epidaurus from Argos.
Ca. 640: Revolt of Aegina: Aeginetan friendship with Argos.
      640–630: Aeginetan raids on Epidaurus.
      630: Seizure of Damia and Auxesia; Periander's accession at Corinth.
      629: Deposition of Procles; Periander controls Epidaurus; Athenian embassy to Aegina.
      629/8: Athenian defeat by Argives and Aeginetans.
      628/7: Abortive coup of Cylon; prominent role of *prytaneis* of the naucraries.
      The other phases may now be fitted smoothly.

Phase 3, the Aeginetan penetration into Arcadia, and phase 4, the Samian attack, should both
precede the time of Pheidon. The last king of Samos was overthrown at a time shortly after the
foundation of Perinthus,[26] early in the sixth century at the latest. The construction of the first
specialized warships in 704 should mark the upper limit, and the seizure of power and control of
Aegina by Pheidon, the lower–somewhere between 700 and 680 for phase 4– would be
suitable.[27] Phase 3 should precede phase 4, since it is associated with Pompus and his son Aeginetes, the latter of whom is placed a generation before Charilaus, well before Theopompus and the
Messenian Wars. The conventional date should be about 840, although a lowering into the early
part of the eighth century is possible. No date can be assigned as yet to phase 1, except that it
should be in sub-Mycenaean or in the early Dark Ages.

Phase 10, the introduction of coinage, cannot be set much before 600,[28] at a time when Aegina
was independent of both Argos and Epidaurus, the possessor of a powerful fleet, and was trading
widely. The crediting of the first mint to Pheidon is no longer believed.

The *temenos* in Naucratis was established sometime between 600 and 570.[29] Smilis can be
assigned to the latter half of the sixth century.

Thus the phases can be dated as follows:

1. Eleventh or tenth century B.C.: Dorian settlement of Aegina from Epidaurus.
2. Until mid-seventh century: Epidaurian control of Aegina.
3. Early eighth century: Aeginetan friendship with Arcadia, under Epidaurian and Argive sponsorship.
4. Early seventh century: Samian raid.
5. Ca. 680–665: Pheidon of Argos controls Aegina and Epidaurus.
   660: Accession of Cypselus of Corinth.
   Ca. 650/45: Accession of Procles of Epidaurus; separation of Epidaurus from Argos.
6. Ca. 640: Revolt of Aegina from Epidaurus.
7. 640–630: Aeginetan raids on Epidaurus.
   Ca. 630: Seizure of Damia and Auxesia.
   630: Accession of Periander.
   629: Deposition of Procles.
8. 629/8: Athenian raid and defeat.
   628/7: Abortive coup of Cylon.
9. Ca. 625–480: Banning of Athenian imports to Aeginetan and Argive shrines of Damia and
   Auxesia.

---

[26] Plut., *Quaest.Graec.* 57 = *Mor.* 303E – 304C.

[27] I doubt that Samian filial feelings would lead it to assault a rebellious Aegina out of loyalty to Epidaurus, *pace* Jeffery
(1976), 213.

[28] Amit (1973), 13 f.; Hopper (1976), 113; Jeffery (1976), 135, 150.

[29] Amit (1973), 13 f.; Hopper (1976), 113, 120; Jeffery (1976), 53.

10. Ca. 600: Aeginetan coinage introduced.
11. 600–570: *Temenos* in Naucratis.
12. 550–520: Smilis.
13. 519: Exiles from Polycrates defeated.
14. 505: Alliance with Boeotia.

University of Alberta   R. J. BUCK

BIBLIOGRAPHY

M. Amit (1973).	*Great and Small Poleis.* Brussels.
A. Andrewes (1949).	"The Corinthian Actaeon and Pheidon of Argos," *CQ* 43, 70–78.
A. Andrewes (1956).	*The Greek Tyrants.* London.
J.N. Coldstream (1968).	*Greek Geometric Pottery.* London.
J.N. Coldstream (1977).	*Geometric Greece.* London.
J. Ducat (1961).	"Note sur la chronologie des Kypsélides," *BCH* 85, 418–25.
J.G. Frazer (1898).	*Pausanias' Description of Greece.* London. Reprinted, New York 1965.
A.W. Gomme (1945–).	*Commentary on Thucydides,* 1–3, and 4 with A. Andrewes and K.J. Dover, Oxford.
R.J. Hopper (1976).	*The Early Greeks.* London.
W.W. How & J. Wells (1928).	*Commentary on Herodotus*[2]. Oxford.
G. Huxley (1958).	"Argos et les derniers Temenids," *BCH* 82, 588–601.
F. Jacoby (1923–).	*Die Fragmente der griechischen Historiker.* Leiden.
L.H. Jeffery (1976).	*Archaic Greece.* London.
T. Kelly (1976).	*A History of Argos.* Minneapolis.
M. Miller (1970).	*Sicilian Colony Dates.* Albany.
S.I. Oost (1972).	"Cypselus the Bacchiad," *CP* 67, 10–13.
R. Sealey (1976).	*A History of the Greek City States 700-338 B.C.* Berkeley and Los Angeles.
J. Servais (1969).	"Herodote et la chronologie des Cypsélides," *AC* 38, 28–81.
R. A. Tomlinson (1972).	*Argos and the Argolid.* London.
C.H. Waldstein (1905).	*The Argive Heraeum.* New York and Boston.

THE COLLOQUIAL STRATUM IN CLASSICAL ATTIC PROSE

In a modern language the differences between what people say and what they write are quite easily observed and described. In particular, the invention of the tape-recorder has given us access to an ocean of words uttered in a more relaxed way than can usually be achieved in the presence of stenographers. This material can be quantified, analysed and categorised objectively without any reference to the spontaneous reactions which are expressed in praise or blame according to aesthetic (and therefore idiosyncratic) criteria, and without dependence on the selective recollection which is determined by such reactions. We remain free to detest the linguistic habits of those who begin every answer with "Well, . . ." or every narrative sentence with "So . . ." or punctuate every explanation with a repeated "you see" – indeed, we are free to detest everyone's linguistic habits except our own – but the frequency of such phenomena in the transcripts of discussions and interviews makes it senseless to carp at the educational attainments of all those who use them.[1] When we turn to the language of a previous age, the possibility of distinguishing between the spoken and the written language is immensely reduced, and in the case of some cultures may be reduced to nothing. From the past we have only written utterance, and no written utterance can be treated as entirely spontaneous and unconsidered; the act of writing takes time, and therefore gives time, and it entails an awareness, however ill-formed, of a future reader who will receive the message in the sender's absence and therefore without further amplification or explanation by the sender.

In the case of classical Attic literature (and no doubt in the case of some other past literatures as well) a further difficulty is created by the fact that, judged by the standards of modern conversation (whether English or Modern Greek), such of it as has been transmitted to us is technically sophisticated and structurally elaborate. Yet we have the strongest reasons to believe that at some other periods in history of Greek the difference between genres of literature in respect of their distance from speech could be very great indeed. The relation between modern spoken Greek, the poetry of Theodoros Prodromos in the twelfth century A.D. and the sum total of evidence for ancient Greek enables us to assess the relative distance of Prodromos and his contemporary Anna Komnena from twelfth-century speech and compels us to wonder how far Anna's work was intelligible to those who lacked a literary education. Similarly, the abundance of private letters and documents from Roman Egypt in the early imperial period, considered in relation to earlier literature and modern speech, affords us at least a starting-point for a hypothesis about the linguistic differences between an oration given by Dio of Prusa and the whispered comments of members of his audience; and natural curiosity leads us on to speculation about a Periclean funeral-speech. It is an area of speculation in which ancient writers on style and rhetoric give us no significant assistance,

---

[1] No one would regard Mr. John Freeman or the late Lord Birkett as inarticulate, but a transcript of part of their famous dialogue televised in 1959 (H. Montgomery Hyde, *Norman Birkett* [London 1964] 577ff.) reveals eight successive utterances beginning with "Well, ..."

partly because they too are looking back to a past era in ignorance of its conversational idiom, and partly because they do not maintain a distinction between vulgar words for things and words for vulgar things.[2]

Within the ancient evidence available to us there is one clear and important distinction to be drawn. We possess on the one hand much literary portrayal of conversation, composed by skilled writers who wished to be admired for their artistry. We possess on the other hand utterances composed by people who wanted simply to communicate instructions, requests or sentiments. The relation between the former category and actual speech depends on the writers' attitudes to realism and to the function of art. The relation between the latter category and actual speech depends partly on the writers' beliefs about what is functionally efficient or socially acceptable in any given genre of communication,[3] and partly also on the fact that since they read less and write less than the artist the linguistic sources on which they can draw, other than conversation, are more restricted. The distinction is clear enough in modern English. In many people's speech certain words which until recently it was illegal to print are of very frequent occurrence. A novelist portraying conversation may well sow them thickly, but the people who use them freely in speech tend to avoid them in writing messages and letters; conversely, the uneducated often use stilted clichés and formulae in writing which are equally alien to their speech and to that of their more educated contemporaries.

Evidence of the second category from Athens in what I propose to call the "central" period, i.e., 430–300 B.C., is in short supply;[4] many of the most interesting graffiti and dipinti are earlier or non-Attic or both, and the overwhelming majority of private documents is post-classical and comes from Egypt. Difference of time and place is a factor not to be ignored in dealing with colloquial language. My grandfather would have been surprised by the dentist's exclaiming "Smashing!" or "Fantastic!" when he complied with a request to open his mouth a little wider, and a foreigner who heard in Lancashire, "They wouldn't do well there, wouldn't strawberries," would be mistaken if he adopted this sentence-structure in talking with natives of Surrey.[5] Nevertheless, if a putative colloquial phenomenon in Attic of the central period is found in relevant contexts in another region or period, a tilt is given to the balance of probability in assigning it to the colloquial register. Contrasts between the colloquial and the literary in modern languages also have analogical value, in proportion to the breadth of their distribution in cultures which use languages comparable in structure with Greek and adopt comparable attitudes towards language and literature.[6] Finally, any system of contrasts constructed for Greek merits confidence to the extent to which it resembles a system constructed independently for Latin.

It is time now to review the main types of evidence.

Category I: Literary Portrayal.

(A) Attic of the Central Period.

(1) One thinks first of those portions of Socratic dialogues which introduce or separate passages of sustained exposition and philosophical argument; Demetrios, *Eloc.* 297f. (cf. 224 and 226) says of this genre ἐξέπληξαν τῷ τε μιμητικῷ καὶ τῷ ἐναργεῖ. But passages of reported speech in forensic oratory (e.g., Lys., 1.16) must not be overlooked, and it is arguable that the great

---

[2] Cf. "Longinus," *Subl.* 43, with D.A. Russell's comment *ad loc.*

[3] Demetr., *Eloc.* 223–235 lays down rules for the style of letters; rules of that kind tend to have an effect, however fragmentary, at all levels of society.

[4] I treat 430 B.C. as the starting-point in order to include as "central" our earliest extant Attic comedies and prose.

[5] Both examples are genuine and heard by me during 1977. I should add that the dentist is Welsh and my Lancastrian friend an Old Harrovian.

[6] Cf. J. B. Hofmann, *Lateinische Umgangssprache*[2] (Heidelberg 1936) *passim,* and E. Hermann, *Griechische Forschungen* 1 (Leipzig and Berlin 1912).

quantity of conversation in Xenophon's *Anabasis* and *Cyropaedia* might be at least as important, for our present limited purpose, as the Socratic material. Assessment of the genuinely colloquial element in it may be helped by reference to the way in which Xenophon on occasion gives dialectal colouring to a reported utterance by a non-Athenian. In *An.* 6.6.34 the Spartan Kleandros says ἀλλὰ ναὶ τὼ σιώ ... ταχύ τοι ὑμῖν ἀποκρινοῦμαι, using a distinctively Spartan oath (cf. Ar., *Peace* 214, *Lys.* 81, 86, etc.) which recurs in *HG* 4.4.10, where a complete sentence of the Spartan Pasimakhos is given in dialect: ναὶ τὼ σιώ, ὦ Ἀργεῖοι, ψευσεῖ ὑμὲ τὰ σίγμα ταῦτα. Kleandros proceeds to offer sacrifices in the hope of obtaining divine approval for leadership of the force which Xenophon has offered him, but θυομένῳ ... οὐκ ἐγίγνετο τὰ ἱερά (6.36). He reports this to Xenophon and the other commanders by saying ἐμοὶ μὲν οὐ τελέθει τὰ ἱερὰ ἐξάγειν. That verb τελέθειν appears as a substitute for the normal Attic γίγνεσθαι in the words of another Spartan, Kheirisophos, at *An.* 3.2.3: δεῖ ἐκ τῶν παρόντων ἄνδρας ἀγαθοὺς τελέθειν; it is a favourite word of Theokritos (e.g., 5.18) and occurs both in Epikharmos (170.17 Kaibel) and a Doric inscription (*Tabulae Heracleenses, DGE* 62.1.111). If a touch of authentic dialect appealed to Xenophon,[7] touches of authentic colloquialism may have appealed to him no less, but perhaps we should not look for more than could fairly be called a touch. After all, Kleandros' Spartan oath in *An.* 6.6.34 introduces not the declaration ἀποκρινίομαι (as we might have hoped from the Spartan sentence in *HG* 1.1.23, etc.) but ἀποκρινοῦμαι, a fact which suggests that for Xenophon dialect was a means of achieving occasional dramatic effect; cf. Kebes' Boeotian oath ἴττω Ζεύς in *Phd.* 62a, where Plato adds τῇ αὐτοῦ φωνῇ εἰπών. Serious Greek artists and writers were willing enough to portray what was wicked or frightening, but we should not expect them often to sacrifice elegance and articulateness to realistic portrayal of what they thought clumsy, socially despicable or distractingly quaint.

(2) Comic dialogue, although in verse and admitting its own poetic conceits, much sophisticated word-play and much parody of serious poetry, may reasonably be supposed to contain a colloquial element, partly because its subject-matter is so often alien to that of serious literature: domestic, mundane and physiological. It readily uses obscene words, familiar to us from some classes of Category B but excluded from prose (and the occurrence of the verb βινεῖν in *CGF* 138.8 and 254.1 shows that the distinction between Old and New Comedy in this respect is not absolute). It is surprising, but it seems on present evidence to be a fact, that comedy did not exploit the humorous potentialities of solecism and malapropism in the language of slaves or illiterate citizens. The existence of grammatical deviations which can fairly be called solecisms is attested by archaic dipinti (e.g., δέχε = δέχου, Kretschmer 89 no. 61 [black-figure]) and classical curse-tablets (e.g., καὶ [γ]υνὴν τὴν Ἐργασίωνος, Peek 91−93 no. 3.71f.). Yet even the Sausage-seller of *Knights*, whose hold on reading and writing is shaky (188f.), speaks as well as anyone else. The conversation of the slaves in *Frogs* 738−813, where we might expect humorous exploitation of linguistic contrast between slaves and masters, is not demonstrably marked by solecism or vulgarity; for example, the idiom μὴ ἀλλὰ πλεῖν ἢ μαίνομαι "I'm just crazy about it!" (751) echoes the words of Dionysos himself (103). Foreigners and speakers of dialect are certainly caricatured linguistically, but that is a different matter.[8]

(3) In certain cirumstances Attic tragedy may make a positive contribution. It is well known that phenomena characteristic of portrayal of conversation in prose or comedy sometimes occur in tragedy (especially in Euripides) at moments when the situation encourages us to think that a character is speaking angrily, rudely or flippantly.[9] That being so, a phenomenon found in a passage of which the emotional tone makes colloquialism appropriate deserves to be considered as possibly colloquial even when more direct evidence is lacking.

---

[7] L. Gautier, *La Langue de Xénophon* (Geneva 1911) 22−47, esp. 26−28; J. Wackernagel, *Hellenistica* (Göttingen 1907) 7−11, 29−34.

[8] Dover, *RCCM* 18 (1976) 357−371.

[9] Stevens, 10−18, 23f.

18   K. J. DOVER

(B) Earlier Period: Attic Vases.

On some Attic black-figure and (predominantly early) red-figure vases words are shown issuing from the mouths of the people portrayed or elsewhere on the surface but plainly intended by the painter to be associated with the picture. Such words must be classed as artistic portrayal of conversation, not as the direct expression of the painter's sentiments. A black-figure plaque (Athens, National Museum, Acropolis collection 2560) shows a vintage-scene accompanied by ἤδη κανῆ πλέα, then μετὰ κἀγώ (sc. οἴνου πλέως ἔσομαι),[10] followed by κἀγὼ τ[and ἐκφεφορ[. The first utterance reminds us of Ar., Ach. 946 ἤδη καλῶς ἔχει σοι (said when the sycophant has been packed up for export), and the second and third recall Frogs 414–5 ἐγὼ δ' . . . χορεύειν βούλομαι. – κἀγώ γε πρός. Adverbial μετά, however, common enough in Herodotos (μετὰ δέ), is not attested from Attic comedy or prose. On the red-figure pelike (Leningrad 615a, ARV 1594),[11] the sight of the first swallow of spring is greeted by one speaker with the words ἰδοὺ χελιδών, to which a second speaker adds νὴ τὸν Ἡρακλέα. This accords with Ar., Frogs 182f. καὶ πλοῖόν γ' ὁρῶ. – νὴ τὸν Ποσειδῶ, κἄστι γ' ὁ Χάρων οὑτοσί, and with the ready use of oaths "by Herakles" and "by Poseidon" in comedy, though not in Plato (where Alkibiades' drunken, hectoring μὰ τὸν Ποσειδῶ in Symp. 214d is unique). A black-figure homosexual courting scene of familiar type (Boston, Museum of Fine Arts 08.30d)[12] contains the sequences of letters αρενμι and ιδορεν (or ιαορεν?). If these are to be interpreted as ἄρρην εἰμί and ἰδοὺ ἄρρην the first utterance is presumably spoken by the youth; the second may possibly reinforce it, but an alternative interpretation is suggested by the comic idiom in which a speaker repeats the word or phrase of the previous speaker and prefaces it with a contemptuous ἰδού, e.g. Ar., Knights 343f. ὁτιὴ λέγειν οἷός τε κἀγώ ... – ἰδοὺ λέγειν ("Whaddya mean, speak?"). If that idiom was current in the sixth century B.C., ἰδοὺ ἄρρην is the vase-painter's cynical comment on the youth who allows himself to be courted;[13] the vase thus combines evidence of category I (B) with evidence of category II (B) (1). The scornful ἰδού is not used in Plato even when characters such as Thrasymakhos and Kallikles are being rude to Socrates; nor is any other kind of ἰδού, except in the words which a certain Leontios, according to Resp. 440a, addressed to his own eyes: ἰδοὺ ὑμῖν, ἔφη, ὦ κακοδαίμονες, ἐμπλήσθητε τοῦ καλοῦ θεάματος (where καλοῦ is sarcastic,[14] κακοδαίμονες is predominantly comic,[15] and ἰδοὺ ὑμῖν has a parallel in Ar., Ach. 470 ἰδού σοι, words accompanying the gift demanded in 469 φυλλεῖα δός).[16]

(C) Hellenistic Period.

Some Hellenistic poetry, notably Herodas and Theokritos 14 and 15 (cf. parts of 4, 5 and 10), ostensibly portray the conversation of uneducated people. Theokr., 14.8 παίζεις, ὦγάθ', ἔχων exemplifies the kind of support to be found in this area for the designation of an Aristophanic and Platonic usage as colloquial; cf. Ar., Birds 341, Lys. 945 ληρεῖς ἔχων, Frogs 202 and 524 οὐ μὴ φλυαρήσεις ἔχων, Pl. Euthd. 295c ὅτι ἔχων φλυαρεῖς καὶ ἀρχαιότερος εἶ τοῦ δέοντος, Grg. 490e ποῖα ὑποδήματα; φλυαρεῖς ἔχων. It is significant that the last example shows also the scornful ποῖος common in comedy,[17] and Euthd. 295c (on which Socrates comments, "I realised that he was getting annoyed with me,") the dismissive ἀρχαῖος "not with it," "square" (e.g. Ar., Wasps 1336 ἀρχαῖα γ' ὑμῶν, ironic in the mouth of the rejuvenated and outrageous old Philokleon).

---

[10] Kretschmer (90) understands πίομαι, but he interpreted the first utterance as ἤδη κἀνέπιε⟨ν⟩. J.D. Beazley, AJA 39 (1935) 477f. concurs in πίομαι, although rejecting κἀνέπιεν in favour of κανῆ πλέα.

[11] Kretschmer, 91; E. des Places in Mélanges Bidez (Brussels 1934) 274f.

[12] Emily Vermeule, Antike Kunst 12 (1969) 10f.

[13] Dover, Greek Homosexuality (London 1978) 146.

[14] Stevens 55; add Eur., Med. 514, Pherekrates, fr. 149.

[15] Stevens, 14f.

[16] The idiom is related to the attachment of a dative pronoun to a demonstrative; e.g., Hdt., 5.92. η 4 τοιοῦτο μὲν ὑμῖν ἐστι ἡ τυραννίς.   [17] Stevens, 38f.

Category II: Documents.

(A) Attic of the Central Period.

(1) Private Documents.

Most Attic graffiti and dipinti are considerably earlier in date than Aristophanes and will therefore be considered together in (B) (1) below. Some messages incised on potsherds (Lang, nos. 18, 22, 35, 38) are also early. A fourth-century letter on lead (Wünsch, 11f.)[18] helps to confirm that the morphological basis of Attic literary prose was identical with that of ordinary communication, but its contribution to our knowledge of colloquialism is questionable. A private contract relating to the sale or loan of a house (Peek, 88f., no. 168) is cast, like the depositions interspersed in some Demosthenic speeches, in formal terms and belongs linguistically with (A) (2) below. Curse-tablets, some of which are certainly to be dated well within the central period,[19] show a smattering of solecisms (cf. p. 17, above),[20] and some of them even a non-Attic dialectal colouring. Occasional obscenities (Wünsch, no. 77b. 1 ψωλή, κύσθος; cf. Ar., Lys. 979, 1158) link their language to that of comedy, but the occurrence of καὶ ἔργα [κ]α⟨ὶ⟩ ἔπεα in Wünsch, 84b.2 (cf. ε]πεα in Peek, 91–3 no. 3.20) side by side with γλῶτ⟨τ⟩αν (84b.1, 3) reminds us that in a curse the writer is handling a religious formula to which he might sometimes (and to us, unpredictably) judge poetic forms appropriate. This may account also for μήποτε (alien to Attic prose) rather than μηδέποτε in Wünsch, 64.3 καὶ μήπο[τ]ε αὐτὸς εὖ πράττοι, 78.3; cf. the heartfelt curse of Ar., Peace 3 καὶ μήποτ' αὐτῆς μᾶζαν ἡδίω φάγοι, where μηδέποτ' would have been permitted by comic metrical practice.

(2) Public Documents.

In Ar., Thesm. 431f. the woman who has proposed in the "assembly" of women that Euripides must somehow be destroyed (the substance of her γνώμη is given in 428–431 νῦν οὖν ἐμοὶ ... δοκεῖ ... ὅπως ἀπολεῖται) concludes: ταῦτ' ἐγὼ φανερῶς λέγω, τὰ δ' ἄλλα μετὰ τῆς γραμματέως συγγράψομαι. If this is as close a parody of procedure as the rest of the scene, it seems that what we read in an Attic decree, introduced by ὁ δεῖνα εἶπε, is not the unaided composition of the proposer. Until the 360's the secretary of the assembly was changed for every prytany, so that we have no chance of detecting, in such decrees as remain to us, the individual style of a given secretary, nor of assessing his linguistic competence. Thereafter the possibility becomes less remote, and on the strength of IG 2/3.² 110.16 ὅπως ἂν ἐάν του δέηται τυγχάνῃ and 111.17–19 ὅπως δ' ἂν καὶ οἱ ὅρκοι καὶ αἱ συνθῆκαι ἃς συνέθετο Χαβρίας ... ὑπὲρ ... Κείων οὓς κατήγαγον ... κύριαι ὦσι we might attribute to Nikostratos of Pallene, secretary in 363/2, a liking for certain types of hypotactic construction. Yet we must never forget the professional under-secretaries who will have done more than anyone to mould Attic official style. The establishment of formulae in this style was slow and by no means complete even in the fourth century, as we can see by contrasting IG 2/3.² 26.9f. καὶ ν[υνὶ] καὶ ἐν τῷ προτέρῳ χρόνῳ with 77.14 καὶ νῦν καὶ ἐν τῷ πρόσθεν χρόνῳ, or 107.10f. τοὺς] προέδρους οἳ ἂν λάχωσιν προεδρεύειν εἰς τὴν πρώ[την ἐ]κκλησίαν with 128.10 τοὺς μὲν προ[έδρους οἳ ἂν τυγχάνωσι π]ροε[δ]ρεύον[τε]ς [ε]ἰς τὴν πρώτ[η]ν ἐκκ[λησίαν. Nevertheless, it was one of the determinants of the genre from the very first. Such evidence of colloquial language as documentary inscriptions may afford is to be sought in their preservation of (presumably local Attic) forms lost in literature, e.g., IG 1.² 898.1, 900.1, 901.1, 2/3.² 4960.7 δεῦρε = δεῦρο,[21] 2/3.² 1522.30 (et saepe) κάτροπτον = κάτοπτρον. It is possible that such forms once existed in Attic

---

[18] A. Wilhelm, JOAI 7 (1904) 94–105; W. Crönert, RhM 65 (1910) 157f.

[19] On the dating cf. Wilhelm (above, note 18) 106–121, and L. H. Jeffery, ABSA 1 (1955) 74f. on material from the Kerameikos.

[20] For an analysis of the linguistic data cf. E. Schwyzer, NJbb 5.3 (1900) 244–262 and W. Rabehl, De Sermone Defixionum Atticarum (Diss. Berlin 1906).

[21] Cf. A. J. Beattie, Trans. Philol. Soc. (1949) 3.

literary texts but were purged in transmission; rather as Demosthenes must surely have said and written Κερσεβλέπτης (as in *IG* 2/3.² 126.10, 17, 20) but the manuscripts of his text have Κερσοβλέπτης under the irresistible influence of χερσο- and the predominant pattern of substantival compounds. At phonological and morphological level the stonecutter's language may come through, or at any rate his predilections in spelling (e. g., the indiscriminate initial aspirates of *IG* 1.² 374).

(B) Earlier Period.

(1) Attic Graffiti and Dipinti.

Graffiti are largely derogatory and make much use of the Aristophanic abusive term καταπύγων (e.g., Lang, no. 20), to which we must add the feminine (as yet unattested in literature) καταπύγαινα (*SEG* 13,32); cf. *IG* 1.² 921.4f. λαιϰ[ασ]τ[ρια] ~ Ar., *Ach.* 529, 537. By contrast, most dipinti on vases are laudatory, acclaiming someone's beauty. The predicate καλός may be intensified in several ways: simple repetition, καλὸς καλός (Havana, *ARV* 1570); καλὸς ναί (Oxford 333, *ARV* 1602 ~ 26); καλὸς ναίχι (Copenhagen 127, *ARV* 138); καλὸς κάρτα (Compiègne 978, *ABV* 674); καλὸς νὴ Δία (Palermo, *ABV* 675). This handful of expressions turns out, when their history and affinities are explored, to show up the gaps in our evidence and the fragility of inferences. Repetition of an evaluative word and its reinforcement by an oath are echoed in Ar., *Eccl.* 213 εὖ γ' εὖ γε νὴ Δί' εὖ γε (representing rapturous applause). Repetition of καλός recurs in Alexandrian erotic poetry:[22] *Anth. Pal.* 12.62.1 καλὰ μὲν καλὰ τέκνα (*sc.* youths) τέϰεσθε 130.1 εἶπα 'καλὸς καλός', and cf. [Theokr.] 8.73 καλὸν καλὸν ἦμεν ἔφασκεν. Kallim., *Epigr.* 30.5 reinforces it by ναίχι: σὺ δὲ ναίχι καλὸς καλός (cf. *Epigr.* 53.3). Since ναίχι is also a feature of New Comedy dialogue (Men., *Epit.* 872.f. — οὐ σὲ τὴν νύμφην ὁρῶ . . .; — ναίχι, *Sam.* 296 ἐμέ τις κέκληκε; — ναίχι — χαῖρε δέσποτα), we should expect to find it in Old Comedy, bridging the gap between archaic dipinti and Hellenistic poetry, but we do not; only the Scythian policeman in *Thesm.* uses it (1183 *al.* ναίϰι), no doubt because it can be exploited to illustrate his inability to aspirate unvoiced stops. In the Platonic corpus it is confined to *Hipparch.* 232a, and it appears just once in tragedy (Soph., *OT* 684 — ἀμφοῖν ἀπ' αὐτοῖν; — ναίχι. — καὶ τίς ἦν λόγος;). It must be said plainly that these passages have nothing in common to distinguish them from the occasions on which ναί is used.[23] If the history of ναίχι is obscure, that of κάρτα is no less so. Commonplace in fifth-century Ionic prose, it is virtually confined in Attic to tragedy; Plato uses it once (*Ti.* 25d πηλοῦ κάρτα βραχέος) and Aristophanes once, in combination with an undoubted colloquialism (cf. p. 17, above), *Birds* 342 τοῦτο μὲν ληρεῖς ἔχων κάρτα. Presumably κάρτα, like adverbial μετά (cf. p. 18, above), belonged to that part of the common Ionic-Attic lexicon which went out of use in Attic in the course of the fifth century;[24] in *Birds* 342 it is virtually an archaism, in *Ti.* 25d quite strongly archaising.[25]

(2) Non-Attic Graffiti and Dipinti.

This class is characterised, like its Attic counterpart, by much obscenity, in which some regional variation of vocabulary is noteworthy: οἴφειν "copulate" (e. g., *IG* 12.[3]537) and the noun οἰφόλης (e. g., *SEG* 15.523 [Tenos]) are quite alien to the Attic vocabulary of sex. (Conversely, if βενεοι in *DGE* 412.1 (Elis) is rightly interpreted as = βινοίη, it shows that one of the grossest words in Ionic and Attic was permissible in an archaic religious law of the Eleans).

---

[22] Cf. also (non-erotic) Pind., *Pyth.* 2.72f.

[23] W. Schulze, *Kleine Schriften* (Göttingen 1934) 706 treats ναίχι as an outright vulgarism. I learn from Professor Morpurgo Davies that Eduard Fraenkel's agreement with Schulze on this matter was by no means as unqualified as might appear from *Due Seminari di Eduard Fraenkel* (Rome 1977) 52. Neither Schulze nor Fraenkel mentions Menander, and though Fraenkel cites the Kallimakhos passages he does not consider their relation to a tradition of homoerotic formulae.

[24] Cf. Dover in *Wege der Forschungen* 265 (1975) 127 on θωᾶν and θωά.

[25] It is not impossible that Plato wished to offset "mud" (cf. *Prm.* 130c) by an elevated word; cf. note 2 above.

(3) An Early Ionic Letter.

A letter written on lead and found on the island of Berezan, at the mouth of the Bug,[26] has much of interest to tell us about Ionic, but one feature of its structure is relevant also to early Greek (including Attic) prose literature. The writer says (6–9): "He protests and says that there is no connexion between himself and Matasys. And he says that he is a free man and that there is no connexion between himself and Matasys. Whether[27] there is any connexion between him (*sc.* Matasys) and Anaxagoras, they themselves know." Just this kind of repetition occurs in a forensic speech, Lys., 1.17: "I was at once thrown into a turmoil, καὶ πάντα μου εἰς τὴν γνώμην εἰσῄει, καὶ μεστὸς ἦ ὑποψίας, when I thought of how I'd been locked in my room and remembered that the courtyard door and the street door made a noise that night – it had never happened before – and I thought my wife had make-up on; ταῦτά μου πάντα εἰς τὴν γνώμην εἰσῄει, καὶ μεστὸς ἦ ὑπο-ψίας." Dobree, observing the normal dislike of Attic prose for pure repetition, deleted ταῦτα . . . ὑποψίας, but the Berezan letter simultaneously justifies the retention of the words by modern editors and alerts us to the possibility of deliberate naivety of style in other parts of Lys., 1. Comparable repetitiousness in [Xen.] *Resp. Ath.* 2.11f., perhaps an ambitious attempt at rhetorical effect in 11 (where the question ποῖ διαθήσεται ἐὰν μὴ πείσῃ τὸν ἄρχοντα τῆς θαλάσσης is posed twice), but rambling and loquacious in 11 ἐξ αὐτῶν . . . 12 τὸ δὲ τῇ, encourages us to look for a colloquial element in the sentence-structure of early prose in general;[28] cf. (D) and p. 22, below.

(C) An Ionic Letter of the Central Period.

DGE 736 (*SGDI* 4, pp.865f.), from Olbia,[29] is a good companion-piece to the Attic letter mentioned in (II)(A)(1), and seems to offer an Ionicism familiar from Herodotus:[30] παρὰ Ἀτάκους εἰς τὸ οἴκημα· ἢν γὰρ διδῷ· εἰ δὲ μή, παρὰ Ἀγάθαρχον κτλ. "(. . .) into the room (hired? borrowed?) from Atakes – if, that is, Atakes allows; otherwise, to Agatharkhos . . . . " Interpretation of other details of the text is controversial; its punctuation, mainly systematic but with one bizarre lapse (3 ὑ:μ[ᾶς]) recalls early Attic public documents.

(D) Private Documents of the Hellenistic Period.

Private letters and messages from Ptolemaic and Roman Egypt provide support for the identification of some classical Attic phenomena as colloquial,[31] e.g., *POxy* 2844 (s. 1 p.C.) μὴ οὖν ἄλλως ποιήσῃς, a formula of earnest invitation, entreaty or admonition, familiar in Plato (e.g., *Smp.* 173e) and represented in Aristophanes by *Birds* 133.[32] A strikingly vulgar message from the first century A.D. (*POxy* 3070) says: εἰ διδῶς (ΗΔΙΔΥC) ἡμεῖν τὸ πυγίσαι καὶ καλῶς σοί ἐστι, οὐκέτι οὐ μὴ δείρομέν σε ἐὰν δώσῃς ἡμεῖν τὸ πυγίσαι. The repetition of the protasis is, as it happens, a feature of the earliest prose literature:[33] Anaxagoras B12 "if it were not on its own but were mixed with something else, it would participate in everything, if it were mixed with something else"; cf. (less blatantly) Diogenes of Apollonia B2 "if the present components of the universe . . . , if any of them were different from another . . . , they could not in any way be blended . . . nor could any plant . . . come into being, if it were not so constitued as to be the same."

[26] J. Chadwick, *PCPS* 199 (1973) 35–37.

[27] I interpret ματατασυεδετι as Μα[τα]τάσυ⟨ι⟩. ε(ἰ) δέ τι (Ματά⟨συι. Μα⟩τάσυι δὲ τί Chadwick; Ματάσυι · τί δὲ ed. pr. [Vinogradov]).

[28] On colloquial aspects of the language of the "Old Oligarch" cf. F. Pfister, *Philologus* 73 (1914/16) 558–562.

[29] A. Wilhelm, *JOAI* 7 (1904) 94–105; Crönert (above, note 18), 158–160.

[30] Denniston, 67f.

[31] Cf. D. Tabachovitz, *MusHelv* 3 (1946) 144–179.

[32] Ed. Fraenkel, *Beobachtungen zu Aristophanes* (Rome 1962) 69f.

[33] D. Fehling, *Die Wiederholungsfiguren und ihr Gebrauch bei den Griechen vor Gorgias* (Berlin 1969) 148f.

In (II)(B)(3) and (D) we have seen a glimmer of affinity between the sentence-structure of non-literary utterance and the sentence-structure of prose literature in its emergent stage or in a deliberately unsophisticated style. The relation between the complex structures of Attic prose and the way people usually talked is crucial to the formation of any clear view of the contrast between the two, and narrative is the genre in which the contrast may be most easily drawn. Consider the sentence with which the narrative opens in Xen., *Anab.* 4.1.5, a text read by many modern learners of Greek early in their careers: "When it was about the last watch and there was left of the night enough for them to cross the plain in darkness, then, having broken camp at the passing on of a command, going on their way they arrived at daybreak at the mountain." In what form did one of Xenophon's soldiers communicate this same datum to his friends or his grandchildren?

In considering possible structures for spoken narrative it is worthwhile to take some examples from cultures which were entirely non-literate until the era of colonialism and compare them with examples from the unlettered stratum of a literate culture.

(1) The first example, from the Solomon Islands,[34] illustrates narrative sequence in a language which makes virtually no use either of connectives or of subordinate clauses.

> It was nut-time. Her mother, her father, went to the garden. Kanupea went. There she saw Kirikoputu. She called, "Sister, come on, we will pick nuts, we will gather in". Kirikoputu said, "Ah, I have no arms, I have no legs! Now what shall I do?" She said. She refused. "Oh, sister, I will give you my arms, my legs" said Kanupea. She gave her arms. She gave her legs. They went. They picked.

(2) Igorot, a language of the Philippine Islands,[35] makes much use of connectives translatable as "then" or "so".

> Then the rice and the crabs are cooked. Then I begin eating. And then comes my companion. Then we eat together, because we are very hungry. Then we start. Then we go to Dagupan, a large town. And then they do not provide for us.

(3) A modern folktale from Cyprus[36] mixes connected clauses with asyndeta irregularly.

> They reached the boy. The giant dismounted. He takes him. He cut off the head of the boy. And he took the girl and returned back. He took the girl inside. He also went to pasture his horse. The girl recovered from her grief, and took his head, and put it in her bosom, and took up the body, and went. She attached the body there to the head.

(4) Each of the two last sequences contains one subordinate clause tacked on to a main clause: "because we are very hungry" and "to pasture (νὰ βοσσήσει) his horse." Spoken narrative can easily accommodate a string of such subordinate clauses,[37] as in this example from a Modern Greek dialect of Asia Minor:[38]

> And anger seizes the king. He goes home. He takes his daughter. He leads her to a desert place, and puts her there. He returns to (νά) bring much wood, to (νά) burn it, to (νά) kill his daughter and that (νά) the ash-seller may not marry her.

(5) Spoken narrative may compensate, artistically speaking, for a monotonous simplicity of structure by frequent movement between the past tense and the present (as in [3]), and also by rhetorical questions; this development is a positive characteristic of oral delivery, as in the following example from the Dodecanese.[39]

---

[34] G. C. Wheeler, *Mono-Alu Folklore* (London 1926) 73.

[35] C. W. Seidenadel, *The Language of the Bontoc Igorot* (Chicago 1909) 525.

[36] Brian Newton, *Cypriot Greek* (Hague/Paris 1972) 167.

[37] In *Eloc.* 10–15 Demetrios might seem to be contrasting a string of this kind with more elaborately planned hypotaxes, but his examples suggest that he has in mind a succession of short main clauses. His § 21, on the opening of Pl., *Rep.*, is more relevant.

[38] R. M. Dawkins, *Modern Greek in Asia Minor* (Cambridge 1916) 284f.

[39] J. Zarriftis, ed. (tr. R. M. Dawkins), *Forty-five Stories from the Dodecanese* (Cambridge 1950) 31.

But when he was sixteen, the old man died, and he was unprotected. Who is to look after him? The old woman? – who herself wanted people to look after her! He leaves his books then, and he seeks work, to support his mother and himself. But what work is he to take up? A craft? He needed to learn it first.

(6) Many languages in New Guinea have developed a system of participles and "sentence-medial" tenses,[40] the operation of which is shown by the following examples from Kâte:[41] *mulâ kiopo* "having spoken, I wept"; *mulâ kiove'*, "having spoken, he wept"; with change of subject, *mume kiopo* "when he had spoken, I wept"; *mupe kiove'* "when I had spoken, he wept" (different forms are used for other temporal relations between the two actions or events). How this works in narrative is best shown by literal translation:

Later. having seen (*part.*) a kalophyllum tree, climbing (*part.*) up it, he having arrived (*sent.-med. tense*) at the top, straightway having broken off (*part.*), it slinging him away (*sent.-med.*), sailing (*part.*) through the air, having fallen (*part.*) downwards, having pierced (*part.*) a hole in the ground, he having gone down in (*sent.-med.*), fire mounted up (*sent.-final tense*). It burns (*sent.-final*) always.

These specimens of narrative are not in themselves conversation, for they were told by people deliberately transmitting a story, but much conversation is narrative in character, and the specimens illustrate the range of resources in structural types upon which Attic Greek could draw. One of the fundamental differences between speech and writing is that a writer has time to plan ahead and a reader, if he loses the thread, can retrace his steps and pick it up again. We have seen in (II) (B) (3) and (D) some reason to think that a person unaccustomed to large-scale written composition becomes uneasy when his sentence exceeds a certain modest length and restates what he has already stated. Mere complexity, as assessed by counting up subordinate clauses and participles, is not so important a difference; the speaker of specimen (4) could, in theory, go on indefinitely adding νά-clauses, one at a time, and start a fresh sentence at any moment of his own choosing, and similarly the Kâte story-teller in specimen (6) never has to look more then a couple of words ahead in deciding whether a participle, sentence-medial tense or sentence-final tense is appropriate.[42] The composer of an Attic decree, on the other hand, may have to fix his eyes on a distant horizon when he embarks on an elaborate ἐπειδή–clause; *IG* 2/3.² 111.27–41 (again Nikostratos is the secretary [cf. p. 19]) provides an unusually complicated example:

ἐπειδὴ δὲ Ἰουλιητῶν οἱ παραβάντες ...
        καὶ πολεμήσαντες ...
        καὶ θανάτου αὐτῶν καταγνωσθέντος κατελθόντες ...
τάς τε στήλας ἐξέβαλον
    ἐν αἷς ἦσαν ἀναγεγραμμέναι ...
καὶ τοὺς φίλους τοὺς Ἀθηναίων,
    οὓς κατήγαγεν ὁ δῆμος,
τοὺς μὲν ἀπέκτειναν
τῶν δὲ θάνατον κατέγνωσαν ...,
Σατυρίδου καί Τιμοξένου καὶ Μιλτιάδου,
    ὅτι κατηγόρουν Ἀντιπάτρου,
        ὅτε ἡ βουλὴ ἡ Ἀθηναίων κατέγνω αὐτοῦ θάνατον
        ἀποκτείναντος τὸν πρόξενον ...
        καὶ παραβάντα (*sic*)[43] τοὺς ὅρκους ...
φεύγειν αὐτοὺς κτλ.

[40] A. Capell, *A Survey of New Guinea Languages* (Sydney 1969) 82–86.

[41] G. Pilhofer, *Grammatik der Kâte-Sprache in Neuguinea* (Berlin 1933) 35–38, 172.

[42] In modern Amharic, by contrast, an everyday message may reveal quite elaborate syntactical planning on the part of its composer; cf. E. Ullendorff, *The Challenge of Amharic* (London 1965) 14f.

[43] Here the stonecutter – or possibly even the composer – loses his way, for the sense requires παραβάντος.

When Plato portrays a speaker as launched on a sentence of comparable size, he sometimes makes him lose track of the syntax and start afresh, as in *Smp.* 177bc, 182d 183c, 218ab. But even much less complex sentences, such as we find by the score in literary narrative, require a degree of planning which was probably (to judge by modern Greek folktales) alien to speech, e.g. (an example selected at random), Thuc. 4.101.3 μετὰ δὲ τὴν μάχην ταύτην καὶ ὁ Δημοσθένης ... ὡς αὐτῷ τότε πλεύσαντι .... οὐ προυχώρησεν, ἔχων ..., ἀπόβασιν ἐποιήσατο κτλ.

Narrative which is predominantly cast in short units tends to develop substantial boundary-markers ("then", "so", etc.), and one of the most striking differences between narrative in Old Comedy and the narrative speeches of tragedy is the use made by the former of εἶτα, κᾆτα, ἔπειτα and κἄπειτα, which are virtually absent from the latter.[44] Thus we find in the speech of the disguised old man in Ar., *Thesm.* 481–9 οὗτος ... ἔκνυεν ... κᾆτ᾽ εὐθὺς ἔγνων· εἶτα καταβαίνω ... ὁ δ᾽ ἀνὴρ ἐρωτᾷ ... κᾆθ᾽ ὁ μὲν ἔτριβε ... ἐγὼ δέ ... ἐξῆλθον ... εἶτ᾽ ἠρειδόμην κτλ. It is agreeable to find exactly the same phenomenon in Lys., 1.14, the reported words of a wife whose adultery was remarkably like that of the imaginary wife in *Thesm.*: ἔφασκε τὸν λύχνον ἀποσβεσθῆναι τὸν παρὰ τῷ παιδίῳ, εἶτα ἐκ τῶν γειτόνων ἐνάψασθαι. Connective εἶτα figures in some Aristophanic passages where the syntax is anomalous, notably *Ach.* 23f. ἀωρίαν ἥκοντες εἶτα δ᾽ ὠστιοῦνται πῶς δοκεῖς (πῶς δοκεῖς has colloquial associations),[45] *Clouds* 409 ὀπτῶν ... κᾆτ᾽ οὐκ ἔσχων, 623f. λαχών ... κἄπειθ᾽ ... ἀφῃρέθη. Adverbial καί in the construction *ποιήσας καὶ ἀπῄει is virtually unknown, and "apodotic" δέ in similar circumstances is attested only when the participial clause is substantial enough to separate the participle from the verb by several words.[46] The Aristophanic passages represent a (colloquial?) fusion of (1) *part.* εἶτα *verb* with (2) *verb*$_1$ κᾆτα (or εἶτα [δέ]) *verb*$_2$.

It would not be surprising if some of the earliest surviving specimens of Greek literary narrative showed some affinity with the basically paratactic structure postulated for speech,[47] and Akousilaos of Argos (*FGrHist* 2) F22 does so:

> Καινῇ δέ ... μίσγεται Ποσειδῶν.
> ἔπειτα (οὐ γὰρ ἦν ...) ποιεῖ αὐτόν ... ἄνδρα ἄτρωτον,
> ἰσχὺν ἔχοντα ...
> καὶ ὅτε τις αὐτὸν κεντοίη ...,
> ἡλίσκετο ...
> καὶ γίγνεται βασιλεὺς οὗτος Λαπιθέων
> καὶ τοῖς κενταύροις πολεμέεσκε.
> ἔπειτα στήσας ...
> ἐκέλευεν ...
>]σι δ᾽ οὐκ ἦν ...
> καὶ Ζεὺς ἰδών ...
> ἀπειλεῖ
> καὶ ἐφορμᾷ ...
> κἀκεῖνοι αὐτὸν κατακόπτουσιν ...
> καὶ ἄνωθεν πέτρην ἐπιτιθεῖσιν σῆμα
> καὶ ἀποθνήσκει.

---

[44] Dover, *Lysias and the Corpus Lysiacum* (Berkeley and Los Angeles 1968) 84 f.

[45] Stevens, 39.

[46] Denniston, 181 f. and 308 f.

[47] S. Trenkner, *Le Style KAI dans le récit attique oral* (Assen 1960) 16–21; S. Lilja, *On the Style of the Earliest Greek Prose* (Helsinki 1968) 73–100.

We value Greek culture mostly for its achievement in the arts and its intellectual confrontation of some enduring problems. Preoccupation with the way in which Greeks expressed themselves when they were not achieving anything of great worth or exercising their intellects very hard might therefore be criticised as the product of trendy cant about "real life." Yet the relationships obtaining in any culture between literature and speech, illuminating as they do the writers' own conceptions of the status and function of literature, ought to be of concern to historians and literary critics. In the case of the Greeks there is abundant reason to think that their arts were firmly rooted in the attitudes and values of ordinary life, and to catch from time to time the sound of their voices enables us to judge how far, and in what circumstances, a conceptual relationship between art and life was reinforced by a formal relationship.

Corpus Christi College,   K. J. DOVER
OXFORD.

An earlier draft of this paper was given in Christ Church, Oxford, as the 1977 Gaisford Lecture , and an earlier version still at the Royal Society of Edinburgh in March 1977.

Reference is made to the following works by author's name only: J. D. Denniston, *The Greek Particles,* revised edition (Oxford 1954); P. Kretschmer, *Die griechische Vaseninschriften* (Gütersloh 1894); Mabel Lang, *Graffiti in the Athenian Agora* (Princeton 1974); W. Peek, *Inschriften, Ostraka, Fluchtafeln* (= *Kerameikos: Ergebnisse der Ausgrabungen* 3; Berlin 1941); P. T. Stevens, *Colloquial Expressions in Euripides* (= *Hermes* Einzelschriften 38 [1976]); R. Wünsch, *Defixionum Tabellae Atticae* (= *CIA* Appendix; Berlin 1897).

ON THE LOCATION OF MT. TISAION*

The point of departure for Polybios' well-known excursus on fire-signalling (10.43–47) is his description of a system of communication established by Philip V of Macedonia in 208 B.C.

καὶ τὴν μὲν δύναμιν ἐν τῇ Σκοτούσῃ πάλιν ἀπέλειπε, μετὰ δὲ τῶν εὐζώνων καὶ τῆς βασιλικῆς ἴλης εἰς Δημητριάδα καταλύσας ἔμενε, καραδοκῶν ⟨τὰς⟩ τῶν ἐναντίων ἐπιβολάς. ἵνα δὲ μηδὲν αὐτὸν λανθάνῃ τῶν πραττομένων, διεπέμψατο πρὸς Πεπαρηθίους καὶ πρὸς τοὺς ἐπὶ τῆς Φωκίδος, ὁμοίως δὲ καὶ πρὸς τοὺς ἐπὶ τῆς Εὐβοίας, καὶ παρήγγειλε διασαφεῖν αὐτῷ πάντα τὰ γινόμενα διὰ τῶν πυρσῶν ἐπὶ τὸ Τίσαιον. τοῦτο δ'ἐστὶ τῆς Θετταλίας ὄρος, εὐφυῶς κείμενον πρὸς τὰς τῶν προειρημένων τόπων περιφάσεις.

(10.42. 6–8)[1]

Livy's version of the same event is also worth quoting, for according to him Philip . . . ipse in Tisaeo . . . speculam posuit, while those whom the King had sent to Phokis, Euboia, and Peparethos were to pick out . . . loca alta . . . unde editi ignes apparerent.[2]

Philip's arrangements were simple, as Polybios further makes clear.

> To take the case I just mentioned, it was possible for those who had agreed on this to convey information that a fleet had arrived at Oreus, Peparethus, or Chalcis, but when it came to some of the citizens having changed sides or having been guilty of treachery or a massacre having taken place in the town, or anything of the kind, things that often happen, but cannot be foreseen — and it is chiefly unexpected occurrences which require instant consideration and help — all such matters defied communication by fire-signal.
>
> (10.43. 7–9)[3]

Yet in the emergency of the occasion it was enough for Philip that from his residence at Demetrias he could in this way monitor the threatening moves of the Romans and Pergamenes.

The hub of the system was the relay-station established by Philip on Tisaion, which Polybios describes in the text quoted above as "a mountain in Thessaly, well situated to provide wide-ranging views of the places mentioned," that is, of Peparethos (modern Skopelos), Phokis, and

* Some debts should be acknowledged publicly, and I am glad to record how much I owe to Malcolm McGregor, a master-teacher, loyal colleague, and patient friend. In this slight return I hope that he will recognize two qualities borrowed from his own scholarship, respect both for ancient texts and for personal observation. But he will also recognize that I, in common with so many others who have attended the American School of Classical Studies in the past thirty years, have learned from another exemplary teacher, colleague, and friend, Eugene Vanderpool. And it is to him that I owe the subject of this essay. I thank them both.

[1] In translating this passage in *The Loeb Classical Library,* W.R. Paton (*Polybius, The Histories* 4 [London and Cambridge, Mass. 1925, reprinted 1960] 207) unaccountably substituted Boiotia for Euboia. F. W. Walbank made the same mistake in the first edition of *Philip V of Macedon* (Cambridge 1940) 94, but noted the correction in the reprint published by Archon Books in 1967.

[2] Livy 28. 5. 16–17.

[3] Translated by W. R. Paton (above, note 1) 209.

28 C. W. J. ELIOT

Euboia. Despite Polybios' reference to Thessaly, modern critics have been unanimous in placing Tisaion in Magnesia. F. W. Walbank's comment on this passage represents orthodoxy.

> τὸ Τίσαιον: modern Mt. Bardhzogia (130 m.), opposite Artemisium in the southernmost part of the Magnesian peninsula, where it runs east and west. Alexander of Pherae had made it the main point of a fire-signalling system (Polyaean.vi.2.1). See Leake, *NG,* iv.396 f.; Bursian, i.100; Wace, *JHS,* 1906, 148−9 (putting it further east on the main peninsula between Lavkos and Platania, just above C. Sepias); Stählin, *Hell. Thess.* 55; *RE,*'Tisaion', col. 1467. It is odd that P. reckons it part of Thessaly rather than of Magnesia.[4]

Map. Location of Mount Tisaion.

[4] *A Historical Commentary on Polybius* 2 (Oxford 1967) 258. Walbank's figure for the altitude of Bardzogia is incorrect. The source of his error is probably F. Stählin, *Das hellenische Thessalien* (Suttgart 1924) 55, where the same height is recorded. Stählin, however, later published the correct information, 644 m., in the article on Tisaion in *RE* noted by Walbank. E. Meyer's entry on Tisaion in *Der kleine Pauly* 5 (Munich 1975) 865−866 recapitulates traditional views and references.

What is the evidence that justifies so easy a disregard of Polybios' word? As far as Stählin and Walbank are concerned, the deciding text seems to be Polyainos (*Strategemata* 6. 2. 1).

> Alexander [of Pherai], when Leosthenes was besieging Panormos, not daring to engage openly in a sea-fight against all the Athenian ships, sent a message by a skiff at night to those soldiers within, to the effect that, if some of the ships abandoned the patrol, in addition to the previously agreed upon fire-signal they were to raise a second to those in Magnesia, and the latter to those at Pagasai.

As a result of these arrangements, when the fire-signals were raised and the message thus sent from Panormos on Peparethos to Pagasai by means of a relay in Magnesia, Alexander was able to surprise the Athenians and defeat them. Since Stählin and Walbank assume that both Alexander in 361 B.C. and Philip in 208 B.C. chose the same place for their relay-station, and since neither scholar questions the correctness of Polyainos' account, it necessarily follows for them that Tisaion was located in Magnesia.

The remaining literary evidence does nothing to support such a conclusion; one text seems to contradict it. Tisaia and its headland were clearly a traditional element in the landscape passed by the Argonauts as they sailed from the Gulf of Pagasai into the open sea beyond. But none of the three citations[5] is so detailed that one can infer the position of Tisaia, whether on the right or left of the gulf's mouth, a lack of precision reflected in the scholiast's gloss on the mention of Tisaia by Apollonios Rhodios[6] − Τισαίη ἀκρωτήριον Θεσσαλίας ἢ Μαγνησίας, τινὲς δὲ τῆς Θεσπρωτίας − (even poetic vagueness hardly warrants the last suggestion). A notice of Τίσαι λιμήν has also been claimed in pseudo-Skylax's description of the Magnetes following the place-name Ὀλιζών.[7] The text, however, has Ἴσαι λιμήν, and, even though this constitutes the only reference to such a harbour, it is the reading accepted by Stählin and Wace, who do not reject it on the grounds of its uniqueness or resemblance to Tisaion − Tisaia.[8] Without other evidence to prove the location of Tisaion in Magnesia, I see no case for emending pseudo-Skylax's text.

Beyond these several references that leave the question of Tisaion's location in either Thessaly or Magnesia unsettled, there is a final mention of Tisaion in Appian, *Mithridateios* 35, where, though the manuscripts preserve Τίδαιον, the emendation Τίσαιον proposed by J. Schweighäuser in 1792 is now the accepted reading.[9] The events described by Appian occurred in 86 B.C., when Sulla was beseiging Athens.

> And at the same time Arkathias, son of Mithridates, invading Macedonia with another army, with no difficulty prevailed over the few Romans who were there, reduced the whole country, and, after entrusting it to satraps, himself advanced on Sulla, until he fell sick and died near Tisaion.

From this brief mention, one can assume that Tisaion was placed in the vicinity of one of the routes from Macedonia to Attica. Since it is clear that Tisaion-Tisaia was on one side or other of the mouth of the Gulf of Pagasai, that is, in Magnesia or Thessaly, and since no land route passes through the former, the evidence of Appian supports the plain statement of Polybios that Tisaion was in Thessaly.

---

[5] Apollonios Rhodios, *Argonautica* 1. 566−568; Valerius Flaccus, *Argonautica* 2. 6−7; E. Abel, *Orphica* (Leipzig and Prague 1885) *Argonautica* 460 (462).

[6] C. Wendel, *Scholia in Apollonium Rhodium vetera* (Berlin 1935) 49, with reference to line 568.

[7] Skylax, *Periplus* 65, s.v. Magnetes, in C. Müller, *Geographici Graeci Minores* 1 (Paris 1855) 51.

[8] F. Stählin, *RE* 9. 2 (1916) 2050, s.v. Ἴσαι λιμήν, and A. J. B. Wace, "The Topography of Pelion and Magnesia," *JHS* 26 (1906) 149.

[9] P. Viereck and A. G. Roos, *Appiani Historia Romana* 1 (Leipzig 1962) 449.

The topographical inferences that can be drawn from these literary references to Tisaion-Tisaia can be summarized: Tisaion was a mountain in Thessaly from which one could see Peparethos, Phokis, and Euboia (Polybios), forming a headland near the mouth of the Gulf of Pagasai (Apollonios Rhodios, Valerius Flaccus, *Orphica*), and in the area of a highway linking Macedonia and Athens (Appian). By these criteria, Tisaion must be sought near Pteleon among the heights that separate the major north-south route passing to the east of Othrys from the Gulf of Pagasai.

Despite the opposition of the literary evidence, the case for placing Tisaion in Magnesia, perhaps even for assuming a single location used by both Alexander and Philip, would still be a convincing one if it could be shown that only in Magnesia would it have been possible for a relay-station to perform the services demanded by Philip. But no such claim can be made; and there is at least one height in Thessaly that meets all the requirements.

* * *

If one looks south down the length of the Gulf of Pagasai from Demetrias, whether from the acropolis or the fortification walls nearest to the "palace," one sees in the distance, as if marking the entrance to the gulf, two prominent heights, the higher, twin-peaked, to the right in Thessaly, the lower, a ridge-backed chain, to the left in Magnesia. No other mountains catch the eye so immediately.

The eastern of these two heights is Bardzogia, also called Sarakiniko, Walbank's Tisaion, with an altitude of 644 m.[10] According to David Cole, who "spent two hours on the summit" in the spring of 1972, although the view from the top fulfils the requirements of Alexander's signalling system, there are on the other hand "no traces of ancient occupation; given the exposed nature of the place and the many crevices, this may be understandable. Furthermore, blocks may have been confiscated for use in fortifications erected to the west during the Revolution . . . ."[11] This lack of material evidence would have worried Stählin, who recognized not only that fire-signalling was frequently associated with roofless platforms, but also that locations in Magnesia other than on Bardzogia had to be considered seriously. Thus he wrote: "The remains of such a tower will have to be found on Bardzogia in order to decide conclusively the question of Tisaion."[12] Though one may question this insistence on the finding of remains, Stählin was nevertheless right in his caution, for Bardzogia, however prominent, is not the only Magnesian height that could have served Alexander's purpose, as Wace was aware when he suggested that a peak "a little north of Platania" be identified as Tisaion;[13] nor could it, or Wace's candidate, have served Philip's purpose as reported by Polybios, for, while Peparethos and Euboia are visible from both, neither is "well situated to provide wide-ranging views" of Phokis.[14]

To the east of Bardzogia, as if marking the western edge of the entrance to the Gulf of Pagasai, is Mt. Chlomon (Khlomón), the second of the two prominent heights that one sees from Demetrias when looking south. Chlomon lies directly north of the Thessalian village of Pteleon; its highest point, with an altitude of 893 m., is the western limit of a curving ridge that slopes down to a

[10] Both this figure and that for Chlomon below are taken from Sheet G. 8 Vólos, 1:250,000, published by the British War Office in 1945.

[11] David Cole's observations are recorded in an unpublished "School Paper" contained in *Papers of the American School of Classical Studies 1972*, available in the Blegen Library. I am very grateful to Mr. Cole for permission to quote from his study. Moreover, it is proper to note that his explorings, no less than mine, have made this paper possible.

[12] Stählin (above, note 4), 55.

[13] Wace (above, note 8), 149.

[14] Views of Phokis from Bardzogia are largely blocked off by the higher hills at the north-west end of Euboia, Lichas on the promontory opposite the Malian Gulf, and Telethrion immediately east of Aidipsos. Between these two mountains, however, there is a gap, which might have allowed communication between Bardzogia and Varvas north-east of Elateia.

secondary peak at the east. In late summer, 1972, I climbed this steep-sided height and explored the ridge. I can, therefore, testify that here we have a mountain that provides the "wide-ranging views" demanded by Polybios' words: to the east Magnesia, Skiathos, and Skopelos; to the south-east Euboia; and to the south the ranges north of Elateia and Hyampolis in eastern Phokis, particularly another Mt. Chlomon.[15]

Stählin would have been interested in my further discoveries on Thessalian Chlomon, whatever their meaning. Although I did not find remains of a signalling tower, I did note that spaced along the ridge linking the two peaks were remains of half a dozen man-made stone cairns of rubble construction and similar size, each circular with a flat top somewhat smaller in diameter than the base. These truncated cones have a maximum height of five feet and an average diameter of about three. Some stand almost as they were built; others are partially destroyed. None presents evidence that makes clear their date and purpose. Thus, there is no compelling way of associating these stone markers with Philip's signalling system, even though the possibility must be freely admitted.[16] At the very least, however, this series draws attention to the fact that someone held Chlomon's ridge to be important.

*   *
*

In seeking the location of Mt. Tisaion, I have concentrated on Bardzogia and Chlomon, the two principal heights on either side of the entrance into the Gulf of Pagasai, the two most prominent features of the distant landscape as one looks south from Demetrias. If I am justified in so limiting my search, one or other ought to be Tisaion. Of these two Bardzogia has been the choice of most scholars; yet it is a choice that goes against the evidence. My candidate is Chlomon, a mountain situated in Thessaly (Polybios), immediately east of a route linking Macedonia and Attica (Appian), from whose summit there are "wide-ranging views" of Peparethos, Phokis, and Euboia (Polybios).

Mount Allison University   C. W. J. Eliot

---

[15] Because of haze I was unable to ascertain how close to Chalkis one can see from Chlomon. It is my impression from the maps that the western edge of Mt. Kandilion stands in the way, and that an intermediary station would have been needed. Moreover, one might assume from Polybios' text that Philip had charged those of his officers in Phokis to report the arrival of a fleet at Chalkis.

[16] My caution is, I believe, justified: I do not want a circular argument; I do not know what structures, if any, were required for Philip's signalling system; and I am aware that Greece's northern border as established in the summer of 1832 must have met the Gulf of Pagasai near Chlomon.

POLITICS IN EARLY ATHENS

> Even in a daylight battle each combatant is just barely aware of what is going on directly
> opposite himself; but in a night battle, how could anyone know anything for certain?

Few scholarly controversies fit Thucydides' classic description of ignorant armies clashing by night (7.44.1) so well as the continuing disagreement over the politics practised by the Athenians of the Marathon generation. From the differing pictures drawn of political activity in the early fifth century, one would think that recent commentary had drawn from entirely different sets of testimonia and that scholars were, in effect, flailing away at each other in the dark. And yet the testimonia are all the same. Appeals are regularly made to the authority of identical authors so predictably that one need not even glance at the footnotes. This situation exists because, after all the meager testimonia for the period are collected, it is still necessary to make certain assumptions about the nature of the political struggle. From the literature it becomes immediately obvious that curiously different assumptions are being made.

The forms and vocabulary proposed by Aristotle, for instance, retain their old popularity. They assume some kind of spectrum of political sympathies, from one-man rule to the whim of the mob, plus the inevitable political parties endeavoring to put their programs into effect. One cannot deny that these forms existed: after all, there *were* monarchies and aristocracies and democracies of every variety in ancient Greece. But to take groups of human beings, label them with Aristotelian political sympathies, and then make assumptions about their political behavior, is to invite difficulties, if not for the political scientist, at least for the historian. I illustrate with the argument of an article published a few years ago in a respected journal. Here are all the radical democrats and conservative Areopagites that previous generations found so useful for simplifying Athenian politics. The author proposed that the reform of the archonship in 488/7 was introduced by radicals in order that "political activity would intensify around the other officials in power," namely, "politicized ambitious *strategoi* of the left."[1] Although the author did not clarify *his* underlying assumptions about Athenian politics, it would seem clear that he accepted the Aristotelian – Marxist concept of horizontal class structure, with nobles and commons eternally at odds, a predictable spectrum from right to left and an occasional maverick aristocrat taking the side of the Demos. I confess that those "politicized, ambitious *strategoi* of the left" might even have startled Aristotle.

Other scholars have seen the absurdity that can result from such an extension of Aristotelian political logic. They have rejected such horizontal divisions of the body politic into rich versus poor, or the Few versus the Many. Using what might be called the reasoning of cultural anthropology, they have pictured the early Athenians divided vertically, with the various noble families

---

[1] R. W. Wallace, "Ephialtes and the Areopagus," *GRBS* 15(1974) 259–269, cit. 260, 263. I could quote many other examples of what might be called the *CAH* doctrine of Athenian politics, but I believe Ernst Badian has exhausted the possibilities of that genre in his excellent, corrective article, "Archons and *Strategoi*," *Antichthon* 5 (1971) 1 ff.

enjoying the support of partisans drawn from all social and economic classes.[2] This is far more sensible and has parallels as well: it has long been recognized that political activity in the Roman republic followed this sort of configuration. Since the kinship structure of the ancient Latin tribes bears a close relationship to early tribal organization in the Greek world, it is reasonable to assume that political loyalties developed along lines of kinship in the same way.

But the study of Roman family politics is made possible by a far greater mass of data. It is possible to detect patterns in the behavior of families like the Cornelii or the Claudii. Neither the Greek system of nomenclature nor the surviving data lend themselves to this kind of analysis. Therefore, while a vertical division of political activity in early Athens seems far more reasonable than a horizontal one, we lack the data to make further assumptions about factions and loyalties. To illustrate, we do not even know for certain whether the archon of 489/8 was the famous Aristeides or a younger relative with the same name.[3] The human intellect intuitively seeks structure, rules of logic, a framework on which to focus its concepts. Is there a conceptual framework we can use to reason about early Athenian politics?

First, I would propose that politics, at least in its rational aspect, is simply disagreement about government, or more precisely, about the exercise of authority within a governmental structure. I further believe it is possible to define the various functions of government during the approximate century between the Solonian reforms and the Persian Wars. If we can clarify just how controversy arose over the exercise of authority within each governmental function, we shall have put political behavior in a more precise perspective than that offered by the Aristotelian forms. Aristotelians will protest that disagreement occurs over the *form* of government as well as its *functions*. But since for the period under discussion there is evidence for debate over functions and virtually none for disagreement over form, I may be forgiven for concentrating on the former.[4] Finally, we should remember that there is a less than rational side to politics: proud men simply wished εὐδοκιμεῖν and to be πρῶτοι.[5] They strove to do so within the cultural constraints of their society – constraints that had a great deal to do with the style and methods of their political behavior. A brief analysis of cultural patterns is therefore indispensable.

Government in the archaic community tends to be a logical outgrowth of social structure. As the community grows, it becomes obvious that certain functions need to be performed by a central authority – functions that are too complex, too difficult, or require a greater investment of labor and resources than can be supplied by a few tribal leaders on their own initiative. The governmental functions of the early Athenians can be studied under the following heads: relations with the Gods, relations with neighbors, relations with each other.[6]

It is difficult to perceive controversial elements in the practice of Athenian religion. Authority over the various cults was unquestionably a matter of heredity: priests and priestesses continued in direct succession from a divine ancestor or at least a founding family hallowed by tradition and legend. Overall responsibility had once been vested in the king, subsequently in the archon basi-

---

[2] Summary of the "party" vs *genos* controversy in W. R. Connor, *The New Politicians of Fifth-Century Athens* (Princeton 1971) 5–18; for the latter view, Jochen Martin, "Von Kleisthenes zu Ephialtes," *Chiron* 4 (1974) 7–12; cf. D. J. McCargar, *Historia* 25 (1976) 394f; R. Sealey, *CSCA* 2 (1969) 268f; C. Mossé, *AC* 33 (1964) 401ff.

[3] P. T. Bicknell, "The Archon of 489/8," *RFIC* 100 (1972) 164–172.

[4] Admittedly there is contemporary comment (if not debate) about tyranny as a form, e.g., Hdt., 5.92. I also recognize that the distinction between function and form is not always clear. Tacit recognition of the existence of a central authority within a society indicates a sort of consensus over form, as does the acceptance of such things as that authority's assuming the family's obligation to exact retribution for homicide.

[5] As Theopompus said of Cimon, *FGrHist* 115 F 89, in Athenaeus 533 C.

[6] Cf. E. Badian, *Publicans and Sinners* (Ithaca 1972) 14, commenting on governmental functions in the emergent Mediterranean city state: "to maintain the favour of the Gods for the community; to defend it against foreign enemies . . . and to keep the peace inside it." Public works is another recognizable function, but for the period under discussion it remained with a few exceptions a matter of private rather than public initiative; see note 19 below.

leus and his *epimeletai* (*Ath. Pol.* 57.1–2). The general trend in Greek governments was for a traditional exercise of authority to become a rational one, to use the terminology of Max Weber, or in Greek terms, for *themis* to give way gradually to *nomoi*. At the very beginning of the period under discussion Solon performed the invaluable service of codifying religious law, from crimes that offended the Gods to the minor details of defining the right sort of sacrificial animals.[7] The earliest Eleusinian regulations seem to show that procedural changes continued to go on in public, although it is impossible to determine the extent to which the public was actually consulted about the community's most sacred cult.[8] On other matters of religious policy, debate could be lively: at the very end of our period we see the oracles of Apollo being debated before the full Assembly with the advice of a private citizen being accepted over that of the *chresmologoi* (Hdt., 7.143). Testimony is rare for abuse of religious authority. The most shocking instance occurred when Hipparchus rejected the sister of Harmodius from a religious procession, an occasion to which I shall return.[9]

The subject of Athenian foreign relations may be further subdivided into war, diplomacy, and the establishment of cleruchies. It would appear from the meager evidence that decisions about war and diplomacy did not become binding upon all Athenians until the end of the period under consideration. The long, drawn-out struggle with Megara over the island of Salamis would seem, from the details preserved by Plutarch, to have been waged by that limited number of troops that could be raised by those noble families who saw profit or opportunity in a conquest of the island (*Sol.* 8–9). During most of the later sixth century, war, diplomacy and colonization became private ventures directed or encouraged by the tyrant Peisistratus and his sons.[10] Not until the Cleisthenic tribal reorganization do we see a process by which the entire population of Attica could be mobilized. It was possibly such a mobilization that repelled two invading armies on the same day, leading to Herodotus' famous remark about *isegorie*.[11]

Shortly after the expulsion of the tyrants *angeloi* were sent to ask an alliance with the Persians and, believing themselves to be plenipotentiary, they agreed to give earth and water (Hdt., 5.73). This perhaps reveals the attitude of individual aristocrats that they were still competent to speak for the whole community, a misunderstanding we might expect in this period of transition. The first foreign policy debate to be decided in the full Assembly (so far as we know) resulted in the expedition to aid the Ionian revolt in 499 (Hdt., 5.97). This event and the full mobilization for the Marathon campaign seem to show that the Athenians had by now a well developed military and diplomatic apparatus. For a long time, however, we can see throwbacks to an earlier era. Many Athenians, for instance, seem to have remained uncommitted to the war with Aegina. On the other hand, we see Cleinias coming to Artemision like a great warlord with his own ship and crew (Hdt., 8.17). Themistocles too commanded a small body of private troops in the aftermath of the Salamis campaign (or so Hdt., 8.110.2, 112.1 would lead us to believe). The notion of war as a matter of *condottieri* countenanced by fellow citizens – a typically aristocratic approach to war through the ages – had not entirely died out.

When we examine the question of authority in military and diplomatic affairs, it becomes even clearer that the Athenians had not really begun to think out an organized system. The king had

---

[7] E.g., Plut., 25.1; Arist. Byz. in *Etym. Gud.* 164,11 Reitz.

[8] See the comments of C. W. Fornara, *Translated Documents of Greece and Rome* 1, *Archaic Times to the End of the Peloponnesian War* (Baltimore 1977) no. 75 (*IG* 1.² 6/9, *SEG* 10.6).

[9] We can also see an instance of religious policy directed against an entire family in the tradition about the pollution of the Alcmeonids (Hdt., 5.71; Thuc., 1.126).

[10] The conquest of Sigeion, Miltiades in the Chersonese and Lemnos, the protectorate over Plataea in 519. Testimony and comment in L. Piccirilli, *Gli arbitrati interstatali greci* (Pisa 1973) nos. 7, 9.

[11] Hdt., 5.78, discussion in Meiggs and Lewis, *GHI²* 15. See H. van Effenterre, "Clisthène et les mesures de mobilisation," *REG* 89 (1976) 1–17.

once been the leader in war; the polemarch had taken over this duty. Generals came to be elected
(*Ath. Pol.* 22.2) and commands were sometimes distributed on an *ad hoc* basis, like Melanthius in
the Ionian revolt, or Miltiades in the ill-fated Parian campaign, but we are by no means certain
about the measure of authority shared by polemarch and individual *strategoi* – and perhaps the
Athenians were not either, as we see at Marathon.[12]

Of as much concern to Athenians as anything else having to do with war and diplomacy was the
disposition of spoils after a successful campaign. I would assume that the land taken from Chalcis
in 506 was assigned to cleruchs by a process of διανομή under the authority of the victorious general; this procedure is suggested by the practices followed by Cimon in the first campaigns after
the Persian Wars.[13]

It was in what we should call the administration of justice that Athenians, like all other Greeks,
felt most threatened by an arbitrary and unjust exercise of authority. From the time of Hesiod's
bribe-swallowing nobles, all Greeks were concerned with systems that would arbitrate internal
disputes and dispense justice in the fairest possible manner. Unjust punishment would have been
the most serious concern, but who can doubt that the most common sort of grievance was dispute
over property (including the inheritance of property) and that the most common source of resentment was the suspicion that conflict of interest or outright bribery had influenced the decision.
Once again we can see a steady progress in replacing a traditional system with a rational one. By
the beginning of the period under consideration these concerns had been at least partially met by
Dracon's codification of the laws and by Solon's creation of a regular system of courts (*Ath. Pol.*
9.2). Theoretically, everyone now knew what the law was and could calculate his chances of
obtaining – or avoiding – justice. Tradition claimed that Peisistratus both preserved and advanced
the cause of impartial justice. We are told that he obeyed the laws himself (Thuc., 6.54.6). He also
created a board of circuit judges (δικασταὶ κατὰ δήμους), according to *Ath. Pol.* 16.5, in order to
keep farmers from coming to town with their suits, but more likely for the purpose of eroding, in
the demes, the traditional role of the largest landowner as a court of first resort.[14]

Although we have virtually no testimony to procedures for settling disputes in the first decades
after the Peisistratids,[15] later Athenian practice shows that the steady trend was to dilute the possibility of arbitrary or corrupt judgments by bringing as many people into the decision making
process as possible.[16] It is in the category of administration of justice that we see the first hint of
disapproval of a *form* rather than a *function* of government. Greeks everywhere opposed the institution of tyranny because it was under this form of government that injustice was most likely to
occur.[17]

In any modern government, a system of public finance is required to keep the functions of
government operating. The literary testimony gives a picture of Athens enjoying a vigorous
commercial economy during the time of Solon (e.g., Plut., *Sol.* 22.1); in such an atmosphere we
should expect some forms of taxation, a public treasury, and regular disbursements for public

[12] Hdt., 6.109–110; Badian (above, note 1), 31 f. reminds us that A. Hauvette had made the same point many years ago, *Hérodote historien des guerres médiques* (Paris 1894) 255. N. G. L. Hammond, "Strategia and Hegemonia," *CQ* 19 (1969) 121–123, is too confident that the Athenians already had a smoothly operating system.

[13] E.g., Ion, *FGrHist* 392 F 13 in Plut., *Cim.* 9.1; see also W. K. Pritchett, *Ancient Greek Military Practices* 1 (Berkeley and Los Angeles 1971) 85 ff.

[14] A standard interpretation: C. Hignett, *A History of the Athenian Constitution to the End of the Fifth Century B.C.* (Oxford 1952) 115; D. Kienast, "Die innenpolitische Entwicklung Athens im 6. Jahrhundert," *HZ* 200 (1967) 269.

[15] In this study I have limited consideration of testimonia to the earliest possible authorities. Anecdotes about Aristeides and Themistocles acting as judges (Plut., *Arist.* 4.2 on Aristeides; *Praec. ger. reip.* 807 AB on Themistocles), for instance, must be regarded as hopelessly compromised by the opportunities for contamination between the dramatic date and that of Plutarch.

[16] See, e.g., A. R. W. Harrison, *The Law of Athens* 2 (Oxford 1971) 2 f.

[17] The classic example of Cypselus and Periander is offered by the Corinthian spokesman in Hdt., 5.92.

purposes. Yet archaeologists recognize that such a picture is highly anachronistic. Numismatists have in fact shown that the Athenians at the time of Solon had not even yet begun to strike their own currency.[18] We should be safest in assuming that most public expenses were handled by liturgy: those not assumed by the Peisistratids were shared out among the wealthier families and were accepted by them as a traditional honor rather than an obligation to avoid.[19] The only regular public revenues we can identify with certainty are the incomes from the Laurium silver mines; the haphazard sort of distribution that was suggested in 483 demonstrates that public finance must still have been in its infancy in Athens at that time.

We now turn from the functions of government to those persons who tended to exercise authority within those functions. One must make an important distinction between the politically active Athenian and the modern politician. The latter tends to be a person who believes he is capable of statesmanlike resolution of the problems of society and therefore wishes to occupy a statutory position of power so he can deal with these problems – or at least be seen pondering them – as they come along. But the experience of the Peisistratids instilled in Athenians a deep mistrust of statutory positions and the exercise of authority *per se*. There were therefore no equivalent positions of power in the Athenian community. Not only did the Athenians eliminate offices that could have lent themselves to the abuse of executive authority, they even feared private individuals whose influence appeared to be growing at an excessive rate, as the practice of ostracism makes clear. What then was so attractive about political activity to an ambitious Athenian?

For the introduction to a study of Athenian society in the late sixth century, I once surveyed the present state of research not only in our literary evidence but in a number of archaeological fields – the architecture of the period, the sculpture, the ceramic evidence, numismatics and epigraphy.[20] In doing so, I hoped to get a picture of a cross section of Athenian society, its standards and its values. Insofar as any cross section was concerned, the survey was disappointing because our evidence is almost entirely elitist in character. The fine painted pottery, the many dedications of sculpture on the Acropolis, the imposing statues of youths and maidens found all over Attica, the highly ornate grave memorials, all are products of and for the elite classes of Athens. But as a testimonial of the lifestyle and the values of this elite, at least, the study was highly revealing.

The lasting impression was of a small but growing urban center dominated by an ostentatious timocracy. Under the Peisistratids, an aristocracy of birth began to be challenged in conspicuous display by a growing class whose status was measured in wealth. We are in fact told that such a class played an important role in Solon's day, but the rest of our evidence clearly shows that they rose to real prominence under the Peisistratids.[21] Since what they had in common with those of noble birth was the desire to show off their wealth, their accomplishments, their τιμή, in short, it is accurate to call their society a timocracy. It was what has been called a "shame culture," if I may use that ugly but instructive term: a society dominated not by motives of economic gain and certainly not by political ideology, but by pride, honor, self-esteem and the respect of others – that *philotimia* that is still echoed in the *philotimo* of the modern Greek. Like Cimon, a generation later, the Athenian elite wished money only that they might spend it and they spent it in order to gain honor and repute (Gorgias in Plut., *Cim.* 10.5). Their ostentation is clearly represented in hairstyles and dress, statues, dedications and gravestones, in the beautiful pottery they commis-

[18] Current controversy centers around a high or low chronology for the Wappenmünzen, but the earliest dates proposed are well after the traditional date of the Solonian reforms, e.g., C. M. Kraay, *NC* ser. 7, 2 (1962) 417.

[19] For instance, the dromos of the Panathenaia, A. Raubitschek, *DAA* nos. 326–328; J. Travlos, *PDAA* 2.

[20] "Society and Politics in Peisistratid Athens," presented to the annual meeting of the Association of Ancient Historians, Berkeley, May 1976.

[21] I repeat, however, Badian's warning against assuming an active antagonism between landowning aristocracies and *nouveaux riches* as a universal state of affairs in all ages, *AJAH* 1 (1976) 105.

sioned and in the foreign artists, musicians and poets they invited to their city and patronized. These attitudes were not limited to the elite either of wealth or of birth. On the Acropolis were dedications by persons of humbler station, including a laundress.[22] And an analysis of the coarse pottery from the Agora shows a demand among Athenian housewives for imported, mould-made washbasins, probably for no other reason than vogue, for such items not only could be but were produced domestically at what must have been a much lower price. The housewife, in her own way, was mimicking the young noble who spent half a year's income on a pedigreed horse or on a *kouros* dedicated on the Acropolis: both were spending money to win the admiration of peers.[23]

It is only reasonable to assume that pride, honor and repute were the overriding considerations in the political arena as well. Under the Peisistratids, of course, opportunities to make or influence policy were severly limited. Nevertheless, we know that archons and other officials continued to be chosen or appointed, priesthoods and judicial positions continued to be filled, and, so far as we know, the tribes and phratries continued to elect respected men to positions of leadership. The expulsion of the tyrants and the constitution of Cleisthenes did not completely change governmental institutions and functions; they simply broadened the opportunities for community leadership to a degree that had been impossible, or at least dangerous, under the Peisistratids.

From this perspective, we can almost define politics in early Athens as one of those activities which in Aristotle's scheme did not produce an end result but which was an end in itself, like flute playing.[24] I say almost, because there were some notable exceptions. But, for the most part, political success was measured in terms of the respect and attention one attracted when speaking as a private citizen in council or before the Assembly.[25] This respect was gained by service in many other ways: as a just arbitrator of disputes, as a priest in one of the cults of Attica (although this was limited by heredity), as an eager performer of liturgical duties, like the production of a tragedy. Respect and honor were also won by continual expenditure upon what we might call creative ostentation: patronage of a famous musician, regular commissions of fine pottery, perhaps most typical, dedicating a *kouros* or *kore,* sculpted of island marble by a master artist and set up on the Acropolis to advertise both the wealth and the piety of the donor.

Thus we see political activity as just one of many other activities undertaken in the ritual pursuit of honor and esteem – εὐδοκιμεῖν and to be πρῶτος. It is not surprising that these values played such an important part in Greek politics. Sociologists have pointed out the importance of these qualities today, not only in Greece but all around the Mediterranean.[26] In these societies, in these sunny climates, so much activity goes on out of doors. Ostentation and public display are taken for granted and members of the community are accustomed to inspect each other critically every day for minor successes or failures of style. The competition is not always good-natured; our sources continually remind us of the Greek tendency to *phthonos* – obsessive envy. There are finite limits to everything; therefore the honor earned by one man diminishes the amount available to others.[27]

I have tried to define in this paper a rather novel conceptual framework for Athenian politics in the generation before the Persian Wars. I believe that discussion of political activity is fruitless

[22] *DAA* 380 (*IG* 1.² 473).

[23] B. Sparkes and L. Talcott, *The Athenian Agora* 12, *Black and Plain Pottery* (Princeton 1970) 42, 219.

[24] Arist., *Eth. Nic. init.*; cf. *Mag. Mor.* 1211ᵇ 27 (where flute playing is the example). According to Plutarch, Solon believed all activities should have a goal (quoted by his suppositious disciple Mnesiphilus in *Sept. sap. conv.* 156 B); this doctrine would surely include political activity and it is interesting to note that it was supposedly passed on in a direct philosophical *diadochê* to Themistocles (Plut., *Them.* 2.6). This theory probably derived from the stories about Themistocles' unusual political style, as noted below.

[25] Note the definition of such a citizen in Jane F. Gardner, ed., *Leadership and the Cult of Personality* (Toronto 1974) xv.

[26] See particularly the introductiom to J. G. Peristiany, ed., *Honour and Shame. The Values of Mediterranean Society* (Chicago 1966).

[27] In all fairness to the Athenians, this attitude is not unknown to other eras and societies; some observers have been so unkind as to note its existence among academics.

unless, first, we describe as exactly as possible the functions of government and why disagreement is likely to arise over those functions; second, we ascertain whether a specific political figure is taking a stand on a particular issue because he believes certain actions are necessary for the well-being of the community, or whether he believes that a well-chosen issue offers a forum that will enhance his reputation as a wise, well spoken, and stylish community leader – a leader, in other words, who wishes the appearance and the prerogatives of leadership without actually having to do any leading. This conceptual framework can only serve as a speculative model and must be tested against all the political events in early Athenian history. I offer two examples.

The supreme realist Thucydides missed the point, I believe, when he belittled the affair of Harmodius and Aristogeiton as inconsequential in the downfall of the tyrants (δι' ἐρωτικὴν λύπην, 6.59.1). Hipparchus had publicly ejected the sister of Harmodius as a *kanephoros* in a sacred procession and for Harmodius only death could avenge the dishonor. It is exactly such a thing, a public insult to the maiden daughter of an old and honorable family that may have started the other families thinking. If the Peisistratids did not respect the *philotimia* of the Gephyraioi, how long would it be before others were so insulted?

I believe this model also helps to explain the reputation Themistocles gained as an unusual and aggressive politician. A century and a half later, Aristotle concluded that he must have been ideologically a radical democrat.[28] Using the criteria I have just described, however, I think we can see that Themistocles caused such controversy because every time we encounter him he is actually trying to get something accomplished. For years he was successful and had his moments of glory. But he also made innumerable enemies simply because his success seemed to threaten the *philotimia* of others. He eventually learned to his chagrin that taking a stand on the issues meant, in Athenian terms, that he must continue to pick the right issue and continue to be successful: that political popularity is a fragile thing and is far better maintained by the appearance of leadership than by its exercise.

University of California, Santa Barbara   FRANK J. FROST

[28] As I showed in "Themistocles' Place in Athenian Politics," *CSCA* 1 (1968) 110–112.

IN SEARCH OF A POLYPRAGMATIST

ὥστε εἴ τις αὐτοὺς ξυνελὼν φαίη πεφυκέναι ἐπὶ τῷ μήτε αὐτοὺς ἔχειν ἡσυχίαν μήτε τοὺς ἄλλους ἀνθρώπους ἐᾶν, ὀρθῶς ἂν εἴποι.[1]

The opponents of Athens at the time of the Peloponnesian War were united in the view that the Athenians were polypragmatists, every man-jack of them. The Athenians themselves were of the same opinion. Not only did Euphemos boast as much to the Kamarinaians (τῆς ἡμετέρας πολυπραγμοσύνης καὶ τρόπου[2]), but the humour of Aristophanes' *Birds* exploits the characterisation. Pisthetairos and Euelpides (two more typical Athenians you could not find) are doomed to failure in their search for a τόπος ἀπράγμων,[3] for no sooner will they find it than their true nature will assert itself and they will take over the universe.[4] You cannot change Athenian nature.

In the face of such unanimity it is surprising to find modern commentators taking a different approach. The wealthy were the first to be acquitted. "It is well known that from time immemorial the rich men of Athens were the peace party, while the demos was always eager for war."[5] Next the *demos* itself was subdivided. Studies of the so-called "Constitution of the Five Thousand" have developed the idea that the ὅπλα παρεχόμενοι represented a moderate group in Athenian society, men who were opposed to imperialism and radical democracy alike. They wanted a return to the honourable days of Kimonian *hegemonia,* the restriction of the franchise and the abolition of pay for magistrates.[6] Thus by a process of elimination the only supporters of radical democracy and the Athenian empire were the landless thetes, the men who, in the view of current theory, dominated the assembly and whose muscles moved the triremes.[7] Supposedly their livelihood (τροφή) was at stake.[8] These, then, were the true polypragmatists. Chalk one up to the Old Oligarch.[9]

But any theory that agrees, either in whole or in part, with the distorted viewpoint of that tormented outsider demands reconsideration. To begin with the wealthy. "It is well known that from time immemorial the rich men of Athens were the peace party . . . ." Here is an intriguing notion. If it is true, rich Athenians were a rare breed, for it goes against the grain of everything we have come to know about the involvement of money and the interests of the monied class in territorial annexation, imperial expansion and war itself. Why were they different? The answer involves the source of their wealth. Wealth in antiquity was based upon possession of land, it is argued, and the possessors of this form of wealth were not interested in trade.[10] In fact, they despised it. Conse-

---

[1] Thuc., 1. 70. 9.   [2] Thuc., 6. 87. 3.   [3] Ar., *Birds* 44.

[4] For this and other references to Athenian πολυπραγμοσύνη see V. Ehrenberg, "Polypragmosyne," *JHS* 67 (1947). See also J. de Romilly, *Thucydide et l'Impérialisme athénien* (Paris 1951) 72.

[5] W. Jaeger, *Demosthenes: The Origin and Growth of his Policy* (Berkeley and Los Angeles 1938) 77.

[6] See, for example, F. Jacoby, *FGrHist.* 3B Suppl. 1. 95–97. For other bibliography on the Constitution of the Five Thousand and for a refutation of the view that a moderate party continued to exist in the fourth century see my article, "The Theramenes Myth," *Phoenix* 28 (1974) 101–111.

[7] See *CAH* 5. 109–112.   [8] Cf. Aristotle, *Ath. Pol.* 24.   [9] Pseudo-Xenophon, *Ath. Pol.* 1. 2.

[10] This distinction underlies the division (in, for example, *CAH* 5. 109–110) between the wealthy landowners as leaders of the "conservative" farmers and the demagogues as leaders of the urban proletariat, whose existence is predicated upon the industrialisation and commercialisation of Athens.

quently they had little to gain from the Athenian empire and could hardly be enthusiastic about a war whose purpose was the preservation of that empire. Their ideal was ἀπραγμοσύνη and they themselves were ἀπράγμονες.[11]

Such, at least, was their propaganda. In addition they called themselves βέλτιστοι and σώφρονες to set themselves apart from the many (the *demos* in its narrower sense), whom they characterised as κάκιστοι and who they claimed ruled over them *en masse* like a tyrant, in both the assembly and the law courts.[12] We tend to sympathise with this poor frustrated minority, helpless to make itself heard in the direct democracy of Athens in the latter part of the fifth century. Perhaps we are naive.

In the first place the antipathy between 'the Few' and 'the Many' was most likely of a social and economic nature, not political at all. In a socio-economic analysis of fifth-century Athenian society 'the Few' can best be defined as the liturgical class,[13] that group that by virtue of its wealth was required to make several more or less voluntary contributions to the operation of the state, such as providing a chorus for a dramatic or dithyrambic presentation or maintaining a trireme for a year. They are sometimes equated with the aristocrats, but, though many of them were of noble birth (like Kimon, Perikles, Alkibiades), this was not true of them all. Kleon's family, for example, belonged to the liturgical class, but was not of noble origin.[14] Nor is it true to say that they were all owners of large estates, *i.e.,* that their wealth depended on property. Kleon, again, serves as an example, for his family wealth was based upon ownership of a tannery. In case Kleon seems a bad model, it is as well to point out that the same is true of his opponent in politics, Nikias. Nikeratos, his father, like Kleainetos, the father of Kleon, was the founder of the family's wealth, which was based upon exploitation of the silver mines and hiring out slaves for mining.[15] Neither Kleon nor Nikias was ἀπράγμων, nor was their opposition in politics based upon disparity in wealth or the sources of their wealth. It was most likely personal.

To a large extent the liturgical class can be equated with the upper two of Solon's property-classifications, the *pentakosiomedimnoi* (the very wealthy, who numbered 300 in the fourth century) and the *hippeis,* whose number was in the region of 1000. Their total would hardly be much more than it was in the fourth century–1200. These were the men whose sons had the time and money to take part in *symposia,* to hire the services of flute-girls and to indulge in the pleasures (whatever they were) of homosexual love. In these meetings they sang *skolia,* songs that commemorated the past glories of the aristocratic state. This does not mean that they were anti-democratic. One of the most popular songs, for example, was the Harmodios-*skolion,* yet Harmodios and Aristogeiton had long since become popular democratic heroes. Sometimes they drank too much and got sick. In public they flaunted their wealth by wearing expensive clothes, training horses for the great Hellenic festivals and, later, by paying for an elitist education from the sophists.[16] For all this they made themselves unpopular with the mass of Athenians, who were prejudiced against excessive displays of wealth, as can be seen in the career of Alkibiades.[17] His was no isolated case, though perhaps extreme. Abuse of wealth is portrayed in the *Clouds.* Strepsiades, the countryman who has moved to the town (as so many must have done), has married a fashionable towngirl. He is out

---

[11] But see J. de Romilly (note 4 above), 72.

[12] Cf. pseudo-Xenophon, *Ath. Pol. passim* (especially 1. 1–10). See also G. Grossman, *Politische Schlagwörter aus der Zeit des Peloponnesischen Krieges* (Zurich 1950) *passim.*

[13] Cf. J. K. Davies, *Athenian Propertied Families* (Oxford 1971) xx.

[14] See Davies (note 13 above), no. 8674 *s. v.* Κλέων Κλεαινέτου Κυδαθηναιεύς.

[15] Davies (note 13 above), no. 10808 *s. v.* Νικίας Νικηράτου Κυδαντίδης.

[16] For a characterisation of this class see V. Ehrenberg, *The People of Aristophanes*[2] (New York 1962) 95–112.

[17] This prejudice underlies Nikias' attack on Alkibiades (Thuc., 6. 12. 2), against which Alkibiades is at pains to defend himself (Thuc., 6. 16). The same prejudice is manifest in the law courts, where the best evidence is from the fourth century. Cf. D. Brown, *Das Geschäft mit dem Staat* (Hildesheim 1974) *passim.*

of his class with her. Not only was she from the town, she was also from the wealthy. In fact the latter is the point. Pheidippides, their son, apes the ways of the sons of the wealthy and Strepsiades is eaten out of house and home. The underlying prejudice reflects an antipathy not so much between town and country as between classes. The ways of the wealthy and the ways of the city have become confused. It is easy to see how this could come about. Since, as Gomme has pointed out,[18] many of the members of the wealthy class were enrolled in city demes (and even those who were not had homes in the city), the type of behaviour they indulged in was considered typical of the *asteios* and formed much of the basis for the antipathy, such as it was, between townspeople and country-people (*agroikoi*).

Not that all the wealthy flaunted their εὐδαιμονία. It was necessary only that some did in order to create a prejudice. Likewise most lower-class Englishmen had until recently a fairly clear stereotype of a member of the upper class, a stereotype that was based more upon prejudice than fact in the majority of cases. That this prejudice existed is evident not only from comedy, but also from oratory, two media that allow us to perceive the prejudices of the people, though reflecting them in different ways.[19] It was in the law courts that the wealthy claimed to be most tyrannised. Obviously they were on the defensive, for they were at great pains to counter the accusations of their opponents (against whom they used the same accusations, because they too were usually wealthy) that they were profligate, loath to pay their taxes or perform their liturgies and, of course, homosexual. These accusations were playing upon the prejudices of the jury and it was in regard to them that the wealthy developed the representation of themselves as a group that was overburdened by its financial obligations to the state and concerned only with peace and inactivity (ἀπραγμοσύνη).[20]

For they were not inactive. While their wealth may have caused them some embarrassment and certainly involved them in financial obligations, it had its advantages. One of these was that it left them free to take part in the activities of the city-state to an extent quite disproportionate to their number. It was from this class that the politicians of fifth- (and fourth-)century Athens almost invariably arose and that the *strategoi,* the *tamiai,* the ambassadors and other leading magistrates were chosen.[21] They all worked within the democratic constitution and found an outlet for their polypragmatism in its service. Their reward was prestige, honour, in Greek political terms, τιμή. Even the individual members of the 400, about whom more will be said later, were so motivated (κατ᾽ ἰδίας δὲ φιλοτιμίας οἱ πολλοὶ αὐτῶν τῷ τοιούτῳ προσέκειντο, Thuc., 8. 89. 3). The involvement of the wealthy in the greatness of Athens was, therefore, assured, for as it increased so did the prestige of her servants.

Not surprisingly they were equally committed to the empire. From Aristeides, who seized the opportunity,[22] through Kimon, who encouraged the allies in their lethargy,[23] to Perikles, who told the Athenians what empire really meant and cast his vote for war,[24] to Kleon, who echoed Perikles' sentiments,[25] and Alkibiades, who proposed the Sicilian expedition, the wealthy, whether landed or 'industrialist,' were intimately associated with Athenian imperialism. Even Nikias played

---

[18] A. W. Gomme, *The Population of Ancient Athens* (Oxford 1933) 37–38.

[19] Comedy used popular prejudice in order to tease its audience, oratory frankly exploited it.

[20] See D. Brown (note 17 above), *passim.* If one accepts K. J. Dover's assertion, *Aristophanic Comedy* (Berkeley and Los Angeles 1972) *frontispiece,* that the majority of Aristophanes' audience were peasant farmers and, on the other hand, the common assumption that the jurors in the law courts were essentially townspeople, then the homogeneity of popular prejudice is assured, for in both one finds the same glorification of the Men-of-Marathon and their ways (parodied in comedy, of course); the same criticism of popular politicians; and the same innuendo against the wealthy, that they were profligate, loath to pay their taxes and homosexual.

[21] This was argued long ago by J. Sundwall, *Epigraphische Beiträge zur sozialpolitischen Geschichte Athens im Zeitalter des Demosthenes (Klio, Beiheft* 4 1906) 74. The same conclusion can be drawn from J. K. Davies' more comprehensive and methodologically sound analysis referred to above (note 13).

[22] *Ath. Pol.* 22. 4.

[23] Plut., *Kimon* 11. 2.   [24] Thuc., 2. 63 and 1. 141. 1.   [25] Thuc., 3. 37 1–3.

his part and, though Thucydides the son of Melesias opposed the use of allied money for the buildings on the Akropolis, there is no evidence that he opposed the decree of Kleinias or the decree of Klearchos or any of the other administrative measures of the early 440s. He was a politician in search of a cause and he lost. They were all polypragmatists.

Nor was it only concern for their individual honour that motivated the involvement of the wealthy in the greatness of Athens. They did have economic interests. Though it is quite likely that the main beneficiaries of the economic stranglehold on Aegean trade exerted by the Peiraeus were metics, it is hard to believe that some of Kleon's hides or Hyperbolos' lamps did not find their way to the *emporia* of the empire. Likewise, after the Coinage Decree established the Athenian owl as the standard currency throughout the empire, exploitation of the silver mines of Laureion became an increasingly lucrative business. Nikias could not fail to profit. Furthermore, there were less visible forms of gain to be made from Athens' trading supremacy. Studies of the Athenian investors of the fourth century have shown that the wealthy knew how to put their money to work.[26] They did not need to consult Isokrates.[27] The most profitable form of investment was in maritime ventures. It was also the most risky. Only the very wealthy could run that risk. It strains credibility to believe that they learned to exploit this source of gain only after the fall of the Athenian empire. Finally, the evidence of the decree of Aristoteles shows that it was not only klerouchs who owned land in allied territory;[28] many individual Athenians did too. So wealthy Athenians were benefiting at all levels from the economic supremacy of Athens in the days of her empire. If they strove to play down their share in the profits and to persuade the less wealthy Athenian that he was the main beneficiary of the proceeds of empire, this is not untypical of the propaganda of their kind. They needed the rowers more than the rowers needed them. So much for the Old Oligarch. Wealthy Athenians were no different from their counterparts throughout the centuries.

But, if we find the rich guilty of polypragmatism, we cannot for that reason absolve the less wealthy, the *demos* in its narrower sense. For such was the nature of Athenian democracy that while Perikles (or his like) might propose and while he might be chosen to execute, the *demos* decided. While their leaders (the wealthy) may have succeeded in imposing their views by virtue of their mastery of the art of rhetoric, there can be no doubt that the majority in the assembly believed in the Athenian empire and were prepared to fight for it. To be sure, in the dark days of the plague they wavered and Perikles was called to account,[29] but this was only a momentary weakness. Their resolve soon hardened. Even after the failure of the Sicilian expedition, they were united in their decision to continue the war.[30] It seems, then, that there was no peace-party in Athens during the Peloponnesian War, that the Athenians were all polypragmatists.

This could, however, be an insensitive reading of the situation. Maybe 'the Many' were not as cohesive a body as this interpretation would imply. Perhaps there was a minority group, whose views were consistently outvoted by the rest of the *demos* that was united in opinion with 'the Few.' This group has frequently been discerned and identified with the peasant farmers of Attika,[31] the ὅπλα παρεχόμενοι. In political terms they have been dubbed 'moderates.' The argument goes that since they were subsistence-farmers with no surplus capital they could not invest in trade like the wealthier landowners. The empire brought them no profit.[32] Their land was their livelihood

[26] See L. Casson, "The Athenian Upper Class and New Comedy," *TAPA* 106 (1976) 29–59. More to the point is: Wesley Thompson, "The Athenian Investor," *Rivista di Studi Classici* 26 (1978) 403–423.

[27] Isok., *Areiopagitikos* 31–35.

[28] *IG* 2.² 43 (Tod, 123) lines 25–46. Cf. Andokides, *On the Peace* 15.

[29] Thuc., 2. 59.

[30] Thuc., 8. 1. 3.

[31] See, for example, *CAH* 5. 110.

[32] This is, of course, naive. Much of their produce, such as oil, wine, honey, made its way to the corners of the empire in the pottery produced by the potters of the Kerameikos, carried by traders whose enterprises were financed by the capital of the very wealthy. Thus they were able to live in some style; cf. *Hell. Oxy.* 17. 5.

and their land was being laid waste by the Spartan incursions. Naturally they opposed the Peloponnesian War and resented those who had voted for it. Their resentment was particularly sharp against the landless majority who outvoted them, because these had assumed a more influential position in the state through their domination of radical democracy (especially since the introduction of pay for magistrates) and through their importance to the imperial system as rowers of the triremes. As hoplites the peasant farmers idealised the great days of Marathon, when hoplites had saved Athens, and had been hostile to the growing dependence of Athens upon her navy since the time of Themistokles.[33] This shift of influence had robbed them of their significance and created a major split amongst 'the Many' of Athenian society. To restore their influence this group wanted a restriction of the franchise to property-owners, abolition of pay for magistrates and, above all, the end of the Peloponnesian War. Evidence for the existence of this 'moderate' or 'conservative' group has been found in the so-called 'Peace-Plays' of Aristophanes[34] and, of course, in their supposed involvement in the Revolution of the Four Hundred of 411/0.[35] Our search for the real Athenian polypragmatist seems to have yielded the opposite. We have found the apragmatists.

This all sounds very logical and much has been made of this dichotomy between town and country, hoplite and rower. It is traced back to the time of Themistokles. Aristeides, his opponent, was the champion of the hoplites. After all, did he not command the hoplites on Psyttaleia? But the evidence for this antagonism is late, largely in Plutarch,[36] and Plutarch can only quote Plato.[37] It should not be forgotten that Miltiades, the victor of Marathon, immediately led the Athenians on a naval expedition to Paros. He felt no shame, nor did they object. And where was Aristeides when the Ionians approached him to found a naval confederacy? On board ship. And did he, in deference to his hoplite supporters, turn down the offer? Of course not. The evidence for an ideological clash between Themistokles and Aristeides is lacking. They even collaborated in the building of the walls of Athens. The cause of their opposition was personal ambition, the struggle to become προστάτης τοῦ δήμου.

We should also scrutinise the other evidence more closely. To begin with Aristophanes: in three plays, *Acharnians, Peace* and *Lysistrata,* he appears to advocate the advantages of peace. Since his comic hero is often the peasant farmer, it is arguable that he is depicting and supporting this man's desire for an end to the war. We should exclude *Peace* from the discussion. This play celebrates a peace that is as good as signed. It is not propaganda. Every Athenian was happy to make peace in 421, for it did not involve Athens in any loss of sovereignty. No sensible man fights war for its own sake. Peace with profit is clearly preferable. This is a far cry from proposing peace at a time when the city is at a low ebb in its fortunes. That is tantamount to surrender. Yet that is what Aristophanes seems to do in *Acharnians* and *Lysistrata.* If this is true, he was a peace-propagandist, and we might believe that there was a group to whom and for whom he was speaking.

The historical situation at the time of these two plays is the most convincing argument against this theory. When Aristophanes produced the *Acharnians*, the Athenians had little to be happy about. Their land had been invaded, their crops burnt and their trees cut down. How greatly this distressed them we learn from Thucydides.[38] In addition there had been the plague and the revolt of Mytilene. Plataia had fallen. On the credit side they had overpowered Poteidaia and suppressed the revolt of Mytilene. But, besides the successes of Phormion in the Gulf of Korinth, Athens'

---

[33] Cf. *CAH* 5. 111, based upon pseudo-Xenophon, *Ath. Pol.* 1. 2.

[34] *CAH* 5. 110.

[35] Cf. note 6 above.

[36] In his lives of *Themistokles* and *Aristeides, passim.* See especially *Aristeides* 2. Against this, of course, is the testimony of Aristotle, *Ath. Pol.* 23 and 24, where Aristeides is a popular leader. The view that Aristeides and Themistokles were ideologically opposed is sensibly rejected by Gomme and Cadoux in their article on Aristeides in the *Oxford Classical Dictionary.*

[37] Plut., *Themistokles* 4. 4.

[38] Thuc., 2. 21.

war-effort was not prospering. The war was not going to be over "by Christmas." Morale was low. So Aristophanes produced a play that proclaimed the advantages of peace. As a statement of the obvious it would have fallen very flat. As a comedy it was hardly likely to win a prize. It is insensitive to read war-time comedy in this way. Aristophanes is allowing all Athenians (not just one group) to realise their secret desire in fantasy, laugh at it and then return to the Lamachan reality of night-time guard duty. That he is not making propaganda for peace becomes evident in the subsequent period. After the victory at Pylos Athens was in a much stronger bargaining position, yet Aristophanes turns to different topics and we hear no more of peace.

The case of the *Lysistrata* is even clearer. The Sicilian expedition had ended in complete disaster, the allies were restless, Dekeleia was occupied, the state was almost bankrupt, and yet the Athenians resolved to continue the war. To men in this mood of desperate resolution Aristophanes thought it would be a funny idea to advocate peace? Not likely! Once again the Athenians are being teased by a ridiculous and fantastic realization of their innermost wishes. Aristophanes' 'Peace-Plays' are no evidence for a *group* in Athens that wanted peace with Sparta. On the contrary they are evidence that on these two occasions *all* Athenians longed for peace, but were resolved to fight on, not least the hoplites, the men of Acharnai, the Men-of-Marathon.[39]

One point that has emerged from the study of Aristophanes is, however, worth emphasising. The type of Athenian most prominently and favourably represented in the comedies is the peasant-farmer. It is a reasonable inference that this type comprised the majority of the audience. This is not surprising for Thucydides expressly tells us that at the beginning of the Peloponnesian War the majority of the Athenian population lived on and off the land.[40] Whether we set the proportion at two-thirds or three-quarters, they were the majority.[41] They were not outnumbered by the landless city-thetes. Quite the reverse. So, in theory, the peasant-farmers of Attika should have formed the dominant majority in the assembly, as they did in the theatre, and, in that case, it was their prejudices, attitudes and opinions that triumphed. In particular, they supported radical democracy, they approved of the empire, and they voted for war. So they were polypragmatists.

There are, however, many who think this was not the case. They feel that the distances that had to be travelled by the men of the country would have been an effective deterrent from attending the assembly. The city-mob, being on the spot, packed the meetings and dictated policy.[42] This division of opinion on the nature of the dominant majority in Athenian politics arises from the assumptions of a basic rift between town and country, not only spatially (in distance), but mentally (in attitude). This I believe to be quite unfounded.[43]

To deal with the matter of distance first — Attika is not large. Even the settlements at its furthest extremities are hardly more than thirty miles from Athens. A deme like Acharnai, the most populous deme in Attika, is less than ten. Of course, we, "who are hardly capable of walking to the corner drug-store," are naturally put off by such distances. But this was not the case even a generation ago, when children often walked so far to school, and certainly it was not so in antiquity. A couple of hours' walk would see an Acharnian in town. Maybe he arrived late and breathing of garlic (as Aristophanes says in the *Ekklesiazousai*[44]), but arrive he did. No doubt, under normal circumstances, the farmer on the extremities would think twice about travelling thirty miles for an assembly, but it is idle to suggest that he would not have undertaken such a journey when the question was one of war or peace.

[39] *Ibid.*   [40] Thuc., 2. 14. 1 and 2. 16. 1.

[41] Cf. Gomme (note 18 above), 47 and V. Ehrenberg (note 16 above), 86.

[42] Most simply stated in *CAH* 5. 110.

[43] Cf. V. Ehrenberg (note 16 above), 83: "The barriers between them (*sc.* town and country) were not nearly so high as some scholars seem to believe."

[44] Aristophanes, *Ekklesiazousai* 290 f. That Athenians were prepared to walk such distances is shown, for example, by the case of Diokleides, who got up before dawn (despite his mistake in the time he clearly meant to leave before dawn) to walk the 20 miles to Laureion to collect a fee for a mine-slave (Andokides, *On the Mysteries* 38).

But, one might object, a farmer cannot afford to take time off. A farmer's work is never done. True, but not true. If his crops are vines and olives, there are many periods when there is little to do.[45] Furthermore, the Attic farmer had a slave to take care of the everyday needs of his plot of land and to cultivate any vegetable crops that might be grown between the vines. There was another side to a farmer's business. In a primitive economy, when there was as yet no middleman, the farmer needed to be his own salesman. Much of his livelihood was made by selling his goods in the city's *agora*.[46] A trip to the town for the assembly could easily be combined with business.

For the period, however, when the dichotomy between city-thete and country-peasant is most commonly assumed, that of the Peloponnesian War, the above argument is irrelevant. On several occasions the Spartan army invaded Attika and the country-folk were forced to take refuge in the town. The consequent hardship we learn from Thucydides,[47] but their presence is assured. In the last part of the war, after the occupation of Dekeleia, they were permanently present. The thetes, on the other hand, if they were the only Athenian citizens who rowed the ships, which I find hard to believe, were often out on campaign. Surprising, then, if they were radically opposed on matters of policy, that Athenian policy did not change radically.

This brings me to the second point, the idea that the thetes in the town and the farmers in the country differed fundamentally in their attitudes to democracy, the Peloponnesian War and the empire. To begin with democracy: there was only one occasion in the fifth century, and none in the fourth before the end of the Lamian War (322), when the Athenians voted to abrogate that form of government. The Thirty Tyrants, who ruled for a short period at the end of the Peloponnesian War, were forced upon the Athenians by Lysander. They quickly got rid of them, though it was a long time before they forgot. The occasion I am referring to is the Revolution of the Four Hundred in 411/0 B.C. The situation was this: the fleet was away in Samos; a group of upperclass intelligentsia, inspired by a teacher of rhetoric, the sophist Antiphon, instituted a reign of terror that produced fear and mistrust amongst the people; they were joined by others from the fleet at Samos, who had been promoting oligarchy there. They did all the talking in the *boule*, and all the talking in the assembly. Those of democratic inclination dared not speak. Finally this group put before the assembly a motion that anyone might propose whatever he wished without fear of indictment. This was, in essence, to do away with the *graphe paranomon*, the king-pin of democracy. The motion passed. They proceeded to form a council of 400, whose task was to publish a list of 5000 (more or less[48]) propertied citizens, who should, under this constitution, enjoy the franchise. There was to be no pay for magistrates. The Four Hundred never produced the list, instead they ruled as oligarchs. From the very beginning they made overtures for peace to the Spartans.[49] The Spartans, to their credit, were wise enough to realise that these people did not represent the view of the Athenians as a whole, and did not negotiate. All this comes directly from Thucydides.[50] To cut a long story short, the Athenians soon realised what the Four Hundred were up to and restored the democracy. Some scholars have seen in the mention of the Five Thousand (ὅπλα παρεχόμενοι) the implication that there were five thousand propertied men, who were interested in a restriction of the franchise. They argue that these must be the men who were being

---

[45] Cf. V. Ehrenberg (note 16 above), 79.

[46] Cf. V. Ehrenberg (note 16 above), 77. These farmers would have to arrive before dawn, or maybe the night before, since activity in the *agora* began before the sun was up. Cf. Aristophanes, *Acharnians* 20f., where Dikaiopolis complains that people who are already engaged in business in the *agora* try to avoid being interrupted for a dawn meeting of the assembly (ἑωθινῆς ἐκκλησίας).

[47] Thuc., 2. 17.

[48] Not more than 5000, Thuc., 8. 65. 3; not less than 5000, Aristotle, *Ath. Pol.* 29. 5.

[49] This does not mean they were ideologically opposed to war, rather that, like other minority groups in city-state politics, they had to look outside for support.

[50] Thuc., 8. 63. 3–8. 71. 3.

hurt by the war and opposed the democrats' insistence on continuing it. Nothing could be further from the truth.

Thucydides is abundantly clear on this. The Four Hundred were an isolated group. They enjoyed no support. There was no liaison between them and the Five Thousand, because the latter did not exist as an identifiable entity—they had not yet been catalogued. This is all too often over-looked by those who write about the Constitution of the Five Thousand and assume that they had a corporate identity and a platform of demands that went with it. The Five Thousand were merely a figment of the propaganda of the Four Hundred,[51] they were not a reality until after the overthrow of the oligarchy,[52] and then they turned out to be closer to nine thousand in number.[53] The Four Hundred silenced the voice of democracy by their terrorist tactics alone. Who were these voiceless people? They were the same as those who later restored the democracy. Since the fleet was away in Samos, the supporters of democracy at home must *ipso facto* be the rest of the citizen body that was not serving on board ship at that time. It follows that there was no radical disagree-ment on the nature of the constitution between these two parts of the *demos*. The only undemo-cratic element was the Four Hundred, and they were motivated by private interest.

The same incident can serve as an answer to the question whether there was a difference of opinion amongst 'ordinary' Athenians about the war. Even the Spartans could see that the Four Hundred spoke for themselves alone. The men in the city no less than the fleet at Samos were committed to continuing the war, as Thucydides tells us at the beginning of book eight. There was no peace-party in Athens, except a small group of over-educated aristocrats. From this same group came the Thirty Tyrants. They had studied under the sophists, many with Sokrates. Their actions only confirmed the prejudice of 'the many' against the higher education offered by the sophists to those who could afford it. We should not be surprised at the verdict of the jurors of the restored democracy, who condemned Sokrates in 399 B.C.

The question regarding the attitude of these two sections of the Athenian *demos* to the empire revolves around 'the profits of empire.' The common assumption is that the thetes were the real supporters of empire, because they gained their livelihood from it, both from the income they received for rowing the triremes and from the various payments the state made for minor magis-tracies, jury duty, etc.[54] The farmers, on the other hand, did not derive their livelihood from this source and were consequently not well disposed towards the empire, especially when the empire involved them in a war. We have already seen that the thetes were not the only ones to benefit (if they did) from the proceeds of empire. The rich gained as much as anyone, most likely more. Next to them were the metics.[55] This, of course, need not mean that the thetes did not profit from the Athenian empire, but the idea that they did is based upon two facile assumptions that are accepted too uncritically. The first is that there was a large number of thetes, enough to man a fleet of, say, 100 triremes (*i.e.*, 20,000) without drawing upon the farming community. Only thus can it be claimed that they were distinct in their attitudes to naval enterprises. The second is that a thete, by virtue of having no property, had no other source of income and was sitting around in the taverna (*vel sim.*) waiting to sign on for the Sicilian expedition or the like. Neither of these assumptions is appealing.

A. H. M. Jones, in his study of fourth-century society,[56] has argued most convincingly that, out of an adult male population of 21,000, only 12,000 were of the thetic class, barely enough to man

---

[51] Thuc., 8. 66. 1: ἦν δὲ τοῦτο εὐπρεπὲς πρὸς τοὺς πλείους, ἐπεὶ ἕξειν γε τὴν πόλιν οἵπερ καὶ μεθίστασαν ἔμελλον.

[52] Thuc., 8. 92. 11 and Aristotle, *Ath. Pol.* 32. 3.

[53] [Lysias], *Pro Polystrato* 13.

[54] *CAH* 5. 110–111.

[55] So, too, did the farmers of Attika, cf. note 32 above.

[56] A. H. M. Jones, *Athenian Democracy* (Oxford 1960) 75–96.

sixty triremes, if they all turned out. If we accept Gomme's tentative figure for thetes in 431, there were possibly 50% more at that time, but already by 425 their number had dropped to *c.* 12,000. In relationship to those of hoplite census and over the thetes increased from a ratio of 3:4 in 431 to 2:2 in 400.[57] This is not surprising. Not only does Thucydides tell us that at the beginning of the Peloponnesian War the majority of the Athenians still made their living off the land, but the natural progression from country to town, exacerbated by the war, is sure to have swelled the number of the thetic class proportionally to the rest of the citizen-body in the fourth century. Nevertheless, after 425 there were never enough thetes to man a sizeable expedition and, if the Athenians did provide all the manpower for their navy, it follows that many from the farming community would be called upon. This must certainly have been the case also in the early fifth century, especially at Salamis, Athens' finest hour, when as many as 40,000 rowers were pressed into service.[58]

For the period of the Peloponnesian War, however, the evidence suggests a different story. A recent study of the Athenian naval administration shows that for this period, while the Athenians provided the experienced *nautai*, who were professional sailors, the bulk of the manpower came from other sources—metics, volunteers from the allied states and slaves.[59] The experienced *nautai* were, most likely, from the thetic class, but their number was very far from being enough to represent the dominant voice in the assembly.[60]

There remains one other possibility, that a large number of thetes had an interest in the preservation of the Athenian empire because they had come to depend for their livelihood upon state income, not for military service, but for holding magistracies and for jury duty, and upon state support for attending the theatre and, later, the *ekklesia*. This common assumption, that full democracy depends upon the tribute of empire, is belied by the evidence of the fourth century. Further, it is based on the naive belief that a landless person has no other means of support than the generosity of the state. In the first place, as Jones has shown for the fourth century,[61] many members of the thetic class did own some land, though not enough to sustain themselves and their families. They supplemented their income by hiring themselves out as labourers during part of the year. Furthermore, since the time of Solon, those who could not derive a livelihood from the land had been encouraged to learn a trade. Many thetes will have been small shop-owners or skilled craftsmen, who had some investment in slaves and stock and sufficient income from their trade to maintain themselves. For the period of Jones' study the dividing line (in wealth) between the thete and the lower levels of the hoplite census was negligible. Further, the majority of the 6000 liable for the *eisphora* were little better off. If one excepts the very wealthy few at the top, the great majority of Athenians in the fourth century had a property-rating of between 20 and 30 minae. There is no reason to believe the situation was different in the fifth century. Consequently, there were very few citizens indeed who lived wholly on state pay. Nor was there a sufficient difference in wealth between the majority of the landed and the landless to motivate a radical difference of opinion on such major issues as the nature of the constitution, the war or the empire. They were united in their common antipathy towards 'the Few,' who were very wealthy, their leaders in war and peace. In sum, we must reject not only Jaeger's assertion that "the rich men of Athens were the peace party," but also the view that the proletariat were any more warmongering than the peasants.

---

[57] See Gomme (note 18 above), 26.

[58] That is, allowing 200 rowers for each of 200 triremes.

[59] Borimir Jordan, *The Athenian Navy in the Classical Period* (Berkeley and Los Angeles 1972) 210–267.

[60] One should also note that the view that the Athenian *nautai* were all from the urban proletariat is not persuasive, for this would mean that the Athenians made no use of the men in the coastal demes, who were likely to have most naval expertise. Cf., for example, the origin of the sailing families cited by Jordan, 221 and note 39.

[61] The following details are taken from the work of A. H. M. Jones cited above, note 56.

Finally, one could be contentious and point out that, during the Peloponnesian War (more particularly from 412 onwards), those thetes whose income was derived from city-based activities[62] were less affected by the deprivations of war, less available for state service and less in need of state support than the farmers and thetes from the country, who were deprived. For this reason it is likely that the latter were in the majority not only in the theatre, but also in the *ekklesia*, and that they served more frequently as magistrates in Athens and the empire and as jurors in the law courts, even as rowers in the triremes. For these were the men with the time and the need.

In conclusion, it appears that, with the exception of a few self-seeking and ambitious rich men, who hoped to capitalise upon a period of Athenian weakness, there was no part of the Athenian *demos* that did not wholeheartedly support the democratic constitution and the empire. The judgement of their contemporaries was correct: the Athenians were all polypragmatists.

University of British Columbia   PHILLIP HARDING

---

[62] We should remember that not all thetes lived in the city, just as not all city-dwellers were of the thetic class.

PHILIP AND OLYMPIAS (337/6 B.C.)

In 357 B.C. Philip II of Macedon married the Molossian princess, Olympias.[1] Romantic writers portray them as childhood lovers on Samothrake,[2] though Satyros indicates that this was a political union (ὁ δὲ Φίλιππος αἰεὶ κατὰ πόλεμον ἐγάμει, *ap.* Ath., 13.557B). Whatever the original nature of their relationship, Olympias' position was greatly enhanced when in the following summer she gave birth to Alexander.[3] Arrhidaios, Philip's other son by the Thessalian Philinne, soon showed signs of mental disorder;[4] subsequent wives failed to produce male offspring.[5] Before long Olympias was unrivalled at the Court, though not solely by virtue of her splendid son. She was a woman of indomitable spirit; neglected by her husband, she transferred her affections to Alexander. And she was determined that he should rule.

[1] Who killed Philip of Macedon? Or rather, who instigated his murder? It is a vexed question, and the case against each "suspect" has in turn been argued and re-argued vigorously: Pausanias, the sons of Aëropos, the Great King, Olympias, even Alexander himself. Space does not permit another full-scale treatment, nor does such an approach seem necessary to me. I should like, rather, in this essay to characterise the relationship between Philip and Olympias, and to consider anew the plausibility of the charges against her. For full discussions of the death of Philip, some of which will be cited by author, see the following works: G. Grote, *A History of Greece* 11 (London 1869) 317–327; A. Schaefer, *Demosthenes und seine Zeit* 3 (Leipzig 1887) 1–102, esp. 62–72; U. Koehler, "Über das Verhältnis Alexanders des Großen zu seinem Vater Philipp," *Sitzungsberichte der Akademie der Wissenschaften, Berlin* (1892) 497–514; H. Willrich, "Wer ließ König Philipp von Makedonien ermorden?" *Hermes* 34 (1899) 174–183; E. Badian, "The Death of Philip II," *Phoenix* 17 (1963) 244–250; J. R. Hamilton, "Alexander's Early Life," *Greece & Rome* 12 (1965) 117–124; K. Kraft, *Der "rationale" Alexander, Frankfurter Althistorische Studien,* Heft 5 (Frankfurt 1971) 11–42; J. R. Ellis, "Amyntas Perdikka, Philip II and Alexander the Great: A Study in Conspiracy," *JHS* 91 (1971) 15–24; A. B. Bosworth, "Philip II and Upper Macedonia," *CQ* n.s. 21 (1971) 93–105; J. Rufus Fears, "Pausanias, The Assassin of Philip II," *Athenaeum* 53 (1975) 111–135; J. R. Ellis, *Philip II and Macedonian Imperialism* (London 1976) 211–227.

[2] Plut., *Alex.* 2.2.

[3] According to Plut., *Alex.* 3.8, Philip learned the news of Alexander's birth at the same time as he received word of his victory in the horse-race at Olympia. Plut., *Mor.* 401B says that Olympias was originally called Polyxena, then Myrtale (cf. Justin, 9.7.13); G. H. Macurdy, *Hellenistic Queens: A Study of Woman-Power in Macedonia, Seleucid Syria and Ptolemaic Egypt, The Johns Hopkins University Studies in Archaeology* 14 (Baltimore 1932) 24, believes that Olympias took her name, which "appears for the first time as a proper name as a name of this queen," to commemorate the simultaneous birth of Alexander and the Olympic victory. See also H. Berve, *Das Alexanderreich auf prosopographischer Grundlage* 2 (Munich 1926) 283–288, no. 581, *s.v.* Ὀλυμπιάς; H. Strasburger, *RE* 18.1 (1935) 177–182, *s.v.* "Olympias (5)." Stratonike, a fourth name attributed to her by Plutarch (above), must belong to her final year and the victory over Hadea-Eurydike (see D.S., 19.11) rather than to her maiden years (so Macurdy, 24; Berve, 2.283); cf. *Chiron* (1981).

[4] See Berve (above, note 3), 2.385–386, no. 781, *s.v.* Φίλιππος Ἀρριδαῖος; J. Kaerst, *RE* 2.1 (1895) 1248–1249, *s.v.* "Arridaios (4)." For his mental state see App., *Syr.* 52; Justin, 13.2.11; 14.5.2; D.S., 18.2.2; Plut., *Alex.* 10.2; 77.7–8; Porphyr. Tyr., *FGrHist* 260 F2; Heidelberg Epit. 1; Plut., *Mor.* 337D. According to Plut., *Alex.* 77.8, his mental condition was induced by drugs given to him while he was still a child by Olympias, an implausible tale, deriving perhaps from the fact that Olympias was later responsible for his death (D.S., 19.11). For Philinne see Satyros, *FHG* (Müller) 3.161 = Ath., 13.557B–D; for her alleged low birth see Justin, 9.8.2 (*saltatrix*); 13.2.11 (*scortum*); cf. Ath., 13.578A; Plut., *Alex.* 77.7. Beloch, *GG²* 3.2.69; G. T. Griffith, "Philip of Macedon's Early Interventions in Thessaly (358–352 B.C.)," *CQ* n.s. 20 (1970) 70–71, and Ellis, *Philip II* 61, rightly consider her to be of good family, probably the Aleuadai. For Philip's marriage to Philinne in 358 (against C. Ehrhardt, *CQ* n.s. 17 [1967] 297) see Berve, 2.385 and Ellis, *Philip II* 212.

[5] Justin's claim (9.8.3) that Philip had numerous sons is a rhetorical exaggeration. See my comments in *RhM* forthcoming. A son named Karanos (Justin, 11.2.3) did not exist: see my "Philip II, Kleopatra and Karanos," *RFIC* 107 (1979) 385–393. And cf. now G. L. Cawkwell, *Philip of Macedon* (London 1978) 206, note 5.

For twenty years of stormy wedlock she endured Philip's lengthy campaigns, numerous amours and political marriages. But not in silence. She was a jealous and passionate woman who, if she could not be his only wife, meant to be his only queen. And in this cause she enlisted even Alexander, as Plutarch tells us: αἱ δὲ περὶ τὴν οἰκίαν ταραχαί, διὰ τοὺς γάμους καὶ τοὺς ἔρωτας αὐτοῦ [sc. Φιλίππου] τρόπον τινὰ τῆς βασιλείας τῇ γυναικωνίτιδι συννοσούσης, πολλὰς αἰτίας καὶ μεγάλας διαφορὰς παρεῖχον, ἃς ἡ τῆς Ὀλυμπιάδος χαλεπότης, δυσζήλου καὶ βαρυθύμου γυναικός, ἔτι μείζονας ἐποίει, παροξυνούσης τὸν Ἀλέξανδρον (Alex. 9.5). The complaints were clearly not confined to Olympias herself: we might consider in this context Plutarch's anecdote (Apophthegmata Philippou 22 = Mor. 178E−F), which claims that Alexander had complained to his father because he was producing children by other wives. Nevertheless, Olympias suffered no harm, other than to her ego, until 337, when Philip married Kleopatra, the niece of Attalos.[6]

Attempts to attach political significance to this union have met with only limited success.[7] It may well have been an irrational act, an act of love. On this the ancient sources, at least, are unanimous.[8] The adjective "domestic" is perhaps nowhere more aptly used of state-politics than in ancient Macedonia. And Philip's household problems were, as Plutarch says, "a type of state-illness that originated in the women's quarters" (Alex. 9.5). Like Alexander after him, he was liable to the criticism that he was "a more illustrious man in war than he was after a victory."[9]

At any rate, he married Kleopatra. Probably it was nothing more than an infatuation. Kleopatra's relatives may have seen it as a way of supplanting Alexander and his Epeirot mother; for they resented the latter as much for her origins as for her uncompromising personality. But what Attalos wished for under the influence of wine was far removed from what Philip had intended. Alexander had proved himself his father's son at Chaironeia, in Athens and at home; indeed Philip encouraged his son's popularity (Φίλιππος ὑπερηγάπα τὸν υἱόν, ὥστε καὶ χαίρειν τῶν Μακεδόνων Ἀλέξανδρον μὲν βασιλέα, Φίλιππον δὲ στρατηγὸν καλούντων. Alex. 9.4).[10] Attalos' prayer for *legitimate* heirs from this union of Philip and Kleopatra was a tactless utterance.[11] That the drunken bridegroom turned upon his own son in a fit of passion is also understandable, especially in the Macedonian context.[12] In the morning, Philip will have been awake to the political realities of the situation. But by then it was too late: Alexander was bound for Illyria via Epeiros, where he would leave Olympias with her brother.

[6] Satyros *ap.* Ath., 13.557D−E; Ath., 13.560C; Arr., 3.6.5 (who calls her Eurydike); Justin, 9.7.12; Plut., *Alex.* 9.6−7. The relationship is confused by Justin, 9.5.8−9 and D.S., 17.2.3, who call her Attalos' sister (cf. Ps.-Kall., 1.20 τὴν ἀδελφὴν Λυσίου Κλεοπάτραν; clearly Ἀττάλου is meant); Jul. Val., 1.13 has Kleopatra as Attalos' daughter; D.S., 16.93.9 makes her his aunt. See Berve, 2.94, no. 182, *s.v.* Ἄτταλος and 2.213−214, no. 434, *s.v.* Κλεοπάτρα. Cf. also O. Hoffmann, *Die Makedonen: ihre Sprache und ihr Volkstum* (Göttingen 1906) 157, 219.

[7] A. B. Bosworth, *CQ* n.s. 21 (1971) 103, sees in Philip's marriage with Kleopatra the attempt of a junta from Lower Macedonia to gain power. Thus Pausanias and the Lynkestians represent the disgruntled Upper Macedonian faction. Bosworth makes much (97−98) of early connexions between Upper Macedonia and the kingdom of the Molossians in order to support his claim that Attalos' "reference to legitimate heirs must mean that Cleopatra came from Lower Macedon . . .". (102). She may have been from there, but surely the distinction is between Macedonian (Kleopatra) and non-Macedonian (Olympias) queens. Against Bosworth see Ellis, *Philip II* 303−304, note 23, who rightly points out that we do not know anything about Parmenion's origin; he may himself have been Upper Macedonian (Koinos, his son-in-law, was of Greek ancestry and commanded the *pezhetairoi* from Elimiotis: Berve, no. 439).

[8] Plut., *Alex.* 9.6: [Κλεοπάτρα], ἣν ὁ Φίλιππος ἠγάγετο παρθένον, ἐρασθεὶς παρ' ἡλικίαν τῆς κόρης. Ath., 13.557D: ἔγημε Κλεοπάτραν ἐρασθεὶς τὴν . . . Ἀττάλου δὲ ἀδελφιδῆν.

[9] Curt., 8.9.1: *semper bello quam post victoriam clarior.*

[10] P. Green, *Alexander of Macedon* (Harmondsworth 1974) 93, thinks that this was Alexander's own propaganda: "It is not hard to guess who started *that* rumour−or who put it about that Philip was 'delighted' by such a compliment to his heir."

[11] Ellis, *Philip II* 214 ff., disbelieves Satyros' anecdote, which almost all scholars accept without question.

[12] We need only to think of Alexander's murder of Kleitos (see Berve, 2.206−208, no. 427 for full references); but cf. also Philip's shameful conduct after Chaironeia (D.S., 16.87.1−2).

Some time later, Demaratos of Korinth, a *xenos* of the Argead house and a diplomat of his own state, arrived, perhaps to congratulate Philip on his most recent matrimonial effort, but more likely to inform him of the state of preparation and the mood of the League-allies with respect to the proposed expedition against Persia. Philip's question concerning the relations of the Greek states was, therefore, not an idle one, but the matter of business on which Demaratos had come.[13] And the latter scarcely needed to remind Philip that the disorders of his own household were of equal importance to the success or failure of his Persian campaign. One had only to think of Jason of Pherai. Through the agency of Demaratos, Alexander was urged to return from Illyria, but there is no mention of Olympias by name.[14]

Justin (9.7.7) speaks of her activities in Epeiros in the following manner: *Olympias quoque fratrem suum Alexandrum, Epiri regem, in bellum subornabat pervicissetque, ni filiae nuptiis pater generum occupasset.* Modern scholars have been reluctant to see any attempt on Philip's part at a reconciliation with Olympias: the marriage of their daughter (also called Kleopatra) to Alexandros of Epeiros was intended to secure the latter's support for Philip, drawing him away from his sister's pernicious influence.[15] But, unless we attribute to the princess an "Electra complex," there is little reason to suppose that this marriage would do anything but bind Philip's Epeirot family even more closely.[16] Philip could not have hoped to isolate Olympias in this way. With her son as regent of Macedonia, her brother king, her daughter queen of Epeiros, Olympias might have been expected to excercise considerable authority. Philip, if anyone, knew what the woman was capable of, and he must have recognised that a reconciliation with Alexander would remain hollow if Olympias were excluded.[17]

But, in order to understand Philip's relations with Olympias, we must return to the marriage with Kleopatra. "Entire households," writes Athenaios (13.560C), "were overturned on account of women: for example, that of Philip, Alexander's father, by his marriage with Kleopatra." Why did he marry Kleopatra? And when? Philip was an astute politician who had won hegemony over Greece as much by diplomacy and bribery as by force. Now, on the eve of his Persian expedition, he contracted a disastrous marriage, shattering the very stability that he so needed at home during his absence. Modern treatments have failed to produce cogent arguments to show that this marriage was politically oriented.[18] In fact, it was politically so inopportune that there can be little doubt that Philip was not acting rationally. Thus our sources draw attention to two facts: he married Attalos' niece because he had fallen in love with her, and this caused trouble at home with Olympias. Previous unions, made for political reasons, had been tolerated only grudgingly by Olympias.[19] But this was a personal matter: Philip simply preferred the young Kleopatra to his

[13] Berve, 2.133, no. 253, *s.v.* Δημάρατος.

[14] See note 35 below.

[15] Badian, 246: "Philip's action is, of course, very significant. . . . it is interesting to see him taking deliberate steps to deprive Olympias (and, by implication, Alexander) of possible influence there [*i.e.*, Epeiros]." Cf. Droysen, *Geschichte des Hellenismus*[3] 1 (Basel 1952) 69; Fears, 128: "By tieing the Molossian more closely to the Argead house, Philip sought to protect himself from whatever influence Olympias might seek to exercise over her brother." I draw the line at Green's claim (93) that Alexander "might . . . find some attraction in an incestuous marriage . . . ."

[16] Recognised by Kraft 18: "Man müßte schon ein völlig unerweisliches besonderes Naheverhältnis der Tochter zum Vater, ja Haß gegen die eigene Mutter und gegen den Bruder Alexander unterstellen, damit die junge Kleopatra diese Rolle hätte spielen können, ganz abgesehen davon, daß sie als Persönlichkeit schwerlich der Mutter gewachsen sein konnte." Cf. Ellis, *Philip II* 304, note 32; C. Bradford Welles, *Alexander and the Hellenistic World* (Toronto 1970) 14: "Olympias had agreed to the marriage . . . ."

[17] W. W. Tarn's well-known statement that "it is doubtful if he ever cared for any woman except his terrible mother" (*CAH* 6.397) is to the point. Cf. Alexander's alleged claim (Plut., *Alex.* 39.13) that one tear from his mother could wipe out ten thousand letters of complaint against her.

[18] See note 7 above. Nor is it probable that Philip was motivated by "the belief, justified or not, that Alexander and Olympias were engaged in a treasonable plot to bring about his overthrow" (Green 91). The cause of Alexander's *self-imposed* exile was his (and, by extension, Olympias') dishonour at the wedding-feast; cf. Kraft, 17-18.

[19] Plut., *Alex.* 9.5; *Mor.* 141B-C; 178E-F.

Epeirot wife, now in her late thirties.[20] Justin is certainly incorrect in claiming that Philip divorced Olympias on a charge of *stuprum*; this has a suspiciously Roman discoloration. And no respectable historian could believe that her unusual fascination for snakes (if this is, in fact, true) ever formed the basis of a serious charge of adultery.[21] Olympias was still at the Court—though apparently not at the actual wedding-feast—when Philip married Kleopatra, as she had been when he wedded Nikesipolis of Pherai and Thracian Meda.[22] Nor did Philip ever challenge his son's position—much less his paternity!—or drive him into exile. It was only the manner in which the Attalos-faction interpreted the marriage that created the rift between Alexander and his father.

For the date of the wedding we have no precise evidence; although Philip's activities in Central Greece and the Peloponnesos make it unlikely that it occurred before spring 337.[23] Moreover, A. Schaefer may be correct in assigning Alexander's Illyrian campaign, which he conducted after Chaironeia and in Philip's absence, to the spring of 337, thus postponing the wedding-date further to at least summer of that year.[24] Now, according to Justin (9.5.8–9), Philip had only recently (*nuper*) married Kleopatra when Parmenion, Attalos and Amyntas led the advance forces into Asia at the beginning of spring 336 (*initio veris*). There is perhaps some corroboration in Diodoros (16.93.9), who correlates Attalos' departure with the first mention of Philip's new wife (τῆς ἐπιγαμηθείσης γυναικός) in a way that recalls the sense of Justin's statement. Furthermore, we are told that Kleopatra's child was born shortly before Philip's assassination: καὶ γὰρ ἐτύγχανε παιδίον ἐκ τῆς Κλεοπάτρας γεγονὸς τῷ Φιλίππῳ τῆς τελευτῆς τοῦ βασιλέως ὀλίγαις πρότερον ἡμέραις (D.S., 17.2.3.) This accords well with Justin's description of Kleopatra's daughter (Europe), who was murdered by Olympias *in gremio matris* (9.7.12).[25] Therefore, since Philip's death could not have occurred before the beginning of July 336 B.C.,[26] Kleopatra was no more than five or six months pregnant when her uncle left Macedonia at the beginning of spring. And, if we assume that she became pregnant reasonably soon after the marriage was consummated, then her union with Philip, and Alexander's flight, would belong to late summer, or even early autumn, 337.[27]

Alexander was soon recalled from Illyria, and Philip knew that Olympias could not be allowed to linger in Epeiros with a brother who was no match for her powerful personality. The winter saw the Illyrian problem resolved and negotiations carried on with Epeiros.[28] Alexander had gone to seek the support of the Illyrian chiefs, no doubt with the intention of leading them against Macedon in the spring. After the reconciliation with Alexander, Philip dispelled any rumours of Macedonian weakness by conducting a war against Pleurias (?),[29] probably in late winter (Feb./

---

[20] Berve, 2.283: "gegen 375 geboren," following C. Klotzsch, *Epirotische Geschichte bis zum Jahre 280 v. Chr.* (Diss. Friedrich-Wilhelms-Universität, Berlin 1910) 58, note 1.

[21] Plut., *Alex.* 2.6–3.4; Justin, 9.5.9 (*expulsa Alexandri matre Olympiade propter stupri suspitionem*); 11.11.3.

[22] Satyros *ap.* Ath., 13.557C–D; Plut., *Mor.* 141B–C, probably a reference to Nikesipolis.

[23] See Schaefer, 37 ff.; C. Roebuck, "The Settlements of Philip II with the Greek States in 338 B.C.," *CP* 43 (1948) 73–92; also T. T. B. Ryder, *Koine Eirene: General Peace and Local Independence in Ancient Greece* (Oxford 1965) 150–162; Grote, 11.315–317 also outlines Philip's settlement in Greece, but thinks (318, note 4) the marriage with Kleopatra belongs to 338. See again my "Philip II, Kleopatra and Karanos" (note 5 above).

[24] Schaefer, 63, with note 3; Curt., 8.1.25.

[25] Paus., 8.7.7 describes, in rather sensational fashion, the deaths of Kleopatra and her child, whom he wrongly calls a son.

[26] It belongs to the year of Pythodelos' archonship, 336/5 B.C. (Arr., 1.1.1 has Pythodemos, D.S., 16.91.1; Pythodoros), and *IG* 2.² 1.240 reveals that in the tenth prytany of the preceding year (in which Phrynichos was archon) Philip's death was not yet known in Athens. See K. J. Beloch, *GG*² 3.2.59–60; C. Bradford Welles, *Diodorus of Sicily* 8 (Loeb Classical Library, Cambridge, Mass. 1963) 100, note 1; Ellis, *Philip II* 306, note 53.

[27] Thus Schaefer, 66, note 3: "Die Hochzeit mit Kleopatra mag in den Spätsommer fallen"; and most recently Cawkwell (note 5 above) 178 "autumn 337." Cf. A. R. Burn, *Alexander the Great and the Middle East* (Harmondsworth 1973) 47, who places Philip's return to Macedonia in the summer of 337.

[28] Plut., *Alex.* 9.14 mentions only Alexander's recall; but cf. Kraft, 19; and also note 34 below.

[29] Lenschau, *RE* 21 (1951) 239, *s.v.* "Pleurias," accepts a battle "einige Zeit vor 336," but assumes that the name "ist wohl

March 336). This campaign has been dated, by those who do not conflate it with the campaign against Pleuratos (344/3), to the summer of 337; but this date is dependent upon the notion that Philip married Kleopatra in the spring of that year.[30] Some time later came Aristokritos, the ambassador of the Karian satrap, Pixodaros, who sought to wed his eldest daughter to a son of Philip, though it is doubtful that Pixodaros himself chose the mentally deficient Arrhidaios.[31] If Alexander's exile consumed the winter of 337/6, the Pixodaros-affair must date to the spring of 336: this coincides conveniently with the arrival of Parmenion, Attalos and Amyntas (presumably the son of Arrhabaios[32]) in Asia—which may have induced Pixodaros to seek a marriage-alliance with Philip—and the opening of the sailing-season.[33]

And Olympias? Attalos' departure gave Philip the opportunity to attend to his domestic problems. Now he recalled Olympias from Epeiros, hoping to soothe her wrath with the impending marriage of her daughter to Alexandros. Justin (9.7.10) implies that she was never recalled by Philip, but his account is marred by internal contradictions.[34] Plutarch mentions the services of Demaratos of Korinth in three separate passages (*Alex.* 9.12–14; *Mor.* 70B–C and 179C); in one of these he says that Philip was reconciled with both Alexander and Olympias: ἐπεὶ δὲ διενεχθέντος αὐτοῦ πρὸς Ὀλυμπιάδα τὴν γυναῖκα καὶ τὸν υἱὸν ἧκε Δημάρατος ὁ Κορίνθιος . . . . ὁ δὲ [sc. Φίλιππος] συμφρονήσας ἐπαύσατο τῆς ὀργῆς καὶ διηλλάγη πρὸς αὐτούς (*Mor.* 179C).[35] But Philip's plans were disrupted by two unexpected complications: Attalos, just before his departure for Asia, had sexually abused (or, at least, instigated the attack on) Pausanias of Orestis, one of the King's *somatophylakes*,[36] and Aristokritos arrived with proposals of marriage from Pixodaros.

Kurzform für Pleuratos." See N. G. L. Hammond, "The Kingdoms in Illyria *circa* 400–167 B.C.," *ABSA* 61 (1966) 245, with note 27; also Fears 144, note 11; Ellis, *Philip II* 302, note 3. See further note 40 below.

[30] Ellis, *Ibid.*

[31] While Badian (245) correctly gauges Alexander's insecurity by his actions in the Pixodaros-affair (cf. also Hamilton, 121), he makes too much of the words Πιξώδαρος . . . ἐβούλετο τὴν πρεσβυτάτην τῶν θυγατέρων Ἀρριδαίῳ . . . γυναῖκα δοῦναι, arguing that Pixodaros clearly understood that Alexander was in disfavour at the Macedonian Court. But this argument collapses when one takes into account Plut., *Alex.* 10.3: καὶ Πιξωδάρῳ μὲν οὐ παρὰ μικρὸν ἤρεσκε ταῦτα τῶν προτέρων μᾶλλον. ὁ δὲ Φίλιππος αἰσθόμενος κτλ. Pixodaros (μέν) liked this arrangement (that is, a marriage-alliance with Alexander) better—would he not have rejected it, if he thought Alexander was in disfavour?—but Philip (δέ) was greatly troubled by the prospect of his Crown Prince marrying a mere Karian (Καρὸς ἀνθρώπου, cf. J. R. Hamilton, *Plutarch, Alexander: A Commentary* [Oxford 1969] 26). Now it may be that Pixodaros chose Arrhidaios "because he had no idea that Alexander was a possible candidate" (Fears, 127) and did not himself "overrate his eligibility as a potential ally" (Green, 99). I am inclined to believe, however, that Plutarch compresses the affair and that Pixodaros simply sought an alliance (without specifying which of Philip's sons he wanted), in response to which Philip offered him (gladly, we may assume) Arrhidaios. Pixodaros may not even have known the truth about his would-be son-in-law, for Alexander sent Thessalos with the message ὡς χρὴ τὸν νόθον ἐάσαντα καὶ οὐ φρενήρη. Cf. Burn (note 27 above), 49.

[32] See Berve, 2.29–30, no. 59, *s.v.* Ἀμύντας, 2.80, no. 144, *s.v.* Ἀρραβαῖος.

[33] A. T. Olmstead, *History of the Persian Empire* (Chicago 1948) 490, thinks Pixodaros' offer came after the advance-force reached Asia. Ellis, *Philip II* 305, note 40, argues that this "makes Pixodaros' abandonment of the projected alliance a little harder to explain." There are two plausible motives for Pixodaros' change of heart: the truth about Arrhidaios (note 31 above) or the death of Philip in the summer of 336, which appeared to remove the threat of a Macedonian invasion.

[34] Justin argues, on the one hand, that Olympias incited Pausanias to murder Philip (9.7.1, 8; cf. Plut., *Alex.* 10.5) and that she even supplied horses for the assassin's escape (*Olympias certe fugienti percussori etiam equos habuit praeparatos,* 9.7.9), but then clearly implies that she was not in Macedonia for her daughter's wedding (9.7.10). The evidence of Plut., *Alex.* 10.1, 5; *Mor.* 179C suggests strongly that she had returned; cf. Green, 524, note 63; Ellis, *Philip II* 217; Kraft, 19.

[35] The passage is adduced by Kraft, *ibid.* Badian, in his review of Kraft, *Gnomon* 47 (1975) 53, claims that Plut., *Alex.* 9.13–14 states "that *only* [my emphasis] Al. was allowed to return." This is inaccurate: Plutarch, in the *Life*, mentions Alexander only, but we cannot infer from his silence that Olympias was *not* recalled, a point clearly contradicted by the *Moralia*. And it is certainly a dangerous, if not fallacious, argument that "the anecdote in the *Moralia* has to be complete in itself, not historically accurate . . . . In the Life, on the other hand, Plutarch is concerned with the *facts* . . . ." (Badian, *ibid.*).

[36] See Berve, 2.308–309, no. 614, *s.v.* Παυσανίας, also note 43 below; cf. *LCM* 4.10 (Dec. 1979) 215–216.

The story of Pausanias of Orestis smacks of the sensational: it is a sordid tale of homosexual lust, rape and vengeful murder. Yet, while it undoubtedly suffers from embellishments, much remains that is highly plausible. There are three main parts: (i) the quarrel of the two Pausaniases over Philip's affections and the heroic death of one of these; (ii) the rape of the Orestian by Attalos' muleteers (or by Attalos himself, so Justin, 9.6.4−8); and (iii) the murder of Philip. Pausanias of Orestis had been a lover of Philip, but his namesake soon supplanted him as Philip's favourite.

> "When he saw the king was becoming enamoured of another Pausanias . . . he addressed him with abusive language, accusing him of being a hermaphrodite and prompt to accept the amorous advances of any who wished. Unable to endure such an insult, the other kept silent for the time, but, after confiding to Attalus, one of his friends, what he proposed to do, he brought about his own death voluntarily and in a spectacular fashion. For a few days after this, as Philip was engaged in battle with Pleurias, king of the Illyrians, Pausanias stepped in front of him and, receiving on his body all the blows directed at the king, so met his death" (D.S., 16.93.4−6).[37]

The story continues that, as a consequence, Attalos invited Pausanias of Orestis to dinner, where, having filled him with wine, he handed the young man over to his muleteers, who sexually assaulted him (παρέδωκεν αὐτοῦ τὸ σῶμα τοῖς ὀρεωκόμοις εἰς ὕβριν καὶ παροινίαν ἑταιρικήν).[38] Pausanias later complained of the outrage to Philip, who would not punish Attalos on account of their relationship and the latter's appointment to the command of the advance forces that were to be sent to Asia.[39] Finally, some months later, instigated by the sophist Hermokrates (so D.S., 16.94.1) or by Olympias (Justin, 9.7.1; Plut., *Alex.* 10.5), Pausanias murdered Philip.

Now the preamble about the two Pausaniases has a suspicious duplicity: two young men, both named Pausanias, lovers of the King. Like Olympias, Pausanias of Orestis was jilted by Philip and insulted by Attalos. But modern scholars have been troubled more by the chronological difficulties: the confusion (or rather conflation) of the battles with Pleuratos (344/3) and Pleurias (337/6), and the vexed question of why Pausanias waited so long for his revenge *and then struck down Philip, not Attalos*, have led many to reject the Pausanias-story outright.[40] Recent discussions by K. Kraft, J. Rufus Fears and J. R. Ellis have corrected some misconceptions, but the entire affair is, I think, more satisfactorily explained by my slightly revised chronology.[41] Philip's battle with Pleurias the Illyrian followed the marriage with Kleopatra and, as it appears, Alexander's recall from Illyria, where he caused the unrest that necessitated the campaign. This was late winter, that is, February or early March 336. In this battle the first Pausanias fell. Immediately thereafter, upon their return to Macedonia, the Orestian was victimised by Attalos, who was already designated commander of the advance forces in Asia and left Macedonia at the beginning of spring.[42] Philip, we are told by Diodoros (16.93.9), attempted to console Pausanias by advancing him through the ranks of the σωματοφυλακία.[43] And, at this time, he also recalled Olympias from Epeiros.

The woman was implacable. Her dishonour and the rival Kleopatra, who now bore the dynastic name Eurydike and showed visible signs of her pregnancy,[44] remained foremost in her mind. She

---

[37] The translation is that of C. Bradford Welles (note 26 above), 97.

[38] D.S., 16.93.7. Justin, 9.6.6 has Attalos directly involved: *Nam perductum in convivium solutumque mero Attalus non suae tantum, verum et convivarum libidini velut scortorum iure subiecerat ludibrium omnium inter aequales reddiderat.*

[39] D.S., 16.93.8−9.

[40] Thus Badian, 247; cf. Hamilton, *Plutarch, Alexander* (note 31 above) 27−28.

[41] Kraft, 33−35; Fears, 120−122; Ellis, *Philip II* 302, note 3.

[42] Justin, 9.5.8−9.

[43] Justin, 9.6.7−8 seeks a stronger motive for Pausanias' attack on Philip, alleging that Pausanias was angry at the King because he made fun of his complaint and had, moreover, honoured Attalos.

[44] For the dynastic name "Eurydike" see my "Kleopatra or Eurydike?" *Phoenix* 32 (1978) 155−158.

regarded Philip's almost deferential treatment of Attalos as a further insult, a threat to Alexander's *Erbrecht*. We may assume that she was receptive to the pitiful laments of Pausanias. Blinded by her hostility, she completely misread Philip's intentions and played upon the insecurities of her son. The matter came to a head with the arrival of Aristokritos from Karia. Philip decided that Arrhidaios was as much as a Karian princess could reasonably hope for, but, according to Plutarch, this caused new talk and revived accusations, which originated with Alexander's companions and his own mother: αὖθις ἐγίνοντο λόγοι καὶ διαβολαὶ παρὰ τῶν φίλων καὶ τῆς μητρὸς πρὸς Ἀλέξανδρον, ὡς Ἀρριδαῖον ἐπὶ τῇ βασιλείᾳ Φιλίππου γάμοις λαμπροῖς καὶ πράγμασι μεγάλοις εἰσοικειοῦντος (*Alex.* 10.1). Unless we assume that Olympias was influencing Alexander and his companions by letter—Plutarch, who records numerous details of Alexander's correspondence, knows nothing of it—, she was again in Macedonia, perhaps entrusted with her daughter's wedding-arrangements but not fully at peace with Philip. To her mind, his concessions amounted to "too little too late."

The companions of Alexander—Harpalos, Nearchos, Erigyios, Ptolemy[45]—were exiled by Philip, who also demanded the extradition of the actor Thessalos, whom Alexander had used as his negotiator with Pixodaros. He appears to have come to no harm, however, and it is possible that Philip did not live to see him extradited.[46] The banishment of the "companions" (does *philoi= hetairoi*?) shows that Philip took the matter seriously; their interference was detrimental to his attempts at re-establishing stability at the Court. Ptolemy's history, which was very likely the source of Arrian's brief notice of this incident (3.6.5–6), places an interesting emphasis not on the Pixodaros-affair (which is not specifically mentioned), but on the dishonour of Olympias. And this may suggest that these men represented a political entity that favoured Olympias.[47]

Philip was in a dilemma: to retaliate against Olympias would surely destroy any hope of regaining Alexander's confidence, yet the woman had become his avowed enemy. What part she played in Philip's assassination may well be irretrievable, owing to the distortions of a hostile tradition; for certainly she was not guilty of all the crimes imputed to her by Justin.[48] A convincing case has been made recently for Pausanias' personal motive, but this does not mean that Olympias could not have instigated the murder.[49] For this there is a strong tradition in antiquity, and indeed Olympias could have hoped for better treatment with Alexander on the throne than she was receiving from Philip. No one questions that she was responsible for the cruel murder of Kleopatra and her daughter Europe, a most vindictive and unnecessary act.[50] And, if we are correct in assuming that she returned to Macedonia in the spring of 336, she was in a position to do great harm. Her hatred was directed against the woman who had displaced her as wife and queen, and against the man who had allowed that to happen. "Dies Teufelsweib hat hinlänglich gezeigt, dass sie zu allem fähig war . . . ."[51]

University of Calgary   WALDEMAR HECKEL

[45] Plut., *Alex.* 10.4; Arr., 3.6.5 adds Laomedon, Erigyios' brother. Schaefer, 65, note 2 believes that Arrian correctly dates the banishment of these companions to the time of Philip's wedding; cf. Kraft, 26–27, with note 36 on p. 27. See, however, Hamilton, *Plutarch, Alexander* (note 31, above) 27; Badian, *Gnomon* 47 (1975) 54: the Pixodaros-affair is the proper context. Burn (note 27, above), 48, 50, has them leaving Macedonia on two separate occasions.

[46] Berve, 2.180, no. 371, *s.v.* Θέσσαλος.

[47] Hamilton, *Greece & Rome* 12 (1965) 120: "It is noticeable that among Alexander's close friends were few of the greater Macedonian nobility." They shared this feature with Olympias. Nor were they all contemporaries of Alexander: Erigyios was certainly much older (Berve, 2.151–152, no. 302 does not indicate this); see Curt., 8.4.34: *Erigyius, gravis quidem aetate, sed et animi et corporis robore nulli iuvenum postferendus . . . . canitiem ostentans . . .*

[48] Justin, 9.7.8–14; cf. the comments of Ellis, *Philip II* 224–225.

[49] See note 41 above.

[50] Justin, 9.7.12; Paus., 8.7.7; Plut., *Alex.* 10.7. I see no reason to disbelieve that Alexander was displeased with his mother over this matter.   [51] H. Willrich, *Hermes* 34 (1899) 175.

THUCYDIDES AND HELLANIKOS

In 1.89.1, tracing the growth of Athenian power in the period of the Fifty Years, Thucydides begins his digression with the words: Οἱ γὰρ Ἀθηναῖοι τρόπῳ τοιῷδε ἦλθον ἐπὶ τὰ πράγματα ἐν οἷς ηὐξήθησαν. As so often is the case, it is virtually impossible to convey fully all the implications of the Thucydidean Greek in a single English sentence. We may translate as follows: "The Athenians in such a way as this attained the position in which they became powerful" or "attained the position of power in which they found themselves." But it is important to stress, for my subsequent discussion, that other connotations are inherent in the text, that is, "The Athenians in such a way as this faced the circumstances" or "undertook the actions in which they became powerful."[1]

Thucydides then goes on to mention briefly the events surrounding the engagements at Mykale and Sestos; he becomes more expansive and personal in his account of Themistokles' rebuilding of the walls of Athens and completing the walls of the Piraeus and in his review of Pausanias' unsuccessful career as commander of the Hellenic forces. After explaining the recall of Pausanias' successor Dorkis and the assumption by Athens of leadership, Thucydides then provides a terse and factual sketch of essential details concerning the organization of the Delian League.

At this crucial point Thucydides leads into a second preface before the continuation of his Pentekontaetia (97.1). In order to emphasize the nature of the transition let us look at the text beginning with 96.2:

> καὶ Ἑλληνοταμίαι τότε πρῶτον Ἀθηναίοις κατέστη ἀρχή, οἳ ἐδέχοντο τὸν φόρον· οὕτω γὰρ ὠνομάσθη τῶν χρημάτων ἡ φορά. ἦν δ᾽ ὁ πρῶτος φόρος ταχθεὶς τετρακόσια τά-λαντα καὶ ἑξήκοντα. ταμιεῖόν τε Δῆλος ἦν αὐτοῖς, καὶ αἱ ξύνοδοι ἐς τὸ ἱερὸν ἐγίγνοντο. ἡγούμενοι δὲ αὐτονόμων τὸ πρῶτον τῶν ξυμμάχων καὶ ἀπὸ κοινῶν ξυνόδων βουλευόν-των τοσάδε ἐπῆλθον πολέμῳ τε καὶ διαχειρίσει πραγμάτων μεταξὺ τοῦδε τοῦ πολέμου καὶ τοῦ Μηδικοῦ, ἃ ἐγένετο πρός τε τὸν βάρβαρον αὐτοῖς καὶ πρὸς τοὺς σφετέρους ξυμμάχους νεωτερίζοντας καὶ Πελοποννησίων τοὺς αἰεὶ προστυγχάνοντας ἐν ἑκάστῳ.

> And then first the Athenians established the office of Hellenic treasurers, who received the tribute. For tribute was the name given to the money collected. The first assessment of tribute was four hundred and sixty talents. Their treasury was on Delos and the meetings of the council were held in the temple. The Athenians, leading the allies who were at first autonomous and debated policy in councils shared by all, through

---

[1] See A. W. Gomme's note in *A Historical Commentary on Thucydides* 1 (Oxford 1945) 256 (hereafter *Comm.*) for a realization of the implications in this sentence. Gomme translates: "arrived at the situation in which they had become so powerful." But, as Gomme appreciates (quoting Croiset), τὰ πράγματα also imply the deeds or actions (*les actes*) of the Athenians through which by 432 they had become powerful. There is no need to insist, with Gomme, that ηὐξήθησαν be interpreted as a pluperfect in order to believe that this preliminary statement is intended as a preface for the whole Pentekontaetia. It is an aorist, possibly ingressive; see H. D. Westlake, "Thucydides and the Pentekontaetia," 41, with note 15 in *Essays on the Greek Historians and Greek History* (Manchester and New York 1969), first published in *CQ* n.s. 5 (1955) 54, note 6.

war and the management of affairs during the period between this war and the Persian undertook such [or so many or so great] actions which resulted from their encounters with the Persians, their own allies in revolt, and those Peloponnesians who came into contact with them on frequent occasions.

Once again the compression of ideas in the words τοσάδε ἐπῆλθον ἃ ἐγένετο . . . αὐτοῖς is similar to that found in the initial statement of theme and purpose in 89.1, quoted above. I have translated them: "The Athenians undertook such [or so many or so great] actions which resulted from their encounters." Yet they also convey the meaning: "The Athenians attained such greatness which resulted from their encounters."[2] Thus Thucydides artfully echoes in his second preface not only the words (ἦλθον ἐπί) but also the duality of thought initially expressed in 89.1; but here he writes in terms of the subsequent years of the Pentekontaetia, which are concerned with the character of events and actions after the formation of the Delian League that now have become his concern.[3] It is in this second preface too that Thucydides for the first time sets the chronological framework of roughly fifty years for his digression.[4]

The reiteration of theme has been inextricably bound within the structure of the narrative in both style and content. So much so that the transition in content, although clear in import, becomes awkward grammatically—a point worth stressing in view of the argument to follow. The reference in the participle ἡγούμενοι is to the Athenians, as sense demands, but the reader must look beyond the two previous sentences to find them mentioned, and in the dative case at that; the immediately antecedent αὐτοῖς should logically refer to the allies as a group and not the Athenians alone.

Next follow the lines concluding the second preface (97.2), which are most crucial for the basic thesis of this paper; I shall translate them as literally as possible, avoiding in my rendition any preconceived notions, on the basis of the scholarship, of what they are supposed to mean, particularly in their reference to Hellanikos:

ἔγραψα δὲ αὐτὰ καὶ τὴν ἐκβολὴν τοῦ λόγου ἐποιησάμην διὰ τόδε, ὅτι τοῖς πρὸ ἐμοῦ ἅπασιν ἐκλιπὲς τοῦτο ἦν τὸ χωρίον καὶ ἢ τὰ πρὸ τῶν Μηδικῶν Ἑλληνικὰ ξυνετίθεσαν ἢ αὐτὰ τὰ Μηδικά· τούτων δὲ ὅσπερ καὶ ἥψατο ἐν τῇ Ἀττικῇ ξυγγραφῇ Ἑλλάνικος, βραχέως τε καὶ τοῖς χρόνοις οὐκ ἀκριβῶς ἐπεμνήσθη· ἅμα δὲ καὶ τῆς ἀρχῆς ἀπόδειξιν ἔχει τῆς τῶν Ἀθηναίων ἐν οἴῳ τρόπῳ κατέστη.

I have written about these events and I have made the digression in my account for the following reason: this topic has been omitted by all before me and they have treated either Hellenic events before the Persian wars or the Persian wars themselves; the one who has also touched on these events in his Attic history, Hellanikos, has mentioned them briefly and with chronological imprecision; at the same time he also provides [or these events also provide] demonstration of the way in which the power of the Athenians was established.

We shall return to these lines shortly but at this point I need to comment upon the nature of the rest of the excursus as well as the excursus as a whole. That Thucydides' treatment of the Pente-kontaetia, particularly in chapters 98–117 which follow, leaves much to be desired is generally

---

[2] Following the scholiast (ed. Hude) who interprets the τοσάδε as referring to the events Thucydides is about to relate.

[3] For theories about the relationship of the two prefaces see Gomme, *Comm.* 363, note 1 and Westlake, "Thucydides and the Pentekontaetia," 41–42. I feel no compulsion to agree with most editors who consider 89.1 to be intended as an introduction to 89–96 alone and not the entire excursus. Gomme maintains that both prefaces (89.1 and 97.1) "cover all the ground," but the specific context of 97.1 and the additional information given as the chapter proceeds make it clear that this second preface belongs exactly where it is; thus I am in sympathy with Westlake's conclusion that it "is in no sense an alternative preface to the whole excursus."

[4] This framework is reiterated even more precisely after the conclusion of the excursus (118.2).

acknowledged. Compared to the standards apparent in all the rest of his work and in view of his own statements elsewhere about method, accuracy and chronological precision, his digression comes as a shock; for example, there are glaring omissions and it is brief, imprecise and possibly, on occasion, inaccurate.[5] In fact, ironically enough, Thucydides' criticism of Hellanikos for brevity and chronological impreicison could apply equally well to his own account. How are these disturbing considerations to be explained? I cannot believe that Thucydides himself was unaware of the obvious inadequacies of his own treatment of the Fifty Years. I maintain that, at the conclusion of this second preface, he offers an acknowledgement that he has used the only literary source available to him for the period of the Fifty Years as a whole, namely the *Atthis* of Hellanikos.

Both sections of the excursus are so inextricably bound together in thought and grammatical structure that, even if the two parts do indeed reflect different stages in conception or execution, it is impossible for the reader to determine the interval of time involved or the order of composition.[6] I can only agree with Westlake's conclusion that "the whole excursus as it now stands was put together at the same time, the marked difference between the two parts being due to the limitations of the sources then available to Thucydides."[7] As we shall see, however, neither can any conclusive date be established for the writing of the excursus as a whole.

It is also important to be aware of the nature of these striking differences between the two sections of Thucydides' Pentekontaetia. Despite the few slight similarities that may be detected between the annalistic and factual treatment of the first part (particularly evident in its opening and closing sections)[8] and that of the second, their overall character and mood are essentially quite different. The first section is dominated by the careers of both Themistokles and Pausanias; and here the flowing narrative with its emphasis on intimate, dramatic details and with its romantic colouring bears an unmistakable resemblance to that of the later, even more expansive excursus dealing with the two men, towards the conclusion of Book 1 (128-138). Both accounts of Pausanias and Themistokles, which show affinities and dovetail so neatly, must be essentially from the same origin, that is, drawn from the same source. That this source was literary has been fully and convincingly argued by Westlake, the most likely but not necessarily the only candidate being Charon of Lampsakos. The style of Charon, as far as we can determine, is eminently Ionic or Herodotean, like that of Thucydides' uncharacteristic treatment of Themistokles and Pausanias; Charon definitely wrote about Themistokles and there is good reason to believe he also gave an account of Pausanias; and no real chronological problem clouds the assumption that Thucydides could have consulted the works of Charon.[9] Scepticism has often been expressed concerning

---

[5] Gomme (*Comm.* 361−413) offers an excursus of his own, which focuses upon the inadequacies of the Pentekontaetia.

[6] For example, Gomme (*Comm.* 363, note 1) infers that the initial section (89−96) may be "in fact the beginning of a rewriting of the whole excursus." Westlake ("Thucydides and the Pentekontaetia," 41−42) objects, observing that, if Thucydides were to have rewritten 98−117 on a scale comparable to that of 89−96, the result would have been a digression of disproportionate and "unmanageable length." Yet substantial improvements could have been made in 98−117 which would not necessarily involve the inclusion of lengthy additional material. In other words, the excursus could be unfinished. Westlake himself (60) concludes that Thucydides "doubtlessly intended to revise the excursus."

[7] Westlake, "Thucydides and the Pentekontaetia," 42; but nevertheless he believes (39) that the reference to Hellanikos is a later insertion. I am indebted to his perceptive analysis of the distinctive characteristics evident in the two sections of Thucydides' excursus, as well as that of Gomme (note 5 above).

[8] The initial, brief treatment of Mykale and Sestos may be derived from the fuller account of Herodotus (9.114-118) but these events may have also been mentioned by Hellanikos in his *Atthis*. We should expect too that Hellanikos said something about both Pausanias and Themistokles, however briefly; and it has been assumed, although it is by no means inevitable, that Thucydides' mention (93.3) of Themistokles' year of office (probably the archonship) is derived from Hellanikos; see Robert J. Lenardon, *The Saga of Themistocles* (London 1978) 35−36, with notes 39 and 40. That Thucydides used Hellanikos for his Pentekontaetia (especially 97−118.2) will be argued subsequently.

[9] Westlake, "Thucydides on Pausanias and Themistocles−A Written Source?," *CQ* n.s. 27 (1977) 95−110. Westlake is cautious in his identification of Charon as Thucydides' source for Pausanias and Themistokles. At any rate, he (96) has abandoned his former belief that Thucydides obtained his information solely "from his own research relying on

much of what Thucydides records about both Themistokles and Pausanias. But Thucydides, as he himself realizes, was handicapped by the limitations and availability of his literary as well as oral sources, particularly for the history of the past, which he nevertheless felt compelled to include because of its illustrative significance.[10]

When we turn to the second section of Thucydides' excursus on the Fifty Years, following the second preface with its reference to Hellanikos, we find, as I have mentioned above, an obvious and startling change in the overall character of the writing, both in treatment and style. This section (98–117), which covers a period of about forty years, is only a little over twice the length of the preceding chapters (89–96), dealing with an interval of roughly two years.[11] This second part with its bare summary of events generally, although not always, reads like a catalogue. Individuals are usually given little prominence; major battles and events are often only mentioned; important facts are omitted; the discussion does not always seem to be properly focused in terms of the theme or themes enunciated in the preface; and the chronology is sketchy. Once again the conclusion seems virtually inevitable: Thucydides, as he has told us, is now heavily dependent on the sole, literary source available to him for this period in its entirety, the brief and chronologically imprecise account of Hellanikos.

Such a natural interpretation of Thucydides is, of course, not new, and certainly at one time would not have been considered in the least iconoclastic.[12] But it has been studiously and emphatically rejected in recent years because of arguments postulated by Ziegler in an article published in 1929. Ziegler's hypothesis has been so clearly and concisely reiterated by Adcock that it is to Adcock's support of Ziegler that I now turn.[13]

Adcock, following Ziegler in his exegesis of Thucydides' text (97.2, quoted above), maintains that the second sentence which alludes to Hellanikos, is a late insertion: "it is inconsistent with the preceding statement with its emphatic ἅπασιν" and in the last sentence "the subject of ἔχει refers back to the first sentence and not to the second sentence. Thus the second sentence interrupts the grammatical construction of the passage." According to this argument, Thucydides originally said:

> I have written about these events and I have made the digression in my account for the following reason: this topic has been omitted by all before me and they have treated either Hellenic events before the Persian wars or the Persian wars themselves; at the same time my digression also provides a demonstration of the power of the Athenians.

---

popular tradition and an oral information" and is now convinced that his evidence was literary. Of course Thucydides may have incorporated sources of different kinds in his treatment of the first section of the Pentekontaetia, but that he relied heavily on a literary source for Pausanias and Themistokles which he considered the most authoritative (i.e., Charon in his *Persika* or the *Chronicle of Lampsakos* or both) is a reasonable conjecture; Thucydides seems more confident about his information for Themistokles in Athens (over which he personally had better control, e.g., 93.1–6) than that for Themistokles' subsequent career. For the fragments of Charon see Jacoby, *FGrHist* 3 A(262). For the links between Charon's and Thucydides' treatment of Themistokles, see also Lenardon (above, note 8), 137–138, 140–141, 149–150.

[10] See Lenardon (above, note 8), 14, 97, 123, 128–131, with note 210; and Westlake, "Thucydides on Pausanias and Themistocles," 96–97.

[11] See Westlake, "Thucydides and the Pentekontaetia," 42, with note 18.

[12] See Benjamin D. Meritt, H. T. Wade-Gery and Malcolm F. McGregor, *The Athenian Tribute Lists* 3 (Princeton 1950) 160–161 (hereafter *ATL*), who acknowledge Thucydides' debts to Hellanikos; also Gomme (*Comm.* 363–364, note 1), who quotes, apparently with approval, from a résumé of the arguments put forth in a paper by Harrison (*Cambr. Univ. Reporter* March 2, 1912): "some of the deficiencies and disproportions of Thucydides' narrative of the Fifty Years may be due to features of the *Atthis* of Hellanikos."

[13] F. E. Adcock, *Thucydides and his History* (Cambridge 1963) 122–123; see also "Thucydides in Book I," *JHS* 71 (1951) 11. K. Ziegler, "Der Ursprung der Exkurse im Thukydides," *RhM* 78 (1929) 58–67, especially 66, note 2 (which is worth quoting in full): "Vielmehr scheint es mir, daß der Satz über Hellanikos eine nachträgliche Einfügung ist, gemacht nach dem Erscheinen der Ἀττικὴ ξυγγραφή. Denn die Aussage τοῖς πρὸ ἐμοῦ ἅπασιν ἐκλιπὲς τοῦτο ἦν τὸ

Subsequently, after Thucydides had completed his Pentekontaetia, the *Atthis* of Hellanikos was published; therefore he added his reference to it because his statement that no one previously had dealt with the period was no longer valid; and we can detect the insertion because of the inconsistency and awkwardness of the text.

Let me say immediately that this interpretation of Thucydides provides him with a feeble reason for singling out Hellanikos as an available source for the period; he is, after all, the only historical writer ever identified in the entire history; furthermore Ziegler's argument also does little justice to the implication of Thucydides' criticism of Hellanikos' treatment. How can Thucydides dare to condemn Hellanikos for his brevity and chronological inaccuracy in the face of his own account? What are we to assume Hellanikos' *Atthis* was like? Can we imagine that Thucydides would have read, criticized, and *ignored* an annalistic account by archon years, such as that, for example, reconstructed for Hellanikos by Jacoby (who believes in Ziegler)?[14] If we assume that Thucydides added his reference to Hellanikos with the unfulfilled intention of revising his excursus on the basis of his reading of the *Atthis,* then, his criticisms seem curious and ill-advised.[15]

Therefore the conclusion that the reference to Hellanikos provides a *terminus ante quem* rather than a *terminus post quem* for the composition of the whole excursus (because it was added after Thucydides had written the Pentekontaetia) bears consequences that are far reaching and important and by no means merely confined to the problems of the chronology of the composition of Thucydides' *History.* They have in fact a direct bearing upon our conception of his historical methods in general, the nature and purpose of this excursus in particular, and its relationship to Hellanikos. If Thucydides did not write his Pentekontaetia after Hellanikos, he did not know or use Hellanikos' account at the time of composition and we cannot explain the nature of Thucydides' digression on the assumption that he did follow Hellanikos. Therefore we would have to conclude that Thucydides does not reflect the content and style of Hellanikos' *Atthis* in any way and it would be impossible to say that one of Thucydides' purposes is to modify or correct Hellanikos.

The major contention of this article is that there is no compulsion on the basis of grammar, syntax, or logic to accept Ziegler's thesis. Thucydides read Hellanikos, used his account, and tells us so. Only on this assumption can we adequately explain the character of Thucydides' whole excursus; the change in style evident in its two sections reflects a shift in source. His critical mention of Hellanikos is in keeping with what we know about the personality and character of Thucydides as an historian from the rest of his work. Indeed his use of Hellanikos confirms a growing awareness (or should it be re-awareness?), which has been succinctly expressed and confirmed by Westlake in his "second thoughts" about the sources for Thucydides' account of Pausanias and Themistokles: "though explicitly or implicitly critical of other historians, he [Thucydides] did not hesitate to make considerable use of their works wherever he thought that his own work would benefit therefrom."[16] In addition, as far as Hellanikos is concerned, it is legitimate to look at Thucydides in an attempt to determine the content and scheme of Hellanikos' *Atthis*

χωρίον wird ja durch die Worte τούτων δὲ ὅσπερ καὶ ἥψατο ἐν τῇ Α. ξ. Ἑλλάνικος aufgehoben. Das ist schwerlich so aus einem Guß. Auch wird die Härte des Anschlusses der Worte ἅμα δὲ καὶ τῆς ἀρχῆς ἀπόδειξιν ἔχει usw, zu denen jeder Leser, so wie der Text jetzt lautet, zunächst Ἑλλάνικος als Subjekt nimmt, beseitigt, wenn sie ursprünglich an den vorangehenden Satz anschlossen."

[14] If, on the basis of Ziegler, we are to imagine that Thucydides revised his excursus after reading Hellanikos, the argument becomes academic to an extreme. Jacoby's reconstruction of Hellanikos' *Atthis* will be discussed in the text below.

[15] Cf. Westlake, "Thucydides and the Pentekontaetia," 60; he conjectures that Thucydides wrote the Pentekontaetia in exile and, upon returning to Athens, added his reference to Hellanikos with the intention of revising his excursus now that "Athenian sources were available to him." Is Hellanikos of Lesbos among these Athenian sources or was his intended revision to be based on evidence other than that of Hellanikos and thus confirm his criticism of the *Atthis* ? Surely these tortuous arguments should be abandoned.

[16] Westlake, "Thucydides on Pausanias and Themistocles," 96–97; cf. notes 9 and 10 above.

(particularly for the period of the Fifty Years), which we must imaginatively reconstruct on the basis of the most meagre and fragmentary evidence.

Thus I must return to a reexamination of my interpretation of chapter 97.2 in Thucydides, if only because Ziegler's view has won such persistent acceptance. Adcock feels that his argument is "beyond doubt" and quotes Jacoby in confirmation;[17] even Westlake, as he expresses his realization of Thucydides' dependence on literary sources continues to believe that the reference to Hellanikos is "almost certainly a late insertion" and comments on the wide acceptance of this conclusion.[18] In the face of all this support, surprising though it may be, Ziegler's hypothesis demands further, more searching refutation.

I have translated Thucydides 97.2 as follows:

> I have written about these events and I have made the digression in my account for the following reason: this topic has been omitted by all before me and they have treated either Hellenic events before the Persian Wars or the Persian Wars themselves; the one who has also touched on these events in his Attic history, Hellanikos, has mentioned them briefly and with chronological imprecision; at the same time he also provides [or these events also provide] demonstration of the power of the Athenians in what way it was established.

An examination of the Greek text, quoted above, reveals that the inconsistency between ἅπασιν and the following mention of Hellanikos is surely not serious; it may represent careless writing in its lack of strict logic, but the notorious style of Thucydides is full of examples more difficult than this. Ziegler is over-sensitive on this point. The first sentence is immediately qualified and this qualification could have been added at any time. One could argue along these lines, but I prefer to maintain that Thucydides' choice of expression is most deliberate and emphatic. Gomme's translation, which I have followed, gives the proper emphasis: "The one who *has* touched on the subject in his *Atthis*."[19] Similarly in English one might say (inconsistently to be sure but with point): "Everyone has neglected this period but there is one who *has* touched on it, namely Hellanikos." I shall explain, in a moment, the reasons for Thucydides' unique, conscientious and emphatic reference to Hellanikos. Let us look first at the concluding sentence of 97.2 and the passage in its entirety.

The subject of ἔχει may come ultimately from the first sentence but it can definitely be supplied from the second; it is most immediately Hellanikos but it also can easily be derived from τούτων. The implied subject, I believe, includes *both*; and the conflation of ideas is expressed with characteristically Thucydidean brevity. Crawley captures the essential meaning when he translates the subject of ἔχει as "the history of these events," which should include the accounts of both Hellanikos and Thucydides. The insistence that the first sentence must supply the subject of the third does not in itself prove the second sentence an insertion. We need only compare the syntax of ἡγούμενοι explained above, or has there been tampering with the text there too? I doubt it.

At the risk of some repetition, I offer two paraphrases of Thucydides' thought in order to suggest the many implications of the syntactical compression of his text.[20]

1. I have written this digression because the topic has been neglected by everyone except Hellanikos; he is the only literary source available and, although his treatment is inadequate, neverthe-

---

[17] *FGrHist* 7 5 (= 3B 1.5); cf. also N. G. L. Hammond, "The Composition of Thucydides' History," *CQ* 34 (1940) 150, who thinks the whole of this section with its reference to Hellanikos has been inserted.

[18] Westlake, "Thucydides on Pausanias and Themistocles," 108, note 72; he cites O. Luschnat, *RE* Suppl. 12 (1971) 1145; cf. note 7 above.

[19] Gomme, *Comm.* 280. I do not, however, consider Thucydides' criticism of Hellanikos to be in any way "superficially . . . capricious" (362, note 2).

[20] Cf. *ATL* 3, 160–161.

less he does demonstrate the growth of Athenian power [my vital theme iterated above, 89.1 and 97.1; and therefore I am dependent upon his account].

2. I have written this digression because the topic has been neglected by everyone except Hellanikos, whose treatment is inadequate. [Therefore I must deal with this neglected subject and improve upon Hellanikos.] By so doing, my account [like that of Hellanikos] offers a demonstration of the growth of Athenian power [my vital theme iterated above, 89.1 and 97.1].

We are now better able to appreciate Thucydides' reference to Hellanikos. Thucydides, true to his character as an historian, reflects his scrupulous concern for factual accuracy and chronological precision that we see so often in his work.[21] His attitude towards and treatment of evidence in the Archaeology provide a specific and informative parallel; he is disturbed by the difficulty of his sources for this early period (Homer, for example), but he does the best that he can to determine the truths essential for an introduction to his *History*. Here in the Pentekontaetia he tells us, unhappily, that the only literary source available for the period is brief and chronologically imprecise, but nevertheless it provides him with the necessary basis for tracing the growth of Athenian power, one of his major concerns in book 1 and throughout his *History*. These are the reasons for the nature of his critical reference to Hellanikos and why Hellanikos alone, among his many sources, has been singled out and identified with this kind of emphasis. Thucydides, aware of the limitations of his own excursus, offers not only an apologetic explanation but a justification as well.[22]

The theory that Thucydides' reference to Hellanikos is a later insertion has been championed by some in the belief that Thucydides' excursus must have been written early and that he could not have seen Hellanikos' *Atthis* until after his return to Athens, ca. 403. Ziegler himself[23] maintains that the digressions in Thucydides, which are concerned with past history, represent the result of investigation undertaken before 431 and later incorporated into his history of the Peloponnesian War. But this hypothesis fails to resolve our problems and, whatever research may have been done earlier, the excursuses in general and the Pentekontaetia in particular must have been composed in their present form after the outbreak of the war.[24] In fact no real consensus exists among scholars for the date of the Pentekontaetia. It cannot have been completed much before 432, but beyond that various reasons (often linked to subjective theories about the composition of book 1 and the *History* as a whole) have inspired different conclusions: Adcock suggests it was composed "not long after the first Conference at Sparta"; others believe it belongs later to a period when Thucydides was absent from Athens; still others insist he wrote it after his return from exile.[25]

The argument that Thucydides could not have seen the *Atthis* of Hellanikos before his return from exile is also inconclusive. It rests upon the testimony of two fragments (4 F 171 and 172 =

---

[21] Westlake's observation ("Thucydides and the Pentekontaetia," 42) that Thucydides was not particularly interested in the chronology of the Pentekontaetia and errors in Hellanikos' *Atthis* is misleading. Thucydides was, it is true, concerned primarily with the illustration of Athenian power, as he tells us, but he was also by nature obsessed with the need to get the facts right, whenever and insofar as he was able.

[22] There are of course problems concerning chronological and factual accuracy elsewhere in Thucydides' *History*, about which scholars have been dubious. The excursus on Pausanias and Themistokles offers, as we have seen, a notable example. But the Pentekontaetia is unique because of the number and nature of its obvious deficiencies, which have become notorious. Westlake ("Thucydides and Pausanias," 95, note 5) quotes the judgment of R. Meiggs (*The Athenian Empire* [Oxford 1972] 465): if Thucydides' excursus had "been written by any other Greek historian, it would not have been taken seriously."

[23] Ziegler (above, note 13), especially 63.

[24] See Westlake, "Thucydides and the Pentekontaetia," 55, with note 65.

[25] Adcock, *Thucydides and His History,* 22; Gomme (*Comm.* 362) suggests that Thucydides wrote the Pentekontaetia at a time when he did not have a "list of archons readily accessible . . . either when in command in Thrace or after his exile." Westlake, "Thucydides and the Pentekontaetia," 43 and 59–60, believes in the period of exile ("perhaps not long after the Peace of Nicias") not because of "chronological deficiencies," but because of "distinctive features"; he lists (39, note 1) Patzer, de Romilly, and Schmid-Stählen for the view that the excursus must belong after the return from exile.

232a F 25 and 26) attributed to Hellanikos, both of which come from the scholia to Aristophanes (*Frogs*) and refer to events that are dated by the archonship of Antigenes (407/6).[26] Serious doubts have rightfully been cast upon the evidence afforded by these fragments.[27] Yet, even if we agree that the work referred to is the *Atthis* and that it ended with the year 404/3, it is by no means improbable that a section or sections of Hellanikos' history including the Fifty Years was available to Thucydides.[28] At any rate Thucydides affords no clear evidence that he knew Hellanikos' treatment of the Peloponnesian War.[29] Thus, the best that we can conclude is that Thucydides may have consulted the *Atthis* at some time after 406 or 403 but he may also very well have done so earlier. Once again the date of his reference to Hellanikos and the composition of the Pentekontaetia remains flexible.

Before considering some of the possible borrowings by Thucydides from Hellanikos, we must first review what the *Atthis* of Hellanikos has been imagined to have been like.

Jacoby has formulated, through lengthy and in large part hypothetical arguments, a reconstruction of this work, which in its essentials, he feels, cannot be seriously doubted.[30] His theories, although steeped in an extensive and profound knowledge of the whole range of Greek historiography, must be based, fundamentally, upon the meagre evidence of the fragments of Hellanikos himself (twelve quotations from his *Atthis* are preserved, with a total of some twenty-five or thirty when we include those without a title)[31] and the later character of the *Atthis* (the history of Athens) as we know it in its evolution at the hands of Athenian writers (the Atthidographers) in the period ca. 350−263. Jacoby maintains that it was the foreigner Hellanikos of Lesbos, a contemporary of Thucydides, who created the first *Atthis,* establishing at the outset not only the basic content but also the annalistic structure of subsequent *Atthides.* He relied both on "living memory" and on documents (the most important being the archon list) but "had in the main to

---

[26] I am, of course, particularly dependent upon Felix Jacoby's edition and discussion of the fragments of Hellanikos (*FGrHist* 4 and 323a with commentary and notes) and his *Atthis, The Local Chronicles of Athens* (Oxford 1949), as well as Lionel Pearson's *Early Ionian Historians* (Oxford and Connecticut 1939) 152−235 and *The Local Historians of Attica,* (APA Monographs, 11, Philadelphia 1942) 1−48 and 145−163), all of which provide essential bibliography; so does Kurt von Fritz, *Die Griechische Geschichtschreibung* 1 (Berlin 1967), who devotes to Hellanikos (476−522) a chapter that is strongly influenced by Jacoby's theories.

[27] For the attempts to eliminate the reference to Hellanikos in this testimony, see Pearson (*Early Ionian Historians* 153−154) and Jacoby (*FGrHist* 3B 1.5, with note 44), who remain unconvinced. But scholiasts are not always the most trustworthy source and their information can become garbled not only through their own errors but also through those of textual transmission. The archon's date may, after all, come from Philochoros. Perhaps what makes me most uneasy is that so much has been hypothesized on the basis of so little, i.e., these two fragments such as they are.

[28] I heartily concur with Gomme's scepticism in his reluctant acceptance "out of deference to Jacoby" (*Comm.* 6-7, note 3 and 362, note 2) of the view that Hellanikos himself continued the *Atthis* to 407/6. The chronographic tradition (Pamphila and Apollodoros) may be not too far wrong in having Hellanikos born in 496/5 and die in 412/11; the *Priestesses* (see note 29 below), a late work (like the *Atthis*), seems to have ended ca. 421 (Jacoby, *FGrHist* 3 B 1.9−10; cf. Gomme, *Comm.* [1956] 3.625). Jacoby argues, relying on some dubious evidence, for 479/8−395/4 as Hellanikos' dates (*FGrHist* 3 B 1.3−4); in a similar vein, Alden A. Mosshammer ("The Apollodoran *Akmai* of Hellanicus and Herodotus," *GRBS* 14 [1973] 5) states that Hellanikos could not have been older than Herodotos, on the authority of the scholia to Aristophanes. I agree with Gomme that an edition of Hellanikos' *Atthis* "might have been published long before 406." Equally insubstantial is the thesis that Hellanikos could not have written his treatment of the Fifty Years before a public copy of the archon list was set up in the Agora, which Jacoby dates in 425 (*Atthis* 171, with note 20). For the archon list, see Benjamin D. Meritt, "Greek Inscriptions," *Hesperia* 8 (1939) 59−65.

[29] Thucydides seems to have consulted Hellanikos' works primarily in his digressions upon earlier events (e.g., perhaps in the Archaeology, the excursus on Sicily and his treatment of the Peisistratids), but his debts are not easily identified. It is conjectured that he used Hellanikos' *Hiereiai* (*The Priestesses of Hera in Argos*) for the chronology in 2.2, and 4.133.2, which refers to Chrysis' priesthood at Argos, and elsewhere. Cf. Jacoby, *FGrHist* 3 B 1.9−10, with note 72.

[30] See Jacoby, *Atthis,* which serves as an introduction to his edition of the Greek Local Historians (*FGrHist* 3 B); Jacoby attacks the theories of Wilamowitz (*Aristoteles und Athen* [Berlin 1893]), who postulated a lost chronicle written by an unknown or anonymous *exegetes* and published ca. 380 as the archetype for the later Atthidographers.

[31] Jacoby, *FGrHist* 3 B 1.11.

use his imagination in order to fit a mass of isolated, often contradictory, and mostly undatable evidence into the framework of a continuous history."[32] Hellanikos in the first part of his work extended the list of the kings down to 684/3 and joined to it the list of archons beginning with Kreon 683/2 (which he was the first to publish), arranging his material under the names of the kings and the archons; and "the scanty tradition for the seventh, sixth, and even the fifth century may very well mean that for more or less extensive stretches the *Atthis* was confined to a naked list of eponyms."[33] Through Hellanikos the literary form of the *Atthis* as a "city chronicle" was handed down to his successors.[34]

Jacoby, for all we know, may be right in the essentials of his depiction of Hellanikos' role in the development of Atthidography. But since information is so scarce and ambiguous, final solutions must remain elusive; therefore some of the major problems and the disturbing questions that they raise need to be reviewed, even in cursory fashion, for the purpose of my argument. One may wonder to what extent a strict annalistic form for the *Atthis* originated with Hellanikos; is it possible that in his first attempt to write a history of Athens the chronological scheme may have been more varied, flexible and even inconsistent than Jacoby would allow? The only concrete evidence for Hellanikos' use of archon dates comes from the testimony of the two scholia referred to above;[35] and thus they deserve to be looked at more closely.

We are told in the second (4 F 172 = 232a F 26)[36] that Hellanikos mentioned (φησιν) the minting of gold coinage in the archonship of Antigenes (407/6); according to the first (4 F 171 = 232a F 26) Hellanikos mentioned that the slaves who fought [in the battle of Arginusai?] were given their freedom and enrolled as fellow citizens of the Plataeans when he was narrating the events in the archonship of Antigenes (διεξιὼν τὰ ἐπὶ Ἀντιγένους). Pearson voices the inevitable question of whether this testimony is enough to justify the belief that Hellanikos "recorded the events of each year separately, naming the archon in each case"; he concludes that at least a portion of the *Atthis* was so organized.[37] At what point did this portion begin? If, say, with the treatment of the Peloponnesian War, were any archon dates used earlier? Perchance this sole identification of Antigenes from Hellanikos has survived because it is unusual. Not a likely conjecture to be sure; yet I dread to think of the misconceptions about the nature and consistency of the chronological schemes employed by Herodotos, Thucydides and the *Ath. Pol.* inspired by the sole survival from each work of similar fragmentary reference to a single archon.

Criteria of literary form and genre also raise suspicions.[38] Thucydides, as we have seen, calls Hellanikos' history an Ἀττικὴ ξυγγραφή; whatever this designation may imply, one does not readily conjure up a work that for the period of the Fifty Years consisted of a list of archon names, many of which may have been accompanied by no information whatsoever.

---

[32] Jacoby, *Atthis* v.   [33] Jacoby, *FGrHist* 3 B 1.16.   [34] Jacoby, *Atthis* 89.

[35] The availability of an archon list I do not question, even before ca. 425, when a copy was set up in the Agora (see note 29 above); for Jacoby's arguments see *FGrHist* 3 B 1.14−15.

[36] I have expressed my doubts about this evidence (note 27 above) but it is futile to evade it. Yet, if Hellanikos was not dead by 407/6, these references may come from a work other than the *Atthis*; his antiquarian interests would allow for the insertion of pertinent asides. The *Priestesses* comes to mind; it was definitely chronographic in style and dealt with the Peloponnesian War; we cannot be sure it ended ca. 421 (notes 28 and 29 above). It was by no means confined to Argos in content but a Universal History (see *FGrHist* 3 B 1.9-10 and Pearson, *Early Ionian Historians* 225-231); perhaps it contained some chronological equations such as those given by Thucydides in 2.2. The *Priestesses*, like the *Atthis*, could have been continued by a successor.

[37] Pearson, *Early Ionian Historians* 223 and *The Local Historians of Attica* 24−25.

[38] I am not sure to what extent our attitudes towards the form of his *Atthis* should be influenced by the fact that, among Hellanikos' many works, two are definitely, in a sense, chronographic, the *Hiereiai* (the *Priestesses of Hera in Argos*; see note 36, above) and the *Karneonikai*, a list of victors at the Spartan festival of the Karneia about which we know very little (Pearson, *Early Ionian Historians* 231−232). Jacoby (*FGrHist* 3 B 1.2) assigns only the *Atthis* to a category that he labels Horography, with the *Hiereiai* and *Karneonikai* forming "a group by themselves." Perhaps it should be the other way around.

Perhaps a consideration of the nature of the account of the Peisistratids in the *Ath. Pol.* may offer some help in a theoretical reconstruction of the first *Atthis.*[39] The *Ath. Pol.* provides chronological information for Peisistratos' career that is much more specific than that of Herodotos both in the intervals of time noted and in the insertion of archon dates. It has often been argued that a comparison of the two is instructive in that it provides a kind of test case for the methods of the Atthidographers, which began with Hellanikos. On the basis of Herodotos and oral tradition it would seem that Atthidographers attempted to compute by generations and to establish equations with the archon list in order to offer as precise an account as they could, but the results of their attempts because of both their methods and their sources sometimes turned out to be historically very dubious indeed,[40] particularly for the sixth century or earlier. If we can infer from all this anything about Hellanikos' style and methods, his narrative for the historical period would have contained some archon dates, although not many, and included intervals of time; and, like the *Ath. Pol.*, he would have provided details of various sorts about his subject. As he approached contemporary events, his chronology may have become more consistent in the employment of archon dates, especially for the Peloponnesian War.

In his treatment of the early period, for which the fragments are by far the most numerous (although not numerous enough), it seems clear that Hellanikos included the genealogies of the kings as a framework.[41] It seems equally clear that he wrote a narrative account and his stories and details from myth and history were factual, terse, and prosaic, Apollodoros has been shown to have often followed closely Hellanikos' writings on mythology, which were by no means confined to the *Atthis*, and Pearson, with some justice, observes that "a careful reading of the *Bibliotheca* is essential for anyone who wants to know the character of Hellanikos' work."[42] Hellanikos, therefore, probably composed much more than a mere annotated list of kings for his *Atthis*. From the fragments of his works, and those of subsequent Atthidographers reflecting similar concerns, we should also be aware that his penchant for geneaology and mythology included an interest in aetiology, religious cults, topography, and political institutions and constitutions. When we conjecture what kind of material Hellanikos might include for the historical period, it is worth remembering that in his discussion of the Peloponnesian War he reveals the tenacity of his genealogical pursuits by tracing the ancestry of the orator Andokides back to mythical times.[43]

On the basis of such observations as these, I tentatively conclude that we should imagine that Hellanikos provided for the Fifty Years a terse narrative with some (a few?) archon dates and intervals of time, which to a very great extent was constricted by both the limitations of his sources and methods and his own personal interests in mythological and historical material. This assumption perhaps can best explain why, in the subsequent tradition right down to the time of Plutarch and even after, relatively little of historical and chronological value can be found to supplement and control Thucydides' information; also it would preserve the identity of Hellanikos' *Atthis* as a literary work unified in its stylistic concept and it would more easily account for both Thucydides' criticism of Hellanikos and the consequent shortcomings of his own Pentekontaetia.

[39] The bibliography is voluminous; but see F. Heidbüchel, "Die Chronologie der Peisistratiden in der Atthis," *Philologus* 101 (1957) 70–89, with discussion by von Fritz ([above, note 26] 502–504); also Jacoby, *Atthis* 149–168; M. Lang, "The Generation of Peisistratus," *AJP* 75 (1954); J. S. Ruebel, "The Tyrannies of Peisistratus," *GRBS* 14 (1973) 125–136; and J. G. F. Hind, "The Tyrannis and the Exiles of Peisistratus," *CQ* n.s. 24 (1974) 1–18.

[40] In a youthful exercise, *The Chronology of the Peisistratid Tyranny* (M.A. thesis, University of Cincinnati 1950), I reached the conclusion (which I do not regret) that the Herodotean chronology for Peisistratos is the most trustworthy.

[41] Jacoby, *FGrHist* 3 B 1.16, with note 130; Pearson, *Early Ionian Historians* 224.

[42] Pearson, *Early Ionian Historians* 160.

[43] Pearson, *The Local Historians of Attica* 25–26, commenting upon *FGrHist* 4 F 170 = 323a F 24. For the date of F 24 see note 44 below.

It is to the Pentekontaetia that we must now return, with the realization that Thucydides had before him at the time of composition Hellanikos' treatment, from which unfortunately nothing remains to provide a comparison.[44] My comments cannot pretend to be exhaustive; I shall attempt to dwell upon the most likely possibilities.

Thucydides calls Hellanikos' history brief.[45] We must remember that this criticism is not only confined to the treatment of the Fifty Years as an entity but even further restricted to the treatment of the events in which Thucydides was interested, that is, the actions that the Athenians undertook, which resulted from their encounters with the Persians, and their own allies and the Peloponnesians, and illustrate how their power was established. Thus Thucydides did not intend merely to repeat Hellanikos' version of the period nor did he wish to supplant it. Rather he extracted from it the material that he saw (and wanted us to see) as pertinent to his own purposes. His aim was to accomplish something new (as he had done in the Archaeology) by the thematic emphasis in his selection and organization of material. Hellanikos' account, therefore, could have been of some length and, because of his scholarly and antiquarian interests might have concentrated, in digressions of various kinds, upon many things that Thucydides would consider either irrelevant or dubious.

Thucydides charges Hellanikos with chronological imprecision, and a logical inference has been that we are to relate this charge to comments made by Thucydides elsewhere (5.20.2–3), explaining that he has avoided the system of dating by officials, such as archons, because it is imprecise (οὐ γὰρ ἀκριβές), and prefers to employ summers and winters (that is, campaigning seasons) for his account of the Peloponnesian War. Thus his complaint against Hellanikos may be inspired by the archon dates that he found in the *Atthis*; indeed not a single archon is named in Thucydides' excursus. Yet the problems that Thucydides faced, I think, were more complex. Hellanikos was probably not consistent in his use of archon dates and did not provide him with a complete list; also, in the context of the naming of one archon, Hellanikos very likely resorted to a prevalent habit (found in Herodotos and Diodoros, for example) of recounting an incident or episode in its entirety, thus creating uncertainty about the chronology of individual events. In addition, we do not know what other intervals of time he employed or how he designated them. I can agree, therefore, that Thucydides would be as meticulous as he could about getting the events in the right order by his careful use of temporal particles and the interruption of his narrative to insure a proper chronological sequence,[46] but he was severely handicapped by the chronological shortcomings of Hellanikos. Perhaps he was satisfied that the relative chronology that he produced was enough for his present purposes; certainly we know from other contexts in his *History* that he could have provided a more specific chronology for some of the events in his excursus. The more probable conclusion (also evident from other considerations to follow) is that the Pentekontaetia is unfinished and that Thucydides' narrative often remains closely dependent upon his source. The omission of important facts that seem to us vital to his theme as stated also points in the same direction; Hellanikos did not include them for whatever reasons and Thucydides might have added at least some of them later.

The annalistic, terse listing of events by Thucydides also suggests a reflection of Hellanikos' style, but it may also provide another illustration of his method of extracting only the facts and details for which he was looking. Gomme calls some of these occasional details "picturesque

[44] Cf. FF 24, 28, and 29 with notes (*FGrHist* 323a = 4 F 170, 183, and 18). F 24 belongs probably to 433/2 and 416/5 rather than 446/5; F 28 to 480/79; Jacoby conjectures 455/4 as a date for F 29 and suggests that Thucydides' reference (101.2) to the origin of the Helots is "directed at" Hellanikos.

[45] Hellanikos wrote at greater length about the early period because of his mythological pursuits. According to F 7 (*FGrHist* 232a = 4 F 44) his *Atthis* consisted of four books; on the basis of hypothetical reconstructions of their contents, five have been suggested but Jacoby argues for two with emendation of the text of F 7 (*FGrHist* 3 B 1.14–15).

[46] Convincingly argued at length by the authors of *ATL* (3.158–180); see also Gomme (*Comm.* 361–362).

rather than significant."[47] Westlake, who, as we have seen, eschews a literary source for the Pentekontaetia, takes pains to account for its peculiarities in terms of the limitation of Thucydides'
personal investigation. He observes the lack of prominence given to important individuals, particularly Athenians like Kimon and Perikles, and concludes that Thucydides lacked adequate information about Athenian leaders. He sees in the treatment of the revolt of Thasos, the Helot revolt, and
the battle of Tanagra the influence of Spartan sources and for the campaign against Corinth in the
Megarid he conjectures Corinthian information; and he determines that the informant for the
Athenian expedition to Egypt was a source or sources who "cannot have been wholly Athenian"
and "who, like Herodotus, had travelled to Egypt and had been in contact with Egyptians and
Persians alike."[48] I suggest that this may well have been Hellanikos of Lesbos.[49] This is not to say
that Thucydides has not added material of his own. It is extremely probable that the more expansive treatment of the Samian revolt is to be explained by the fact that it occurred in a time
when he was an adult.

That Thucydides followed Hellanikos for his account of the Fifty Years is made clear by a literal
and sensitive translation of his reference in 97.2. The unusual emphasis of this unique acknowledgement was prompted by the character of Thucydides himself and the nature of his historical
principles. He was not unaware of the inadequacies of his excursus and explains, apologetically,
that he has been dependent upon the only literary source available for the entire period, which,
although brief and chronologically imprecise, nevertheless reveals for him essentials about the
growth of Athenian power.

Thucydides followed Hellanikos closely as he wrote what may have been a preliminary draft and,
although he may have begun to incorporate material of his own, the brevity, lack of proportion and
chronological shortcomings of his excursus betray both his indebtedness to his source and the
limitations of his own personal investigation and knowledge. Thus Thucydides reflects and eluci-
dates some of the characteristics in the form and style of the first history of Athens, the *Atthis* of
Hellanikos, about which, nevertheless, much must remain a mystery because of our limited
evidence.

It is probable that Thucydides made not only some adjustments but also some improvements
upon Hellanikos particularly in regard to chronology and that he intended to revise further at a
later date. We cannot be sure when or where Thucydides consulted the *Atthis* or, if he was dissatis-
fied, why he did not complete a final version of his Pentekontaetia before his death.

We should not be surprised that Thucydides, however critical, would make use of pertinent literature useful for his subject.[50] By his own admission he was very much aware of bibliography and
his *History* bears testimony to the fact that he was a learned man. Modern scholars have too often
been misled by his famous introductory statement (22.2−3, notably at the *end* of his Archaeology)
about his exacting procedures for personal investigation of the facts of the war; but they too often
forget that his standards and methods for the investigation of earlier history had, by necessity, to
be adjusted and compromised. Thucydides could hardly have avoided reading about ancient history, and even for events closer to his own time he could not afford to ignore a Charon or a Hellanikos, for it was neither wise nor possible to attempt to find out everything on his own.

The Ohio State University   ROBERT J. LENARDON

---

[47] Gomme, *Comm.* 363.   [48] Westlake, "Thucydides and the Pentekontaetia," 47.

[49] We know virtually nothing about the life of Hellanikos, but among the many details imaginatively reconstructed from
the fragments is the suggestion that he may have travelled to the west coast of Asia Minor, Cyprus, and Egypt (Jacoby,
FGrHist 3 B 1.9).

[50] Westlake, "Thucydides on Pausanias and Themistocles," 97, observes that the excursus on Sicily (6.2−5) is not "well
suited to the purpose for which it was intended" and that Thucydides follows his major source Antiochos of Syracuse
closely despite the "gross inaccuracies" of his chronological scheme (cf. Gomme, Andrewes and Dover, *Comm.* 4
[1970] 198−210). Westlake also notes Thucydides' debts to Hekataios.

THE ORIGINS OF THE FIRST PELOPONNESIAN WAR

It is a pleasure to contribute to a volume in honour of Malcolm McGregor and to be able to repay in some degree the debts I have contracted over the years to his helpfulness and co-operation, never more strongly manifested than at the time I write. He has always liked the central topic, however apparently well explored, and I hope that he may find something here to interest him in an inevitably simplified investigation of a very central topic indeed, the first major conflict between Athens and Peloponnesian states.[1]

That a topic is central does not mean that it is well studied. About twenty years ago, the Oxford examiners put the question: "Examine Athenian strategy in the First Peloponnesian War." The result was disastrous. As they reported ruefully later, "Of the 52 candidates who answered this question, 38 answered it as if it referred to the Archidamian War. We concluded that we could not fairly penalise this mistake." The candidates were not indeed to be blamed. Their tutors had been anxious to get on to *the* Peloponnesian War, and most of the text-books give up on the First Peloponnesian War, confining themselves to a bald paraphrase of the military operations recorded by Thucydides, without troubling to think much about the implications of these operations. There has been a good deal more solid thinking since 1959, but there may still be more to be said.

Most of the trouble, of course, arises from the fact that our connected tradition rests on only seven pages of Thucydides, pages chiefly composed of a plain narrative of facts, sparing in ascriptions of motive and in general explanation. To my mind, these pages, like the whole of the excursus of which they form part, rank little higher than brief notes; Thucydides may well have wanted to do a good deal more work on them. Fortunately, at the end of the excursus, he is rather clearer about what he has shown, what he regards as the essence of the period.

> All these things which the Greeks did against each other and against the barbarian happened in roughly fifty years between the retreat of Xerxes and the beginning of this war, years in which the Athenians made their empire firmer and themselves attained great power, and the Spartans, seeing this, did not try to prevent them except for short periods, and kept quiet most of the time, being even before this not quick at going to wars unless they were forced, and in part also prevented by wars of their own, until the power of the Athenians was clearly at its height and they were laying hands on their own alliance (1. 118.2).

Two things here are perhaps unexpected. The first need not detain us long. It is of course a fact that, if you wish to select a year for which to draw a map of the Athenian Empire at its greatest extent, and colour as much of the map Athenian colour as you can, you will pick some year during the First Peloponnesian War and not 431, just as you pick the death of Trajan for doing the same thing for the Roman Empire. Both operations are equally delusory. They do not represent Athenian or Roman power at their firmest, and I do not think that there is any widespread desire to

[1] My thanks are due to Prof. A. Andrewes and Mr. G. E. M. de Ste. Croix, who read an earlier version, and to Miss L. H. Jeffery for last minute help.

challenge Thucydides' judgement that in all essential respects Athenian power was at its height in
431.

The second point is more interesting. I have been totally unable to determine who it was who
invented the phrase "The First Peloponnesian War." It is not ancient, and I do not think it goes far
back into the last century. The trouble is that, once established, it may have played a part in creating an expectation that the actual war was a prefiguration of *the* Peloponnesian War and that
Sparta was an important part of it. It is certainly true that a Spartan army was involved in what was
probably the major battle of the war and that a Spartan army took the field and, without fighting,
probably exercised a decisive influence in the last campaign. It is undisputed, I think, that Athens
and Sparta were formally in a state of war after the Battle of Tanagra, with a suspension for the
Five Years' Truce of 451. But it seems to me that there has been a dangerous progression from
chapter headings like: "Der erste peloponnesisch-attische Krieg und die ägyptische Expedition"
(Busolt); and: "Der Ausgang der Perserkriege und der erste Krieg Athens gegen die Peloponne-
sier" (Meyer) to those which prejudge the question: "Der Konflikt der Großmächte" (Beloch);
"Athènes contre Sparte (464−454)" (Cavaignac); and "Athens at war with Persia and Sparta"
(Hammond). These last seem to me, on the evidence of the passage I have quoted, to be in conflict
with Thucydides' view, which is certainly quite incompatible with any proposition like: "From 461
to 446 it was a main object of Athenian policy to attack Sparta and of Spartan policy to attack
Athens."[2] To my mind, Thucydides was quite right; the First Peloponnesian War was not in any
important sense a war between Athens and Sparta at all. Fortunately, a recent paper by Holladay[3]
has carefully surveyed the evidence for Spartan participation, and I can concentrate here on the
preliminaries.

I begin with a simplified account of my attitude to some of the essential elements in Peloponnesian affairs during the thirty years or so before our war starts. With respect to Sparta, the first great
period of the Peloponnesian League ends with an episode of weakness around 500. Sparta's position is notably re-established by her great victory at Sepeia in, say, 494, which knocked out Argos
as a great power for a generation and gave Sparta the prestige she needed for her contribution to
the saving of Greece in 480−79. In the period immediately after the defeat of Persia, there is
evidence for disagreement in the highest levels at Sparta as to the desirability of pursuing an
aggressive foreign policy outside the Peloponnese. There is also good evidence of increasing or
revived difficulty with her allies in Elis and Arcadia. These troubles are persistent, give rise to at
least two major battles, and continue at least until, if they do not overlap with, the major threat to
the Spartan position caused by the revolt of her Helot and Messenian subjects after what may have
been a very destructive earthquake in the winter of 465/4. This revolt was extremely serious. How
long it must be reckoned with as a factor in Spartan policy is not certain. The treatment of the
problem in *The Athenian Tribute Lists*[4] is still the most persuasive of those which bring the revolt
to an end in 461 or 460 by emending Thucydides' text, but despite my earlier adhesion to that
view,[5] I am now inclined to think that it went on longer than that and was still going, though
perhaps in a rather minor way, until 456. If so, it will certainly have overlapped the opening phases
of our war and have been an element in it.

Into this Spartan history, there interlocks from time to time the history of Argos, and here all is
nearly dark. The battle of Sepeia was followed by some change of regime at Argos. After an

[2] But see the important remarks by de Ste. Croix, *The Origins of the Peloponnesian War* (henceforth *OPW*) (London
1972) 50−51, 180, for whom Thucydides is certainly wrong. He attributes Thucydides' failure to include the First War
in his great design to his lack of information and to the fact that Sparta's allies did most of the fighting. For him, the
lack of Spartan participation is due to military considerations, not to lack of will.

[3] *JHS* 97 (1977) 54−63. What Holladay has to say in 61 note 40 and 63 runs close to my own guesses about the importance of the Persian War for Spartan attitudes in my *Sparta and Persia* (Leiden 1977) 63.

[4] 3. 162−8.   [5] *Historia* 2 (1953/4) 412−8, but see *Sparta and Persia* 46.

unknown length of time, there was counter-revolution, the new regime was thrown out and its members retired to Tiryns. At some time in the middle of the 460s Argos fought and captured Tiryns and Mycenae. The regime at Argos, probably the new regime rather than the counter-revolution, though this is by no means securely established, certainly co-operated to some extent with the anti-Spartan movement in Elis and Arcadia. The most thorough study, that by Forrest,[6] does not allow the counter-revolution a very long life, but I have no great confidence in this view.

These matters have been much explored. My interest here is in opening up newer ground in the exploration of the policy of the second city of the Peloponnesian League, Corinth, the great Greek city of whose inner life we know far the least.[7] To go back a little again, the historical evidence is clear in showing that, for thirty years or so, from 518 to about 488, it was an important part of Corinthian policy to nourish the growth of Athenian power[8] and there is no doubt that the main reason for this was to set Athens against Aegina, at that time the dominant naval power in the Saronic Gulf. The symbol of this attitude is the remarkable act of lend-lease by which, perhaps in the year of Marathon, Corinth sold Athens 20 ships for use against Aegina at 5 drachmae apiece.[9] The political contrast with the period of the First Peloponnesian War is marked. At the beginning of that war Corinth is straining every resource to support Aegina against Athens. Her change of front seems to be due to a simple calculation of the balance of power; Athenian power, which increased greatly thanks to the shipbuilding programme before Xerxes' invasion and the success during it, now far outweighs Aegina's.[10]

That Corinthian policy in this period has its self-assertive elements has been seen most clearly in her relations with Northwestern Greece and in her attempts to strengthen her control over her colonial dependencies, attempts which start, with the case of Leukas, in the 470s.[11] For matters which concern us directly, we must start with an anecdote in Plutarch's life of Cimon, which has long been seen to rest on an eyewitness account by Ion of Chios.[12] Cimon was marching back from Sparta[13] and took his army through Corinth. A Corinthian named Lachartos complained to Cimon that he had brought in his army without asking the city's permission.[14] He said that it was customary to knock at other people's doors and not come in until invited by the master of the

---

[6] *CQ* n.s. 10 (1960) 221–32. My general difficulty with this treatment is a doubt about the way in which the sons of the slain allow their class-feelings to lead them to the side of the Spartans who killed their fathers; my particular problem is the need to make them lose control again after their coup in time for their opponents to make the alliance with Athens. R. A. Tomlinson, *Argos and the Argolid* (London 1972) 107 sees a more balanced situation at Argos, with the scales tipping from time to time.

[7] The only useful treatment I know of this period which puts Corinth in the centre of the picture is W. Grüner, *Korinths Verfassung und Geschichte, mit besonderer Berücksichtigung seiner Politik, während der Pentekontaetie* (Diss. Leipzig, Colditz n.d. circa 1875), intelligent but incomplete.

[8] de Ste. Croix, *OPW* 211.

[9] I deliberately keep trade out of the text. Corinthian friendship for Athens in this period is after all the most powerful warning that one cannot write political history from pots, since it is not all that long since Attic pottery had driven Corinthian off the world market. Corinthian potters (not necessarily her traders) had gone bankrupt, but the government did not care. However, it does not follow that Corinth's attitude to Aegina had no element of commercial consideration about it, since we cannot be sure that Aegina did not use her naval strength to promote her own entrepot trade. That Corinth's interests lay more in the West than in the Aegean (de Ste Croix, *OPW* 212) is something that we can hardly know, once the pottery index fails us.

[10] For de Ste. Croix, *loc. cit.*, there is no hostility between Athens and Corinth before the Athenian alliance with Megara. He is right to match Plut., *Them.* 24.1 (Corinth accepts Themistocles' arbitration over Leukas) against Herodotean gossip about 480, but, if Themistocles' decision in favour of Corcyra made him a *euergetes* there, Corinth may at least have been mildly displeased, and I think de Ste. Croix undervalues Corinthian determination to preserve Aegina.

[11] A. J. Graham, *Colony and Mother City in Ancient Greece* (Manchester 1964) 128ff.

[12] Plut., *Cim.* 17.1–2; see most recently F. Jacoby, *Abhandlungen zur griechischen Geschichtschreibung* (Leiden 1956) 156–157 (= *CQ* 41 [1947] 9).

[13] There is no need to consider whether it was from Ion that Plutarch derived his two expeditions of Cimon to Sparta.

[14] Cf. Thuc., 4. 78.2 and Gomme's puzzled note *ad loc.*; perhaps cf. Thuc., 4. 75.2.

house. To this Cimon replied: "But you Corinthians, Lachartos, did not knock at the doors of the Cleonaeans and Megarians, but took a hatchet to them and forced your way in under arms, thinking that all doors were open to those who had the greater power."

With Megara, we are on comparatively firm ground. Border troubles between Corinth and Megara were traditional, and Thucydides (1. 103.4) tells us that the reason why Megara left Sparta and joined the Athenian alliance was that the Corinthians were making war on them because of frontier disputes. There is thus no doubt that one aspect of Corinthian policy between 480 and 460 was an aggressive policy on her northern frontier against Megara, though we cannot tell how early it developed. It should be noticed that Corinth is here acting with hostility against a fellow-member of the Peloponnesian League, with no apparent thought of, or reaction from, a much-preoccupied Sparta.

Cleonae is something different (with no confirmation from Thucydides). It lies between Corinthian and Argive territory. It has a plain of its own, but communications are not particularly difficult either with Corinth or Argos.[15] It falls slightly more logically into the Argolid, but it is as far from Argos as it is from Corinth, and, in a period of Argive weakness like that which followed Sepeia, it would be vulnerable to Corinthian aggression. Cimon's remarks assure us that there had been such aggression. Why would Corinth be interested in Cleonae? At all relevant periods, the only interesting thing about Cleonae is its control of the Nemean Games,[16] a control which it normally exercises under the suzerainty of Argos. The introduction to the Scholia on Pindar's Nemean Odes, however, says that Corinth did once control the Nemean Games.[17] It gives no date, and perhaps we have no right to use the information here. However, we are certainly entitled to believe that the control of the games was an issue in this period of Argive weakness. Diodorus (11. 65.2–3) gives us the reasons which led the Argives to attack Mycenae, probably in 465 or 464.[18] The Mycenaeans had been getting above themselves. They were disputing with Argos about the control of the Argive Heraion, and there is indeed some slight epigraphical confirmation that Argos did lose control of the Heraion in this period.[19] They claimed that they should run the Nemean Games themselves. Presumably this would be resented in Cleonae as well as in Argos, and some 'cross-check' on this is given by the statement in Strabo[20] that Cleonae joined Argos in her attack on Mycenae. Unfortunately the point is neutralised by the evidence of Pausanias that some of the defeated Mycenaeans moved to Cleonae. We may either reflect on the difficulties presented by the use of scattered, secondary sources or suppose that there were two sorts of Mycenaeans, which is likely enough.[21]

[15] Tomlinson (note 6 above), 29–30.

[16] Pind., Nem. 10. 42, 4. 17, Hyp, Schol. Pind. Nem. (Scholia vetera in Pindari carmina, ed. Drachmann, 3 [1927] pp. 3.17, 5.3).

[17] This is the position established by McGregor, TAPA 72 (1941) 277–8, and he was surely right. If I correctly understand S. G. Miller, Hesperia 46 (1977) 9-10, he thinks that there is no evidence even for Argive suzerainty before the end of the fifth century (G. W. Bond, Euripides Hypsipyle [Oxford 1963] 144) and the beginning of the fourth (Xen., Hell., 4. 7.2). Scepticism about Eusebius' attribution of the foundation of the games to the Argives goes back at least to Grote (4. 247 note 1, Everyman edition), and he also argued that the reference to the Cleonaeans in Pind., Nem. 10, which is an ode for an Argive, proved that there was no dispute over the games at the time between Argos and Cleonae and that Argive control therefore started after circa 460. It seems to me safer to distinguish between actual running of the games and suzerainty. That in D.S., 11. 65.2 the Argives regard Mycenaean claims to the games as an affront seems to me to show that they already claimed such suzerainty. The physical transfer of the games to Argos which Miller's excavations at Nemea are currently suggesting is a different matter again; the abandonment of the site seems too late to concern us here. For the date of Nem. 10, see Forrest (note 6 above), 228.

[18] For the date I follow Andrewes, Phoenix 6 (1952) 3 and Forrest (above, note 6), 231–2, who is less confident. Tomlinson (note 6 above), 104–8, inclines to prefer Diodorus' date of 468/7, but this only derives from Diodorus' method of laying out his material and is not evidence.

[19] Mitsos, Ἐπετηρὶς τῆς Ἑταιρείας Βυζαντινῶν Σπουδῶν, 21 (1953) 150–1, Forrest (above, note 6), 230.

[20] 8. 6.19, p. 377.

[21] Pausanias (7.25.6) appears to contrast those who moved to Cleonae with the demos.

It seems most economical to associate these two pressures on Cleonae and the Nemean Games and to suggest that Mycenae was in some sense an instrument for Corinthian pretensions and aggressions in the northern Argolid. The attack on Cleonae is sufficient evidence for these aggressions, even if Mycenae was playing an entirely lone hand, which seems hard to believe. The evidence which is missing here, of course, is direct evidence of Corinthian support for Mycenae. It is tempting to supply some. Olympia has produced two helmets and parts of at least six shields with the inscription "The Argives dedicated these to Zeus from their spoils from Corinth."[22] The dedication has most recently been dated 500–475.[23] Kunze and Miss Jeffery, who once followed him, wisely did not offer an occasion for an Argive defeat of Corinth in those years, and I find it hard to think of one. One would certainly have to go back nearly to 500 before the darkness is thick enough to bury these weapons.[24] I am relieved to be told by Miss Jeffery, at least, that she now sees no obstacle to placing this victory around 465.[25]

Does this exhaust the story of Corinthian expansion? I do not think it does, but, to take it further, we have to work back from the opening events of our war itself. The first action in the war was an Athenian landing at Halieis. This was met and defeated by a combined force of Corinthians and Epidaurians. Thucydides' list of Peloponnesians is not exhaustive; we now know that there were Sicyonians there too.[26] Close co-operation between Corinth and Epidaurus continues to be attested in the next phase, when everyone's attention switches to the battle for Aegina. In fact, the Corinthians and Epidaurians seem to be the principal Peloponnesians against whom the Athenians fought at the beginning of the war. We have the right to enquire about this close association between Corinth and Epidaurus. Marriage relations go back to the time of the Corinthian tyranny,[27] but Epidaurus has some sacred obligations to Argos[28] and would be vulnerable by land to her in a period of Argive power. We also have the right to ask why the Athenians were attacking Halieis and, more especially, why the Corinthians, Sicyonians and Epidaurians were there to defend it, the first two at least very far from home. Thucydides does not stop to tell us, and very few have stopped to ask.[29] The answer seems fairly obvious. Profiting again from the period of Argive weakness, Corinth has established fairly strong interest in the eastern Argolid or the area east of the Argolid, whichever way you like to put it. We are indeed at the start of the war, and past the high point of Corinth's power in the Argolid. Argos has recovered far enough to regain Mycenae and Tiryns, but outside the Argive plain itself Corinthian influence will remain strong, and the observation is confirmed by the fact that the Tirynthians expelled by Argos went either to

---

[22] References collected by L. H. Jeffery, *The Local Scripts of Archaic Greece* (Oxford 1961) 162, 169 note 18.

[23] E. Kunze, *Bericht über die Ausgrabungen in Olympia* 5 (Berlin 1956) 36, a slightly lower date, based on a changed view of the London helmet, than that implied in *Bericht* 3 (Berlin 1938–9) 77. The dedication was removed by the middle of the century, which is a separate problem.

[24] Even if, with Jeffery, *Archaic Greece. The City-States c. 700–500 B.C.* (London and Tonbridge 1976) 157–158, one accepts a late sixth-century war of Megara and Argos against Corinth, based on Paus., 6. 19.12–14, who puts it in the tenth century, and the Megarian Treasury at Olympia, neither the weapons nor the lettering can be that old.

[25] So also Forrest (above, note 6), 231, note 2.

[26] As far as I know, the only published references to the greave (Olympia B 2777) found in the south wall of the Stadion in 1940 remain the newspapers Ἑστία and Ἐλεύθερος Κόσμος of 8 May 1971. I conflate published and unpublished texts since the published spellings are impossible: τοὶ Σεχυόνιοι ἀνέθεν τοῖ Δὶ ἐξ Ἀλιέο[ν] Ἀθεναίον h⟨ε⟩λόντες. For the same grouping at the time of the Megarian revolt of 446, cf. Thuc., 1. 114.1. For the development of a Corinthian *Sonderbündniß*, see Grüner (note 7 above) 28. But Sicyonian policies are not invariably aligned with Corinthian after the Thirty Years' Peace; they sent no ships to Leukimme and joined Sparta in attempting to solve the Corinth-Corcyra dispute (Thuc., 1. 27.2–28.1).

[27] Hdt., 3. 50.2. Even E. Will, *Korinthiaka* (Paris 1955) 544 sees Corinthian maritime interests in this marriage.

[28] Thuc., 5. 53, with W. S. Barrett, *Hermes* 82 (1954) 421–442.

[29] Some of the necessary points are made by Jeffery, *BSA* 60 (1965) 53–54, but she has her mind on the Sparta-Argos relationship and does little to explain Corinthian involvement.

Epidaurus or Halieis.[30] The fact that Argos is now once more in the way by land is of course not particularly important to Corinth. Communications from Corinth to Epidaurus and beyond are by sea, and the importance to Corinth of this area lies in having firm control of one coast of the Saronic Gulf, her outlet to the Aegean. As she becomes more and more suspicious of Athens' growth, this becomes more important. The key to the Saronic Gulf is of course Aegina, and we have no means of telling when Corinth made her switch of sides between Athens and Aegina; all we do know is that by the start of our war she and Epidaurus are prepared to regard Aegina as vital. If we move on forty years, we find Thucydides (5.53) rather more ready to illuminate the strategic importance of this part of the world. Alcibiades has promoted a new alliance between Athens and Argos; Aegina is now an Athenian island. Alcibiades and the Argives agree that Epidaurus must be won, a) to keep Corinth quiet, b) because communications between the Athenians on Aegina and Argos would be quicker that way than sailing round Cape Skyllaion.[31] The fall of Epidaurus would mean both the completion of the Athenian ring across the Saronic Gulf and the assurance of communications between the Argive and the Athenian spheres.

We can now return to what is perhaps the major turning-point in the *pentekontaetia*, the Spartan decision to dismiss the Athenian force which had come to help them at Ithome. This finally sealed the failure of Cimon's version of Athenian foreign policy: pursuance of the war against Persia founded on friendship with Sparta. Athens had become too different for the partnership to be possible. Cimon fell and, by formal notice or not, Athens abandoned the Spartan alliance. The pattern of Greek friendships as the Persian invasion had left it was at an end. Within a few months, Athens was in alliance with Argos, neutral in that war and perpetually hostile to Sparta, with Thessaly, pro-Persian in that war (where a Spartan king had met disgrace some fifteen years before), and with Megara, bitterly discontented with the aggression from Corinth which the absence of Spartan leadership had made possible. This, says Thucydides (1. 103.4), was the principal reason why the Corinthians first began to hate the Athenians so bitterly.

What did the new partners want? Some recent treatments attribute their alliance, at least from the Athenian point of view, to fear of Sparta: to worry lest the hostility revealed by the dismissal of Cimon be rapidly transformed into Spartan military action.[32] I find this very hard to believe. On any view, Sparta's Messenian War is not yet over at the time of the alliance with Argos and Thessaly, and, since Athens embarks before long on the Cyprus expedition which turned into the Egyptian expedition,[33] it seems hard to think that full-scale war with the whole Peloponnesian League was envisaged or that Sparta was thought a major threat. I prefer the more normal view, that Athenian policy was expansionist and that the Spartan alliance would no longer be allowed to stand in the way of implementing policies which had been in many Athenian minds for many years. Athens' initial concern will have been to have her final, long-delayed settlement with Aegina. As for the others, I have nothing to add on Thessaly, about which one can never say anything without qualification.[34] Megara wanted security from Corinth and this she got; Athens

[30] Strabo, 8. 6.11 p. 373, following the version of W. Aly, *Parola del Passato* 5 (1950) 244.

[31] I repress the temptation to discuss Thuc., 2. 56.4.

[32] Notably de Ste. Croix, *OPW* 182–3, but already Jeffery (note 29 above), 52; my impression is that this is a very new idea indeed. For de Ste. Croix, Athenian motives are entirely military: Argos to bring hoplites, Thessaly cavalry, Megara a landbarrier against invasion from the south. The only evidence which is produced to show that there might be military danger is the alleged Spartan promise to invade Attica at the time of the Thasian revolt (Thuc., 1. 101.1–2). We do not know that this was the time when this came to be known or believed in Athens; whether it was true is uncertain, but hardly relevant.

[33] I accept de Ste. Croix's contrast between Athens' power by sea and her vulnerability by land, but no one will suppose that fewer than 2000 hoplites went to Cyprus and there may well have been many more; cf. Thuc., 1. 105.3, where the *stratia* which is away in Egypt must in the context be hoplite.

[34] Some suggestions in Jeffery (note 29 above), 52 note 49.

gave her long walls and a garrison. Argos wanted self-respect and at least the re-establishment of her position in her area. If my argument so far is followed, it is clear that the wishes of at least Athens, Argos and Megara brought them into conflict above all with Corinth[35] and her partners Sicyon and Epidaurus. They had no immediate need to come into conflict with Sparta at all.[36] If Sparta was unwilling or unable to defend her allies,[37] she just did not come into question. In the first phase of the war, the campaigning season of 459,[38] she certainly did not. This first phase ends with a major Corinthian defeat outside Megara and the completion of the Athenian blockade of Aegina, of which the Aeginetan capitulation of the next year was only the consummation. Essentially, this first year's campaign had given the allies most of what they had been fighting for. Corinth, it seems to me, had been cured of meddling for some time. Athens had gained control of much of the Saronic Gulf. At some later stage, she improved her position by taking over Troizene[39] and Hermione[40] on the further shore. Halieis too was at some point for a time in hands not friendly to Sparta, though the Tirynthians were not disturbed.[41] Only at Epidaurus had the allies perhaps hoped for more than they achieved.[42]

As wars go on, they are more and more likely to form their own pattern and less likely to throw light on their causes. I have nothing new to add on Sparta's motives for the Tanagra campaign, though I have a preference for taking Thucydides (1. 107.2) at face value and supposing that the only motive was Doris. I am certainly not denying that Sparta was in the war after a fashion thereafter or that Tolmides burnt the Spartans' dockyard at Gytheion. What I am inclined to say is that, once Athens had established her control in Boeotia,[43] her main objective continued to be Corinth and that most of the scattered operations which follow are directed at restricting Corinth's activities in the Corinthian Gulf in the same way as the opening phase had already done for the Saronic Gulf. Someone, perhaps Tolmides,[44] settles Messenian exiles at Naupactus. Tolmides seizes Chalkis from Corinth.[45] Pericles, a year or two later, takes over Achaea and makes an attack on Oiniadai,[46] with which the Messenians were also engaged.[47]

---

[35] That the principal target of the allies was Corinth has been said most clearly by Tomlinson (note 6 above), 113, but I find it hard to believe that there was, at this stage of Corinthian history, any prospect or intention of turning Corinth into a friendly democracy.

[36] The thought has of course suggested itself that Argos ought at this time to have wanted to recover the Thyreatis from Sparta as in 421 (Thuc., 5. 41.2); Jeffery (note 29 above), 53, Tomlinson (note 6, above), 108–9, 111–2. But, as far as we know, no attempt of the kind was made, and the only possible conflict of Argos and Sparta in the Peloponnese at this time was on Argive territory at the battle of Oinoe, carefully discussed by Jeffery, but which may never have happened (Andrewes in B. Levick, ed., *The Ancient Historian and his Materials* [Farnborough 1975] 9–16). Either we have lost something, which is by no means impossible, or the Athenians had made it clear to the Argives how far they were prepared to go.

[37] For de Ste. Croix, *OPW* 187–196, there was no lack of will, and he makes a stronger case for the difficulties in the way of Spartan intervention than Holladay (note 3 above, 61) perhaps allows, though I agree with Holladay that it is the will which needs demonstrating.

[38] *Pace ATL* 3. 177, note 60, but I agree that only one year is involved.   [39] Thuc., 1. 115.1; 4. 21.3.

[40] *SEG* 10. 15 (= *IG* 1.³ 31).   [41] Hdt., 7. 137.2, where a Spartan captures it.

[42] Miss Jeffery reminds me of an Epidaurian proxeny decree for an Argive which could well belong to the 450s (W. Peek, *Neue Inschriften aus Epidauros, Abh. Ak. Leipzig, Ph.-Hist. Kl.* 63.5 [1972] 9, no. 10), but there is no necessary political implication, even if we could be sure of the politics of Philoxenos son of Phylacidas. Epidaurus is certainly on the Corinthian side at the end of the war (Thuc., 1. 114.1).

[43] I allow myself a wicked and irrelevant guess on a problem which has recently been concerning our honorand. In *ATL* List 2, col. IX 9 [Κλαζομ]ένιοι used to be read, but they have had to be abandoned since their appearance in the new fragment of col. VIII. McGregor, ap. Camp, *Hesperia* 43 (1974) 317 and in *Hesperia* 45 (1976) 281, abandons a clear iota and suggests [Κυζζικ]ενοί. Are we so certain that no tribute can have been paid to the Delian League by the epigraphically preferable [ℎερχομ]ένιοι (cf. *SEG* 10. 84.24 = *IG* 1.³ 73.23 for the spelling)?

[44] D.S., 11. 84.7.   [45] Thuc., 1. 108.5.   [46] Thuc., 1. 111.3.

[47] Paus., 4. 25, cf. Jeffery (note 22 above), 205. That the independent position of Oiniadai reflects some Corinthian interest is only a guess; contrast the slightly different view of G. B. Grundy, *Thucydides and the History of His Age* (London 1911) 347–54.

One topic demands slightly closer attention. Thucydides[48] gives both Tolmides and Pericles attacks on Sicyon and minor victories. One would be inclined to dismiss these as minor attacks on Corinth's ally of purely nuisance value, but Plutarch has a rather different story about Pericles: "He was admired and his name renowned in the outside world for his campaign against the Peloponnese with a hundred triremes from Pegae in the Megarid. For he not only sacked much of the coast like Tolmides before him, but he even went a long way in from the sea with the hoplites from the ships, so that everyone else cowered behind their walls at his approach, but the Sicyonians fought him at Nemea, and he beat them soundly and set up a trophy."[49] The orthodox treatment of this passage[50] is to say that Plutarch or his source has confused Nemea with the River Nemea which formed the boundary between Sicyon and Corinth and that Pericles never went inland at all. I dare say this is right, but there is a perfectly passable route inland, and Pericles might have been doing something to protect Cleonae's rights to Nemea.[51]

We are of course affected by the usual frustrations of seeing these events through the eyes of Athens and our inability to get inside Corinth. What I have been describing as Corinthian aggression might have been seen there as a quest for security, and the Corinthians will certainly have felt themselves encircled as the new alliance got going.[52] We might hazard the guess that the renewed interest in the colonies and the border-war with Megara point to some population pressure. We do have a picture of Corinth in this very period, Pindar's Thirteenth *Olympian* of late 464 or early 463, but it does not help us much.[53] Pindar does say:[54] "Among you the Muse, sweet-spoken, among you Ares also, flowers in your young men's spears of terror," but that is a compliment, amply justified by the Corinthian record in the Persian War and more than neutralised by what has been said before about the Hours: "Corinth the rich, forecourt of Poseidon of the Isthmus, shining in its young men. There Law, sure foundationstone of cities, dwells with Justice and Peace,[55] dispenser of wealth to man, her sisters, golden daughters of Themis, lady of high counsels. They will to drive afar Pride, the rough-spoken, mother of Surfeit." I once wondered whether it was Athenian *hubris* which was in mind, and whether Pindar was already assured that, if it came to a showdown, Corinth would stand by her friends in Aegina. That would be a very unfashionable thought for the 1970s and is moreover wrong. Internal Koros and Hubris are things with which Eunomia is amply qualified to deal,[56] and we learn nothing from this poem about Corinth's foreign policy.

Christ Church, Oxford   DAVID M. LEWIS

[48] 1. 108.5, 111.2.

[49] Plut., *Per.* 19.2.

[50] See e.g. Busolt, *Griechische Geschichte* 3. 334, note 4.

[51] Cleonae itself was of course under Argive control in the year of Tanagra (Paus., 1. 29.7) and apparently earlier (see notes 20–21). The start of the route, at modern Assos, seems too close to Corinth for comfort. Whether the Athenians ever came near these parts or not, note the possible Argive victory at Phlius (Jeffery [note 29, above], 53, note 50, slightly more venturesome than *Local Scripts* [note 22 above] 146, note 1).

[52] Cf. E. Meyer, *Geschichte des Altertums*, 4.² 1.556.

[53] I have not yet thought of a way to exploit politically the brilliant expansion of the family background of the victor by W. S. Barrett in R. D. Dawe et al. edd., *Dionysiaca* (Cambridge 1978) 1–20. We now know more about the Oligaithidai than about any other classical Corinthian family.

[54] Richmond Lattimore, tr., *The Odes of Pindar* 2 (Chicago 1976).

[55] Wilamowitz, *Pindaros* (Berlin 1922) 372, thought that Eirene was important because of the developing war between Sparta and Athens. This seems unnecessary and unlikely; that Eirene can be thought of for internal reasons is clear enough from West's commentary on Hesiod, *Theog.* 902: M. L. West, *Hesiod Theogony Edited with Prolegomena and Commentary* (Oxford 1966). Wilamowitz (369, note 1) is surely likely to be right in thinking that the reference to Enyalios in line 106 is athletic. The concluding prayer for *aidos* (line 115) refers to the successes of the family, not to the city; cf. *Ol.* 7. 89, precisely contemporary.

[56] Cf. Solon, 4.32–34: M. L. West, *IEG* 2 (Oxford 1972).

THE THEMISTOKLES DECREE FROM TROIZEN: TRANSMISSION AND STATUS*

The virtually complete decree in Themistokles' name providing for evacuation of Attica and full naval mobilisation has split scholars sharply ever since its discovery by Michael Jameson at the site of ancient Troizen in 1959.[1] Yet the first eighteen lines are unexceptionable, since they were used or paraphrased by such writers as Cicero, Quintilian, Plutarch and Aristeides and add little but colour and rhetoric to the Herodotean account.[2] What follows them, however, was both unexpected and disturbing. Indeed in our whole literary tradition lines 18–47 seem to have been known only to Cornelius Nepos, not hitherto regarded as a very high authority.[3] The first time that we hear of any such decree of Themistokles is in Demosthenes' speech *On the Embassy* (19.303), where he is making his habitual fun of his opponent Aischines. Here he picks on the dramatic, overnight change in Aischines' attitude to Philip of Macedon. Now Philip is Athens' friend and can do no wrong. Yet only yesterday–actually in 348 B.C.–Aischines had been as patriotic and anti-Philip as anyone could have wished. Then he was calling for a Greek crusade against the "barbarian" and backing his appeal with rousing readings of the decrees of Miltiades and Themistokles and of the ephebic oath.[4] Now Aischines' text of the Themistokles Decree apparently stopped at line 18 of the Troizen text, since he links it directly with the battle of Salamis and its pendant was the immediate prelude to Marathon.[5] This opening section alone was known to the rest of the later fourth-century writers and to those who drew on them. Herodotos' dating of events was not questioned nor were his reasons for evacuating Attica. Thus Diodoros, Plutarch and Aristeides all put the decision to evacuate *after* the collapse at Thermopylai, making it stem from the allies' failure even to consider a second line of land defence along the Attic-Boiotian border.[6]

* Malcolm McGregor has always enjoyed vigorous controversy and this particular decree has made a special appeal to him (see *Trans. Royal Soc. Canada*, Series IV, 11 [1973] 236f.). I hope that this slightly irreverent challenge–offered with both gratitude and respect–may seem somehow right for this occasion.

[1] See M. H. Jameson, *Hesperia* 29 (1960) 198–223: Meiggs and Lewis, *GHI* (Oxford 1969) no. 23, pp. 48–52 (later text and short commentary). For a complete early bibliography see S. Dow, *Class. World* 55 (1961/2) 105–108: for a later selective and annotated listing see M. Chambers, *Philologus* 111 (1967) 166–169. Later contributions can be traced through the *Bull. Epigr.* of *REG* under the heading 'Troezen'.

[2] Cic., *Off.* 3.11.48: Quint., 9.2.92: Plut., *Them.* 10.3–4: Aristid., 13.1, p. 225f. Dindorf and 46, vol. 2, p. 256D.

[3] Nepos, *Them.* 2.6–8 with 3.1–2 and *Aristeid.*, 1.5 with 2.1. For low rating of this source see C. Hignett, *Xerxes' Invasion of Greece* (Oxford 1963) 464 and J. Wells, *Studies in Herodotus* (Oxford 1923) 164. See also my Appendix.

[4] *On the Embassy* (19), 302–313. The key sentence (303) runs: τίς ὁ τοὺς μακροὺς καὶ καλοὺς λόγους ἐκείνους δημηγορῶν καὶ τὸ Μιλτιάδου καὶ τὸ Θεμιστοκλέους ψήφισμ' ἀναγιγνώσκων καὶ τὸν ἐν τῷ τῆς Ἀγλαύρου τῶν ἐφήβων ὅρκον; οὐχ οὗτος;

[5] Note 311, ὅς, ὦ γῆ καὶ θεοί, ἐκεῖν' ἃ διεξῆλθον ἐν ἀρχῇ δεδημηγορηκώς, τὸν Μαραθῶνα, τὴν Σαλαμῖνα, τὰς μάχας, τὰ τρόπαια; 312, "Would Greece still be free and belong to Greeks" εἰ μὴ τὰς ἀρετὰς ὑπὲρ αὐτῶν ἐκείνας οἱ Μαραθῶνι κἀν Σαλαμῖνι παρέσχοντο, οἱ ἡμέτεροι πρόγονοι; note also how Aischines himself in his speech *Against Ktesiphon* (4) 181 similarly equates Miltiades conceptually with Marathon, Themistokles with Salamis. For the Miltiades Decree see note 14f. below.

[6] See Diod., 11.13.3–4 with 15.2–17: Plut., *Them.* 9.3–10.10 with 11.5 (Themistokles to Eurybiades at Salamis: "if you betray us *twice*"): Aristid. 13 (pp. 225–231) and 46 (pp. 254–259D).

The Troizen text, however, implies that fifth and fourth century Attic tradition alike have led us badly astray. The decision on evacuation and total naval deployment really came *before* the move northward to the Thermopylai/Artemision stations. Actual evacuation may have been held back – but with contingency plans thoroughly laid – until the Persian advance through central Greece made it urgent.[7] But that leaves the main point unaffected. The Troizen version completely exonerates Athens' allies from the charge of betraying Athens and preferring safety at the Isthmos to honour. What appears in Herodotos as a desperate, scrambled response to crisis becomes sober, conscious and farsighted planning by Athens' leaders. The alternative story that we now possess actually succeeds in enhancing the glory of Athens. What other city would have accepted willed self-sacrifice from the start in the cause of Greek freedom?[8]

How was this version utterly ignored by Theopompos, Ephoros and the Atthidographers? Why much later does the author of the essay *On the Malice of Herodotos* not employ this deadly weapon against his subject's integrity? He has much to say about Herodotos' excessive partiality for Athens and his bias against Corinth and Sparta. But nowhere does he advance the crowning proof – that Herodotos has most unjustly maligned Spartan behaviour after Thermopylai by withholding the truth on the decision to evacuate Attica.[9] Challenging and rewriting Herodotos was a favourite historical game from the later fourth century onwards. It is thus all the more surprising that no one, during this long process of criticism, seems ever to have used the damning evidence of lines 18–47 of the Troizen text.[10]

We may reasonably assume that in the fourth century lines 18–47 were all that was known of the Themistokles Decree and that they circulated quite separately from any other Themistoklean material. Aristotle, Plutarch and Aristeides know of Themistokles' motion for the recall of the ostracised; but it is clearly quite distinct from lines 44–47 of the Troizen text and all three authors separate it from the evacuation decree even in date. They put the recall measure in the archon-year 481/0 B.C. and envisage a straightforward recall to Attica in the interests of national unity. The Troizen text presents us with a baffling, two-stage procedure.[11]

[7] See *GHI* no. 23, lines 40–44: ἐπειδὰν δὲ πεπληρωμέναι ὦσιν αἱ νῆες, τα[ῖ]ς μὲν ἑκατὸν αὐτῶν βοηθεῖν ἐπὶ τὸ Ἀρτεμί-σ[ι]ον τὸ Εὐβοϊκόν, ταῖς δὲ ἑκατὸν αὐτῶν περὶ τὴν Σαλαμῖνα καὶ τὴν ἄλλην Ἀττικὴν ναυλοχεῖν καὶ φυλάττειν τὴν χώραν· On the probable "contingency nature" of the evacuation measures, if decided so early, see Jameson (above, note 1), 203–205 (but some population, he thinks, *did* leave before early June) and *Greece and Rome*, Series 2.8 (1961) 9 f. and 13 f.: C. Hignett (above, note 3) 459, 464 and 467 f.: *GHI* no. 23, p. 52: P. Green, *Year of Salamis* (London 1970) 99–103 (incomplete evacuation at once). M. Chambers contested this line of reasoning in *AHR* 67 (1962) 309 f. and 316 and *Philologus* 111 (1967) 161 f.

[8] This was clearly seen both by the sceptical Chambers (*AHR* [1962] 311 f.; *Philologus* 111 [1967] 166) and by the decree's discoverer and firm champion Jameson (*Greece and Rome* [1961] 10 f.). Jameson writes: "The truth in fact seems more complimentary to both Spartans and Athenians. The Spartans did not betray the Athenians . . . . The Athenians did not act out of panic but deliberately chose the bold policy of Themistokles while Xerxes was still far from their borders."

[9] The essay (Plutarch, *Moralia* 854–874) has generally been seen as the work of Plutarch himself since Holzapfel's important article in *Philologus* 41 (1884) 23–53. But some would still contest this and so I prefer to leave the question undecided. For my purposes here it is immaterial. Even where this essay touches on Themistokles' grand strategy for victory at sea from Artemision to Salamis (867 b–871 e), there is no hint of doubting the basic narrative of Herodotos.

[10] Plutarch's essay provides us with a number of names. Much of the revision corrected some form of Herodotean bias. It is worth quoting here Josephos' revealing words (*Against Apion* 1.16): περίεργος ἂν εἴην ἐγὼ . . . διδάσκων . . . τίνα τρόπον Ἔφορος μὲν Ἑλλάνικον ἐν τοῖς πλείστοις ψευδόμενον ἐπιδείκνυσιν, Ἔφορον δὲ Τίμαιος, καὶ Τίμαιον οἱ μετ' αὐτὸν γεγονότες, Ἡρόδοτον δὲ πάντες. Plutarch in his *Themistokles* (7.1–2) once comes near the Troizen version: παραλαβὼν δὲ τὴν ἀρχὴν εὐθὺς μὲν ἐπεχείρει τοὺς πολίτας ἐμβιβάζειν εἰς τὰς τριήρεις, καὶ τὴν πόλιν ἔπειθεν ἐκλιπόντας ὡς προσωτάτω τῆς Ἑλλάδος ἀπαντᾶν τῷ βαρβάρῳ κατὰ θάλατταν. ἐνισταμένων δὲ πολλῶν ἐξήγαγε πολλὴν στρατιὰν εἰς τὰ Τέμπη . . . . Both the dating and *failure* to persuade disprove any use of the Troizen text.

[11] Arist., *Ath. Pol.* 22.8; Plut., *Aristeid.* 8.1 and *Them.* 11.1 (implies early date, but muddled in first on Xerxes' movements); Aristid. 46 (p. 248D). For Hypsichides' date see T. J. Cadoux, *JHS* 68 (1948) 115–119; C. Hignett, *History of the Athenian Constitution* (Oxford 1952) 336 f. (emends the *Ath. Pol.* τετάρτῳ ἔτει to Plutarch's τρίτῳ ἔτει); M. Chambers,

Taken alone lines 1–18 do not inspire much confidence. Jameson himself saw this. "Had we only the first eighteen lines," he wrote, ". . . it would have been not unreasonable to suspect them of being the creation of the antiquarian enthusiasm of Lykourgan Athens."[12] I believe that he came nearer the truth here than he then realised. There is little in these eighteen lines that could not have been built up adroitly by combining Herodotos, 7.144 and 8.41. In response to the 'wooden walls' oracle, as interpreted by Themistokles, the Athenians after consultation "decided to receive the barbarian when he attacked Greece with every man aboard the ships, trusting in the God, together with those Greeks who were willing." In the second passage we read "After the allies' departure home the Athenians issued a proclamation that every Athenian should save his children and his servants as best he could. Most of them sent them to Troizen, some to Aigina, some to Salamis. They hastened to carry them away to safety because they wanted to comply with the oracle . . . ."[13] Moreover Troizen lines 1–18 are also disturbingly reminiscent of the content of the Miltiades Decree, in whose company they first appear. The fullest paraphrase of that is found in the scholiast on a passage in Aristeides, *On the Four*: "When the Persians were proceeding to attack Attica he drew up a decree that they should not wait for their Greek allies, but abandon the city to the Goddess, leaving old men and women to guard the walls, whilst all the young men were to march out with all possible speed to Marathon." Once again we have the themes of trusting the city to its divine patron, of meeting the enemy in advance of Athens with full manpower, and of giving an independent lead to the rest of Greece.[14]

Now few modern scholars would care to defend the authenticity of the Miltiades Decree. Plutarch knew a text in which the prytanising tribe was noted–and that tribe was precisely Aiantis, the tribe of Kallimachos the polemarch a key figure in the decision-making![15] The post-Herodotean tradition, to which the decree relates, sees Kallimachos' support of Miltiades as crucial. He backed him on the issue of immediate advance from Athens against other generals' advice and thus they could jointly be credited with the ensuing victory. None of this is in Herodotos, who knows only the parallel dispute among the generals at Marathon about the wisdom of launching an attack on the Persian force.[16] The Miltiades Decree is surely spurious embroidery of history. It resulted from the fourth-century urge to rewrite Herodotos and further satisfy Athenian

---

Philologus (1967) 163–5 (482/1 B.C.; keeping the *Ath. Pol.* τετάρτῳ ἔτει, with altered reference point). Chambers' view is hard to sustain, since in *Ath. Pol.* too the exiles are recalled "because of Xerxes' expedition"; Xerxes' army did not even reach its base at Sardis till c. November 481 B.C. See Hignett (above, note 3) 95 with note 6 (based on Hdt., 7.37.1).

[12] *Hesperia* 28 (1960) 222f. 'Euboulan' would probably be preferable.

[13] Hdt., 7.144.3: ἔδοξέ τέ σφι μετὰ τὸ χρηστήριον βουλευομένοισι ἐπιόντα ἐπὶ τὴν Ἑλλάδα τὸν βάρβαρον δέκεσθαι τῇσι νηυσὶ πανδημεί, τῷ θεῷ πειθομένοις, ἅμα Ἑλλήνων τοῖσι βουλομένοισι (and 178: Δελφοὶ δὲ . . . Ἑλλήνων τοῖσι βουλομένοισι εἶναι ἐλευθέροισι ἐξήγγειλαν τὰ χρησθέντα αὐτοῖσι . . .); 8.41: μετὰ δὲ τὴν ἄπιξιν κήρυγμα ἐποιήσαντο, Ἀθηναίων τῇ τις δύναται σῴζειν τέκνα τε καὶ τοὺς οἰκέτας. ἐνθαῦτα οἱ μὲν πλεῖστοι ἐς Τροιζῆνα ἀπέστειλαν, οἱ δὲ ἐς Αἴγιναν, οἱ δὲ ἐς Σαλαμῖνα. ἔσπευσαν δὲ ταῦτα ὑπεκθέσθαι τῷ χρηστηρίῳ τε βουλόμενοι ὑπηρετεῖν . . . .

[14] See Dindorf, vol. 3, p. 542 for the scholion (on Aristid. 46 [vol. 2 p. 219 D = D's own 163.19]): ἐπιόντων γὰρ τῶν Περσῶν ἔγραψε μὴ παραμείνειν τοὺς Ἕλληνας, ἀλλὰ καταλεῖψαι τὴν πόλιν τῇ θεῷ, πρεσβύτας δὲ καὶ γυναῖκας φυλάττειν τὰ τείχη, τὴν δὲ νεότητα πᾶσαν ἐπὶ Μαραθῶνα δραμεῖν.

[15] Plut., *Moralia* 628 e: ἐγὼ δὲ τῷ Γλαυκίᾳ προσετίθην, ὅτι καὶ τὸ ψήφισμα, καθ' ὃ τοὺς Ἀθηναίους ἐξήγαγεν, τῆς Αἰαντίδος φυλῆς πρυτανευούσης γραφείη. For Kallimachos' tribe see *PA* 8008 and *GHI* no. 18 (*IG* 1.² 609). Plutarch alone has the damning prytany (on which see Chambers, *AHR* 48 [1962] 313). Other shorter paraphrases than the Aristeides scholiast (see scholia on Dem., 19.303 in Dindorf, *Dem.* vol. 8, p. 446f.) add nothing new. More interesting is Kephisodotos' use of the decree–as early as 357 B.C.–to advance a patriotic argument. See Arist., *Rh.* 1411a 10: καὶ παρακαλῶν ποτε τοὺς Ἀθηναίους εἰς Εὔβοιαν ἐπισιτισαμένους [ἐπισιτισομένους?] ἔφη δεῖν ἐξιέναι τὸ Μιλτιάδου ψήφισμα. Athens answered the demand for prompt, decisive action: within three days help had reached the Euboians against the Thebans. See Dem., *Against Androtion* 14 with the scholia.

[16] Contrast Hdt., 6.103–110 with Nepos, *Milt.* 4.3–5.4 (5.2 implies that Kallimachos was won over, though–through too much compression?–Nepos omits him) and 'Suda' *s.v.* Ἱππίας β. Obst strangely preferred Nepos to Herodotos: see *RE* 15, col. 1692.

patriotic pride. It suited Aischines' propaganda very well. In such company lines 1–18 of the Troizen text must fall under strong suspicion too. Demosthenes' tone throughout 303–311 of *On the Embassy* is scornful and contemptuous and I find it hard not to feel that some of this falls on Aischines' documentation as well. Demosthenes deigns no more than half-quotations from them and Aischines was clearly hurt in a sensitive place.[17]

At some time between the 320's and c. 270 B.C., where epigraphists would now place the Troizen stele, lines 18–47 were united with 1–18 in an integrated text.[18] It reads now as a whole, with lines 44 f. picking up neatly the *leit motif* of defence against the barbarian found in 14 f.[19] But these added sections are precisely the most suspicious of all. Lines 18–44 contain the details of mobilisation and the disposition of forces between Artemision and Salamis in early summer 480 B.C.; lines 44–47 deal, as we have already seen, with a tentative recall of the ostracised. Both are firmly dated to the archon-year 481/0 B.C.[20] In the section on mobilisation I select just one point. It assumes that 200 ships had to be provided with trierarchs, skilled crews and marines in one operation. But already a Spartan-Athenian force of 10,000 hoplites had been transported by a fleet to south Thessaly for the Tempe campaign and then brought back by sea to the Isthmos, where the new decision on the Thermopylai-Artemision line was taken. This fleet must have numbered around 100 triremes and, in view of Themistokles' presence, we may assume that most of them were provided by Athens. These Attic triremes will have been ready with their trierarchs and trained crews to form the nucleus of the Athenian battle-fleet and the fact that their existence is ignored in lines 18–44 is most damaging to the section's credibility.[21]

The section on the ostracised (lines 44–47) raises equally serious problems. According to this the ostracised are to proceed to Salamis from their exile homes and there await the people's further pleasure. Now Xanthippos was evidently involved in the evacuation of Attica after Thermopylai and he is later found as Athenian general with the fleet at Aigina in winter 480/79 B.C. Diodoros says that Themistokles had been deposed from command at some time after Salamis and that Xanthippos was elected general in his place. But this is surely just a muddle. At the most

[17] Note τίς ὁ τοὺς μακροὺς καὶ καλοὺς λόγους ἐκείνους δημηγορῶν; [303], τίς ὁ πείσας ὑμᾶς μόνον οὐκ ἐπὶ τὴν ἐρυθρὰν θάλατταν πρεσβείας πέμπειν; [304], μὴ βοηθεῖν μηδενί, μὴ κοινῇ μετὰ τῶν Ἑλλήνων βουλεύεσθαι, μόνον οὐ καθελεῖν τὰ τείχη [312]. Besides the absurdity of the embassy to the Persian Gulf (the very antithesis of the two decrees' import) there are direct echoes. Miltiades left the walls to the old and the women to defend; Aischines now might as well be advising Athens to pull the walls down. For Aischines' reaction see his *On the Embassy* (3), 69: ἐπειδὴ δὲ καὶ τὴν δημη-γορίαν μου διαβάλλει, καὶ τοὺς εἰρημένους λόγους ἐπὶ τὰ χείρω διεξέρχεται ... Later he complains (74 f.) that his opponents have stolen for their own use that flowery, patriotic oratory of his that Demosthenes chose to mock: περὶ μὲν τῆς σωτηρίας τῆς πόλεως οὐδ'ἐνεχείρουν λέγειν, ἀποβλέπειν δὲ πρὸς τὰ προπύλαια τῆς ἀκροπόλεως ἐκέλευον ὑμᾶς καὶ τῆς ἐν Σαλαμῖνι ναυμαχίας μεμνῆσθαι καὶ τῶν τάφων τῶν προγόνων καὶ τῶν τροπαίων. Aischines still has a use for these past glories: but Athens needs the ancestors' *wisdom* almost more than their courage.

[18] For the dating of the Troizen stele see S. Dow, *AJA* 66 (1962) 353–368; Hignett, (above, note 3), 459; R. Étienne and M. Piérart, *BCH* 99 (1975) 62 with n. 37 (their Plataian decree of the 250's, probably, has very similar lettering style); M. Chambers, *Philologus* (1967) 159 and 166.

[19] Compare 14 f., καὶ ἀμύνεσ[θαι] τ[ὸμ βάρβαρον ὑπὲρ τῆ]ς ἐλευθερίας τῆς τε ἑαυτῶν [καὶ τῶν ἄλλων Ἑλλήνων] with 44 f., ὅπως δ'ἂν καὶ ὁμονοῦντες ἅπαντες Ἀθηναῖοι ἀμύνωνται τὸμ βάρβαρον.

[20] For the date of the planning of the Artemision operation see Hignett (note 3 above), 453 and 463 (soon after mid-May); for the recall of those ostracised see above, note 11. The Troizen 'halfway' measure must have preceded that formal bill. So Jameson, *Hesperia* 28 (1960) 322.

[21] On this point see the shrewd comments by Hignett (note 3, above), 464 f. On such grounds he could not hold the decree genuine. For Tempe see Hdt., 7.173–175 and for fleet numbers 8.1 (Artemision) and 42–8 (Salamis). At both battles Athens provided 180 ships and 20 lent to Chalkis. The Peloponnesian League had 95 and 108 respectively. Aigina sent 18 ships to the north, but gave 30 nearer home—yet even then kept back some of her fleet (the best section) for home defence. In 430 B.C. 100 triremes were used to transport/escort a force of 4,000 hoplites against the Argolid and Poteideia (Thuc., 2.56.1 f.); in 415 B.C. 40 of the 100 Athenian triremes were troop-carriers and possibly the same proportion of the 34 allied ships. Then there were 2,200 Athenian and 2,900 allied hoplites to convoy. See Thuc., 6.43 and K. J. Dover's discussion of these problems (*Commentary on Thucydides* 4. 308 f.).

Xanthippos was being preferred to Themistokles as Athenian commander with the Greek fleet.[22] Xanthippos may possibly have replaced some other general – dead or disgraced – in the course of 480/79 B.C., but it seems better to accept that he had been general throughout the archon-year and that it was as general that he acted in the evacuation.[23] If lines 44–47 are to be in any way authentic, we must construct a very tight timetable indeed. After hearing of the amnesty proclamation Xanthippos must come from wherever he was to Salamis, there be freed from his ban by the 'second' exiles decree, then be elected general and finally return to Attica to help with the evacuation.[24]

Aristeides proves still more troublesome. We are told by Herodotos that he re-emerged dramatically into history when he sailed clean through the Persian investing lines to Salamis on the night before the battle. Herodotos states unequivocally that he was then a private citizen who had been ostracised by his own people. It was in a private capacity too that he commanded the hoplites who were subsequently landed on Psyttalleia.[25] Some modern scholars have been very sceptical about the whole story. They feel that Aristeides could not just have arrived from ostracism nor could he have commanded hoplites in the battle as a private citizen anyway. He must have been a general, elected like Xanthippos in the summer of 480 B.C.[26] Later in the century, however, private individuals did occasionally command hoplites. The most notable example is Kleon at Sphakteria in 425 B.C. There he joined Demosthenes, who only a little earlier had been allowed ships and troops as a private individual for the fortification of a suitable coastal base.[27]

It seems hardly possible to reject Herodotos' account. But what was Aristeides doing on Aigina? Does the perfect participle ἐξωστρακισμένος – rather than the aorist – imply that his sentence had still not been formally lifted when he came to Salamis? The writer of the second speech against Aristogeiton (ascribed to Demosthenes) thought that the ostracised Aristeides had been living at Aigina as his exile home until the people recalled him.[28] This could be no more than inference from the Herodotean passage, but I suspect that it owed something also to a statement found in the Aristotelian *Constitution of Athens*. We are told there that the recall decree of 481/0 B.C. included a clause ordaining that henceforth "the ostracised should live outside a line from Cape Geraistos to Cape Skyllaion." That surely meant that someone had been living *within* those limits, uncomfortably close to Attica and its unfriendly neighbours – who else but Aristeides at Aigina?[29]

[22] The text runs τοὺς μὲν μεθεστηκότας τὰ [δέκα] ἔτη ἀπιέναι εἰς Σαλαμῖνα καὶ μένειν αὐτοὺς ἐ[. . . . . . 16 . . . .]ωι δόξηι περὶ αὐτῶν· τοὺς δὲ[– – – – –]. The supplement ἐ[κεῖ ἕως ἄν τι τῶι δήμ]ωι δόξηι περὶ αὐτῶν – as in *GHI* no. 23 – looks plausible enough, but one could try ἔ[ως ἂν τελέως τῶι δήμ]ωι δόξηι περὶ αὐτῶν. I cannot see how Meiggs and Lewis get out of this their comment (p. 51) "11.44 ff. order those ostracised, perhaps already back in Athens, to Salamis . . . ." Possibly they were embarrassed by the evidence on Xanthippos. For him see Hdt., 8.131 (at Aigina); Plut., *Them.* 10.10 and Philochoros F.116 = Aelian, *Nat. An.* 12.35) on his evacuation role. Diodoros (11.8.5) shows Sparta skilfully driving a wedge between Athens and Themistokles – the angry Athenians ἀπέστησαν αὐτὸν ἀπὸ τῆς στρατηγίας καὶ παρέδωκαν τὴν ἀρχὴν Ξανθίππῳ τῷ Ἀρίφρονος.

[23] On this see J. B. Bury, *CR* 19 (1896) 414 and 417 f.; J. Beloch, *Griech. Gesch.* 2.² (Berlin 1967) 142 f.; Hignett (above, note 3), 277 and 464.

[24] Jameson (*Hesperia* 28 [1960] 222 with note 52) accounts for his role in the evacuation by having the final decision on the ostracised precede the proclamation (Herodotos' κήρυγμα) that activated the Troizen Decree's first section. This still allows too little time for Xanthippos to have been elected general at or near the normal time. Hignett (note 3 above), 464, rightly saw this as a grave chronological crux.

[25] Herodotos' story and language is clear and consistent (8.79–82 and 95). Plutarch (*Arist.* 8–9.4) follows Herodotos, but with his usual moralising rhetoric. Even Nepos (*Arist.* 1.5 and 2.1) remains close.

[26] See Bury (note 23 above), 417 f.; Beloch, *loc. cit.*; Hignett, *loc. cit.*; G. B. Grundy, *Great Persian War* (London 1901) 388–390.

[27] For these men see Gomme, *Commentary* 3, pp. 471 f. and 437 f. on Thuc., 4.29.1 and 4.3.4.

[28] See 'Dem.,' 26.6: Ἀριστείδην μέν γέ φασιν ὑπὸ τῶν προγόνων μεταστάθεντ' ἐν Αἰγίνῃ διατρίβειν, ἕως ὁ δῆμος αὐτὸν κατεδέξατο. See 'Suda' *s.v.* Ἀριστείδης.

[29] *Ath. Pol.* 22.8: καὶ τὸ λοιπὸν ὥρισαν τοὺς ὠστρακισμένους ἐκτὸς Γεραιστοῦ καὶ Σκυλλαίου κατοικεῖν. ἐκτός is Wyse's correction for the MSS ἐντός; Kaibel preferred to insert a negative in front of κατοικεῖν. Both obtain a meaning

In fact Herodotos' perfect ἐξωστρακισμένος could simply be meant to characterise Aristeides as a man who *had* been ostracised–a status less enviable than that of ex-premier or ex-world champion, but equally lasting and part of the record.[30] I believe that, like Xanthippos, Aristeides was back in Attica after Artemision–if not before–and that he helped with that part of the evacuation which made for Aigina. He may have been encouraged to remain–until it was almost too late to rejoin the main fleet–in order that some responsible Athenian should watch over the refugees and establish a good, working relationship with the Aiginetan authorities.[31] Curiously the post-Herodotean tradition forgets that some Athenian families went to Aigina and this must have facilitated misunderstanding of Herodotos' story of Aristeides.[32]

I am not alone in believing firmly that lines 44–47 of the Troizen text were built up on a combination of this Herodotean passage and the statement in the *Constitution of Athens*. It is very hard to see how responsible Athenian leaders in the early summer of 480 B.C. could have thought up the curious indirect procedure of recalling the ostracised *via* Salamis–by which they would only be fully reinstated when some kind of assembly on the island should pass a second decree.[33] The Troizen text explicitly states that the recall clause was designed to promote harmony in the state against the barbarian. But its failure to indicate how long the returned exiles are to remain in uncertainty is strange, indeed embarrassing. Hignett seems right in claiming that "no procedure can be imagined less likely to promote concord."[34] The linking of internal concord, however, with amnesties runs through the Athenian tradition of 480, 405/4 and 338 B.C. Indeed, as one looks closely, one must be struck with the echoes in the Troizen lines of Andocides 1.77f. and 108f. and with the language of Hypereides' amnesty decree after Chaironeia.[35]

I know that many good scholars jib at the idea of such daring fabrication as condemning lines 18–47 must imply. They rightly want to know when and for what reasons such skilful forgery could have been carried out. There must be some strong purpose behind it. It is clearly no *jeu d'esprit*.[36] We saw earlier that virtually all our tradition links the evacuation of Athens with the

---

required by common sense and the better text of the end of Philochoros' account of ostracism (*FGrHist* 328, F 30 with Jacoby's comments in 3 B (Suppl), Commentary 1, p. 317f. and 2, p. 228 n. 18): καρποῦντα τὰ ἑαυτοῦ, μὴ ἐπιβαίνοντα ἐντὸς Γεραίστου τοῦ Εὐβοίας ἀκρωτηρίου – – – – – [a long lacuna follows in the source from which this comes]. Philochoros was here simply summarising the conditions attaching to ostracism. We should not press him in support of Hignett's assumption (note 11 above, 163 f.) that the residence clause would have been a most inappropriate addition in the amnesty mood of 480 B.C. and must have been there from the start. He thinks that the local historians postdated it under their false impression that Aristeides resided in Aigina during his ostracism.

[30] Such nuances can surely be found with the Greek perfect participle. But the many cases where ὠστρακισμένος *was* used of men still under ban (as Thuc., 1.135.3 and 8.73.3; Arist., *Ath. Pol.* 22.8) misled ancient scholars and some moderns too. In a marginal note on p. 359 of his *Herodotus: a Commentary*, 2 (London 1854), J. W. Blaskesley wrote that the Council of war "is interrupted by the advent of *Aristeides* an Athenian, then under ostracism, who seeks an interview with Themistocles."

[31] Grundy suggested this possibility (above, note 26, 390), but Hignett disagreed with all attempts to salvage history from Herodotos' 'legend' (note 3 above, 408–411). I have refined on Grundy's view, in order to meet Hignett's problems of time.

[32] See the very full citation of the ancient sources and variants by Jameson, *Hesperia* 28 (1960) 210 f. Some stress Troizen almost exclusively, some tell only of Salamis. But the 'Suda' *s.v.* ἀνεῖλε actually says that the Athenians deposited their kin with the Troizenians and the Aiginetans–a late return to Herodotos.

[33] Jameson attempts to deal with these difficulties in *Hesperia* (1960) 222 and *Greece and Rome* (1961) 13 (the aim was "prompt reconciliation," the chosen procedure represented "a generous but at the same time a careful move").

[34] Hignett (note 3 above), 465. Chambers (*Philologus* 111 [1967] 162 f.) recognised the force of this objection and agreed in seeing the Aristeides story as the germ from which this part of the decree grew.

[35] The texts are again conveniently assembled by Jameson in *Hesperia* 28 (1960) 221. Andokides (1.108) insisted that Athens' success against Xerxes was διὰ τὸ ἀλλήλοις ὁμονοεῖν, partly achieved by the amnesty. "Concord" again is linked with amnesty in 405/4 B.C. (*ibid.* 73 and 76: cf. Lysias 25.27). Hypereides' decree is closest (Dem. 26.11): εἶναι τοὺς ἀτίμους ἐπιτίμους ἵν'ὁμονοοῦντες ἅπαντες ὑπὲρ τῆς ἐλευθερίας προθύμως ἀγωνίζωνται.

[36] Down to 1967 the main champions of authenticity are listed in Chambers' bibliography (*Philologus* 111 [1967] 166–9); they include such distinguished names as Berve, Jameson, Lewis, Meritt, Schachermeyr, Thiel.

failure of support from Athens' allies. This may be tendentious and unhistorical, but it remains a fact. That is what the Athenians continued to like to think most of the time throughout the period before Alexander. The long hostility between Sparta and Athens from 431 to 371 B.C. kept such thoughts alive. For the next century there was little cooperation between the two powers and Sparta spent most of it in sullen isolationism.[37] But the hour of destiny finally arrived. The old allies found themselves ranged once more side by side against an external threat to Greek freedom. Encouraged by Ptolemy II and backed by a small Egyptian fleet, Sparta and Athens headed a Greek coalition that aimed to break the dominance of Antigonos Gonatas and that fought the so-called "Chremonidean War" from c. 265 to 262 B.C.[38] In two documents intimately linked with this episode – Chremonides' war decree and the Greeks' decree honouring his brother later at Plataia – the memories of the glorious alliance against Xerxes were deliberately recalled.[39] At this time of unity it would be well to heal the wounds of the past and to be able to remember the events of that former crusade without any sour recriminations such as the Herodotean tradition left. What we have on stone at Troizen surely echoes simply what patriotic Athenian orators and diplomatic envoys were expounding in this changed and heady situation.[40] It is intriguing to note that – in insisting that the evacuation decision must have come before the move to Thermopylai – these shrewd politicians were anticipating some of the more radical of modern scholars.[41]

One possibly unanswerable point remains. Why should the Troizenians have wanted a copy of this "rediscovered" Athenian decree? Some scholars have assumed that Troizen was already in the Ptolemaic sphere during the Chremonidean War and, if this is correct, then sympathy with Athens and a desire of both parties to recall Troizen's helpfulness in 480 B.C. would seem sufficient motive. But the evidence is not good. Inscriptional evidence shows Egyptian interest and even an Egyptian presence at Methana from the time of Ptolemy IV to Ptolemy VI and the change of name to Arsinoe presumably honours Philopator's wife rather than Arsinoe Philadelphos.[42] The numismatic evidence is of the slightest. There is a single bronze coin of Ptolemy II from Troizen, but it is very worn and thus quite different in its status as evidence from the many fresh Ptolemy II coins found at several military installations in Attica. Those surely must be linked with Patroklos' known

[37] For a brief account of all this see A. H. M. Jones, *Sparta* (Cambridge 1967) 67–151 or W. G. Forrest, *History of Sparta* (London 1968) 107–142.

[38] The best recent study of the war is that of H. Heinen, *Historia Einzelschrift* 20 (Wiesbaden 1972) 95–213. He would put the archon Peithedemos and the start of war in 268/7, its end in 262/1 B.C. (Antipatros). See his arguments on pp. 109f. and 201 with note 435 (start); pp. 182–189 (end). Meritt, however, has stood out for 265/4 and 263/2 respectively; see *Hesperia* 26 (1957) 97 with *Athenian Year* (Berkeley 1961) 223 and 233 and *Historia* 26 (1977) 174. A shorter war certainly seems more probable.

[39] See *Staatsverträge* 3 (1969) no. 476 (*IG* 2.² 686f.), lines 7–13; ἐπειδὴ πρότερομ μὲν Ἀθηναῖοι καὶ Λακεδαιμόνιοι καὶ οἱ σύμμαχοι οἱ ἑκατέρων φιλίαν καὶ συμμαχίαν κοινὴν ποιησάμενοι πρὸς ἑαυτοὺς πολλοὺς καὶ καλοὺς ἀγῶνας ἠγωνίσαντο μετ'ἀλλήλων πρὸς τοὺς καταδουλοῦσθαι τὰς πόλεις ἐπιχειροῦντας, ἐξ ὧν ἑαυτοῖς τε δόξαν ἐκτήσαντο καὶ τοῖς ἀλλ[ό]ις Ἕλλησιν παρεσκεύασαν τὴν ἐλευθερίαν. . . . : *BCH* 99 (1975) 51–53, lines 18–24; συνη[ύ]ξησεν δὲ . . . καὶ τὸν ἀγῶνα ὅν τιθέασιν οἱ Ἕλληνες ἐπὶ τοῖς ἀνδράσιν τοῖς ἀγαθοῖς καὶ ἀγωνισαμένοις πρὸς τοὺς βαρβάρους ὑπὲρ τῆς τῶν Ἑλλήνων ἐλευθερίας. . . . This is a convenient text of the new find and the commentary by Étienne and Piérart is full and valuable (pp. 68–71 for this passage).

[40] Étienne and Piérart come near this view (p. 70), recognising that the politicians of the 260's "ont dû être pétris de la littérature de propagandie qui a vu le jour au IVᵉ siècle, lorsque, pour servir des intérêts contemporains, on a récrit l'histoire des guerres médiques: les considerants du décret de Chrémonidès en sont la preuve." They note as significant that the Troizen Decree was inscribed near if not in the 260's, but true to the then prevailing view, add "dont la composition remonte, elle aussi, au IVᵉ siècle."

[41] See for example J. A. R. Munro, *JHS* 22 (1902) 320: E. Obst, *Der Feldzug des Xerxes, Klio Beiheft* 12 (Aalen 1914) 135f.

[42] See K. J. Beloch, *Griech. Gesch.* 4.² 1, p. 612; M. Cary, *History of Greek World: 336–146 B.C.* (London 1965) 135; W. W. Tarn, *CAH* 7.708. The inscriptions *possibly* all belong to Philometer's reign (see note in *IG* 4 on nos. 854f.) despite Hiller's inclination to refer the one from Thera to Philopator's sole reign (*IG* 12.3.466): but the Arsinoe coins, long since proved to belong to Methana by local finds, have the portraits of Ptolemy IV and his queen. See on this *RE* 15, col. 1378, where Ed. Meyer inclines towards putting back the Egyptian connection to the Chremonidean War. For Heinen (note 38 above), 131) this dating is likely enough, though not beyond dispute.

activity as admiral at Sounion and Rhamnous. Nothing justifies us in talking of Methana as a base for Patroklos comparable to Keos.[43] All the same Troizen may have stood on the side of freedom. We know only that Corinth and Megara were firmly held for Gonatas. In the later 270's he had lost most of his Peloponnesian strong-points to Pyrrhos and the Spartan pretender Kleonymos. We hear specifically of Troizen, which Kleonymos took from its Macedonian garrison–imposing a harmost of his own.[44] Gonatas may either have failed to recover it or had it taken from him again by Kleonymos' able nephew King Areos as part of the planning for the Chremonidean War.[45]

Certainly the Troizen version of past history can have had little currency *after* the sad collapse of the promising Greek crusade. Nor did Sparta's later behaviour ever permit its revival. There should be little wonder then that it had such small impact on subsequent writers. If I am right, the Troizen Decree somewhat surprisingly helps us understand better the men who were behind Athens' last real assertion of sovereignty. Helped by scholars and with honourable intentions they reshaped the story of the war with Xerxes to fit more comfortably with present needs. But what was more needed than possibly deluding visions of past grandeur was clearsighted assessment of the realities and odds of the present.[46]

Leeds University   HAROLD B. MATTINGLY

[43] See Mme. Varoucha-Christodoulopoulou, *Congr. Int. Num. Roma 1961,* 2 *Atti* (1965) 225 and *Arch. Eph.* (1961) (= Vol. 3 of studies offered to C. Oikonomides) 323–330. The Troizen piece is described on p. 330 note 6. She shows on Pls. I–II representative bronzes from Attic sites, where the point about relative condition of the Ptolemy II pieces can be appreciated. In general on the Attic finds, the camps and Patroklos' activities see the excellent discussion by Heinen (note 38 above), 152–167–where all the relative literature is cited.

[44] See *RE* 7 A, col. 643 (Troizen); Polyain., 2.29.1; Frontin., *Strat.* 3.6.7 (Cleonymus the Athenian!).

[45] For Areos see *RE* 2, col. 682 f. His rare tetradrachms–cheekily closely copying Gonatas' early Alexander-type coins– almost certainly belong to the Chremonidean War. See the convincing case put by Hyla A. Troxell in *ANSMN* 17 (1971) 67, 70 and 73–80.

[46] It may just be worth noting that Philochoros–historian, scholar, *mantis*–was executed on Gonatas' orders c. 262/1 B.C. for his alleged Egyptian intrigues. See *FGrHist* 3 B no. 328, T 1 and comment.

Appendix

How did Nepos alone of ancient writers come to know of the version of events of 480's B.C. preserved in the Troizen text? He shows this knowledge not only in *Them.* 2.6–3.2, but also in *Arist.* 1.5–2.1. Conceivably Nepos could have known of a transcript of the inscription or at least been made aware of its general drift. He was a close friend of Atticus, who–with his known historical and antiquarian interests (see, in this context, particularly Cic., *Leg.* 2.2.4)–might well have found the Troizen copy or even the presumed Athenian original during his twenty years residence in Athens (Nepos, *Att.* 2–4).

But Nepos' language has no close echoes of the epigraphic text nor does he otherwise use prime material directly. Clearly he consulted no text of the Miltiades Decree, though his account in *Milt.* 4.3–5.2 follows this post-Herodotean tradition (see my note 15 f.). It is here worth nothing that Nepos' version palliates the Spartan failure to send help to Attica in time by stressing Miltiades' determination to lose no precious days before challenging the Persians at Marathon, the army's great eagerness for the fight, and Datis' preparedness to accept the offer of battle under unfavourable circumstances before the Spartans could come up (4.3 and 5; 5.4).

Both versions then may have reached Nepos through a Hellenistic historian affected by the new desire to emphasise the solidarity of Athens and Sparta against the Persians in both wars. There is in fact just such a man – known for his interest in epigraphic evidence, hostile to Herodotos among his other predecessors, critical, long acquainted with third-century Athens through close on fifty years of continual residence. Timaios of Tauromenion was exiled by Agathokles possibly as late as 312 B.C. and remained in his new home Athens till the late 260's, even if he did not die there. For his life and character see most conveniently *FGrHist* no. 566 and comment 526–47; *RE* 6A, cols. 1075–88 (Harder). Some would date his expulsion from Sicily 316/5 B.C., but, whatever date we prefer, we must reckon with the possibility that he did not go straight to Athens as an exile. His historical work seems to have been completed at Athens (see especially F 34 – from the preface to its last section) and certain indications – particularly his famous monograph on Pyrrhos, Antigonos' toughest adversary – suggest that in no case would he have wished to remain there after the Macedonian takeover in 262/1 B.C.

Timaios certainly treated the Persian War, if only – here like Ephoros (see Diod. 11.20–26) – as a pendant to the heroic defence of Greek Sicily by Gelon and Theron. Knowing what we do of his somewhat discursive method, we may assume that it was also brought in by way of digression both before that narrative – evidently in Books 10 and 11 – and later. Similarly reference to Miltiades and Marathon may have been worked in at some appropriate point. Nepos clearly admired Timaios (*gravissimus historicus*) and explicitly quotes his favourable evidence, with that of Thucydides and Theopompos, for Alkibiades (11.1). Theopompos was also his unquoted source for Kimon's recall after only five years of ostracism; compare *Cimon* 3.1 and 3 with Philochoros F 30 and Theopompos F 88 (*FGrHist* no. 115, and comment p. 317). Nepos' account of Timoleon's plot against his brother and of the circumstances of the death of Dionysios I seem likewise drawn from Timaios, though he is not named; compare *Timoleon* 1.4 and *Dion.* 2.4–5 with Timaios F 116 and F 109 (and Jacoby's Commentary p. 584f.). Atticus particularly admired Timaios and presumably had his works in his library, where Nepos could easily have consulted them (Cic., *Att.* 6.1.18). Cicero deferred so far to his friend's partiality as to praise Timaios highly on grounds of style, application and learning (*De Or.* 2.55–58 [13–14]): "apud Graecos autem eloquentissimi homines remoti a causis forensibus cum ad ceteras res illustris tum ad historiam scribendam maxime se applicaverunt . . . minimus natu horum omnium Timaeus, quantum autem iudicare possum, longe eruditissimus et rerum copia et sententiarum varietate abundantissimus . . . ."

From Josephos (*Against Apion* 1.16) it is reasonable to deduce that Timaios was as ready to set Herodotos' history to rights as that of any of his predecessors. Indeed we know from Athenaios (13.32 p. 573 c–d) that he followed Theopompos in giving the story of the womens' prayer to Aphrodite at Corinth in the crisis of 480 B.C. He probably used it to counter Herodotos' suggestions of Corinthian lukewarmness and even incipient disloyalty in the struggle with Xerxes. Certainly the author of the essay *On the Malice of Herodotos* (*Moralia* 871a–c) thus uses it. See *FGrHist* no. 566 F 10 and comment 540f.; it apparently came in Timaios' seventh book, which bears out my earlier suggestion.

KLEON'S ASSESSMENT OF TRIBUTE TO ATHENS

Having worked happily and profitably with Malcolm McGregor for many years on the Athenian tribute lists I take pleasure now in offering as a tribute to the man and the scholar a brief resumé of the evidence for the precise date of the assessment decree of 425/4 and for its association with the demagogue Kleon. I offer also a suggestion for the solution of a minor difficulty in the text of the decree which has troubled me for some time.

It is now evident that this assessment decree belongs in the fifth prytany of the year 425/4.[1] The name of the prytany which dates the first (and principal) decree is not preserved on the stone, but the relative positions of the preserved fragments of the inscription are certain and the number of letters in the name is known as seven. The prytany, therefore, was either Leontis or Aiantis.[2] A new text from the Athenian Agora[3] sponsored by Kleonymos should be dated in the spring of 424. It names the prytany Aiantis. The other prytany with seven letters (Leontis) should therefore be restored in A9, line 3.[4] The prytany Oineis, which was ordered in the *probouleuma* to bring the assessment decree to the *demos* for its vote of ratification, was clearly the fourth prytany of the year, the name being known from the famous *Logistai* inscription (*IG* 1.[2] 324) where it is to be restored, with mathematical certainty, in lines 18–19.[5] The calendar of the year, with Oineis the fourth prytany and with Leontis the fifth prytany, has recently been described by Meritt.[6]

The *probouleuma* of the decree, here referred to as A9 (see note 1), was to have been introduced to the *demos* in the prytany of Oineis. Severe penalties were prescribed if the *prytaneis* did not finish their deliberations and introduce the decree to the *demos* before the end of their term of office.[7] It is evident, however, that the injunction laid upon the *phyle* Oineis to finish its deliberations and introduce the assessment decree to the *demos* was, in fact, not carried out. This was no

---

[1] The decree is published by B. D. Meritt, H. T. Wade-Gery, and Malcolm F. McGregor, *The Athenian Tribute Lists* (*ATL*) 2 (Princeton 1949) 40–43, A9. This followed the publication by the same authors in *ATL* 1 (Cambridge, Mass. 1939) 154–157 and the publication by B. D. Meritt and Allen B. West, *The Athenian Assessment of 425 B.C.* (Ann Arbor, Michigan 1934) 44–47, 64–69, in which the total figure of the assessment championed by Walther Kolbe in 1930 (*Sitzungsberichte der preußischen Akademie der Wissenschaften*, phil.-hist. Klasse 22 [Berlin 1930] 1–24) was acknowledged and verified. I refer now also to the conservative text edited by Russell Meiggs and David M. Lewis, *A Selection of Greek Historical Inscriptions to the End of the Fifth Century B.C.* (Oxford 1969) 188–201 (no. 69).

[2] Meritt and West (above, note 1), *passim* and also Meritt, *AJP* 58 (1937) 152–156 and 59 (1938) 297–300.

[3] B. D. Meritt, *Hesperia* 14 (1945) 115–119.

[4] Meiggs and Lewis (above, note 1), 189, are more conservative and do not commit themselves to the name of the prytany.

[5] The alternative and otherwise epigraphically possible restoration of Aigeis is precluded by the necessary reading of that name in A9, lines 54–55. In the text of the *Logistai* inscription (*IG* 1.[2] 324) published in *CQ* 18 (1968) 89, the restoration in lines 18–19 should be with Oineis rather than Aigeis.

[6] *Proceedings of the American Philosophical Society* 115 (1971) 97–124. The calculations advanced in *ATL* 4 (Princeton 1953) are no longer applicable.

[7] Read in A9 line 34 the name of the prytany as [Οἰνε]ίς and note that the deliberations were to continue without interruption [χουνε]χõς [hέ]ος [ἂν δ]ιαπ[ρ]αχθε͂ι ἐπὶ τε͂[ς καθ' ἑαυτὸ]ς πρυτανείας as specified in line 36. The restoration [καθ' ἑαυτὸ]ς replaces the earlier [εἰρεμένε]ς which has never found favor (Meritt, *Proceedings of the American Philosophical Society* 115 [1971] 112, note 16).

fault of the *prytaneis* for they were supposed to bring the matter to the *demos* "on the second day after the troops return,"[8] and the excuse for their delay was that the troops did not return as expected before the end of their term of office. They were doubtless held not responsible for this unavoidable delay and doubtless no penalty was inflicted.[9] The *probouleuma* was not revised when it was, in fact, brought to the *demos* by the *prytaneis* of Leontis. The urgency which is implied by the injunction to work continuously (see note 7) near the end of the fourth prytany was already out of date. Even as the decree was passed by the *demos,* everyone must have known that this was so. The provisions of lines 33—38 of the *probouleuma* of A9 were a dead letter even before they were adopted. There is thus evident a surprising lack of official interest in the archival accuracy of the record.

I once thought to see another example of careless editing in lines 26—33 of A9 in which provision was made for the timing of future assessments: "in the future announcements concerning the tribute shall be made to the cities before the Great Panathenaia. The prytany which happens to be in office shall introduce the assessments at the time of the Panathenaia" (A9, lines 26—28). The draft of the *probouleuma* which the orator Thoudippos (line 4) presented to the Council clearly envisaged a close connection down through the years between the first prytany of the conciliar year and the month Hekatombaion with its Panathenaia in the festival year. Correspondences between these two types of year show that the Panathenaia, which were on the third day from the end of Hekatombaion, did actually fall within the first prytany in the two Panathenaic years of 422/1 and 418/7 immediately after 425/4, though not again until 406/5.[10] The *probouleuma* of Thoudippos continued (A9, lines 31—33): "And if anyone introduces a motion that the cities shall not be assessed at the Great Panathenaia during the prytany which first holds office he shall be deprived of civic rights and his property shall be confiscated and a tenth given to the goddess." In 1971 I wrote that "the text of the assessment decree is specific, but much of the time it could not have been taken as more than generally applicable." It seems to me now that Thoudippos, with a quite irregular succession of ordinary and intercalary years ahead of him, had as much foresight as could have been expected.

The lacuna of A9, line 17, was filled by Meritt and West[11] and by Meritt, Wade-Gery, and McGregor[12] by reading χσυντα[χσάντον καθάπερ ἐπὶ τῆς τελευτ]αίας ἀρχῆς. Objection to this reconstruction was taken by Béquignon and Will,[13] who urged that the restoration of the verb χσυντα[χσάντον "suppose que le sujet logique et grammatical serait les *nomothètes* de la phrase précédente, ce qui est manifestement impossible," and they proposed instead of χσυντα[χσάντον the verb form χσυντά[χσασθαι, which according to them "supprime ces inconvénients." I question whether there is in fact the ambiguity which they suggest. Surely it is the court and not the *nomothetai* that is to collaborate with the Council, and its function is here so defined. Yet a difficulty remains. Since there is to be a new court, actually nothing is to be done καθάπερ ἐπὶ τῆς τελευτ]αίας ἀρχῆς, nor is there anything to show which earlier ἀρχή is meant. The only simi-

---

[8] ἐχ[σενεγ]κέτο δὲ ταῦτα ἐς [τὸν] δῆμον [*he* Οἰνε]ὶς π[ρ]υτα[νεί]α ἐπει[δὰν *héκει he*] στρα[τιὰ] ἐς τρίτεν ἐμέραν [πρῶτ]ον μετ[ὰ τὰ *he*]ρά. The count for the third day was by inclusive reckoning.

[9] The identity of the expedition to which reference is here made has been much discussed. Meritt and Wade-Gery, *AJP* 57 (1936) 377—394 argued at first that it was Kleon's return from Pylos with the Spartan prisoners. But this is too early for the identification of Oineis as the fourth prytany of the year. The time relationships between the decree and the narrative of Thucydides have been studied by Arnold Gomme, *A Historical Commentary on Thucydides* 3 (Oxford 1956) 478 and Malcolm F. McGregor, *TAPA* 66 (1935) 146—164. McGregor urged that the expedition was that of Nikias against the Korinthia (Thuc., 4.42—45).

[10] The calendar correspondences are outlined in *Proceedings of the American Philosophical Society* 115 (1971) 114.

[11] *The Athenian Assessment of 425 B.C.* (above, note 1) 44.

[12] *ATL* 2. 41.

[13] Y. Béquignon and Édouard Will, *Rev. arch.* 35—36 (1950) 11.

larity in the procedure is that the adjudications are to be brought before the Heliaia just as other cases in the Heliastic court.[14] I believe that the jurors in the new court should be called *heliastai*; hence I restore in line 16 ἐλιαστάς instead of δικαστάς. They were created to afford ample opportunity for adjudications and their duties were to supplement those of the *heliastai* mentioned in line 14. The offending phrase in line 17 is not χσυντα[χσάντον. The new *heliastai* and the Council were to join in making the assessments. But the court in question was something new, and its duties cannot be defined in terms of reference to the "last ἀρχή," whatever that may mean. The difficulty is rather to be resolved by restoring after χσυντα[χσάντον the designation ἐπὶ τῆς νέας καὶ τῆς παλ]αιᾶς ἀρχῆς. This usage of ἀρχή to mean "empire" is well attested, and the comprehensive scope of the "new and the old" is emphasized in line 18 by [*hαπάσας*]. Lines 16–18 now read as follows:

τõν· *hοι* δὲ [νομο]θέτα[ι δικαστέριον] νέον κα[θ]ιστάντον
    χ[ιλίος ἐλιαστάς· τõ δὲ φόρο, ἐπειδ]
ὲ ὀλέζον ἐγ[ένε]το, τὰς [νῦν τάχσες χσ]ὺν τεῖ [βο]λεῖ
    χσυντα[χσάντον ἐπὶ τῆς νέας καὶ τῆς παλ]
αιᾶς ἀρχῆς [πρὸς] μέρο[ς *hαπάσας* τõ Π]οσιδε[ιõ]νος μενός·

This is substantially the text, interpreting ἀρχή as "empire," that was sent to Marcus Tod when he published the first edition of his *Greek Historical Inscriptions* in 1933. Tod notes in his *apparatus criticus* that West and Meritt restored *hαπάσες* rather than *hαπάσας* in line 19. Tod's text was here, in my opinion, an improvement and it was kept in the second edition of his handbook in 1947. West and I puzzled for many days over the text of these lines and I have numerous tentative drafts which have never been made public. I do not now think that they deserve to be. Our uncertain state of mind is clearly illustrated, however, by the statement in our publication of 1934 (p. 59) that Walther Kolbe had persuaded us to interpret ἀρχή correctly as "magistracy" and not as "empire." My qualms about this persist and I can now see no reason to question the meaning of "empire" if it makes good sense in the interpretation of the passage. The meaning of "empire" is cited in Liddell-Scott-Jones from both Herodotos and Thucydides, and, three times in the tribute quota-lists the phrase ἐπὶ Θράικες φόρος (or φόρο) is given, using the prepositional phrase with ἐπί and the genitive of the noun to denote the region of Thrace upon which, as a part of the empire, tribute was assessed (*ATL* 2 [1939] lists 12, 13, and 14, pp. 18–20, of 443/2–441/0). Clearly ἐπί with the genitive can mean "during the time of" or "on the district of" depending on the context.

Reference here is to the growth of the Empire after the last assessment, where one notable increase in number of tributaries came with the Aktaian cities which were taken over by Athens after the subjugation of Mytilene. But there were other additions now as well to be consolidated into the framework of regular tribute assessment. About thirty cities, from all four of the normal tributary districts, make their first appearance in A9. Notable among these are Aspendos and Kelenderis in Ionia-Karia, well within the province of the Great King, and Melos and Pholegandros from the home riding of the Islands. Together with the Aktaian cities these must be counted as the "New Empire." The Aktaian cities formed a kind of appendix to the Hellespontine panel though they were sufficiently homogeneous to be kept separate in a rubric of their own, the Ἀκταῖαι πόλεις.[15]

With the Euxine cities the circumstances were quite different. Not only had they never yet been assessed, they had never been included with other tributary autonomous members of the Empire

---

[14] Lines 13–14: [ἐσαγογέον δὲ *ho* λα]χὸν κα[ὶ *h*]ο πολέμαρ[χος ἀνακρινάντον τὰς δίκας ἐν τ]εῖ ἐλιαίαι [καθάπερ τὰς δίκας τὰς ἄλ]λας τõν ἐ]λιαστõν. The restoration [*ho* ἐσαγογεὺς *ho* λα]χὸν suggested by Béquignon and Will (note 13 above) cannot stand for the particle δέ is omitted at the beginning of the phrase. I have retained their suggested ἀνακρινάντον rather than our earlier χσυνδεχέσθον (see also *ATL* 2. 40; and 4. ix).

[15] For new names in the assessment of A9 see the Register in *ATL* 1. 216–441.

as had the Aktaian cities. Relative amounts of assessment in the several districts were worked out by Meritt and West in 1934 to give the following totals:[16]

Islands	163 tal.	410 dr.	3 obols
Ionia-Karia	450 tal.		
Hellespont	290 tal.		
Aktaian cities	50 tal.		
Thrace	340 tal.		
Euxine	175 tal.		
TOTAL	1468 tal.	410 dr.	3 obols

The total for the Islands is complete, as is also, within narrow limits, the total for the Aktaian cities. The total for the Hellespont lies between 250 and 300 talents and for Thrace between 310 and 350 talents. If the rate of increase over earlier assessments can be applied to Ionia-Karia on the same scale as is found for the other districts of the old empire, then the figure of 450 talents is appropriate for the assessment of Ionia-Karia in 425/4. The sum total of the whole assessment is now known as more than 1,460 talents (final line of A9). The total for the Euxine, therefore, must have been about 175 talents, more even than that for the whole riding of the Islands. It had become in 425/4 a separate and additional major district of the empire.

It is astonishing that this major district is not named in lines 5–6 of the introductory decree along with Ionia-Karia, Thrace, the Islands, and the Hellespont. The answer must be that the addition of the Euxine panel was an afterthought not envisaged by Thoudippos when he drew up the *probouleuma* near the end of the fourth prytany of 425/4. In 1967 Meritt discussed these several panels in the assessment decree[17] and called attention to the complete lack of any reference to a Euxine panel in the decree upon which the list of cities depends. To find any intimation that a Euxine panel was authorized one has to fall back on the instructions given by the assessors to the heralds who were to proclaim the assessment (lines 40–41); [τὰ]ς δ[ὲ πορ]είας τοῖς κέρυχ[σι τοῖς ἰõσι χσυγγράφσαι κατὰ τ]ὸν hόρ[κον τὸς τάχ[τας hέο]ς τ[õ πο]ρε[υθέσ]ον[τα]ι hίνα μὲ αὐ[τοὶ ἄταχτοι ἰõσι·]: "As for the routes of the heralds who are to travel, the *taktai* are to prescribe these, indicating to what point they shall proceed, in order that they may not journey uninstructed."

The orator of the decree which contains this description of the duties of the assessors in defining for the heralds the geographical limits of the Empire was Thoudippos, now identified as Θούδιππος Ἀραφήνιος.[18] He has also been identified with great probability (practically with certainty) as the son-in-law of the demagogue Kleon.[19] Even if the decree was passed only after the return of the troops from the Korinthia (Thuc., 4.42–45) this came so close after Kleon's spectacular triumph at Pylos that his prestige was high and any elective position that he wished could have been open to him. It is very probable that he was one of the assessors. These assessors, ten in number, were to be chosen by the Council (lines 7–9) together with a secretary and an assistant secretary and were to draw up the assessment list within five days. Kleon, of the city deme Kydathenaion, would have represented the phyle Pandionis. They did not, however, conceive the grandiose scheme of levying tribute on the Pontos until they actually began to draw up the list of cities. The making of the list followed close on the heels of the passage of the probouleuma by the Council. Despite the silence of the decree the existence of the list of Euxine cities in the addendum (lines 126–170) makes it certain that the Pontos was included in the travels of the

[16] *The Athenian Assessment of 425 B.C.* (above, note 1) 90.

[17] *GRBS* 8 (1967) 123–129.

[18] Meritt and Wade-Gery, *AJP* 57 (1936) 392, note 36; J. K. Davies, *Athenian Propertied Families* (Oxford 1971) 228–229.

[19] *Ibid.*

heralds,[20] though only eight were provided for in the decree. This is simply another proof that the provisions of the decree were not brought up to date after its passage by the *demos* and another instance of lack of attention to the accuracy of the record. As soon as the Pontos was included in the assessment two more heralds were required, making their number ten, and there were five major districts instead of four in the Empire.

The above discussion, especially the reference to the family relationship between Thoudippos and Kleon, should strengthen the judgement of the authors of *The Athenian Tribute Lists* that the assessment of 425 B.C. belonged to Kleon. The odium of it too belonged to him. We may never know how far he overreached himself in the Pontic venture. There is very little evidence about the actual collection of tribute from this district. In the early summer of 424 the general Lamachos with ten ships sailed into the Pontos to collect tribute from the assessed cities. Apparently he began with Herakleia (A9, line 127) and his ships were anchored at the mouth of the Kales river in the territory of Herakleia when a cloudburst turned the river into a torrent and destroyed them (Thuc., 4.75). Lamachos and his troops had to make their way ignominiously back to Kalchedon by land. The cities of the Black Sea, despite their number and the wealth of some of them, could never have been the fruitful source of revenue that Kleon envisaged.[21] Indeed, it is probable that no city on the south shore of the Pontos was even assessed after the renewal of peace with Persia in 423 B.C.[22]

University of Texas   B. D. MERITT

---

[20] It is now known that the heralds were chosen from the roster of κλητῆρες, Meritt, *Proceedings of the American Philosophical Society* 115 (1971) 113, with note 19.

[21] Meritt, Wade-Gery, and McGregor, *ATL* 3 (Princeton 1950) 345.

[22] *ATL* 3. 116–117.

SOME EARLY ATHENIAN COMMEMORATIONS
OF CHORAL VICTORIES

Although the main outlines of how the Athenian *choregia* worked (in the strict sense: sponsorship of dithyrambic and dramatic choruses) are relatively clear, there is surprisingly little documentation for this typically, though not exclusively,[1] Athenian institution in its early stages. Some important questions still await conclusive answers. It is my purpose here[2] to consider again the early inscriptional evidence, and to suggest answers to some of the questions.

Our knowledge of the fully developed *choregia* comes mainly from the orators. The client for whom Lysias wrote *Oration* 21 gives an account of his public services which included, when he had just turned eighteen, a *choregia* in the tragic competitions (presumably at the City Dionysia of 411/10) at a cost of 3,000 drachmae and, at the Thargelia a little later in the year, another *choregia* at 2,000 dr. for a dithyrambic chorus of men; in the latter competition he says he won a victory.[3] Early in the next archon year (410/9) he sponsored a chorus of pyrrhic dancers at the Great Panathenaia (800 drs.) and in the same year a chorus of men at the Dionysia, with which he was again victorious, "and I expended with the setting up of the tripod (σὺν τῇ τοῦ τρίποδος ἀναθέσει) 5,000 drachmae" (21.2). Subsequent expenditures included 300 drs. for a dithyrambic chorus at the Lesser Panathenaia of 409/8. Returning from military service abroad he served as gymnasiarch for the races at the Prometheia of 405/4 and later in the same year he presented a chorus of boys at an unnamed festival ("more than 15 minae," 1,500 drs.). In the next year, 404/3, he was winning *choregos* for a comedy by Kephisodoros, "and I spent, with the dedication of the equipment (σὺν τῇ τῆς σκευῆς ἀναθέσει), sixteen minae," that is, 1,600 drachmae (21.4). Finally, at the Lesser Panathenaia (probably in the same year) he sponsored a boys' pyrrhic chorus which cost 700 drs.

The speaker's public-spirited generosity included also contributions to trierarchies, *eisphorai*, the equipment of a racing-trireme for competitions at Sounion and various religious embassies and processions, but his catalogue of choral expenditures itself presents an interesting document which calls for comment. We do not know, of course, how many others there were in Athens at the end of the fifth century who could match this young man's record of public service; he claims that of the $10^1/_2$ talent total of the itemized account of his expenditures, "I would not have spent a fourth if I had wanted to discharge my obligations only according to the letter of the law" (21.5). Although perhaps not unique, such largesse will probably have had relatively few equals, especially at a time when Athens' financial capability, both public and private, was extremely straitened. Although the majority of the expenses incurred by Lysias' client were for military purposes, a substantial proportion, almost $2^1/_2$ talents on my calculation, were spent on

---

[1] Evidence exists for an analogous practice in the Attic demes – e.g. Ikaria, Paiania, Aixone and elsewhere; at Eretria; at Thespiai and Orchomenos in Boeotia; at Ceos, Siphnos and Delos.

[2] An earlier version was read to the Seventh International Congress of Greek and Latin Epigraphy in Constanza, Romania (Sept., 1977) and subsequently at the University of Washington, Seattle (November, 1977). It is presented here as a small token of gratitude and affectionate respect to Malcolm McGregor, who read the principal inscriptions with me and rendered assistance and encouragement to my researches.

[3] Lys., 21.2.

performances that were straightforwardly choral, and this in a period of high tension and unrest at Athens, one wonders at a society which would brook no interruption of its normal choral religious celebrations even in such years as those of Alexis and Eukleides must have been. It is worth comparing again (although others have done so previously[4]) the relative costs of mounting the different kinds of chorus. The figure for a tragic chorus (which is confirmed elsewhere in Lysias[5]) is almost twice as much as that for a comic chorus, and that in spite of the larger number of comic choreutai (twenty-four as against, probably, fifteen); the difference may be based on more lavish costuming for the tragic chorus, and perhaps also a longer period of training, during which, as is clear from the separate testimony of Antiphon and Demosthenes,[6] the choregos was expected to defray expenses of food, shelter and tuition, and took upon himself as well (in some cases at least) the actual selection of the chorus; day-to-day supervision must often have been delegated to someone else.[7] The figures given for the two types of choruses at the Lesser Panathenaia are relatively low, 300 and 700 drachmae respectively, while the cost of a chorus for the Dionysia, 5,000 drs., seems rather high, and there is no obvious reason why the figure should be two and one-half times that for a similar chorus at the Thargelia. The high cost of a chorus for the Dionysia can perhaps be explained by the fact that by this time, towards the end of the fifth century, these performances had become extremely elaborate and, calling as they did for near-virtuoso ability to master the intricate dance-patterns and highly involved musical settings, probably required unusually long practice-periods. It is not so easy to explain the discrepancy between choruses at the Dionysia and the Thargelia; what evidence there is points to a figure of fifty for the dithyrambic or "cyclic" chorus,[8] and no distinction appears to be made anywhere in the sources between different sizes of chorus for different festivals. Nevertheless, the inference of this passage in Lysias is supported by the explicit statement of a scholion on Demosthenes (*Lept.* 28): τοῖς δὲ μεγάλοις Διονυσίοις πλείονος αὐτῷ (sc. the choregos) γενομένης τῆς δαπανῆς (than for the Thargelia).

Lysias' client twice includes in his accounting of expenses the phrase "together with the dedication"; this is of particular interest and calls for special comment. The prize for a winning entry in the dithyrambic competitions was a tripod; this is explicitly stated by the Second Hypothesis to Demosthenes' speech *Against Meidias*: τῷ νικῶντι τρίπους τὸ ἆθλον ἦν. These tripods were provided by the Archon Eponymous, who according to the *Ath. Pol.* 56 had general supervision of the major festivals: ἆθλα μὲν ὁ ἄρχων προτίθησιν (Xen., *Hiero* 9.4). These prizes were paid for at public expense; an inscription of 375/4 B.C. lists among expenditures for the years 377/6−375/4 τρίποδες νικητήρια τοῖς χοροῖς, καὶ τῷ ἐργασαμένῳ μισθός (*IG* 2.[2] 1635a A33−4) and they were probably awarded, at least in the first instance, to the choregos rather than his tribe. (When the poet Simonides wrote, perhaps in 477/6, "you won fifty-six bulls and tripods," I suppose that he meant, as he indeed implies in the continuation of the epigram, "that was the number of victorious choruses for which I composed dithyrambs.")

Was the speaker of Lysias 21 obliged to dedicate his prize? What expense could he have incurred sufficient to be included in his expense-account? The answer to the first question is probably "no"; there was no strict obligation, but in those competitions which were primarily tribal (the Dionysia and Thargelia certainly, probably also the Panathenaia[9]) it was to the tribe's

---

[4] Pickard-Cambridge, revised by J. Gould and D. M. Lewis, *Dramatic Festivals of Athens*[2] (Oxford 1968) 87−88; C. Bottin, "Étude sur la chorégie dithyrambique," *R. B. Phil.* 10 (1931) 27 ff.

[5] Lys., 19.29 and 42: 5,000 drs. for two tragic *choregiai*.

[6] Antiphon, 6.11−13; Dem., *Meid.* 16.

[7] Antiphon, 6.13: the defendant says he deputed his son-in-law to "supervise" (ἐπιμελεῖσθαι); cf. *Suda s.v.* ἐπιμεληταί and Dem., *Meid.* 13.

[8] Σ Aischin., *In. Tim.* 10.

[9] Choregic functions are guaranteed for the Lesser Panathenaia by Lys., 21.2; they are suggested for the Prometheia and Hephaesteia by *IG* 2.[2] 1138 and [Xen.], *Ath. Pol.* 3.4.

obvious advantage to have its—or their, in the case of the Thargelia, where there was shared sponsorship of a chorus between two tribes—victory publicized as widely as possible. Here a winning choregos might spend with as lavish a hand as his finances allowed; the flamboyant dedications of Lysikrates (334 B.C.) and Thrasyllos (319 B.C.) come to mind at once. With what is perhaps only a slight exaggeration, Plutarch in one of his essays comments on the excesses of display which led many choregoi to near-bankruptcy.[10] Pausanias (1.20.1) mentions a street called "Tripod Way" which led from the Prytaneion to the theatre, and the Athenian antiquarian Heliodoros wrote c. 150 B.C. a treatise *On Dedications* in fifteen books of which one at least bore the subtitle περὶ τῶν Ἀθήνησι τριπόδων (*FGrHist* 2B, 373).

What of the dramatic victories? Was the prize, too, a tripod? This is harder to determine. Lysias' client mentions the σκευή for whose dedication he paid after his victory in the comic competition, and there is one reference at least to a choregos who dedicated something other than a tripod. Theophrastus' twenty-second character is a Skinflint who νικήσας τραγῳδοῖς ταινίαν ξυλίνην [some sort of carved representation of the victory-fillet, for which cf. Ar., *Ran.* 393] ἀναθεῖναι τῷ Διονύσῳ, ἐπιγραψάμενος αὑτοῦ τὸ ὄνομα. Of the quite numerous inscriptions on Attic tripods or tripod-bases which Amandry has recently assembled and studied anew, not one of them can be shown unequivocally to commemorate a dramatic victory.[11] On the other hand, one or two pieces of evidence seem to show that choregoi occasionally did dedicate tripods,[12] but these are very far from proving that such dedications were the rule; they may have been done at the option of the choregos in imitation of his dithyrambic counterparts. Simonides' fifty-six dithyrambic victories were commemorated, as he himself tells us, by a *pinax* (79.2 Diehl, 182 Page), and Themistokles' dedication as tragic choregos, likewise in 477/6, is explicitly designated by Plutarch (*Them.* 5) a πίνακα τῆς νίκης.

The later history of the choregia is well summarized by Pickard-Cambridge.[13] Towards the end of the Peloponnesian War there are traces of the introduction (though not necessarily as a regular practice) of a shared *synchoregia* (ΣAr., *Frogs* 404). In the latter part of the fourth century the choregia as such was abolished and supervision of choral performances was put in the hands of a publicly appointed ἀγωνοθέτης; inscriptions record victories in which ὁ δῆμος ἐχορήγει (*IG* 2.²3073–3088). Private choregoi, however, reappear sporadically in inscriptions of the Roman period, and there is evidence for dithyrambic competitions at Athens as late as c. A.D. 200.[14]

In the fifth century B.C., when the dramatic and dithyrambic *choregiai* were firmly established, sponsorship of a chorus at one of the major Athenian festivals must have been one of the standard ways a politician had of bringing himself before the public eye. Perikles' first recorded public act was his choregia for Aeschylus with the tetralogy containing *Persae* in 472 B.C.;[15] Perikles would then have been only a year or two older than was Lysias' client in *Orat.* 21 when he sponsored his first chorus. Themistokles' *choregia* for Phrynichus in 477/6 (probably for the set that included *Phoinissai*) has already been mentioned. In this same year, the archonship of Adeimantos, the prize for the men's chorus in the dithyrambic competitions, probably at the Dionysia, was won by the tribe Antiochis. A commemorative epigram survives which names the poet, Simonides, and the choregos, not the famous Aristeides but a homonym, son of Xenophilos; the appearance of the name of this latter individual on an ostrakon from the Kerameikos may indicate his pretensions to

[10] *Mor.* 349 B.
[11] P. Amandry, "Les Trépieds d'Athènes, I. Dionysies," *BCH* 100 (1976) 15 ff.
[12] *IG* 2.² 3099, from Ikaria, was certainly a tripod; see C. D. Buck, *Papers of the American School at Athens* 5 (1886–90) 86; cf. also *IG* 2.² 3097, from Paiania.
[13] *DFA*² (note 4 above) 74.
[14] *Ibid.* 74.3.
[15] *IG* 2.² 2318 line 10.

some kind of political prominence.[16] There is an illustration in *Dramatic Festivals of Athens*[2] of a black-figure neck-amphora of *c.* 460 B.C. depicting a winged victory before a tripod-dedication on whose base is inscribed Ἀκαμαντὶς ἐνίκα φυλὲ Γλαύκων καλός; the likelihood is high that Glaukon is the name of the victorious choregos, and that he is to be identified as the Glaukon son of Leagros who was a colleague of Perikles in the generalship in 441/0 and 433/2, and whose name appears as signatory of the peace-treaty with Samos.[17] Plutarch testifies to Nikias' largesse in out-fitting choruses and mentions his tripod-dedications, though the comment he appends, "he was victorious as choregos many times, and was never defeated" (*Nik.* 3), may be an exaggeration. Choregic victories are attested both for Kleon's father Kleainetos, who won for his tribe Pandionis with a men's dithyramb at the Dionysia in 460/59, and for Kleon's son Kleomedon, whose names occur in retrospective commemorations set up by the tribe at the very end of the century among victorious choregoi for boys' choruses at the Thargelia.[18] The general Demosthenes likewise won a victory for his tribe, Aiantis, with a men's chorus at the Dionysia in 422/1.[19] Some time before 415 B.C. Alkibiades undertook to be choregos for a dithyrambic competition (probably, although not certainly, a boys' dithyramb) which, as may be gathered from the speaker of [*Andokides*] 4, turned into a heated affair; Alkibiades won, but not without resorting to physical violence against one of the competing choregoi, a certain Taureas son of Leagoras and brother of the Andokides who was general against Megara in 446/5 and again against Samos in 441/0, and whose name is probably to be restored as victorious choregos with comedies at the Dionysia of 447/6.[20]

The early inscriptions commemorating choral victories are not numerous, but they show a variety which calls for special comment. The two epigrams by Simonides have already been mentioned, one commemorating the victory of the Akamantid tribe in the men's dithyramb in the archonship of Adeimantos, the other possibly (though not necessarily) from the same year in which the poet made a dedication retrospective of his fifty-six victorious commissions during a long career. Another interesting epigram, wrongly attributed in the Palatine Anthology to "Bacchylides or Simonides," was commissioned apparently by the dithyrambic chorus itself from the tribe Akamantis to commemorate its most recent victory in the competition: οἱ (*sc.* the choreutai) τόνδε τρίποδά σφισι μάρτυρα βακχίων ἀέθλων / θήκαντο (vv. 5–6), and all the relevant personnel are named, Antigenes the poet, Ariston of Argos the fluteplayer, and Hipponikos son of Strouthon the choregos.[21] Mention has already been made of the "retrospective" memorial set up at the close of the fifth century by the Pandionid tribe to honour a number of its most recent victorious choregoi (*IG* 2.[2] 1138).

At the most, however, these glimpses of what must have been a very widespread practice are tantalizingly few, and the origins of the custom of not only dedicating the victory-prize but com-memorating it with a dedicatory inscription or epigram are veiled in obscurity. Hesiod reports that he won a poetry competition at the funeral games of King Amphidamas of Chalkis, and that he dedicated the eared tripod which he received as a prize to the Muses of Mt. Helikon (*Op.* 654 ff.) but the epigram which is preserved in several late sources purporting to be Hesiod's own dedica-tion is unlikely to be genuine.[22] Greater claim to authenticity can perhaps be laid by the epigram

---

[16] Simonides 77.3 Diehl (187 Page, *Epigrammata Graeca* [Oxford 1975]); F. Willemsen, *AD* 23 (1968) *Chron.,* 28.

[17] *DFA*[2] fig. 31 (Brit. Mus. E 298); R. Meiggs and D. M. Lewis, *A Selection of Greek Historical Inscriptions* (Oxford 1969), no. 56, line 30 with p. 153; J. K. Davies, *Athenian Propertied Families 600–300 B.C.* (Oxford 1971) 91.

[18] *IG* 2.[2] 2318 line 34 (Kleainetos); *IG* 2.[2] 1138 lines 23–26 (Kleomedon); Davies 318–319.

[19] *IG* 2[2] 2318 lines 123 f. Xen., *Mem.* 4.4.3 ff.

[20] [And.], 4.20–21 (the speaker, who is perhaps Phaiax son of Erasistratos, boasts at sect. 42 of having discharged the function of tragic choregos without resorting to violence like Alkibiades); see Davies (note 17 above), 29.

[21] *Anth. Pal.* 13.28, Page, 438–449; Pickard-Cambridge, revised by T. B. L. Webster, *Dithyramb, Tragedy and Comedy*[2] (Oxford 1962) 16.

[22] *Anth. Pal.* 7.53, Dio Chrys., 2.11.

recorded by Pausanias (10.7.6) who says it stood on a tripod dedicated in a sanctuary of Herakles at Thebes by the poet Echembrotos for a victory in the Pythian games of 586 B.C.

Ἐχέμβροτος Ἀρκὰς θῆκε τῷ Ἡρακλεῖ
νικήσας τόδ' ἄγαλμ' Ἀμφικτυόνων ἐν ἀέθλοις,
Ἕλλησι δ' ἀείδων μέλεα καὶ ἐλέγους.

How early the practice of holding such competitions came to Athens it is of course impossible to say, but it may have been considerably before the incorporation of a dithyrambic contest in the official state festival of the Dionysia which occurred in the archonship of Lysagoras c. 509 B.C. according to a notice in the Parian Marble (*Ep.* 46). The names of some poets who competed in these early contests have fortunately been preserved: the Hypodikos of Chalcis named by the Parian Marble as first winner with a men's dithyramb; Lasos of Hermione, active according to Herodotus (7.6) towards the end of the Peisistratid tyranny and probably also later, who is said to have instructed Pindar and to have competed against Simonides;[23] Pindar, who won his first dithyrambic victory at Athens in either 497/6 or 496/5[24] and whose dithyrambs comprised two books in the later Alexandrian edition; and Bacchylides, substantial fragments of whose dithyrambs are preserved.

There are very few early Athenian inscriptions commemorating poetic victories. Possible candidates are perhaps to be found in two dedications published by Raubitschek, *Dedications*. No. 319 (Athens, EM 6390) is inscribed on a base which held three tripods, "presumably [Raubitschek writes] the dedication of a victor in three contests":

Χίονις : Οἴ[κλεος : ἀνέθ]εκεν

As Raubitschek further observes, the type of contest and the place where they were held cannot now be determined; he dates the inscription from the letterforms to the end of the sixth century. (My supplement of the patronymic is merely *e.g.*; Raubitschek estimates "ca. 5" spaces vacant.) No. 322 is at first sight rather more promising, since it is in verse:

τόνδε Φίλον ἀνέθεκεν / Ἀθεναίαι τριπόδισκον
θαύμασι νικέσας / ἰς πόλιν Ἀρεσίο

The letter-forms, according to Raubitschek, indicate a date "shortly before 480 B.C." Philon son of Aresios has dedicated his "little tripod" to Athena on the Acropolis for a victory θαύμασι; what the contest was remains a mystery. The word θαύματα is unlikely to be used here in any of its later technical senses of "conjuring, magic tricks," "puppet-shows," "acrobatics."[25] It seems rather to have a more general significance, "amazing feats," "spectacular achievements," and there is even a slight possibility that it points to a dramatic or choral performance; Plato has Socrates refer (somewhat disparagingly) to poets as ones who practice their art ἐνθουσιάζοντες ὥσπερ θεομάντεις καὶ οἱ χρησμῳδοί (*Ap.* 22 C).

From about the same time or only slightly later comes the intriguing dedication of which parts had previously been known (*IG* 1.² 673 and 850), when an additional fragment was discovered in 1956 and published by D. Peppa-Delmousou.[26] Through the great kindness of D. M. Lewis I print the text as it will appear in *IG* 1³.

---

[23] Eustathios, *Prooimion* 296.19 (III 300, 1 Drach.); Ar., *Vesp.* 1410.

[24] *P Oxy* 2438 col. ii, 8–10; cf. D. M. Lewis, *CR* 12 (1962) 201.

[25] Xen., *Symp.* 2.1, 7.203; Plato, *Resp.* 514 B; Theophr., *Char.* 6.6; A. E. Raubitschek, *Dedications from the Athenian Acropolis* (Cambridge, Mass. 1949).

[26] *Ath. Mitt.* 86 (1971) 55 ff. I wish to express my gratitude to Mme. Peppa-Delmousou for drawing the inscription to my attention during the Sixth International Epigraphical Congress in Munich in 1972, and for studying it with me in Athens before the Seventh Congress in September 1977.

[‒ ⏑⏑]ας ho[. . . . .]τον Ἀθένεσ[ιν χο]ρο̑ι ἀνδρο̑[ν]
[‒ ⏑⏑]τες σοφ[ίας] τόνδ' ἀνέθε[κ]εν hόρον
[εὐχσ]άμενο[ς· π]λείστοις δὲ [χ]οροῖς ἔχσο κατὰ φῦ[λα]
[ἀνδ]ρο̑ν νι[κε̑]σαι φεσὶ π[ερ]ὶ̑ τρίποδος.

The "orthodox" supplements for the beginnings of vv. 1 and 2 are [νικέ]σας and [hμερ]τε̑ς respectively,[27] but neither of these is in my opinion compelling. In recent years the suggestion has gained ground that the dedication was by Simonides for his first dithyrambic victory at Athens,[28] but this seems to me to be ruled out by two considerations: (1) an epigrammatist of Simonides' skill and repute will hardly have been unable to accommodate his own name within the epigram, witness the two elegiac commemorations discussed above where his name occurs in an identical place of the hexameter of the sixth and first lines of the two respective epigrams,[29] and, (2) even more important, a date for the inscription soon after 480 (so Raubitschek; Peek; *IG* 1³) all but rules out Simonidean authorship. In fr. 79 (Diehl), Simonides himself reports that by about 477/6 B.C. he had won fifty-six dithyrambic victories; the author of the dedication under discussion says that although he has won prizes "with many choruses elsewhere" (ἔχσο κατὰ φῦλα), this is his first victory at Athens. We are asked to believe that the vast majority, perhaps almost all, of Simonides' fifty-six victories were won outside Athens.

The editors of *IG* 1³ remark, "nomen dedicatoris maturius exspectavisses." This is certainly a reasonable expectation and they are therefore right to look for a suitable supplement in v. 1, although the name they suggest, Diagoras of Melos, seems unlikely on chronological grounds, for what evidence there is places this dithyrambist about the middle of the century.[30] A suitable candidate, however, is I believe to be found in a certain Bacchiadas of Sikyon whose victory at a festival in honour of the Muses at Mt. Helikon[31] and subsequent dedication in the Mouseion there is reported by Athenaeus on the authority of Amphion of Thespiai: Ἀμφίων . . . ἄγεσθαί φησιν ἐν Ἑλικῶνι παίδων[32] ὀρχήσεις μετὰ σπουδῆς, παρατιθέμενος ἀρχαῖον ἐπίγραμμα τόδε·

ἀμφότερ', ὠρχεύμην τε καὶ ἐν Μώσαις ἐδίδασκον
ἄνδρας· ὁ δ' αὐλητὰς ἦν Ἄνακος Φιαλεύς.
εἰμὶ δὲ Βακχιάδας[33] Σικυώνιος. ἦ ῥα θεοῖσι
ταῖς Σικυῶνι καλὸν τοῦτ' ἀπέκειτο γέρας.

Unfortunately it is impossible to suggest a firm date for this Bacchiadas, who is otherwise unknown, but as Pickard-Cambridge observed with regard to this notice in Athenaeus, "the record refers to an early period."[34] Accordingly I restore the epigram as follows:

[Βακχιάδ]ας hό[τε προ̑]τον Ἀθένεσ[ιν χο]ρο̑ι ἀνδρο̑[ν]
[νικο̑ν] τε̑ς σοφ[ίας] τόνδ' ἀνέθε[κ]εν hόρον
[εὐχσ]άμενο[ς· π]λείστοις δὲ [χ]οροῖς ἔχσο κατὰ φῦ[λα]
[ἀνδ]ρο̑ν νι[κε̑]σαι φεσὶ π[ερ]ὶ̑ τρίποδος.

---

[27] *Ath. Mitt.* 86 (1971) 56; W. Peek, *ZPE* 13 (1974) 199. [28] C. Galavotti, *QU* 20 (1975) 165 ff.

[29] F77.5 Diehl (189 Page); 79.1 Diehl (181 Page).

[30] See L. Woodbury, *Phoenix* 19 (1965) 188 ff.: "Diagoras was a poet of the post-Simonidean era who was outlawed in the archonship of Charias" [415/14], 192.

[31] For dedications on Mt. Helikon for victories in games called *Mouseia*, Paus., 9.31.3; Max Mayer, *RE* XVI (1933) 697–8.

[32] Emendation seems essential in light of the epigram that follows. Kaibel proposed ⟨ἀνδρῶν καὶ⟩ παίδων; a member of the audience at Constanza (whose name I regret having failed to obtain) suggested ὑπ' αὐλῶν.

[33] Meineke's emendation for the MSS.' meaningless δ' βαχχίδα seems certain.

[34] *Dithyramb, Tragedy and Comedy*¹ (1927) 24, ²(1962) 15. Against the objection that mention of the fluteplayer is unusual in an early commemoration, I note the choral dedication by the tribe Akamantis, already mentioned (*Anth. Pal.* 13.28, verses 7–8), and the *aulete* portrayed in an early choral scene on a Corinthian aryballos (M. and C. Roebuck, *Hesperia* 24 [1955] 158 ff.; G. Annibalis and D. Vox, *Glotta* 55 [1977] 183 ff.).

As appears from Mme. Peppa-Delmousou's photograph (*AthMitt* 86 [1971] Tafel 43), and as was confirmed by my own examination of the stone in September 1977, the upper-left corner is so badly worn that no traces are visible before the α of ας; preference therefore need not be given to restorations in ρας or σας. It might be objected that supplements ought to take account of left-hand alinement on the stone. It should be pointed out, however, that since the inscription is non-stoichedon the matter is bound to remain in doubt; the favoured supplements (above) in vv. 3 and 4 are in any case of unequal lengths. When I traced my restorations on a reconstructed drawing of the inscription, v. 2 was inset from v. 1 by the space of at most one-half a letter.[35] Of the possible supplements of the second word of v. 1, I now prefer *hó*[τε with *IG* 1³ against my former acceptance of previous editors' *hó*[δε. At the beginning of v. 2 νικõν seems to me to suit both space and sense; the present participle is extremely common (as is its finite equivalent, the imperfect indicative) in victory inscriptions.[36] In the phrase τῆς σοφίας, I take τῆς to be the "possessive" use of the article familiar from Homer,[37] while σοφία is simply "skill, expertise," often but not always poetic.[38] For a non-poetic use in a dedication compare the gold lamp for Athena's statue in the Erechtheion by the sculptor Kallimachos; from the dedicatory inscription the artist's name and the last word survive, −σοφίαι (*IG* 1.² 767; cf. Paus., 1.26.7 σοφία πάντων . . . ἄριστος). For *sophia* in a poetic sense, compare *Anth. Pal.* 13.28.4 (already cited) σοφῶν ἀοιδῶν, Kratinus, F 323K τῆς ἡμετέρας σοφίας κριτὴς ἄριστε πάντων and Kallimachos, *Epigr.* 7.4 (the poet Theaitetos), κείνου δ' Ἑλλὰς ἀεὶ σοφίην [*sc.* φθέγξεται]. The use of *hóρον* at the end of v. 2 is unusual, but perfectly intelligible, and a somewhat similar image occurs once again in the Akamantid dedication: οἳ τόνδε τρίποδά σφισι μάρτυρα . . . θήκαντο (*Anth. Pal.* 13.28.5). (It is not certain that our inscribed base in fact supported a tripod.) In v. 3 [εὐχσ]άμενο[ς seems inevitable, and is amply attested in dedications, although the formula here seems not quite to suit the context; the poet vowed he would make a dedication if and when he won a victory at Athens? In vv. 3−4 the phrase κατὰ φῦ[λα ἀνδ]ρõν, coming as it does after χοροι ἀνδρõ[ν] in v. 1 is either infelicitous or something approaching conscious word-play; neither explanation is completely satisfactory. I have essayed πρόφρων on the basis of *Iliad* A 543 and *Anth. Pal.* 6.137.1, and cf. Pindar, *Nem.* 5.22−3 πρόφρων . . . ἄειδ' . . . Μοισᾶν ὁ κάλλιστος χορός; but our poet perhaps chose to model his phrase on the cliché θνατῶν, ἀνθρώπων, μερόπων φῦλα found in the inscriptions.[39]

Whoever the poet was, he was more accomplished at dithyramb than at epigram (another reason for rejecting Simonidean authorship). The dedication nevertheless constitutes important and interesting evidence for the way poetic victories were commemorated at Athens in the earlier part of the fifth century.

University of British Columbia.   ANTHONY J. PODLECKI

---

[35] I note (without wishing to emphasize unduly) that in the second of the so-called "Marathon Epigrams," also non-stoichedon and from this same period, the first letter of verse 2, ἀνχίαλομ πρεσαι, stands to the left of the beginning of verse 1 by the space of at least one-half a letter (Kirchner, *Imagines* 19).

[36] E.g. (three separate individuals) τραγωιδοῖς χορηγήσαντες / νικῶντες ἀνέθεσαν (*IG* 2.² 3095); . . . με ἀνέθηκε . . . / παγκράτιον νιϙῶν (Friedländer and Hoffleit, *Epigrammata* No. 103); . . . παῖ [δας νικῶν] ἀνέθεκεν (*IG* 1.² 803).

[37] Kühner-Blass, 2.1, sect. 457 d.

[38] Fr. Maier, *Der ΣΟΦΟΣ-Begriff* (Diss., Munich 1970) esp. 24 ff.

[39] See Peek, *ZPE* 13 (1974) 199, with, however, his reservations.

THE DATE OF XENOPHON'S EXILE

Anyone who has had the privilege to be a student of M. F. McGregor cannot help but be aware of the delight he took and continues to take in the chronological problems that pervade inquiry into the history of the ancient Hellenes. In the hope that it will elicit both pleasure and scholarly approval, I offer here a discussion of the date of Xenophon's exile as my tribute to an outstanding teacher and epigraphist.

The question of when Xenophon was exiled has important implications both for an overall view of the chronology of his works and in particular for any theory concerning the composition of the *Hellenica*. Since his relationship to his home state was a peculiar one, it might affect not only when, but also how and why he undertook his literary and historical work. The continued appearance of the view that Xenophon was banished from Athens in 399 for accompanying Cyrus to Persia[1] in spite of several studies arguing the contrary view[2] suggests that there is need to reconsider the exact nature of the relationship between Xenophon and Athens.[3] A careful reconstruction of Xenophon's own career, consideration of the Athenians' domestic and foreign policy in the decade following their capitulation to the Spartans in 404 B.C., and the explicit statements of other ancient authors and Xenophon himself suggest that the most probable date for his exile is late 394 or early 393 B.C.

Xenophon was born into the family of Gryllos, from the class of knights, in the deme of Erchia about 430.[4] Some scholars[5] have seen evidence that he was involved in engagements toward the end of the Peloponnesian War in his accounts of Thrasyllos' campaign in Ionia (*Hell.* 1.2.1–3) and the battle of Arginusai (*Hell.* 1.6.24).[6] During the rule of the Thirty, Xenophon at first sympathized with this form of government and may well have served among the knights, who supported the

[1] J. K. Anderson, *Xenophon* (London 1974) 149, "We may suppose, then, that Xenophon was actually exiled in 399 B.C., as a dangerous 'Socratic' who had fought for Cyrus, the enemy of Athens. . . . Laconism may have seemed to many people to have been Xenophon's real offence, though the charge was 'Service under Cyrus'." D. J. Mosley, "Xenophon," *Oxford Classical Dictionary*[2] 1141, "It was probably in 399, the year of Socrates' death and a time of difficulty for Socratic associates, that Xenophon was formally exiled." Others of a similar view are: W. E. Higgins, *Concept and Role of the Individual in Xenophon* (Diss. Harvard 1971), résumé in *HSCP* 76 (1972) 289–294; H. Baden, *Untersuchungen zur Einheit der Hellenika Xenophons* (Diss. Hamburg 1966) 43–46; Stephen Usher, *Historians of Greece and Rome* (London 1970) 81, 82; H. Erbse, "Xenophon's Anabasis," *Gymnasium* 73 (1966) 485–505.

[2] H. R. Breitenbach, *Xenophon von Athen* (Stuttgart 1966) 1573–1575; E. Schwartz, "Quellenuntersuchungen zur griechischen Geschichte," *RhM* 44 (1889) 161–193; G. Grote, *History of Greece* 7 (London 1872) 343–345.

[3] I would like to thank Professors F. W. Walbank and A. Andrewes for their criticisms of an earlier draft of this paper.

[4] His knowledge of horsemanship and the cavalry is obvious from the technical treatises. He certainly rode during Cyrus' expedition; *An.* 3.3.19; 7.8.6. For his membership in the deme of Erchia see Diogenes Laertios 2.48. His age – he had to emphasize to the Ten Thousand that his age should not be a hindrance to his assuming the strategia in 400; *An.* 3.1.25 and 2.37. Proxenos who was a childhood friend was about thirty years old when he died; *An.* 2.6.20. *An.* 6.4.25: ὁ Ξενοφῶν ἐβοήθει καὶ οἱ ἄλλοι οἱ μέχρι τριάκοντα ἐτῶν ἅπαντες. This may mean, in the light of what was said above, that he was included in this class. Diog. Laert., 2.55: ἤκμαζε δὲ κατὰ τὸ τέταρτον ἔτος τῆς τετάρτης καὶ ἐνενηκοστῆς Ὀλυμπιάδος . . . . (i.e., 401/0).

[5] E.g., Schwartz (above, note 2), 164.

[6] If this is right he could have been born no later than 427 B.C.

oligarchs (*Hell.* 2.3.12; 2.4.2). If he continued to serve against Thrasyboulos and the democrats, as Schwartz suggests,[7] he did so under duress. Several times he explicitly mentions his support for Theramenes' moderate policy (*Hell.* 2.3.55, 56) and indicates his aversion for the later policies of the Thirty by emphasizing their godlessness and greed and by reporting speeches that do likewise.[8] Since their rapaciousness seems almost an obsession with him, his family's property may possibly have been among that confiscated subsequent to Theramenes' death.[9]

After the reestablishment of the democracy at Athens Xenophon was invited by Proxenos, who was a childhood friend, to accompany him in his service with Cyrus (*An.* 3.1.4; 1.1.11). After consulting the oracle at Delphi, not about whether he should go but rather about which god's protection he should seek in order to return successfully, Xenophon left Athens to join the expedition (*An.* 3.1.5−9). It left in the Spring of 401[10] and the battle of Cunaxa[11] was fought in the Autumn. After this, Xenophon assumed one of the leading roles in bringing the troops back to the Black Sea.

Throughout the retreat from Persia Xenophon viewed his leadership as subject to the wishes of Cheirosophos and the Spartans who were at that time the undisputed leaders of the Hellenes.[12] Sparta had been the only Greek state to support officially the designs of Cyrus and even she had done so in secret (*An.* 1.4.3; Diod. Sic., 14.19.5; 14.21.2; 14.27.1). The army reached the shores of the Euxine in the early Spring of 400 and spent the rest of the year returning to the Hellespont. During this time Cheirosophos died and the army began to shrink−first to about 8,000 and then to about 6,000 as some of the men found their way home to their own cities (*An.* 6.4.11; 6.2.16; 7.7.23). Xenophon, too, was already on his way home when, late in 400 B.C., he was appointed commander of the Cyrean army by Anaxibios, the Spartan admiral (who was at that time in charge of most of the coastal regions of the Aegean and the Hellespont); for there was a growing fear that the army would be destroyed by Aristarchos, the new Spartan harmost of Byzantium, and Pharnabazos (*An.* 7.2.8; 7.6.33). Xenophon took up his command and, with the agreement of the remnant of the Ten Thousand, enlisted the army in the service of Seuthes, the Odrysian prince, for the winter of 400/399 B.C. (*An.* 7.2.16−3.14).

In the Spring of 399 B.C. Xenophon's desire to return home to Attica was again frustrated by the combined force of the army's plight because of lack of leadership, the pleas of his comrades not to desert them (*An.* 7.7.57; Diod. Sic., 14.37.1), and new instructions from the Spartans. The army was to cross the Hellespont and for pay, with its command structure virtually intact, to enter the service of Thibron, who was supposed to be defending the Greek cities of Asia Minor against the designs of the Persian satraps, Tissaphernes and Pharnabazos.[13] Xenophon's position of command, his demonstrated concern for his soldiers and, perhaps, his need for their protection in the face of Thibron's enmity (*An.* 7.6.44) kept him in Asia with them until at least the end of the first year of

---

[7] Schwartz (above, note 2), 165.

[8] *Hell.* 2.3.14, 17, 21; 2.4.1, 10. The speeches of Thrasyboulos and Kleokritos; 2.4.13−17 and 20−22 respectively.

[9] *Hell.* 2.3.21; 2.4.1, 10, 13, 21, 40. This would explain why Xenophon would not touch the money for the god which had been entrusted to him (*An.* 5.3.4, 5) when he was in financial difficulties in 399 and had to sell his horse in order to finance his intended journey home (*An.* 7.8.1, 2, 6). He simply could not expect any help from home.

[10] *An.* 1.2.1 and Diog. Laert., 2.55.

[11] The time is calculated by considering the various references to the seasons of the year as they appear incidently in the *Anabasis.* For a discussion of the battle see O. Lendle, "Der Bericht über die Schlacht von Kunaxa," *Gymnasium* 73 (1966) 420−452.

[12] *An.* 3.2.37; 6.1.26−29; 6.2.13; 7.1.27−28; 7.2.8; 7.6.33; for the ascendency of Sparta, *An.* 6.6.9; 7.6.37; *Hell.* 3.1.3. Xenophon emphasizes that he assumed leadership only after the army found itself in dire straits because of the Persian treachery. Before that he had taken no active part in the expedition (*An.* 3.1.4: ὃς οὔτε στρατηγὸς οὔτε λοχαγὸς οὔτε στρατιώτης ὢν συνηκολούθει . . .).

[13] *An.* 7.6.1 for the offer to pay the army and officers; *Hell.* 3.1.3−6 and Diod. Sic., 14.37 for the intentions of the Spartans and Thibron's mandate.

Derkylidas' command (399/8 B.C.).[14] His incidental evaluation of Thibron's leadership and his pointed comment to the Spartan officials reveal that he had stayed with the men and was in a position to criticize and evaluate the leadership of each man.

Of Derkylidas, Xenophon writes: καὶ εὐθὺς μὲν τοσούτῳ διέφερεν εἰς τὸ ἄρχειν τοῦ Θίβρωνος ὥστε παρήγαγε τὸ στράτευμα διὰ τῆς φιλίας χώρας μέχρι τῆς Φαρναβάζου Αἰολίδος οὐδὲν βλάψας τοὺς συμμάχους.[15] The expression καὶ εὐθὺς μέν reveals that this evaluation is of special importance to the author.[16] The καί when used with μέν usually has the force of "even"; of an affirmative leading up to an *a fortiori* argument (in this case left unexpressed) that, if this was already the case at the beginning of Derkylidas' command, how much more was it true at the end of his period of leadership. The μέν is used without the correlative δέ to express absolute certainty on the part of the speaker or writer. Placed after the adverb, as it is here, it takes on the function of an emphatic which stresses the impact of the preceding word. It is a peculiarity of Xenophon's style probably taken from the early poets.[17] Finally, the use of the adverbial of time εὐθύς—meaning forthwith, straightway, immediately—suggests that the writer has very specific knowledge about this new commander's leadership from the outset (a knowledge most likely gained from personal observation and experience). Simultaneously, it also implies that he has similar detailed knowledge about Derkylidas' command as a whole.

The general impression, then, given by this passage is that Xenophon was in a position to compare Thibron's leadership with that of the present commander, Derkylidas, because he had been on hand to observe their day to day conduct of affairs. The passage reads like an eyewitness account. The difference in the treatment of the allies is reported as a fact, something the author knows for certain, and not as something that has been reported to him by an informant; for Xenophon usually indicates when he is quoting the judgement of another person.[18]

It is likely that Xenophon observed the behaviour of both men from close quarters as commander of the Cyrean unit. We have already seen that it was the Spartans' intention to hire the army with its command structure intact. From Xenophon's own words and from an independent source, Diodoros, it is clear that Xenophon held the position of στρατηγός within that structure. Furthermore, Diodoros seems to indicate that, after it undertook service for pay with the Spartans in Asia, the army remained an independent unit (μετὰ Λακεδαιμονίων ἐπολέμουν Πέρσαις).[19] That this arrangement continued until at least the end of Derkylidas' first year as the Spartan representative in Asia is clear.

Xenophon writes: ὁ τῶν Κυρείων προεστηκὼς ἀπεκρίνατο· . . . ἡμεῖς μέν ἐσμεν οἱ αὐτοὶ νῦν τε καὶ πέρυσιν. ἄρχων δὲ ἄλλος μὲν νῦν, ἄλλος δὲ τὸ παρελθόν. This passage is set in the context of a meeting of the soldiers in Asia with Spartan representatives who had come to confirm Derkylidas' second year in command and to censure the army for earlier mistreatment of Ionian Greeks (under Thibron), but also to acknowledge and encourage their improved attitude in the previous year under Derkylidas. From this passage it is immediately evident that the Cyrean unit still has its own leader (ὁ προεστηκώς) and so continues to maintain its own structure of command. This is reinforced by the quoted words (ἡμεῖς ἐσμεν οἱ αὐτοὶ νῦν τε καὶ πέρυσιν), something which could

[14] *Hell.* 3.2.7: ὁ τῶν Κυρείων προεστηκὼς ἀπεκρίνατο· At this point scholars often seem to lose track of Xenophon's career.

[15] *Hell.* 3.1.10. Xenophon's general judgement appears to be supported by Diod. Sic., 14.36.3.

[16] See J. D. Denniston, *The Greek Particles* (London 1954) 359–368, 390.

[17] This use of μέν emphatic in his historical work is, I think, an indication that Xenophon himself is the eyewitness. Nevertheless, the investigation of this idea requires a paper confined to that subject alone and is beyond the scope of this essay.

[18] *Hell.* 4.8.36; 5.3.2; 5.4.7, 24; 6.4.7, 37; 7.1.32; 7.3.3. These statements all occur in the latter part of his history when we are certain that Xenophon was no longer personally involved in the events he narrates.

[19] Diod. Sic., 14.37.4: . . . μετὰ δὲ ταῦτα Θίβρωνος αὐτοὺς μεταπεμπομένου καὶ μισθοὺς ἐπαγγελλομένου δώσειν, πρὸς ἐκεῖνον ἀπεχώρησαν καὶ μετὰ Λακεδαιμονίων ἐπολέμουν τοῖς Πέρσαις.

hardly have been used as a defence of previous actions if there had been a change of leadership within the unit. Thus it appears certain that Xenophon continued to lead the Cyrean army after it undertook service with the Spartans in Asia.

During subsequent years there is no change in the nature of Spartan operations in Asia nor in the command structure of the army until 395 B.C. Then Agesilaos, who had been sent to Asia in 396 B.C. (*Hell.* 3.4.2–4), undertook a reorganization of the entire army and integrated the Cyrean unit into the Spartan command structure by making Herippides, a Spartan, its commander.[20] Xenophon explicitly states that this took place at the beginning of Agesilaos' second year in Asia, while from Diodoros' account it appears that a complete reorganization and unification of the army took place immediately after Agesilaos' arrival in Asia. But a careful scrutiny of Diodoros' narrative method at this point in his history suggests that there is extreme compression (i.e., he continually lumps the events of two or three years together and then gives no account of Greek affairs for a year or two except to mention the name of the Athenian archon).[21] Furthermore, because of the vast expanse of time he is attempting to cover he leaves out certain details (such as Agesilaos' first landing at Gerastos)[22] but in making Ephesos the place where this reorganization occurred he agrees with Xenophon. The misdating of this reorganization can be further explained by Diodoros' attempt to make the Athenian archonship coincide with the Roman consular year. Since there would be parts of two archonships in a given consular year, Diodoros tends to give an account of what happened under both archonships in one year and so finds himself at times including material which in fact sometimes happened during a three-year interval. The passage under discussion is again a part of a narrative (14.79.1–82.1) that covers events of at least two years duration. Finally, it seems unlikely that Agesilaos would begin making immediate and drastic changes in a command structure that had been in existence for three full years, when he was unacquainted with the nature of the enemy he was to face, the location in which the battle was to be fought, and the army he was to lead.

Diogenes Laertios[23] states that Xenophon handed over the Cyrean troops to Agesilaos. Scholars[24] have been quick to point out, on the basis of the last sentence in the *Anabasis*, that he is wrong in attributing the unification to Agesilaos rather than to Thibron.[25] This, however, overlooks the possibility that Xenophon did not relinquish command of the Cyreans until 395, but operated as an intermediary between the Spartan leaders, Thibron and Derkylidas. As has been shown above (p. 104) Xenophon always viewed his command of the Cyrean army as originating with the Spartan high-command and therefore requiring their approval. He gave up this role only when he handed over the army to Agesilaos and there was an official change in the relationship of the Cyrean unit to the Spartan representative in Asia. We can conclude then that Xenophon led the remnants of the army of the Ten Thousand as στρατηγός from 399 until he was relieved of his command by Agesilaos in late 396 or early 395 B.C.

[20] *Hell.* 3.4.20; Diod. Sic., 14.79.2. Xenophon pays special attention to the subsequent behaviour of Herippides (*Hell.* 4.1.20–28). The implied criticism in his narrative may be indicative of some tension between the new and the former leader. On the other hand, Diod. Sic., 14.38.4 indicates that Herippides was indeed a rather rash and brutish man.

[21] E.g., Diod. Sic., 14.19.1–39.6 lumps the expedition of Cyrus, the reign of terror at Athens under the Thirty, the subsequent restoration of the democracy, the return of the Ten Thousand, the expedition under Thibron to Asia and the succession of Derkylidas into two years (401–400 B.C.). Then for the following two years (14.44.1; 14.47.1) there is not a word about Greek affairs. This narrative method is still in use in the passage discussed here; 14.79.1–82.1.

[22] *Hell.* 3.4.4.

[23] Diog. Laert., 2.51: . . . ἦκεν εἰς Ἀσίαν πρὸς Ἀγησίλαον τὸν τῶν Λακεδαιμονίων βασιλέα, μισθοῦ τοὺς Κύρου στρατιώτας αὐτῷ παρασχών.

[24] E.g., Breitenbach (note 2 above), 1574.

[25] *An.* 7.8.24; *Hell.* 3.1.6. The verb Xenophon uses in both passages is an aorist form of συμμείγνυμι – a word which need imply nothing more than adding them to what was already a very diverse and heterogeneous organization; see *Hell.* 3.1.4.

The exact whereabouts of Xenophon during the following year has been the subject of some dispute.[26] What is generally agreed, however, is that Xenophon spent most of his time either in Ephesos or on the march as a friend and personal adviser to Agesilaos. At the beginning of the year the King required Xenophon's expertise to develop and train the new cavalry which he found indispensable if he was to be successful against Tissaphernes.[27] It is tempting to view Xenophon's release from his position as leader of the Cyreans as a means of making him more readily available and therefore more serviceable to Agesilaos, with whom there was a growing friendship (Diog. Laert., 2.51). It was also in this year that Xenophon finally had the leisure to discharge another of his duties, which had been entrusted to him by the Ten Thousand during the return march; namely, to make an offering of the tithe (from the plunder garnered during the expedition) to the gods, Artemis and Apollo (*An.* 5.3.4–6). Diogenes Laertios[28] tells us that since he had the gold with him in Ephesos (γενόμενος δ᾽ ἐν Ἐφέσῳ καὶ χρυσίον ἔχων) he used half the money to send votive offerings to Delphi (τοῦ ἡμίσεος ἔπεμψεν εἰς Δελφοὺς ἀναθήματα). This is supported by Xenophon's own words (τὸ τοῦ Ἀπόλλωνος ἀνάθημα ποιησάμενος) and makes it quite clear that he took advantage of the craftsmen and metalsmiths of Ephesos (to whom he specifically refers in another passage)[29] to make an offering worthy of his own achievements and those of his deceased friend, Proxenos. This project will clearly have required supervision and so kept him in or near Ephesos, but it would also have allowed Xenophon to accompany Agesilaos on his forays into Persian territory at intervals. What is clear is that it was the original intention merely to send these votive offerings to Delphi and that he was proceeding at a leisurely pace with these dedicatory works and still had no definite idea what he intended to do with the portion belonging to Artemis (*An.* 5.3.6). What is implied here is that Xenophon did not expect to return to the Greek mainland in the immediate future, was unaware of the exact situation among the warring states of Greece and was probably busy advising Agesilaos on the proposed march deep into Persian territory.[30]

Because of the recall of Agesilaos, Xenophon found himself returning to Greece in 394 and so was present at the Battle of Koronea.[31] Plutarch says that Xenophon actually fought on the side of Agesilaos (τῷ Ἀγησιλάῳ συναγωνιζόμενος) but this is Plutarch's interpretation of what Xenophon himself wrote (probably *Hell.* 4.3.16; *Ages.* 2.9), for Xenophon is clearly his main source for this account. Xenophon himself takes great pains, when he writes about the Battle at Koronea, to make clear that he was there, as were many others, only because of friendship for Agesilaos,[32] not because of hostility to Athens. He further exonerates himself by pointing out twice that Herippidas was commanding the Cyrean unit which was such a factor in that battle (*Hell.* 4.3.15 and 17). Finally, in another work he writes (*Ages.* 2.10–11): . . . φάλαγγος ὢν Ἡριππίδας ἐξενάγει (ἦσαν δ᾽ οὗτοι τῶν τε ἐξ οἴκου αὐτῷ συστρατευσαμένων καὶ τῶν Κυρείων τινές). This passage was written after 362 B.C. many years following the actual event. Sparta and Athens had been officially friends for at least ten years, and Sparta was no longer viewed as a threat. Yet Xenophon merely says that some of the Cyreans fought at Koronea. If he had been part of that band, he would surely

---

[26] Compare J. K. Anderson (note 1 above), 155–161 with I. A. F. Bruce, *Commentary on Hellenica Oxyrhynchia* (Çambridge 1967) 150–156.

[27] *Hell.* 3.4.15–19; Plutarch, *Ages.* 9.3.4.

[28] Diog. Laert., 2.55. Note the plural ἀναθήματα.

[29] *Hell.* 3.4.17.

[30] *Hell.* 4.1.41–2.3. The first news of the events of 395 B.C. came to Agesilaos (and Xenophon) only in the spring of 394 with the arrival of Epikydidas, when preparations were well underway for the attack on Persia. See also Diod. Sic. 14.83.1, 3; Plutarch, *Ages.* 15.1, 2; Pausanias 3.9.12. Xenophon, *Ages.* 1.36, implies that Xenophon was privy to the plans to invade Persia. That he hated Persia is obvious in all his works; below, note 41.

[31] *An.* 5.3.6; Diog. Laert., 2.51: ἐντεῦθεν (i.e., Ephesos) ἦλθεν εἰς τὴν Ἑλλάδα μετ᾽ Ἀγησιλάου. Plutarch, *Ages.* 18.1.

[32] *Hell.* 4.2.3–8, especially 4: ἀκούσαντες ταῦτα πολλοὶ μὲν ἐδάκρυσαν, πάντες δ᾽ ἐψηφίσαντο βοηθεῖν μετ᾽ Ἀγησιλάου τῇ Λακεδαίμονι.

have admitted it at this time. But the vagueness of the words implies that he himself was not included in that number. Furthermore, to have been the commander of the Cyreans for at least four years and then probably a special adviser to Agesilaos himself would surely have made it difficult, if not impossible, for Xenophon to take up the rank of an ordinary hoplite or even of an ordinary cavalryman, a rank he had never held throughout the existence of the army. On the other hand, he held no position of command since he names all the commanders of the various units and the auxiliary. Hence, it would have been very difficult to find a place for someone of his special status. That he observed the battle is quite clear from his own words and description; that he fought at Koronea is, I think, unlikely.

After the battle, Agesilaos went to Delphi to take part in the Pythian games, to dedicate over one hundred talents as a tithe from the plunder obtained during the Asian campaign and to recover from wounds received in the battle at Koronea.[33] Xenophon, too, at some time made a dedicatory offering in the treasury of the Athenians and had his own name and that of his friend Proxenos inscribed on it.[34] The common view is that this was done in conjunction with Agesilaos' offering of over a hundred talents at the Pythian games[35] after Koronea in 394. As we have already seen, Diogenes Laertios says that he sent votive memorials (ἀναθήματα) to Delphi just before he himself returned to Greece. This means that he would arrive just in time to make the official dedication of the newly prepared votive offering bearing Proxenos' and his own names. Since he was fond of religious ritual[36] and since he knew in the spring of 394 that he and Agesilaos would be returning to Greece during that campaigning season (Hell. 4.2.2, 3) he could certainly have laid plans for such a dedication. In this he may well have been inspired by Agesilaos who could hardly have dedicated the talents in such a lavish manner (Plutarch, Ages. 19.3) without some prior organization.

After this, probably for all his services in the past, he was rewarded by the Spartans, first with a proxeny[37] and then with an estate at Skillos.[38] He seems to have married, before he received the estate, a woman called Philesia who gave birth to two sons, Gryllos and Diodoros. Since they were old enough to fight in the battle of Mantineia in 362 they must have been born before 380. That they were old enough to take charge of the servants when the family left Skillos in 370 after it was overrun by the Elaeans (Diog. Laert., 2.53, 54), and even before this time had taken a leading role in the hunting expedition at the annually held festival in honour of Artemis (An. 5.3.9, 10), suggests a birthdate of at least 385 or, more probably, earlier. Plutarch[39] tells us that shortly after his return to Sparta from Delphi, Agesilaos had Xenophon with him and ordered him to send for his two sons and have them trained in the Spartan system. This passage refers to a time near the approaching Olympics (i.e., 392 B.C.) and before Agesilaos began actively to pursue the war with Corinth. Since the Spartan system took the boy from his parents at age seven, it is likely that Xenophon married while he was still in Asia. Both the summoning of the family to Sparta and the replacing of the proxeny with the estate at Skillos, as tangible proof of Spartan appreciation for his services, suggests that Xenophon found himself at this time without a home or influence in Attica. His exile is the most probable cause.

[33] Hell. 4.3.21; Ages. 1.34; Plutarch, Ages. 19.3; Diod. Sic., 14.84.2.

[34] An. 5.3.5: Ξενοφῶν οὖν τὸ μὲν τοῦ Ἀπόλλωνος ἀνάθημα ποιησάμενος ἀνατίθησιν εἰς τὸν ἐν Δελφοῖς τῶν Ἀθηναίων θησαυρὸν καὶ ἐπέγραψε τό τε αὑτοῦ ὄνομα καὶ τὸ Προξένου . . . .

[35] H. W. Parke, A History of the Delphic Oracle (Oxford 1939) 221–222.

[36] Diog. Laert., 2.56 describes him as εὐσεβής τε καὶ φιλοθύτης καὶ ἱερεῖα διαγνῶναι ἱκανός.

[37] Diog. Laert., 2.51. As Breitenbach (note 2 above), 1575 observes, it is doubtful whether an exile could or would for practical reasons hold a proxeny. Hence, he must not yet have been exiled.

[38] An. 5.3.7; Diog. Laert., 2.52 quoting Deinarchos.

[39] Plut., Ages. 20.2: Ξενοφῶντα δὲ τὸν σοφὸν ἔχων μεθ' ἑαυτοῦ σπουδαζόμενον ἐκέλευε τοὺς παῖδας ἐν Λακεδαίμονι τρέφειν μεταπεμψάμενος . . . . The source for the information in this section appears to be the Spartan records (19.9). In 399 Xenophon was still without children, An. 7.6.34.

The alliance that was established between Sparta and Athens after Leuktra and the presence of Xenophon's sons among the Athenian cavalry at Mantineia in 362 suggests that Xenophon's relations with his home state must have been renewed. That shortly before his death he wrote the *Poroi* which recommends to Athens policies that are essentially the same as those advanced by Euboulos in 355 supports the statement of Diogenes Laertios (2.59, quoting Istros) that Xenophon's exile was lifted by a decree moved by this Euboulos.

This reconstruction of Xenophon's career has attempted to concentrate on that decade (401 – 392 B.C.) in which the exact details have been either vague or in dispute, and has not attempted a chronology of his works or emphasized his activities during the latter part of his life. Nevertheless, certain important conclusions follow, if the reconstruction is correct. First, it has often been wondered why Xenophon did not return home after the expedition of the Ten Thousand. Usually it has been concluded by those who would date his exile to 399 B.C. that he must have been unable to because he had been banished.[40] Here it is suggested that he may not have wanted to, because he had become involved in a war with the Persians whom he despised,[41] and he had probably begun a family during this time in Asia. Second, Xenophon was absent from Athens and the Greek mainland for an uninterrupted period of about seven years. During that time he would hardly have come to the notice of the Athenians until very near the end of that interval, partly because of the slowness of communications, partly because as a politically undistinguished young man he had no following in Athens, and partly because Athens was busy dealing with its own domestic problems and would pay scant heed to what must have seemed to them merely another adventurer. Only when his fame increased and when Athens had once again become interested in foreign policy and conscious of its image abroad, would it begin to scrutinize the actions and behaviour of its citizens in foreign parts. The time when these aspirations for foreign influence again blossomed must now become the object of consideration.

The decade that is of concern here was dominated by the spectre of the reign of terror unleashed by the Thirty Oligarchs in 404/3, when at least fifteen hundred Athenian citizens lost their lives and, perhaps, half the citizen body fled or were banished from the city.[42] The general course of events is well known and need not be repeated here.[43] What is of concern is the general outlook that the Athenians had both toward themselves and toward the Spartans upon emerging from this time of crisis.

The constitutional dilemma was sparked by the treaty which ended the Dekeleian war. Xenophon reports it as follows (*Hell.* 2.2.20):

. . . ἀλλ᾽ ἐποιοῦντο εἰρήνην ἐφ᾽ ᾧ τά τε
    μακρὰ τείχη καὶ τὸν Πειραιᾶ καθελόντας
καὶ τὰς ναῦς πλὴν δώδεκα παραδόντας
    καὶ τοὺς φυγάδας καθέντας τὸν
αὐτὸν ἐχϑρὸν καὶ φίλον νομίζοντας
Λακεδαιμονίοις ἕπεσϑαι καὶ κατὰ γῆν
    καὶ κατὰ ϑάλαττον ὅποι ἂν ἡγῶνται.

What is clear here is that Xenophon is not giving a verbatim report of the clauses in the treaty but merely the highlights of the treaty as they were reported by the Spartans themselves to an assembly of their allies. One can be certain that at this point they would say only what they themselves found particularly pleasing and what would most satisfy their allies. Hence, they ensured their

---

[40] See above, note 1.

[41] See *Cyropedia* 8.8.27. Cf. *Hell.* 4.1.41; *Ages.* 7.7.

[42] Aischines, 3.235; Isocrates, 20.11; Diod. Sic., 14.5.7.

[43] For a narration of events see C. Hignett, *A History of the Athenian Constitution* (Oxford 1952) 378 – 389.

hegemony among the Greek states by the treaty, insisted that the walls should come down and allied the Athenians, by the standard formula, "to have the same friends and enemies," as themselves and their supporters, thereby guaranteeing their allies freedom from threats or attack by Athens. What the Spartans did not mention to their allies, for it might well have created uneasiness, is what Diodoros reports (16.3.2): . . . Ἀθηναῖοι μὲν καταπεπονημένοι ἐποιήσαντο συνθήκας πρὸς Λακεδαιμονίους καθ᾽ ἃς ἔδει τὰ τείχη τῆς πόλεως καθελεῖν καὶ τῇ πατρίῳ πολιτείᾳ χρῆσθαι.

The first clause is merely a quick (and bad) summary of what Xenophon reports in greater detail. However, the last phrase is an indication that the Spartans intended to meddle in the internal politics of Athens, as Lysander had already begun to do elsewhere. It made them the custodians of whatever form of government would exist in Athens. "To employ the paternal constitution" was an extremely vague phrase which gave the Spartans virtually a free hand and yet appealed to the individual Athenian since it was open to every interpretation.[44] It divided the Athenians and allowed Lysander, as the Spartan representative, officially to set up the oligarchy of the Thirty, and, thereby, set in motion the civil strife of the subsequent eight months. During this στάσις Lysander supported the oligarchy, first with a garrison[45] and then, as the crisis neared for the oligarchy, with a loan of 100 talents.[46] In addition, the Spartans attempted to prevent other Greek states from helping any of the Athenian fugitives.[47]

Shortly after this, new ephors were elected at Sparta who, together with the kings, undertook to curtail the influence of Lysander. Pausanias, who was the most conservative of the three Spartan leaders,[48] had a reputation as a friend of democrats (Hell. 5.2.3). He undertook to deprive Lysander of his power, at least in part,[49] by reconciling the Athenians with one another and restoring the democratic form of government.[50] After two skirmishes, which were designed to emphasize Spartan power, he advised both sides in the dispute to propose to the ephors that they be reconciled to each other and live together as friends of the Spartans.[51] These proposals were sent to Sparta along with a statement from the city that the Ten and their supporters surrendered Athens to the Spartans. (The latter was probably an attempt on the part of the oligarchs to sabotage the aims of Pausanias.) Eventually, a commission of fifteen Spartans[52] together with Pausanias effected a reconciliation among the Athenians, from which only the Thirty, the Ten and the Eleven were excluded.[53] What is of extreme importance here is that Pausanias had cut short the aspirations of Lysander for control of the city by establishing a political climate which allowed democracy to be reinstituted. At the same time he was careful to obtain the official sanction of his government

[44] Diodoros reflects the clause as reported by Aristotle, Ath. Pol. 34.3 . . . πολιτεύσονται τὴν πάτριον πολιτείαν. For further discussion of this clause see A. Fuks, The Ancestral Constitution (Westport 1971) 33–51. For its effect on negotiations between Athens and Sparta in 404 see W. James McCoy, "Aristotle's Athenaion Politeia and the establishment of the Thirty Tyrants," YCS 24 (1975) 131–145.

[45] Hell. 2.3.14; Diod. Sic., 16.4.4.

[46] Hell. 2.4.28; Isoc., 7.67; Dem., 20.11.

[47] Deinarchos, 1.25; Plut., Lys. 27.3, 4; Diod. Sic., 16.6.1–3.

[48] See C. D. Hamilton, "Spartan Politics and Policy, 405–401 B.C.," AJP 91 (1970) 294–314.

[49] He was probably also behind the reaction against Lysander's introduction of silver and gold currency into Sparta (Plut., Lys. 17.1) and the trial of Lysander for attempting to bribe the oracle of Ammon (Diod. Sic., 14.13.7, 8).

[50] For Pausanias' intensions see Hell. 2.4.29 (φθονήσας Λυσάνδρῳ), 31 (εὐμενὴς αὐτοῖς ὤν), and 35 (καὶ οὐδ᾽ ὡς ὠργίζετο αὐτοῖς). Plut., Lys. 21.1–3 (οἱ δὲ βασιλεῖς . . . ἔπρασσον ὅπως ἀποδώσουσι τοῖς δημόταις τὰ πράγματα . . .). Diod. Sic., 14.33.6. Agis probably supported Pausanias, at least partially, because Lysander had flaunted his power before him at Dekeleia in 406/5 (Plut., Lys. 9.3).

[51] Hell. 2.4.35–38. Note especially 35: ἀλλὰ διαλυθέντες κοινῇ ἀμφότεροι Λακεδαιμονίοις φίλοι εἶναι.

[52] Aristotle, Ath. Pol. 38.4 says ten.

[53] Hell. 2.4.38; Andokides 1.90; Aristotle, Ath. Pol. 39.6. Even members of the excluded groups, provided they rendered an account of their conduct in office, might find protection under the amnesty. The full text of the amnesty is in Ath. Pol. 39.1–6.

before and while the reconciliation was being fashioned, rather than to present his fellow citizens with a *fait accompli* and then to seek its ratification. From the Athenian point of view, Pausanias and his Spartan supporters became guarantors of the continuation of the amnesty and, therefore, of the democracy in opposition to Lysander and his friends.[54] Therefore, to break the amnesty would have meant a renewal of hostilities and would have offered the Spartan opposition an opportunity to meddle once again in the internal affairs of Athens and, perhaps, to overthrow the democracy.

This recognition of the importance of internal peace and reconciliation for the welfare of the Athenian state developed only gradually. Shortly after the restoration of the democratic assembly, Phormisios, one of the members of the Piraeus party,[55] tried, by means of a motion in the assembly, to limit the rights of Athenian citizenship (πολιτεία) to landowners only and, thereby, would have disenfranchised about five thousand Athenians. This motion, which had the support of the Spartans, was probably a reaction to an earlier attempt on the part of Thrasyboulos to obtain citizenship for all those who had supported the Piraeus party during the civil strife.[56] In a partial speech ascribed to the pen of Lysias[57] there is a discussion of what the Athenian attitude to Sparta should be. At first sight the speaker appears to be very forthright about his antagonism to Spartan interference. He then goes on to speculate what the Spartan reaction will be if Athens rejects the motion. It is quite clear that he is using an argument which Spartans like Pausanias, who pursued a policy of nonintervention,[58] held to, namely that it would be foolish for the Spartans to risk an engagement with the Athenians over this matter merely to limit the democracy slightly. On the other hand, although Phormisios was among those who returned as a fugitive, it is also clear that he belonged to the party of Theramenes[59] and, therefore, probably had ties with Lysander and joined the fugitives only after the death of Theramenes. What is important here, then, is that we have two points of view expressed in the Athenian assembly which may have originated with and would certainly have appealed to differing factions at Sparta. The welfare of the state is linked with the maintenance of democracy and the rejection of policies originating with the Spartan clique led by Lysander. That Phormisios' proposal was rejected suggests that the majority of the Athenians opposed any Spartan interference originating with Lysander but recognized the importance of good relations with Pausanias.

A careful perusal of the extant speeches delivered to Athenian juries during the decade in question[60] reveals a continual committal on the part of the audience (i.e., the jury) to the amnesty and the agreements made with the Spartans in 403 B.C. (These are commonly referred to as οἱ ὅρκοι, meaning the amnesty sworn to by the two Athenian factions, and αἱ συνθῆκαι, referring to the general settlements to which the Spartans and Pausanias were party.)[61] These juries were large and, therefore, usually must have reflected the attitudes of the Athenian populace in general.[62] In a

---

[54] Aristotle, *Ath. Pol.* 38.4 implies that he had a hand in drafting the amnesty: ἐπὶ πέρας γὰρ ἤγαγε τὴν εἰρήνην καὶ τὰς διαλύσεις Παυσανίας . . . . For a further discussion of the undermining of Lysander's work see A. Andrewes, "Two Notes on Lysander," *Phoenix* 25 (1971) 206–227.

[55] Dion. Hal., *Lys.* 32.

[56] Aristotle, *Ath. Pol.* 40.2; Aischines 3.195. Thrasyboulos was merely trying to fulfill a promise that had been made to obtain foreign support against the oligarchs; see *Hell.* 2.4.25. For a discussion of the traditional attitude of the Athenians toward the granting of citizenship to foreigners see Malcolm F. McGregor, *Athenian Policy at Home and Abroad* (Cincinnati 1967) 1–14.

[57] Lysias, 34.6–11. This speech may have been published after the debate as a political pamphlet.

[58] See Hamilton (note 48 above).

[59] Aristotle, *Ath. Pol.* 34.3.

[60] Conveniently listed in R. C. Jebb, *The Attic Orators* 1 (London 1893) xliii–xlv.

[61] E.g., Isok., 18.2, 20, 24, 29; Lysias, 6.40; 18.15; Andokides, 1.103.

[62] Cf. Aristotle, *Ath. Pol.* 41.2, where he emphasizes that the juries after 403 reflected popular opinion. The Athenian attitude to the restoration of democracy is discussed by R. Koerner, "Die Haltung des attischen Demos zu den Umsturzbewegungen nach 412 v. u. Z.," *Klio* 57 (1975) 405–414.

speech written in late 402 by Isokrates for a client, there is a clear indication that the jury viewed the Spartans as being party to the settlement of 403. So the speaker suggests that to vote against him would be a violation of that treaty. He ends with a violent and emotional denunciation of Lysander and the Thirty, who, of course, had no share in the amnesty.[63] This pattern is often repeated in the speeches given throughout this decade. Generally the Spartans and particularly Pausanias are referred to with goodwill. The speakers do not expect hostility from the juries toward Pausanias, though they are vehement in their denunciation of Lysander and the Thirty. It is clear that popular sentiment at Athens at this time viewed it as essential to abide by the agreements made with the Spartans.

As late as 396 B.C. reference is made by the speaker to the goodwill of Pausanias and the Spartans toward the Athenian people,[64] and this argument is intended to help him win the approval of the jury! Yet in the same speech there is reference to the speaker's contribution to the present Athenian navy. What this speech implies is that, although the Athenians were again beginning to rebuild their navy, there was no overwhelming popular anti-Spartan feeling. On the contrary, the oaths and the agreements with the Spartans and Pausanias whereby the democratic process at Athens was confirmed are still viewed as in force and binding in 396 B.C. In fact, in all the extant speeches that were delivered before Athenian juries between 403 and 396 B.C. there is not a single statement that implies or overtly expresses hostility to the Spartans unless it is linked with the *past* actions of Lysander. The speakers always expect the juries to respond positively to appeals based on the agreements made with the Spartans.

Current scholarly opinion[65] has suggested that after the Peloponnesian War there was no philo-Laconian party at Athens. This is undoubtedly true if one means by this that there was no one at Athens who placed the welfare of Sparta above his own city. Nevertheless, it is an oversimplification. The period from 403 to 396 was dominated by "the men of Piraeus." In particular Thrasyboulos' name is referred to more often in our sources than any other. He had already demonstrated a strong committal to the democratic form of government during the oligarchic revolution of 411 B.C. (Thuc., 8.72.4; 8.75, 76). Later, he led the counterrevolution against the Thirty, rejected an invitation to join them as one of the tyrants, took part in the negotiations with Pausanias and, finally, was instrumental in restoring the power of the assembly.[66] Although he lost at least one attempt, and possibly two, to reward all his supporters with Athenian citizenship (above, note 56), this probably won him more support among the common people than it lost for him. Certainly two years later Isokrates referred to him and Anytos as having the greatest power in the city.[67] Many of the existing speeches delivered during this period, and even later, refer favourably to Thrasyboulos and expect to evoke positive reactions from the jury for the speakers.[68] In fact Thrasyboulos' influence continued unchallenged through 396 when he was elected general for 395 (Plut., *Lys.* 29.1). Lysias, in a speech written about 399, outlines the general policy of the men of Piraeus in the following words:

> It is necessary to consider that of the men from Piraeus, those who have the greatest repute, have run special risks, and have done you the most good, already often have

---

[63] Isok., 18.29: . . . εἰς ὅρκους καὶ συνθήκας καταφύγομεν, ἃς εἰ Λακεδαιμόνιοι τολμῷεν παραβαίνειν . . . . Section 60 casts aspersions on Lysander and the Thirty; see J. H. Kuehn, "Die Amnestie von 403 v.Chr. im Reflex. der 18 Isokrates-Rede," *WS* 80 (1967) 31–73.

[64] Lysias, 18.11: ὅθεν Παυσανίας ἤρξατο εὔνους εἶναι τῷ δήμῳ παράδειγμα ποιούμενος πρὸς τοὺς ἄλλους Λακεδαιμονίους τὰς ἡμετέρας συμφορὰς τῆς τῶν τριάκοντα πονηρίας; cf. 15. Section 21 implies that Athens is again building a navy.

[65] Bruce (note 26 above), 52; Raphael Sealey, *Essays in Greek Politics* (New York 1965) 134, 135.

[66] *Hell.* 2.4.2, 35, 39; Plut., *Lys.* 27.3, 4; Diod. Sic., 14.32.5.

[67] Isok., 18.23: . . . Θρασύβουλος καὶ Ἄνυτος μέγιστον μὲν δυνάμενοι τῶν ἐν τῇ πόλει . . . .

[68] E.g., Aischines, 2.176; Dem., 19.280; 20.48; Isok., 18.28; Lysias, 25.28.

advised the majority of the people (τῷ ὑμετέρῳ πλήθει) to abide by the oaths and agreements (τοῖς ὅρκοις καὶ ταῖς συνθήκαις ἐμμένειν) in the belief that this is the defence of the democracy; for those from the city it offers freedom from fear for past occurrences, but for those from Piraeus, in this way, the constitution remains in force for the greatest period of time (25.28).

There can be little doubt that the platform referred to is that of Thrasyboulos and his friends; that platform was clearly based on compliance with the treaties made in 404 and 403 B.C. Thrasyboulos, too, must have viewed Sparta under the leadership of Pausanias as the guarantor of the continuance of the democratic constitution at Athens.

In the years following 398 there was increased anti-Spartan agitation at Athens set in motion by Epikrates and Kephalos.[69] Nevertheless, in 396 Thrasyboulos and his party criticized one particular undertaking (the secret expedition of Demainetos) on the grounds that it would create danger for the city by exposing Athens to the anger of the Spartans (*Hell. Oxy.* 1.2, 3). In consequence they persuaded the assembly to pacify the Spartans. Later that same year Thrasyboulos was re-elected as a general for what was to be a very eventful year. Late in 396 or early 395 B.C. Lysander returned from Asia where he had been snubbed by Agesilaos. At odds, now, with both kings, he determined to rebuild his prestige and attempt to overthrow the kingship and replace it with an elected monarch. The growing dispute with Thebes provided an excellent opportunity to demonstrate once again his martial prowess. He became embroiled in that conflict as a commander of a Spartan invading force which made an attack on Haliartos. He died there fighting against the Thebans.[70]

There were two other armies in the field that day, ostensibly one on each side. Pausanias' army was supposed to support Lysander according to instructions received by a letter (which happened to fall into Theban hands). The Athenian army led by Thrasyboulos had been sent to support the Thebans. Neither army did much fighting, though the excuses offered vary from source to source.[71] There are certain oddities about the Spartan conduct of this campaign. First, the Spartans rarely if ever sent both kings away from Sparta at the same time (*Respub. Lac.* 13, 15). Agesilaos was already in Asia, so the command of Pausanias is extraordinary, since Sparta could not claim to find itself in a dire emergency. Second, when a king was in the field he was commander-in-chief, yet in this instance we find Lysander dispatching the orders to Pausanias (Plut., *Lys.* 28.2). Third, after the battle and death of Lysander, Pausanias did not even attempt to defend himself, but went to live as a suppliant in Tegea (*Hell.* 3.5.25). Fourth, the charge brought against him did not accuse him merely of negligence but also of freeing the Athenian *demos* after having taken it in Piraeus (ὅτι τὸν δῆμον τῶν Ἀθηναίων ... ἀνῆκε). All of this becomes intelligible when one recognizes that the control of Spartan policy had suddenly returned to the friends of Lysander.

This change in Spartan politics had its effect on Athens. Shortly after Lysander went to Phokis to collect an army for the invasion of Boiotia, Thebes began overtures to Athens for an alliance.[72] The party of Thrasyboulos was obviously in a dilemma. They had certain obligations to Pausanias and his friends for the settlement in 403 and they owed Thebes repayment for her early support of the Athenian exiles. On the other hand the radical anti-Spartans must have been delightd with the recent developments. It has been suggested[73] that at this point Thrasyboulos himself proposed the

---

[69] See Sealey (note 65 above), and I. A. F. Bruce, "Athenian Embassies in the early Fourth Century B.C.," *Historia* 15 (1966) 272–281, and "Athenian Foreign Policy in 396–395 B.C.," *CJ* 18 (1963) 289–295.

[70] *Hell.* 3.4.20; 3.5.17–25; Diod. Sic., 14.13.1–8; Plut., *Lys.* 24.2; 27.1–29.3.

[71] *Ibid.* See also Diod. Sic., 14.81.1–3.

[72] *Hell.* 3.5.7: ἐπεί γε μὴν δῆλον τοῖς Θηβαίοις ἐγένετο ὅτι ἐμβαλοῖεν οἱ Λακεδαιμόνιοι εἰς τὴν χώραν αὐτῶν, πρέσβεις ἔπεμψαν Ἀθήναζε . . . .

[73] Sealy (note 65 above), 134 and note 8. The inscription in M. N. Tod, *Greek Historical Inscriptions* 2 (Oxford 1948) 101 does not give any indication of who moved the treaty of alliance.

alliance with Thebes. If he did so, he moved the decree of alliance with hesitation and only because as a politician he recognized that it was the overwhelming sentiment of the electorate. Xenophon's words surely convey both the overwhelming support of the assembly for an alliance with Thebes and Thrasyboulos' own reservations:

> Very many (πάμπολλοι) of the Athenians spoke in favour of the proposal, but all voted to aid them (the Thebans). Thrasyboulos after having reported the decree to them (ἀποκρινάμενος τὸ ψήφισμα) also pointed out that, although the Piraeus was unwalled, they (the Athenians) would run a risk to repay to them (the Thebans) a greater favour than they (the Athenians) had received. "For you," he said, "did not campaign against us, but we will fight with you against them if they should go against you" (*Hell.* 3.5.16).

What had happened to bring about such a sudden, unanimous and dramatic change in Athenian attitudes? Xenophon says merely that the Athenians were eager for war thinking it their right to rule (*Hell.* 3.5.2: νομίζοντες αὐτῶν τὸ ἄρχειν εἶναι). But this is surely insufficient; for the Athenians had held this view from early in the fifth century. Nor would it have disappeared when they lost the Peloponnesian War, and yet they lived quietly and had good relations with Sparta for almost a decade. There had been occasional flare-ups of anti-Spartan activity but these had usually been the result of a small group's machinations and did not have the formal backing of the assembly (e.g., *Hell. Oxy.* 2.1, 2). The unanimity of feeling at this time resulted from an embassy that had been sent to the Spartans to ask them not to go to war with Thebes but to submit their grievances to arbitration. Pausanias (3.9.11) records that the Lakedaimonians sent the embassy away in anger. This embassy, which had the official approval of the Athenian assembly, was probably the initial response of Thrasyboulos and the ruling party to the dilemma in which they found themselves. The treatment of the embassy left Thrasyboulos with no other immediate choice but to follow the dictates of the assembly, which was now clearly in the control of the anti-Spartan extremists, Epikrates and Kephalos, and go to the aid of the Thebans.

Thrasyboulos seems to have been tardy in arriving at the field of battle (*Hell.* 3.5.22). In fact, one account suggests that he was in Thebes guarding the city (Plut., *Lys.* 28.3). Another suggests that he was delaying his arrival until the Spartans should attack, but Pausanias could not attack lest he find himself caught between two armies (Pausanias, 3.5.4). The point is that the appearance of Thrasyboulos kept Pausanias from going to the aid of the other Spartan army and from engaging the Thebans on the following days. Neither wished to attack an old friend in inter-state politics. At the same time neither was particularly enthusiastic about following the new directions which the policies of their home states were taking. The battle of Haliartos thus brought about the death of Lysander, the exile of Pausanias and the decline of Thrasyboulos' influence at Athens. For with Pausanias gone from Sparta, there was no further restraining influence upon the Spartans; the Athenians were forced to look to themselves for the continued existence of the democratic form of government. Thrasyboulos' platform of non-aggression toward the Spartans had now backfired and become outmoded. Although he himself recognized this and began to emphasize a different policy, for the moment (i.e., 395) attacks were made on him in the public courts.[74] His temporary decline was hastened by the defeat of the Spartans at Knidos, the appearance of Konon with a large fleet at Athens, and the rebuilding of the walls in 394 B.C.[75]

---

[74] Lysias, 15.1; 16.15. For his later career see R. Seager, "Thrasybulus, Conon and Athenian Imperialism 396–386 B.C.," *JHS* 87 (1967) 95–115, and S. Perlman, "Athenian Imperial Expansion in the early Fourth Century," *CP* 63 (1968) 257–267.

[75] *Hell.* 4.3.10–13; Diod. Sic., 14.85.2. Thrasyboulos probably set the rebuilding of the walls in motion while still in office. See Tod, *GHI* 2.107A.

One of these attacks is contained in a speech directed against Alkibiades, the son of the Athenian general of the latter part of the Peloponnesian War. The father was a friend of Thrasyboulos[76] and the son had served at Haliartos. He was now directly under attack, in a speech ascribed to Lysias' pen,[77] for serving in the cavalry when, according to his property qualifications, he should have been serving in the hoplite infantry. The general (namely, Thrasyboulos) is indirectly under attack for allowing this transgression of the rules of military discipline and social organization. This appears to be the first criticism of Thrasyboulos in a forensic speech since 402 B.C. and it is connected with the battle at Haliartos. What is even more interesting for our immediate purpose is a statement (by the prosecution) that this is the first indictment of someone for failing to do his duty to the state since the Athenians made peace (i.e., 404/3 B.C.).[78] What this suggests is that for almost the past decade no one has been put on trial for προδοσία at Athens. It also emphasizes that in 395 the Athenians were once more very conscious of their own role in Greek affairs and did not intend to remain passive any longer.

Before we draw any further conclusions about the period in question, it is necessary to consider some of the ramifications of the trial of Sokrates. His trial has often been viewed as part of the political aftermath of the rule of the Thirty. But this, too, is an oversimplification. The main accusers, as is well known, were Meletos and Anytos (Diog. Laert., 2.38), one of those who appear to be allied with Thrasyboulos. Meletos (Andokides, 1.94, 101) was a scoundrel who had supported much that was done by the Thirty. Anytos,[79] a traditionalist and conservative, and a supporter of Theramenes, continued to protect supporters of the Thirty, even after he joined the exiles. On the other hand Sokrates had openly defied the Thirty and could never have been convicted on a charge of pro-Spartanism, before a popular Athenian jury, even if the amnesty had not been in force. Hence, the charge against him was a religious one,[80] and, even though he had incurred the enmity of many powerful Athenians, the only possibility of conviction before an Athenian court lay in charges other than political ones. It is interesting to note that another trial based on religious grounds with Meletos as prosecutor (that of Andokides and the Mysteries) took place in the same year. Andokides took refuge behind the amnesty and was acquitted; Sokrates addressed himself to the charges and lost.

We must conclude then that the evidence from the law courts, the politics of Athens' leading men and the accounts of the ancient historians all imply that between 403 and 395 B.C. no one could be or was condemned for pro-Spartanism. The Athenians, having agreed to have the same friends and enemies as Sparta, followed a policy of pacification toward their conquerors. They supported them with troops on a number of campaigns,[81] and, as long as Pausanias was the dominant figure in Spartan policy affecting the mainland states, avoided antagonizing the Lakedaimonians. They felt no threat to their internal political processes and followed a policy of appeasement while they tried to recover from the ordeal of the Peloponnesian War. In fact, they allowed former supporters of the Thirty to take part in government and even elected them to positions of importance.[82] However, with the return of Lysander to Sparta in 395, they lost their sense of well-being

[76] Thuc., 8.81.1; Plut., *Alc.* 26.6.

[77] Lysias, 14 and 15. See especially 15.1.

[78] The expression (14.4) ἐξ οὗ τὴν εἰρήνην ἐποιησάμεθα could refer either to the original peace treaty signed between Athens and Sparta in 404 (which is not very likely when one considers the events of the succeeding months) or the amnesty and final settlement with Sparta in 403.

[79] Aristotle, *Ath. Pol.* 34.3; Plato, *Meno* 92–94; Isok., 18.23; Lysias, 13.78, 79. At the trial of Andokides (1.150) Anytos was one of his supporters. I think M. I. Finley, *Democracy Ancient and Modern* (London 1973) 91, probably overemphasizes the role of Anytos as an enforcer of the amnesty. From the references just cited, it would appear that his insistence on observing the amnesty was perhaps somewhat one-sided (i.e., to the benefit of supporters of the Thirty).

[80] *Mem.* 1.1.1 and Diog. Laert., 2.40.

[81] *Hell.* 3.1.4; 3.2.25; Diod. Sic., 14.87.7.   [82] Lysias, 16.8; Aristotle, *Ath. Pol.* 38.4.

and once again became embroiled in external conflicts. It was only at this point that banishment and exile became a part of the political scene at Athens.[83]

This brings us to the main problem connected with the life of Xenophon—the date and reason for his exile from Athens. In view of the late date of any other sources (Diogenes Laertios, Pausanias) Xenophon's own words about his banishment must take precedence. In *Anabasis*[84] he links his exile with the battle of Koronea:

τὸ δὲ τῆς Ἀρτέμιδος τῆς Ἐφεσίας, ὅτ' ἀπήει σὺν Ἀγησιλάῳ ἐκ τῆς Ἀσίας τὴν εἰς Βοιωτοὺς ὁδόν, καταλείπει παρὰ Μεγαβύζῳ τῷ τῆς Ἀρτέμιδος νεωκόρῳ, ὅτι αὐτὸς κινδυνεύσων ἐδόκει ἰέναι, καὶ ἐπέστειλεν, ἢν μὲν αὐτὸς σωθῇ, αὐτῷ ἀποδοῦναι· ἢν δέ τι πάθῃ, ἀναθεῖναι ποιησάμενον τῇ Ἀρτέμιδι ὅτι οἴοιτο χαριεῖσθαι τῇ θεῷ. Ἐπειδὴ δ' ἔφευγεν ὁ Ξενοφῶν, κατοικοῦντος ἤδη αὐτοῦ ἐν Σκιλλοῦντι . . . .

He indicates that because he regarded the campaign of Agesilaos to be against the Thebans (τὴν εἰς Βοιωτοὺς ὁδόν) he could foresee only two possibilities for himself—either personal injury of which the ultimate end might be death (ὅτι αὐτὸς κινδυνεύσων ἐδόκει ἰέναι) or an eventual safe return to Asia (ἢν μὲν αὐτὸς σωθῇ).[85] Acting on this analysis he left Artemis' share of the tithe with the priest in Ephesos and ordered that, in the latter event, it should be returned to him, but, if the former happened, the priest was to make a suitable dedication to the goddess. Ἐπειδὴ δέ signifies that neither of the anticipated alternatives took place but rather an unexpected situation developed—namely, Xenophon was exiled from Athens. If this had taken place before the battle it would have been taken into account when the earlier calculations were made. Therefore, one must conclude that Xenophon was not informed of his exile until after the battle of Koronea and that in his mind the two events were connected. Second, both this passage and one by Pausanias (below, note 90) link the gift of the estate at Skillos with his exile. As was demonstrated above (p. 108), the gift of the estate did not occur until 392 B.C. or later. Finally one should consider for a moment the matter of the dedication to Apollo. According to Xenophon this dedication was made in the treasury of the Athenians at Delphi, probably, as we have seen, in the fall of 394. Whether he could or would wish to make a dedication at this treasury after being exiled is not certain, but it seems unlikely.

The later testimonies about Xenophon's exile add some small details and must be considered in the light of Xenophon's own words. Diogenes Laertios' account[86] makes several points, some of them apparently contradictory. First, the exile took place after he had handed over the troops to Agesilaos and become his close friend. Second, the vague phrase παρ' ὃν καιρόν suggests that Diogenes Laertios is himself not quite certain exactly when the banishment took place, but only that it had something to do with Agesilaos' friendship and the increasing expression of anti-Spartan feeling at Athens. The phrase does not imply that the banishment necessarily occurred before the battle of Koronea, which is the next significant event to be recorded in the life of Xenophon. Rather it suggests that the friendship with Agesilaos, to which special reference has just been made, was the critical factor in what follows, namely, banishment for pro-Spartanism (ἐπὶ Λακωνισμῷ). After the Theban-Athenian alliance of 395 and Koronea in 394, this charge amounted to προδοσία, for which the penalty was banishment and confiscation of property (*Hell.* 1.7.22). Before that, as has been shown, such a charge could not have any meaning in an Athenian court or assembly, nor is it likely that it would even have been entertained.

[83] E.g., Andokides, 3; Philochorus, *FGrHist* 328 F149; Dem., 19.191; Pausanias, 6.17.3.
[84] *An.* 5.3.4—7. See note 34 (above) for the first part of the quotation.
[85] That a return to Asia after dealing with the Thebans was the contemplated course of action is clear from *Hell.* 4.2.3, 4.
[86] Diog. Laert., 2.51: ἧκεν εἰς Ἀσίαν πρὸς Ἀγησίλαον τὸν τῶν Λακεδαιμονίων βασιλέα, μισθοῦ τοὺς Κύρου στρατιώτας αὐτῷ παρασχών· φίλος τ'ἦν εἰς ὑπερβολήν. παρ' ὃν καιρὸν ἐπὶ Λακωνισμῷ φυγὴν ὑπ' Ἀθηναίων κατεγνώσθη.

Third, he quotes Istros[87] that Xenophon was banished by a decree of Euboulos and brought back by a decree of the same man. That Euboulos brought about the lifting of the banishment has already been stated, but that he also originally moved the decree to have him banished seems unlikely.[88] H. R. Breitenbach[89] has suggested that there is confusion here between the name of the eponymous archon of the year 394/3 in which Xenophon was probably banished, Euboulides, and the man mentioned in Diogenes Laertios. Whether this is what happened can never be determined with absolute certainty, but this explanation does seem plausible in light of the similarity of the two names.

Finally, Diogenes Laertios (2.58) quotes one of his own epigrams which seems to contradict what he has already said about the exile; for it intimates that friendship with Cyrus was the main reason for Xenophon's expulsion from Athens. The explanation for the two seemingly divergent views in the same author is to be found in their origins. When he discusses the exile, Diogenes Laertios is relying on Xenophon's own words in the *Anabasis* and on the older sources, Deinarchos, Aristotle and Demetrios of Magnesia (2.50, 52, 55). The epigram on the other hand expresses the popular view that was current at the time when Diogenes was active as a writer. This epigram represents a second tradition developed somewhat later in antiquity, possibly from the passage in *Anabasis* 3.1.4, and is also found expressed in Pausanias[90] and Dio Chrysostomos.[91] The passage in Pausanias reveals the romanticized misunderstanding under which this second tradition developed; for it suggests that Xenophon favoured Cyrus who was hostile to the *demos* and opposed Artaxerxes who was supposed to be favourable to Athens. As Grote correctly pointed out,[92] at the time of the expedition of the Ten Thousand both Cyrus and Artaxerxes were hostile to the Athenians. It was only after warfare between the Spartans and the Persians seriously erupted in Asia Minor and Cyrus was already dead that the Persians indicated any goodwill to the Athenians. This was not so much a matter of favour to Athens as support for Konon that came from the satraps, Pharnabazos and Tiribazos, rather than the king himself. The first tangible evidence of Persian support for Athens came in 394 when Konon appeared to rebuild the walls with the help of the fleet and Persian money. All this demonstrates that the tradition that links Xenophon's exile with his friendship with Cyrus is a very romanticized one and that without the events of 394 and his part in them his banishment would probably not have taken place.

On the other hand, after 394 Thrasyboulos, of whom Xenophon speaks admiringly (*Hell.* 4.8.31) had lost control of Athenian policy or, as a result of the treatment accorded Pausanias by his home state, changed his attitude to the Spartans. At this time an alliance with Persia had become an option. With Konon and the fleet in Piraeus, what had formerly appeared as a romantic adventure (the expedition of Cyrus) now took on the appearance of an international incident. At this point in Athenian history both charges, pro-Spartanism and friendship with Cyrus, which formerly made no legal and political sense, could now be pressed and probably were a part of the prosecution's attack on Xenophon.

It remains to consider a few objections that have been raised against the date 394/3 B.C. Xenophon himself has given rise to some of the later speculation by the thoughts he ascribes to

---

[87] 2.59. If this is the Atthidographer (cf. *FGrHist* 334 F32) it means that he may well have discussed more than the prehistory of Attica.

[88] Euboulos was born about 405. Hence he was about 11 years old in 394. See G. L. Cawkwell, "Eubulus," *JHS* 83 (1963) 47–67.

[89] Note 2 (above) 1575.

[90] 5.6.4: ἐδιώχθη δὲ ὁ Ξενοφῶν ὑπὸ Ἀθηναίων ὡς ἐπὶ βασιλέα τῶν Περσῶν σφίσιν εὔνουν ὄντα στρατείας μετασχὼν Κύρῳ πολεμιωτάτῳ τοῦ δήμου.

[91] *Or.* 8.1: Ξενοφῶν δὲ ἔφευγε διὰ τὴν μετὰ Κύρου στρατείαν. J. A. Scott, "Xenophon and Dio Chrysostom," *CW* 18 (1924) 44.

[92] G. Grote, *History of Greece* 7.343 note 1.

Sokrates in advising him to consult the oracle at Delphi (ὑποπτεύσας μή τι πρὸς τῆς πόλεως ὑπαί-
τιον εἴη Κύρῳ φίλον γενέσθαι, *An.* 3.1.4). First, the gist of these remarks is only that friendship
with Cyrus *might* be a cause for ill-will against Xenophon, not that it actually was. Second, as
Sokrates' thoughts they must be considered to share the apologetic nature of most of the other
Sokratic works in the Xenophontean corpus. As H. R. Breitenbach has said,[93] this passage seeks to
defend Sokrates against the charge of corrupting the youth of Athens by showing that he valued
the attitudes of his home state and in difficult positions relied on the guidance of conventional religion. Xenophon mentions this conversation primarily to separate his own exile and reputation at
Athens from the influence of Sokrates. If the Athenians had found fault with the author's conduct
this was not to be ascribed to the teachings of the philosopher; for he was always concerned that
the future course of his pupils should also be the correct one in the eyes of his fellow citizens.[94]
Thus this passage has little value for the consideration of the date of Xenophon's exile. It does,
however, indicate the special concern that Xenophon had for his great teacher.

A second objection has been raised on the basis of *Anabasis* 7.7.57: Ξενοφῶν δὲ οὐ προσῄει,
ἀλλὰ φανερὸς ἦν οἴκαδε παρασκευαζόμενος· οὐ γάρ πω ψῆφος αὐτῷ ἐπῆκτο Ἀθήνησι περὶ φυγῆς.
It has been suggested that οὐ γάρ πω could hardly pertain to the period of five years between 399,
when this activity took place, and 394.[95] However, to consider a period of five years as encom-
passed in οὔπω from a perspective of twenty-five or thirty years later (assuming that the *Anabasis*
was published in the latter part of the third decade)[96] is surely not improbable. All this passage
really tells us is that he had not been banished in the spring of 399 when he returned with the
army to Asia.

A third objection, aimed at the point made above that no one could be exiled for being philo-
Spartan before 396, is based on *Hell.* 3.1.4. Thibron had asked for troops from Athens for the
campaign in Asia. The Athenians sent him 300 cavalry νομίζοντες κέρδος τῷ δήμῳ, εἰ ἀποδημοῖεν
καὶ ἐναπόλοιντο. To argue that this statement indicates anti-Spartan feeling at Athens, as some
have done,[97] is to misplace the emphasis. What the passage does express is that there was still a
deep-seated suspicion on the part of the commons toward the supporters of the Thirty. This is a
matter of internal hostility and has only little to do with the *demos'* attitude to Sparta. After all they
did send troops (cavalry) at this time and again (hoplites) to accompany Agis in 398.

Our discussion, then, has led to the conclusion that Xenophon's exile must have taken place
after Koronea in 394 B.C. From the time he left Athens in 401 until the battle against the Thebans
and their allies it is unlikely, though not impossible, that he returned to Athens. When he left, he
was still undistinguished and his exploits with the Ten Thousand would require some time to
become recognized. The implications for his home state of his part in the expedition would also
not be apparent immediately. Moreover, during this time Athens followed a policy of appeasement until 395. The extant speeches from jury trials of this period reflect a genuine desire on the

---

[93] Note 2 (above) 1773–1774. W. P. Henry, *Greek Historical Writing* 194–200, has discussed how a defense of Socrates is
inherent in the account in *Hell.* 1.7.1–16.

[94] For an analysis of a similar kind of apology that the author advances in the *Memorabilia* see H. Erbse, "Die Architek-
tonik im Aufbau von Xenophons Memorabilien," *Hermes* 89 (1961) 257–287.

[95] B. Krüger, "Prüfungen der Niebuhrischen Ansichten," *Histor. Philol. Studien* 1 (1850) 244 ff. and 2 (1851) 276 ff.,
quoted by Baden (note 1 above) 6, and Breitenbach (note 2 above) 1575.

[96] The apologetic nature of the work requires that certain views about the actions of the army and its generals should
have become known and circulated throughout the Greek States. (See A. Gwynn, "Xenophon and Sophaenetus," *CQ*
18 [1929] 39–40 and J. Mesk, "Die Tendenz der Xenophontischen Anabasis," *WS* 43 [1922–23] 136–146.) This would
require a considerable amount of time. In addition, the indications about the ages of his sons (*An.* 5.3.10), and the
special explanation for his audience, that the Spartans were the most powerful (6.6.9), which implies that
this is no longer the case, suggest a date of composition in the 370s or even later. For a different approach see A.
Kappelmacher, "Xenophon und Isokrates," *WS* 43 (1922) 212–213.

[97] Baden (note 1 above) 45.

part of the populace to make the democratic process work. Pausanias and his Spartan friends were the guarantors that the assembly would remain the final authority in Athenian affairs. Most of the leading politicians at Athens (i.e., the men of Piraeus) worked in concord with Spartan moderates and were prevented from carrying out any overt forms of anti-Spartan legislation or policy by the threat that such actions would cause Sparta to revive and support the policies of Lysander. When control of Spartan policy did return to Lysander and his friends, and shortly thereafter Konon managed to swing Persian support to the Athenians (albeit for only a short time), attacks were soon made on important political figures as part of the struggle for control of Athenian policy. It is in these circumstances and at this time that the explicit statements by ancient writers about Xenophon's exile make sense. It is probable that he was banished from his home state in the archonship of Euboulides late in 394 or early in 393. For absolute certainty we need, what for Malcolm McGregor was always definitive in solving problems in Greek History, an inscription.

Champlain College, Lennoxville   PETER J. RAHN

ANDOCIDES AND THUCYDIDES

There is little doubt that Thucydides knew of Andocides; he may even have known him. And yet, he did not mention him by name even in the one passage[1] in which he clearly refers to him. One wonders whether this was written after Andocides delivered (and published) the speech[2] in which he revealed the famous scene in prison,[3] an early case of plea-bargaining. There is a slight but perhaps not insignificant link between the accounts given by Andocides and Thucydides; both authors emphasize the calming effect the revelations of Andocides had on the hysterical atmosphere prevailing at that time in Athens.[4] Thucydides may not have believed all that Andocides had said, but he surely agreed with him that he had saved the situation at that time. It is, therefore, the more remarkable that Thucydides kept from his readers the identity of this man, if he knew it.[5]

Less than ten years after the speech on the Mysteries (1), Andocides delivered (and presumably published) his oration on Peace with the Lacedaemonians (3) which shows clearly, I think, that he had read Thucydides. At the very beginning of the speech (3.2), he invited his audience to look back at their peaceful relations with the Lacedaemonians in the past, because one must use the past as containing sure signs (τεκμήρια) of the things to be in the future (περὶ τῶν μελλόντων ἔσεσθαι). This is exactly what Thucydides claimed to be his great contribution:[6] those who wish to observe the past and what will once again happen in the future (τῶν μελλόντων ἔσεσθαι) ". . . will consider my work sufficiently useful." Umberto Albini[7] has called attention to the passage in Thucydides (un concetto tucidideo) and to other similar passages in the same speech of Andocides[8] and in the later works of other orators. Special consideration deserves a statement by Lysias[9] because it reflects the same attitude to the utility of historical knowledge and employs the same terminology as do Thucydides and Andocides; unfortunately, the speech which may be dated "soon after"[10] 403 B.C., is considered by Kenneth Dover[11] a hypothetical defence, "a paradigm of the defence speeches which Lysias wrote for men who remained in the city."[12] The speaker urges the court to keep in mind[13] what happened (γεγενημένων) under the Thirty in order to take better counsel (ἄμεινον . . . βουλεύσασθαι). After giving the pertinent historical evidence, he adds[14] the advice: using the examples of previous events (τοῖς πρότερον γεγενημένοις παραδείγμασι χρωμένους) you must take counsel concerning what will happen in the future (χρὴ . . .

---

[1] Thuc., 6.60.2.   [2] Andoc., 1.   [3] Andoc., 1.48–69.
[4] Thuc., 6.60.3 and 5 = Andoc., 1.51, 56, 58, 59, 66, 68, with the repeated mention of suspicion, ὑποψία.
[5] This point has been neglected by R. Seager, *Historia* 27 (1978) 223.
[6] Thuc., 1.22.4.
[7] Umberto Albini, ed., Andocide, *De pace* (Florence 1964) 55.
[8] Andoc., 3.29.
[9] Lys., 25.21–23.
[10] Donald Lateiner, *Lysias and Athenian Politics* (unpublished Stanford Dissertation 1971) 79.
[11] Kenneth Dover, *Lysias and the Corpus Lysiacum* (Berkeley 1968) 189.
[12] Lateiner, (above, note 10) 85.   [13] Lys., 25.21.   [14] Lys., 25.23.

βουλεύεσθαι περὶ τῶν μελλόντων ἔσεσθαι). George Kennedy, in his discussion of Andocides 3,[15] referred to a passage in Aristotle's *Rhetoric*[16] which looks like a paraphrase of the statements in the orators, and which he considered "derived from sophistic rhetoricians." If this were true, Thucydides would be addressing himself to political orators and would be telling them that his work will not only be useful to them as a reliable record of past events which in some way will again take place in the future, but that in fact it will be a lasting possession (κτῆμα ἐς αἰεί—a storehouse) rather than a beautiful composition to be heard and enjoyed but once.

The realization that Andocides and Lysias, and of course Isocrates,[17] accepted Thucydides' concept of the utility of history confirms the traditional interpretation of the historian's famous statement.[18] Even more important is the application of this concept by Andocides to the issue at hand, namely to the Peace with the Lacedaemonians. The orator chose the same period of Athenian history to show that the Athenians prospered whenever they were at peace with the Spartans[19] as Thucydides had chosen[20] to reveal the Athenians as daring and aggressive and the Spartans as quiet and conservative—just as the Corinthian had described them.[21] Evidently, the same events can be made to teach different lessons, and I think that Andocides was quite aware of this, and so was Isocrates after him.[22]

Of all the pleas for peace of the Classical Period,[23] Andocides' alone develops the theme that Athens should make peace with Sparta because the Athenians benefitted greatly in the past whenever they were at peace with the Lacedaemonians. Considering the novelty of this argument, it is not surprising that Andocides was less accurate than persuasive; he did not win his argument, and most modern readers have rejected his account because it is very much at variance with that of Thucydides and Ephorus.[24] Only Wesley Thompson has made a valiant and on the whole successful attempt "to show that Andocides' account is not really so confused and erroneous as scholars have imagined."[25] The two worst mistakes are the statements[26] that it was Miltiades the son of Cimon (and not Cimon the son of Miltiades) who brought about the peace which closed the war which raged in Euboea (and not in Boeotia). Thompson suggested[27] that Andocides reversed by mistake the "War in Euboea" and the "War because of Aegina," while Johan Henrik Schreiber defended the "Euboean War."[28] The confusion of Cimon with his father is the more perplexing because the orator Aeschines repeated the entire passage of Andocides[29] including this obvious mistake.[30]

Aeschines defended the Peace of Philocrates by reviewing the events of Athenian history since the victory of Salamis in order to show that whenever Athens was at peace, the Athenian democracy was well off. This historical summary begins earlier and ends later than the account of Andocides, but for the period covered by Andocides Aeschines follows him very closely, adding

[15] George Kennedy, *AJP* 79 (1958) 41.

[16] Arist., *Rh.* 3.16.11 = 1417b.

[17] C. H. Wilson, *Greece and Rome* 13 (1966) 56.

[18] See now W. R. Connor, *CJ* 72 (1977) 289–298, and R. Leslie, *ibidem* 342–347.

[19] Andoc., 3.3–9.

[20] Thuc., 1.89–117.

[21] Thuc., 1.70.2–3.

[22] Isoc., 1.34; 2.35; 4.141; 6.59, all mentioned by Albini, and 8.11.

[23] Ar., *Ach.* and *Pax*; Xen., *Hell.* 6.3 (Kallias' speech); Isoc., *De Pace*.

[24] Diodorus; see now H. D. Westlake, *Phoenix* 31 (1977) 325–329.

[25] Wesley Thompson, *TAPA* 98 (1967) 489.

[26] Andoc., 3.3.

[27] Thompson, 488.

[28] Johan Henrik Schreiber, *SymbOslo* 51 (1976) 28.

[29] Andoc., 3.3–9.

[30] Aeschines, 2.172–176.

nothing and using often the very same words.[31] The emphasis of Aeschines is, however, on peace in general, and on Athenian Democracy in particular, while Andocides stresses the benefits which the Athenians enjoyed whenever they were at peace with the Lacedaemonians.

Although Aeschines may have used Andocides directly, both orators follow in substance the Athenian popular tradition which Thucydides already sought to correct. This is indicated by a number of significant agreements between Andocides and Thucydides. Both mention the possession of Megara and Pega,[32] the Five Years' Peace,[33] the building of the walls,[34] and the Thirty Years' Peace;[35] what is more striking, there are several correspondences between the second speech of Pericles[36] and the speech of Andocides[37] showing that both relied here on the popular and patriotic tradition concerning the greatness of Athens: the treasure of coined silver on the Acropolis,[38] the numbers of horsemen, archers and triremes,[39] and the revenue from the tribute.[40] Thompson, who examined these details carefully, came to the conclusion that Andocides used the book of Hellanicus,[41] and Schreiber also offers Hellanicus as a source for the "popular version of Athenian history."[42] I think both Andocides and Hellanicus relied on what Aristotle called the Populars (δημοτικοί), and that Thucydides' criticism of Hellanicus[43] would apply equally well to the accounts given by Andocides and Aeschines.

One of the reasons for attributing the "ancient tradition" represented by Andocides (and Theopompus) to Hellanicus was Thompson's decision that this account must be the work of a chronographer who made "a serious effort to order the events of the Pentekontaetia in a chronological sequence,"[44] but he did not consider for a moment that Andocides and Theopompus may have the correct story of Cimon's ostracism, return and death. And yet, many years ago, I tried to show that Thucydides agreed with the story,[45] and Schreiber has gone a long way in the same direction.[46]

The preceding sketchy remarks are offered to a friend of forty years who has taught us a great deal about the history of the very period treated by Thucydides and Andocides, the Pentekontaetia. My modest conclusions are: Andocides knew the history of Thucydides, he accepted Thucydides' view of the utility of history, but he offered a summary of Athenian history which followed the very same popular tradition which Thucydides had set out to correct.[47]

Stanford University   A. E. RAUBITSCHEK

[31] See Thompson, 483, note 2.

[32] Thuc., 1.103.4 = Andoc., 3.3.

[33] Thuc., 1.112.1 = Andoc., 3.4.

[34] Thuc., 1.107.1 and 108.3 = Andoc., 3.5.

[35] Thuc., 1.115.1 = Andoc., 3.6.

[36] Thuc., 2.13.

[37] Andoc., 3.

[38] Thuc., 2.13.3 = Andoc., 3.7 and 8.

[39] Thuc., 2.13.8 = Andoc., 3.7 and 8.

[40] Thuc., 2.13.3 = Andoc., 3.9.

[41] Thompson, (above, note 25) 483–490.

[42] Schreiber, 29 (above, note 28) and especially in a still unpublished monograph entitled "Kimon-Studies."

[43] Thuc., 1.97.2.

[44] Thompson, 489.

[45] A. E. Raubitschek, *Historia* 3 (1955) 370–380; *AJA* 70 (1960) 37–38.

[46] Johan Henrik Schreiber, *SymbOslo* 52 (1977) 29–36.

[47] I have benefitted greatly from the criticism generously offered to me by Bob Connor, David Lewis, Lionel Pearson, Wesley Thompson; how fortunate to have such friends!

EPHIALTES, *EISANGELIA*, AND THE COUNCIL

Omne *ignotum pro magnifico.* The earliest extant author to talk about the attack of Ephialtes on the Areopagite Council is Aristotle. Although the work of Ephialtes aroused controversy in his lifetime, there is no indication that it continued to be discussed later in the fifth century. It seems to have become a subject of argument and reconstruction about 356 when Isokrates composed his speech *Areopagitikos.*[1] Aristotle has transmitted the wisdom of his contemporaries, and his account of the reforms of Ephialtes (*Ath. Pol.* 25.2) is in one way precise and in another unhelpful. He says that Ephialtes took some powers away from the Areopagite Council and gave some of them to the Five Hundred and the others to the Assembly and the *dikasteria.* He fails to specify what these powers were, beyond calling them "additional" and saying that in virtue of them the Areopagos had exercised guardianship of the constitution, but such language sounds like a cover for ignorance.

Hence, in modern times a question: What were the powers transferred by Ephialtes to the other organs? Current hypotheses may be divided into two classes. On the one hand some scholars suppose that Ephialtes carried out extensive reforms in a conscious and somewhat doctrinaire attempt to transform Athenian public life.[2] Others, however, have tried to discover a precise and limited change which may be attributed to Ephialtes, a change which may have had wider effects than its author anticipated but did not amount to a general overhaul of the constitution. Thus H. T. Wade-Gery has argued that Ephialtes transformed the popular court from a court of appeal to a court of first instance.[3] I have urged that the reforms of Ephialtes were solely concerned with *euthynai,* the procedure for calling officals to account when they laid down office.[4] Recently, however, P. J. Rhodes has offered a detailed defense of the larger conception of the reformer's work.[5] While he accepts the hypothesis, derived from W. S. Ferguson, about *euthynai,* he also holds that Ephialtes transferred extensive judicial functions from the Areopagos to the Council of Five Hundred. Until 462, he supposes, the latter body was merely probouleutic; its judicial competence was limited to internal discipline and *dokimasia* of next year's councillors. Until that date, on this hypothesis, the Council of the Areopagos had judicial competence for *eisangeliai* and for *dokimasia* of archons and it judged a group of cases which Rhodes has classified together as "official jurisdiction." But, he holds, Ephialtes transferred jurisdiction of these three kinds (*eisangelia, dokimasia* of archons, "official jurisdiction") to the Council of Five Hundred.

---

[1] E. Ruschenbusch, "Ephialtes," *Historia* 15 (1966) 369–376.

[2] For an outstandingly clear statement of this view, see F. Schachermeyr, *Perikles* (Stuttgart, Berlin, Köln, Mainz 1969) 25–33. C. Hignett entitled a chapter of his *History of the Athenian Constitution* (Oxford 1952) "The Revolution of 462."

[3] *Essays in Greek History* (Oxford 1958) 180–200.

[4] "Ephialtes," *CP* 59 (1964) 11–22 = *Essays in Greek Politics* (New York 1967) 42–58.

[5] *The Athenian Boule* (Oxford 1972) 144–207; a summary of the changes attributed to Ephialtes is given on pages 203–205.

The thesis is impressively argued and the present paper sets out to test it. It is a pleasure to offer such an inquiry to a scholar who has welcomed constantly the expression of divergent views and who has concentrated attention on large issues and on the large implications of apparently small issues. Reconstruction of the work of Ephialtes has implications for understanding the whole political scene in fifth-century Athens. The clue to the matters of jurisdiction studied by Rhodes is to be found, I believe, in a revised understanding of *eisangelia*.

EISANGELIA

Study of the procedure called *eisangelia* must start from some remarks of Hypereides in the speech *For Euxenippos*. The orator alludes to the *nomos eisangeltikos* and cites clauses from it (7−8); these provided for *eisangelia* "if anyone overthrows the *demos* of the Athenians, or conspires for overthrow of the *demos*, or gathers together a *hetairikon*, or if anyone betrays a city, or ships, or a force of infantry or sailors, or being an orator fails in return for bribes to give the best advice to the *demos* of the Athenians." Starting from this observation, and encouraged by some remarks in the Byzantine lexica, many scholars have tried to draw up a finite list of offences which could be prosecuted by *eisangelia*;[6] they have assumed, that is, that this procedure was available for a limited number of offences specified in the *nomos eisangeltikos*. This assumption leads to difficulties.

In the first place the statements of Hypereides in the same speech demand closer scrutiny. Evidently the clauses which he quotes stood in the law, but he does not say that his list is complete. Indeed his argument is tendentious. In the opening sections of the speech he says that in the past *eisangelia* was used for major crimes but recently it has been used improperly for petty offences. He gives examples of petty offences prosecuted of late by this procedure: Diognides and Antidoros were charged with hiring flute-girls above the legal rate of pay, Agasikles was accused of having himself enrolled in the wrong deme, and now Euxenippos is prosecuted for his report to the *demos* of a dream which he had in the temple of Amphiaraos. It appears from the speech that in fact the prosecution charged Euxenippos under the clause about failing to give the best advice to the *demos*. Even so Hypereides' reference to petty offences may suggest that the Athenians were not so eager to restrict *eisangelia* to the major offences which he specifies as he might have wished.

A more serious difficulty arises from studying the views of Hellenistic scholars as reported in the Byzantine lexica. A learned note distinguishes between the opinions of Kaikilios and Theophrastos.[7] The former said that *eisangelia* was available against "new and unwritten offences." Theophrastos, however, gave a list of offences for which *eisangelia* was available as summarized in the note, and his list overlaps that of Hypereides. The same note mentions the prosecution of Themistokles by Leobotes as according with the opinion of Theophrastos, and, after discussing other questions, it concludes: "The subject is treated in the discourses of the sophists." Evidently Hellenistic scholars inherited no uniform tradition about *eisangelia*; it was a question for research. This could not have come about if a law had been extant giving an exhaustive list of the offences which could be prosecuted by *eisangelia*.

---

[6] For example, Th. Thalheim, "Zur Eisangelie in Athen," *Hermes* (1902) 339−352; J. H. Lipsius, *Das attische Recht und Rechtsverfahren* (Leipzig 1905−15) 176−211; A. R. W. Harrison, *The Law of Athens: Procedure* (Oxford 1971) 50−59; M. H. Hansen, "Eisangelia: The Sovereignty of the People's Court in the Fourth Century B.C. and the Impeachment of Generals and Politicians," *Odense University Classical Studies* 6 (1975) 12−20.

[7] *Lex. Rhet. Cant.,* s.v. *eisangelia*; quoted by Harrison (above, note 6) 51, note 1. This note is clearer, more discursive, and more informative than the notes offered by Polux (8.51 f.; also quoted by Harrison) and Harpokration (s.v. *eisangelia*), but they too preserve some echo of the tradition that *eisangelia* was available for offences not defined by law.

The third reason for challenging the assumption that *eisangelia* was available for a limited number of specified offences is that scholars making this assumption have had to add repeatedly to the list of offences. Thus Thalheim (above, note 6), who treated the question with exemplary rigor, started from Harpokration's note, which distinguishes three kinds of *eisangelia*,[8] and added several more. A fourth kind, he supposed, was actions before the Council against officials for illegal conduct; a fifth was available against offences concerning things which stood under the special supervision of the Council, for example, naval equipment in the dockyards. Thalheim argued that additional laws created three further kinds of *eisangelia*: the procedure was available against anyone who deceived the *demos* by false promises, who harmed the allies in the Second Athenian League, and who committed offences on embassies.[9] More recently Hansen (above, note 6, 16) has made Hypereides' citation of the *nomos eisangeltikos* his starting point and asserted thence that *eisangelia* was available for precisely three offences, namely, treason, attempts to overthrow the democracy, and acceptance of bribes by orators to make proposals to the Assembly; but Hansen has had to admit that the procedure of *eisangelia* before the Council embraced not only these three offences but any offence committed by a magistrate or by a citizen performing a public charge.[10]

There is adequate evidence that all of these miscellaneous charges could be the occasion for *eisangelia*. Surely the list would be still longer if there were more evidence. Accordingly some scholars have proposed a view like that of Kaikilios, that there was no statutory limit to the types of offence for which *eisangelia* was available. Thus Bonner and Smith wrote: ". . . the law was intended only to insure the use of the process in certain political cases . . . . The law never forbade that offenses other than those mentioned in the law should be tried by *eisangelia*, but merely made certain that these specified offences should be so tried"; they also noted that *eisangelia* came to be used for trivial offenses, as Hypereides complained.[11] Following them, Rhodes has urged accepting "the non-specific strand" in the tradition on the law of *eisangelia*; he holds that this procedure could be employed against "any major public offence."[12] Indeed even the words "major" and "public" may be too restrictive; the speaker of [Demosthenes] 47 had recourse to *eisangelia* before the Council in seeking redress for a fistfight in the doorway of a private house (41–44), although it must be admitted that the fight arose from a dispute about the public charge of the trierarchy.[13]

---

[8] Harpokration's first type of *eisangelia*, "where the first hearing is before the Council or the *demos*," is the type studied here. His second kind was a procedure before the archon for injury to an orphan; Aristotle (*Ath. Pol.* 56.6) calls the procedure in such cases a *graphe*; Isaios, 11, calls it indifferently *graphe* (31, 32, 35, cf. 28) and *eisangelia* (6, 15). Harpokration's third kind of *eisangelia* was available against an arbitrator (*Ath. Pol.* 53.6).

[9] Against officials: *Ath. Pol.* 45.2; cf. Ant. 6.12 and 35. Concerning naval equipment: *IG* 2.² 1631, lines 398–401; cf. Dem., 51.4. Deceiving the *demos* with false promises: [Dem.], 49.67, cf. Dem., 20.135. Thalheim inferred *eisangelia* for actions harming the allies in the Second League from *IG* 2.² 43 (= Tod, 123) lines 51–63; 111 (= Tod, 142) lines 37–40; and 125 (= Tod, 154); but the word does not occur in these passages. *Parapresbeia: eisangelia* was the procedure employed against Philokrates (Dem., 19.116; Aischin., 3.79); it is also mentioned in general terms as appropriate for charges against ambassadors (Aischin., 2.139; Dem., 19.103). Harrison (above, note 6, 53–54) follows Thalheim in trying to list the offences for which *eisangelia* was available.

[10] Above, note 6, 28; *Ath. Pol.* 45.2; [Dem.], 47.41–44.

[11] R. J. Bonner and G. Smith, *The Administration of Justice from Homer to Aristotle* 1 (Chicago 1930) 294–309; the quotation is from page 307 and the comment from 309.

[12] Above, note 5, 162–164.

[13] Hansen (above, note 6, 19–20) argues against Bonner and Smith and Rhodes; he insists that all known cases of *eisangelia* fall under the headings of treason, attempt to overthrow the democracy, and corruption among orators, as defined in the laws on *eisangelia*. He notes that putative exceptions dissolve on closer scrutiny; thus the act committed by Leokrates may not have been an offence defined in the laws, but the prosecution tried to call it treason, and in the trial of Lykophron the prosecution misrepresented adultery as an attempt to overthrow the democracy. But Hansen has subsumed an excessively large variety of offences under the term "treason"; and it appears from Thalheim's study that the lists of offences given by Hypereides and Theophrastos are far from complete. In 415 Pythonikos was said to *eisan-*

If indeed the law on *eisangelia* had a "non-specific strand," it was in harmony with other Athenian laws on criminal procedure. One may call to mind the *graphe hybreos*. This charge is attested as admissible "if anyone commits *hybris* against anyone, whether against a child or a woman or a man, from among free persons or slaves, or does anything unlawful (*paranomon*) against any of these."[14] It has been plausibly suggested that the law on *hybris* was passed in the time of Perikles when the value of money had decreased since the age of Solon and the old laws providing for compensation in fixed amounts of valuables no longer sufficed. Essentially the new law empowered the court to assess the penalty, and, because of its second clause, "if anyone does anything unlawful against any of these," this law was so general as to embrace all offences against the person. The law on *eisangelia* may have completed its list of offences with a clause of comparable generality.

This conclusion has a bearing on the origin of *eisangelia* (and hence on Ephialtes). Some scholars (Thalheim, Bonner and Smith, Hansen) have supposed that the law in almost its final form was passed in or about 411/10, later changes being small. It must be admitted that the clause against gathering together a *hetairikon* seems appropriate among the reforms following the overthrow of the Four Hundred. Doubtless the provisions about *eisangelia* were reenacted, perhaps modified, when the laws were codified in 403–399. For the earliest stage in the development of *eisangelia*, historians have often relied on a remark of Aristotle (*Ath. Pol.* 8.4); he says that Solon passed a law of *eisangelia*, whereby the Council of the Areopagos should try persons who drew together for the purpose of overthrowing the *demos*.[15] Hansen (above, note 6, 17–19) has rightly questioned the truth of Aristotle's statement. As he points out, the wording of Aristotle's remark, in which the phrase *katalysis tou demou* is essential, is quite unlike the language of Solon's poems. One may add that the crucial phrase, *katalysis tou demou*, is quite unlike the diction of those among the allegedly Solonian laws which have the best claim to be considered authentic, for example, the law of amnesty.[16] Hansen suggests persuasively that the fiction of a Solonian law of *eisangelia*, empowering the Areopagos to try charges of subverting the constitution, was concocted in the second half of the fourth century; for in that period there was speculative and tendentious discussion of the powers of the Areopagos, the slogan *patrios politeia* was current,[17] and a new procedure, called *apophasis* and somewhat resembling *eisangelia*, was introduced, a procedure in which the Areopagite Council took part.

More plausibly Aristotle (*Ath. Pol.* 4.4), describing the condition of Athens before Solon, says: "A person suffering injury was allowed to make a report (*eisangellein*) to the Council of the Areopagites, declaring what law was transgressed by the injury." This statement occurs in suspicious proximity to the spurious "constitution of Drakon," but it is not intrinsically objectionable; even if it rests on conjecture, the conjecture is in accord with what may be presumed about the history of

---

gellein when he told the Assembly that Alkibiades had performed the Eleusinian mysteries in a private house (Andok., 1.14, 27, cf. 11); surely the Athenians called this offence neither treason nor an attempt to overthrow the democracy nor corruption among orators, but *asebeia*.

[14] Dem., 21.47; Aischin., 1.15. My understanding of the law on *hybris* is drawn from Ruschenbusch, "Hybreos Graphe. Ein Fremdkörper im athenischen Recht des 4. Jahrhunderts v. Chr.," *Zeitschrift der Savigny-Stiftung für Rechtsgeschichte* 82 (1965) Romanistische Abteilung 302–309. Cf. Lipsius (above, note 6), 420–429.

[15] Confirmation should not be sought in *Ath. Pol.* 25.3–4 where Aristotle says that Themistokles told the Areopagite Council that some people had drawn together for the purpose of overthrowing the constitution; the anecdote of Ephialtes in shirt sleeves on the altar is not admissible as historical evidence.

[16] Plut., *Sol.* 19.4 = F 70 in Ruschenbusch, *Solonos Nomoi: Die Fragmente des solonischen Gesetzeswerkes mit einer Text- und Überlieferungsgeschichte* (*Historia*, Einzelschriften 9 [1966]). For its authenticity see Ruschenbusch, *Historia* 9 (1960) 132–134.

[17] This slogan did not arise as early as the late fifth century; see the important argument of K. R. Walters, "The 'Ancestral Constitution' and Fourth-Century Historiography in Athens," *American Journal of Ancient History* 1 (1976) 129–144.

eisangelia (see below, p. 133). For the present all that need be said is that Aristotle's statement does not necessarily imply an enabling law which created *eisangelia*; Aristotle merely says that people could bring their complaints to the Areopagite Council (a reasonable thing to do in archaic conditions), not that a law authorized them to do so. The procedure of *eisangelia* is first attested with certainty in the prosecution of Themistokles by Leobotes.[18] Some other famous trials of the first half of the fifth century may have followed the same procedure. In particular the first trial of Miltiades may be instructive. The charge is said to have been tyranny in the Chersonese; this is credible if the later law of *eisangelia* had a "non-specific strand." The trial was conducted, according to Herodotos (6.104.2), before a *dikasterion*; this may be important for reconstructing the procedure of *eisangelia* (see below, pp. 130 – 131), for there is no need to suppose that Herodotos' term for the court is anachronistic.

Rejecting a Solonian origin, Hansen holds "that the *eisangelia* was a democratic institution introduced by Kleisthenes" (p. 19). This hypothesis proves to be the answer to a false question, if one follows a different line of thought. One may start from Hansen's important observation (p. 10) that the Athenians were much more interested in procedural law than in substantive law. They devoted far more thought and ingenuity to devising procedures than to laying down substantive rules. The generality of the law on *hybris* illustrates their indifference to the substantive issue of defining offences. Scholars studying the early history of *eisangelia* seem to have supposed that the Athenians thought about actual or possible offences of treason or subversion and consequently devised a procedure to deal with these. But it would be more in accordance with Athenian habits to devise a criminal procedure without having any specific charge in mind. That is, if anyone in Athens thought that an act deserving punishment had been committed, he could report his information to an appropriate authority; he did not necessarily have to specify a substantive provision of criminal law against which the alleged act offended; he reported the act because he found it outrageous and deserving of punishment. There were procedures available, such as *eisangelia, graphe,* and *endeixis,* so that the authority receiving the information could hear pleas on both sides, the suspect could defend himself, and a verdict could be reached. These procedures were defined and distinguished from one another, not by the nature of the alleged offence, but by the identity of the authority receiving the first information. If the information was given to the Assembly or the Council of Five Hundred, the procedure was *eisangelia*; if it was given to one of the nine archons, the procedure was *graphe*; if it was given to the Eleven, the procedure was *endeixis.*[19] If offences concerning the state were often reported to the Council or the Assembly, this was a matter of convenience.

For the purpose of the present inquiry, the crucial point is that a procedure can arise by custom without specific enactment to lay it down. Hence to suppose that Kleisthenes (or Solon) introduced *eisangelia* is to answer a false question. If someone in Athens believed that Miltiades had exercised tyranny in the Chersonese or that Alkibiades had performed the mysteries in a private house, he could report his suspicions and his grounds to the Assembly. This does not mean that a statute had specified the Assembly as the proper body to receive such allegations. The information was given to the Assembly merely because a meeting of the Assembly happened to be conveniently available. Clearly information about profanation of the mysteries did not necessarily have to be reported to the Assembly and lead to *eisangelia*; it could alternatively be the subject of a *graphe asebeias,* the information being reported to the *archon basileus* (*Ath. Pol.* 57.2).

---

[18] Krateros, *FGrHist* 342, F 11; Plut., *Them.* 23. Krateros calls the procedure *eisangelia.*

[19] My thinking has been helped much by G. M. Calhoun, *The Growth of Criminal Law in Ancient Greece* (Berkeley 1927) 57–62 and Ruschenbusch, "Untersuchungen zur Geschichte des athenischen Strafrechts," *Graezistische Abhandlungen,* Band 4 (Köln und Graz 1968) 73.

In all probability *eisangelia* did not arise from an enabling statute. As soon as the community of Athenian citizens was strong enough to punish acts threatening its welfare, it could receive information alleging that such acts had been performed. In classical Athens the peculiar feature of almost all forms of procedure (all, that is, except the procedures for homicide and related offences) is that each case was heard in two stages. At the first stage the party initiating the suit approached an executive or legislative organ, often one of the nine archons, and that organ conducted a preliminary hearing called *proanakrisis*.[20] Unless it became clear at the *proanakrisis* that there was no case against the defendant,[21] the suit then passed to its second stage, which was a hearing before a *dikasterion*. The word for the process of transferring the case from the first organ receiving it to the *dikasterion* was *ephesis*. This word can best be translated "transfer" or "reference"; it is much wider in meaning than "appeal." *Ephesis* could indeed come about in consequence of appeal by a disappointed litigant, but it could occur because of other causes, and in many circumstances it was compulsory.[22] *Ephesis* to the *dikasterion* was the safeguard of individual liberty and security against arbitrary behaviour by magistrates and public bodies. The modern doctrine of the separation of the powers was unknown. Instead it was taken for granted that any public authority, which we might call legislative or executive, should have some power, of the kind which we would call judicial, to enforce its will and to remedy wrongs; the citizen's guarantee against abuse of that judicial power was *ephesis* to the *dikasterion*.

Eisangelia may be defined as the criminal procedure in which the first of the two stages is a hearing before the Council of Five Hundred or the Assembly. Hansen has clarified the subject by insisting on the procedural distinction between *eisangelia* to the Council and *eisangelia* to the Assembly.[23] In *eisangelia* to the Council, the Council voted at the first stage to decide whether there was a *prima facie* case against the accused; such a decision was called a *katagnosis*, and, after it had been taken, the case was sent to the *dikasterion* for the second stage of the trial.[24] In *eisangelia* to the Assembly, a preliminary vote was taken by the Council, whether on its own initiative or on instructions from the Assembly, but the measure passed by this preliminary vote was a *probouleuma*, not a *katagnosis*; the action taken by the Assembly on this *probouleuma* was the first stage of the hearing, and afterwards the case usually went to a *dikasterion* for the second stage.

It is important to observe that both in *eisangelia* to the Council and in *eisangelia* to the Assembly the second and final stage of the trial was a hearing before a *dikasterion*. On this point there is substantial agreement as concerns *eisangelia* to the Council; the case was referred to a *dikasterion*, unless the penalty voted by the Council was less than 500 drachmas (see note 24). Concerning *eisangelia* to the Assembly, it is admitted that cases were most often referred to a *dikasterion* for final decision, but many people believe that the Assembly itself could and occasionally did sit as a court and issue a final verdict. Attempting a comprehensive survey, Hansen (p. 51) finds that in eighty-six cases of *eisangelia* to the Assembly the final decision was

---

[20] *Ath. Pol.* 3.5; Wade-Gery (above, note 3), 173, 175.

[21] Even the nine archons had a modest power to dismiss a case on these grounds: Harpok., s.v. *anakrisis*.

[22] Ruschenbusch, "Ephesis. Ein Beitrag zur griechischen Rechtsterminologie," *Zeitschrift der Savigny-Stiftung* 78 (1961) Romanistische Abteilung 386–390, and "Heliaia. Die Tradition über das solonische Volksgericht," *Historia* 14 (1965) 381–384.

[23] Above, note 6, 21–28. He draws on *Ath. Pol.* 45.2; 59.2–4; Dem., 24.63; [Dem.], 47.42–43; Xen., *HG* 1.7; *IG* 1.² 110 = Meiggs and Lewis, 85, lines 39–47; *IG* 2.² 125 = Tod 154 lines 6–10.

[24] But the Council could impose a fine up to 500 drachmas without allowing *ephesis* to the *dikasterion*. This rule is known from [Dem.], 47.43; cf. *IG* 1.² 76 = Meiggs and Lewis 73, lines 57–59. I follow Rhodes (above, note 5, 147, 164, 171) in understanding the rule about 500 drachmas thus. Hansen (above, note 6, 24) interprets the rule differently, saying "the Council was empowered to pass the final verdict in the second type of *eisangelia* if the accused was sentenced to a fine of 500 dr. maximum and if he did not appeal against the Council's verdict." I cannot follow Hansen on this, since I am not persuaded that *ephesis* in *Ath. Pol.* 45.2 means "appeal" rather than "compulsory transfer." But the question is immaterial for the present argument.

taken by a *dikasterion*, and in eleven such cases the final decision was taken by the Assembly. But concerning these eleven cases one must be on one's guard against a possible gap in the evidence. Extant sources hardly ever give a full report of the whole course of a trial. It may be that in some of the eleven cases the issue was heard by a *dikasterion*, after the Assembly had voted, but the guilt of the accused had become so evident in the hearing before the Assembly that the decision of the *dikasterion* was a foregone conclusion, and so the extant sources only mention the more memorable stage of the trial. This may be true of the trial of Timotheos in 373/2; the meeting of the Assembly was memorable, not least because Jason and Alketas were present; the accused withdrew into the service of the Persian King soon afterwards, and the extant source of information is a speech ([Demosthenes] 49) delivered eleven years later. It may also be true of others among Hansen's eleven cases, for example, of the second trial of Miltiades; Herodotos (6.136) says that he was accused before the *demos* and that the *demos* voted to inflict a fine of fifty talents; evidently the hearing before the Assembly was politically decisive, but that does not exclude the possibility that a formal hearing before a *dikasterion* followed. In only one case is it certain that the final verdict was issued by the Assembly without even the formality of a hearing before a *dikasterion*; that case was the trial of the generals after the battle of Arginousai. This occurrence was not a model of correct procedure; indeed it was the only occasion (as far as known to me) when the Assembly accepted the doctrine that the *demos* may do as it pleases.[25]

Since *eisangelia* was a proper trial and the accused enjoyed the safeguard of *ephesis* to the *dikasterion*, one may regret the habit, common among writers of English, of translating *eisangelia* with "impeachment." The only similarity arises because the legislature played a part in both procedures. But *eisangelia* conformed to the two-stage pattern of criminal (and civil) proceedings in Athens, so that the accused had some chance of a fair hearing. Impeachment is a procedural monstrosity, more political than judicial, the misshapen offspring of the mother of parliaments, now happily obsolete in the land of its birth, but preserved as a fossilized relic in the Constitution of the United States and revived irresponsibly from time to time for strictly partisan reasons.[26]

To sum up. In classical Athens someone who believed that a crime or outrageous act had been committed could report his information to the Council of Five Hundred or to the Assembly. He might think one of these bodies particularly appropriate to receive the report if the alleged act affected the public interest. To make such a report was *eisangellein*. In the archaic period such reports may often have been made to the Council of the Areopagos, but this practice ceased when that body became impaired in personnel in consequence of the unforeseen effects of the change of 488/7 in the mode of selecting the nine archons.[27] Instead the reports were habitually made to the Assembly or the Council of Five Hundred, once meetings of those bodies became conveniently frequent. A *nomos eisangeltikos*, listing specific offences but including a general clause, may have been passed ca. 411/0; doubtless such a law was enacted or reenacted in the codification of 403– 399. There is no need to suppose that a statute of Solon or of Kleisthenes or of any other legislator created *eisangelia* and specified the organ to receive the reports. Likewise there is no good reason to suppose that a statute of Ephialtes transferred the function of hearing *eisangeliai* from one organ to others; judicial procedure can develop by practice and custom without statutory change.

---

[25] I have avoided deliberately the obscure question of the origin of the *dikasteria*. For divergent views see Wade-Gery (above, note 3) 173–179, 182–197; Ruschenbusch (above, note 19), 78–82; Hansen (above, note 6), 51–52. The *heliaia* was the parent of the *dikasteria* and bore some relationship to the assembled *demos*; but the nature of the relationship between 6,000 sworn jurors aged at least thirty years and the whole body of adult male citizens is not yet clear.

[26] I thank Thomas G. Barnes for discussing this point with me; he is not to blame for the inadequacy of my presentation. I admit to being one of those who have translated *eisangelia* with "impeachment."

[27] Wade-Gery (above, note 3, 105–106) argued that the reform of 488/7 led to a decline in the quality of the personnel of the Areopagos. But a different view can be defended; see E. Badian, "Archons and *Strategoi*," *Antichthon* 5 (1971) 1–34.

"OFFICIAL JURISDICTION"

Rhodes has collected together a group of cases, heard by the Council of Five Hundred, under the heading "official jurisdiction" and has sought to distinguish them from *eisangelia*. But the group is highly miscellaneous. Under this heading Rhodes notes that the Council could try officials on its own initiative or in response to a report made to it by a private person (above, note 9). It had jurisdiction over offences concerning the tribute of the Delian League.[28] It judged offences concerning naval equipment in the dockyards (above, note 9). It supervised public works and reported offences concerning them to the Assembly, so that the case would be referred to a *dikasterion* if the *demos* condemned the accused.[29] It had jurisdiction over some religious offences concerning the Eleusinian mysteries.[30] Sometimes the Assembly instructed the Council to investigate unusual offences and refer them to a court.[31] As indicated above (note 24), the Council's power to penalize was limited to a fine of 500 drachmas; if any greater penalty was at stake, the case was referred to a *dikasterion*. No account need be taken here of the Council's power to imprison people who failed to pay debts due to the state on time;[32] that should be regarded, not as a judicial power to issue a verdict, but as a mode of administrative coercion intended to compel payment.

Rhodes believes that "official jurisdiction," originally less extensive than in the fully developed constitution, was exercised until 462 by the Council of the Areopagos but was transferred by Ephialtes to the Council of Five Hundred. Moreover he thinks that the "official jurisdiction" of the Five Hundred, increasing with the growth of public business, influenced the development of *eisangelia*. That is, he thinks that Ephialtes may have intended *eisangeliai* to be heard by the Council of Five Hundred with reference to the *demos* sitting as a court; but the Assembly, being short of time, may have ordered the Council to send such cases on to a *dikasterion*, and the Council itself may have referred the cases to a *dikasterion* by assimilating *eisangelia* to its "official jurisdiction."

Enough has been said above against the last part of this thesis. The practice of referring *eisangeliai* to a *dikasterion* is to be explained by the privilege of *ephesis* to the *dikasterion*; this privilege was unrestricted (except in homicide and related cases) and according to Athenian tradition it was created by Solon.[33] If the procedure of *eisangelia* arose in the archaic period, as seems likely (cf. Calhoun, above, note 19), it is more likely to have provided the pattern for the growth in "official jurisdiction" of the Council than vice versa.

The word *eisangelia* is used in extant sources for some types of case which Rhodes classifies as "official jurisdiction." It is used, for example, for trials of offences concerning naval equipment. A somewhat crucial question arises in relation to the Council's authority to try officials. Aristotle (*Ath. Pol.* 45.2) says: "The Council judges most officials and especially those who have charge of money. Its verdict is not final but subject to *ephesis* to the *dikasterion*. Private citizens too may make a report (*eisangellein*) against any of the officials whom they wish, alleging that he does not observe the laws; officials in these cases too enjoy *ephesis* to the *dikasterion*, if the Council votes for their condemnation." Here Aristotle indicates two kinds of charges that were made against officials and that came before the Council. The one kind was charges initiated by the Council. The

[28] Meiggs and Lewis 46, lines 31–43, 69, lines 38–40 and 48–50.

[29] *Ath. Pol.* 46.2.

[30] *IG* 1.² 76 = Meiggs and Lewis 73, lines 57–59; Andok., 1.110–116.

[31] *SEG.* 12.32 = A. G. Woodhead, *Hesperia* 18 (1949) 78–83; *IG* 1.² 110 = Meiggs and Lewis, 85, lines 39–44.

[32] *Ath. Pol.* 48.1.

[33] *Ath. Pol.* 9.1. The tradition may be right, But I refrain from asking what "Solon" means in this context and await an inquiry into the authenticity of the extant laws attributed to him.

other was charges initiated by private citizens, who brought their complaints to the Council. Charges of this latter kind could be called *eisangeliai*, since Aristotle uses the verb *eisangellein* of them. Were charges of the first kind, those initiated by the Council itself, also *eisangeliai*? Criticizing Rhodes, Hansen has argued convincingly that they were.[34]

Thus some at least of the cases now classified as "official jurisdiction" of the Council could properly be called *eisangeliai*. It is possible that all cases so classified belong to the procedure of *eisangelia*. Indeed this conclusion can scarcely be avoided if it is true that the *nomos eisangeltikos* did not restrict *eisangelia* to a limited list of specified offences. Even if that hypothesis is mistaken, the difference (for example) between *eisangelia* to the Council on a charge of treason and trial before the Council and a *dikasterion* of an offence concerning the tribute of the Delian League is merely verbal; the procedure was the same. The true historical question concerns the hypothesis that Ephialtes transferred "official jurisdiction" from the Areopagos to the Five Hundred. Here the miscellaneous character of "official jurisdiction" should give pause. Clearly cases of these different types first came within the purview of the Council of Five Hundred at different times. In some cases enactments were passed ordering the Council to take cognizance of offences of a specified kind; this possibility is illustrated by decrees concerning the tribute of the Delian League (above, note 28); the Assembly considered the Council a convenient body to deal with such matters. In other instances it may have become customary for the Council to receive cases of a specifiable kind, simply because individual complainants on their own initiative reported their information to the Council; the informer, like the Assembly, considered the Council a convenient body to deal with such matters. This may account for the Council's share in dealing with offences concerning public works. In the archaic period it is not unlikely that "official jurisdiction" of a less extensive character was exercised by the Council of the Areopagos, although doubtless its verdicts were subject to *ephesis* to the *dikasterion* (*heliaia*?), once that Solonian privilege had been asserted. Later the Council of the Areopagos ceased to exercise "official jurisdiction"; the reason is that, when the personnel of that body deteriorated, the Assembly and individual informers no longer considered it a convenient body to deal with their complaints; they did not need Ephialtes to tell them that.

EPHIALTES

So far it has been maintained in this paper that the development of *eisangelia* and of "official jurisdiction" (whether they are the same or different) can best be explained by considerations of practice, custom and convenience, not by the specific enactments of a legislator such as Ephialtes. Possibly a general hypothesis could be enunciated: in constitutional history custom precedes statute. That is, a practice arises by custom and, if it is not challenged, it remains customary and subject to changes of custom; but if it is challenged, it is regulated, modified or reaffirmed by statute.

Of the changes attributed by Rhodes to Ephialtes there remains, apart from the matter of *euthynai*, the transfer of the *dokimasia* of the nine archons from the Areopagos to the Five Hundred. In the time of Aristotle (*Ath. Pol.* 45.3; 55.2−4) the *dokimasia* of the nine archons was conducted by the Council of Five Hundred in the first instance and then passed by *ephesis* to the *dikasterion*. Since the nine archonships were a much older institution than the Five Hundred, and since the Council of the Areopagos consisted of former archons, it is reasonable to suppose that originally the Areopagite Council conducted the *dokimasia* of the archons. The change must have required specific enactment and it may well have been proposed by Ephialtes, for by 462 the Council of the Areopagos had had twenty-five years to deteriorate and to become unfit for scrutinizing the incoming archons.

---

[34] Above, note 6, 49−50. The argument depends on the law of Timokrates quoted in Dem., 24.63.

If Ephialtes changed the procedure for hearing *euthynai* and for *dokimasia* of archons, his goal becomes clear. He was concerned about the way officials performed their tasks; the two procedures bearing on the performance of officials were *dokimasia*, which tested their formal qualifications, and *euthynai*, where they were called to account for their shortcomings. To classify him among "radical democratic leaders" does not explain his work;[35] he was a man seeking to remedy abuses of a perhaps extensive but certainly limited and specifiable kind.[36]

University of California   RAPHAEL SEALEY
Berkely

[35] R. W. Wallace, "Ephialtes and the Areopagos," *GRBS* 15 (1974) 259–269; the offending phrase occurs on page 266. One may deplore such language as "ambitious *strategoi* of the left" (263). It has become popular of late; one is told that the career of Kallias, husband of Elpinike, showed a "shift to the Left" (J. K. Davies, *Athenian Propertied Families* [Oxford 1971] 259) and one reads of "a political diabole of Right Wing origin" (506). Even in present-day political contexts the terms "right" and "left" belong to propaganda, not analysis.

[36] P. J. Rhodes, "ΕΙΣΑΓΓΕΛΙΑ in Athens," *JHS* 99 (1979) 103–114 appeared while this article was in press.

GREEK VIEWS OF REALITY AND THE DEVELOPMENT OF RHETORICAL HISTORY

I should like to point out, how remarkable a thing is this creation of scientific history by Herodotus, for he was an ancient Greek, and ancient Greek thought as a whole has a very definite prevailing tendency not only uncongenial to the growth of historical thought but actually based, one might say, on a rigorously anti-historical metaphysics. History is a science of human action: what the historian puts before himself is things that men have done in the past, and these belong to a world of change, a world where things come to be and cease to be. Such things, according to the prevalent Greek metaphysical view, ought not to be knowable, and therefore history ought to be impossible.[1]

It is certainly true that from the Ionians to the Eleatics it is hard to find a theory of knowledge, or of physics or metaphysics, that is suitable for historical enquiry unless it be found in Heraclitus or more certainly in Protagoras and the Sophists.[2] I think it is not too unfair to claim that history in the fifth century was an application of Sophistic thinking. It is hard to conceive of the existence of Herodotus' histories unless we assume that he took the view, consciously or not, that man was in some way "the measure"; that what a man perceived was true, at least for him, and that what he remembered perceiving could still have some truth, or at least be worth recording–be ἀξιόλογος, as Herodotus puts it.

Thucydides, of course, carried on the tradition of Herodotean empiricism; but with a twist. "It will be enough for me . . .," he says in his famous introduction, "if these words of mine are judged useful by those who want to understand clearly the events which happened in the past and which (human nature being what it is–κατὰ τὸ ἀνθρώπινον) will, at some time or other and in much the same ways, be repeated in the future. My work is not a piece of writing designed to meet the taste of an immediate public, but was done to last for ever."[3] Dionysius of Halicarnassus said that, in

[1] R. G. Collingwood, *The Idea of History* (Oxford 1973, first published 1946) 20.

[2] Collingwood's comments are valid particularly if we take Parmenides as a typical Greek thinker (see *DK* f. 8, and J. S. Kirk and J. E. Raven, *The Presocratic Philosophers* [Cambridge 1971] 269–278). Heraclitus had at least placed some confidence in the senses (*DK* ff. 55, 107; Kirk and Raven, 189) and seems to have regarded change as part of the scheme of reality (Kirk and Raven, 196–199). Protagoras' views on education, the teachability of *arete*, clearly commit him to a belief in the reality of meaningful change as part of the human experience; and his famous relativism certainly places high priority on the value of sense-data (see W. K. C. Guthrie, *The Sophists* [Cambridge 1971] 65, and 183–188). My remarks on Heraclitus and Parmenides reflect the interpretation of Martin Heidegger, *An Introduction to Metaphysics*, R. Manheim, tr. (New York 1961) 107–109.

[3] Thuc., 1.22.4. Raubitschek's interpretation, ". . . those who wish to observe the past and what will once again happen in the future [human nature being what it is] will consider my work sufficiently useful," "Andocides and Thucydides" (above, 121–122), is surely the correct one. The usefulness of the work emerges from the inevitability of some form of historical repetition κατὰ τὸ ἀνθρώπινον. The translation quoted in the text is that of Rex Warner in the Penguin series (Harmondsworth 1959) 24.

this passage, Thucydides makes history "philosophy teaching by examples."[4] If Thucydidean history is philosophical, it most closely resembles the thought of Heraclitus. Thucydides seeks permanent or repetitive truth behind the multifarious display of historical fact, the abiding and permanent amidst the changing and transient, an enduring truth that sounds remotely Eleatic. Even while Sophistry was at its height, and historical enquiry at its zenith in the ancient world, Greek thought was already beginning to crawl back into its Parmenidean shell.

This is not to deny the anthropocentric quality of Thucydides' history. For him the pattern of truth is only discernable through a careful study of humanity κατὰ τὸ ἀνθρώπινον. The great difference between Herodotus and Thucydides lies in their sense of personal responsibility for what is set down on paper. "My business," said Herodotus in book seven, "is to record what people say, but I am by no means bound to believe it—and that may be taken to apply to this book as a whole."[5] Herodotus separates himself from his material; he does not claim always to know what happened, only to know what people say happened. No such disclaimers to knowledge come from Thucydides' pen. He is at pains to convince us that he is telling the truth; hence his elaborate explanation of his critical method in his introduction which aims to convince the reader that he has successfully taken the various reports of his sources and extracted the truth from them. Therefore, he reports nothing but what he feels he knows. But if true knowledge is of things that are repeatable in the future, then truth is not simply the testable veracity of each individual fact. What the historian claims to know is not a body of specific facts, but repeatable patterns. Truth is not of the particular, it is of the repetitive or categorical.

Thucydides' concern to make his work a possession for all time seems to have led him to the realization that he must convince his reader that what he writes is true and reliable knowledge. This seems to have led him to reflect upon what is called today "historical method." His reflections deserve to be seen as a forward step in the art of scientific historical reporting.

> Thucydides had set up a new standard and proposed a new model for historical investigation. He taught the Greeks to write contemporary political history; this was the permanent result of his work. But the secret of his critical methods may be said to have perished with him; it has been reserved for modern students fully to appreciate his critical acumen, and to estimate the immense labours which underlay the construction of his history but are carefully concealed like the foundation stones of a building. Influences came into play in the fourth century which drove history along other paths than those which he marked out; the best of the principles which his work had inculcated did not become canonical; and historical treatment was not sympathetic under the new intellectual constellations.
>
> The age succeeding his death was perhaps not favourable to the composition of political history. The engrossing intellectual interest was then political science, and the historical method had not been invented. The men who might otherwise have shone as historians were engaged in speculations on the nature of the state. They were eagerly seeking an answer to the speculative question: What is the best constitution? Only three historians of note arose in this period; they were more or less under the influence of Thucydides, but at long intervals behind.[6]

So, in J. B. Bury's view, history became the activity of lesser minds in the century after Herodotus and Thucydides. The historian now becomes little better than a hack writer ". . . drawn under the pernicious influence of rhetoric."

---

[4] Dion. Hal., *Ars Rhet.* 9.2 (398).

[5] Hdt., 7.152.3.

[6] J. B. Bury, *The Ancient Greek Historians* (New York 1958, first published 1908) 150–151.

Not that rhetorical history is of itself necessarily bad: Thucydides and Thomas Babington Macauley could be called rhetorical historians, to name but two (not mentioning Bury himself). No, "One does not mean by that, the cultivation of a clear, and rythmical style; one means the tendency to seek first of all and at any cost what may be called rhetorical effects."[7] Here, of course, we are invited to put the blame on Isocrates, the reputed master of many historians, and particularly of Ephorus and Theopompus. The reason for the turn to rhetoric, it is urged, was that certain historians, especially Ephorus and Theopompus, ". . . determined to win the public ear. It was not enough to write; they wanted to be read."[8]

Bury's view is well reasoned, and rooted in a thorough knowledge of the thought of the fourth century. It is little wonder that it has been repeated in slightly varied form from time to time in compendious studies of ancient historiography.[9] However, there are ways in which I think it almost as misleading as it is helpful; and I think it can certainly be argued that it by no means answers all of the important questions. Therefore, it may be worthwhile to take Bury's proposals and apply them carefully to what is known of the work of the three major historians: Callisthenes, Ephorus, and Theopompus.

We may begin with Callisthenes, for he resembles Bury's rhetorical model most obviously. The large fragment describing the visit to the oracle of Ammon reveals the main features of his style. Here Alexander succumbs to one of his well-known longings, and leaves for the oracle. On the way the party becomes lost in a storm, but is saved by the miraculous intervention of two ravens (κόρακες) who appear and act as guides. Once there, Alexander hears the pronouncement that he is son of Zeus, and other things are revealed to him by signs.[10]

Callisthenes was quickly recognized in antiquity for what he was: an irresponsible flatterer of Alexander's vanity. He probably hoped that learned Greeks would be diverted by a "subtly allusive" quality in his style, while the ignorant Greek would be suitably overawed by Alexander's divine majesty. For the choice of two ravens seems to me, at least, to be highly evocative of an item recorded by Herodotus in book two. There the oracles of Ammon in Lybia and Dodona in Epirus were founded by two black doves (πελειάδες μελαίνες) from Thebes in Egypt, or so the priestesses at Dodona said. The two black birds, whether they be doves or ravens, provide a link between Epirus, Olympias' home (and Alexander's own "back yard," so to speak), and the oracle in Lybia. The plan of Callisthenes seems to have been: Alexander was to be sold as a divine, or semi-divine being to the ignorant; and to the educated Greek he was to be made respectable by being given a rich historical background, full of hitherto unsuspected links with venerable Hellenic traditions. "Who controls the past," said George Orwell, "controls the future."[11]

One famous incident in Callisthenes' life deserves consideration in this connection. According to the story Callisthenes, already the acknowledged leader of the page-boys, and suspect because of his resistance to the act of *proskynesis*, was asked to deliver a speech praising the Macedonians. This he did brilliantly, and was pelted with garlands. But praising the great, and condemning the villain calls for only limited rhetorical skill. Could he prove himself as an orator by taking these same Macedonians and vilifying them? It is said that Goebbels had performed a similar trick at a party of senior Nazis. He had argued for the restoration of the monarchy, and even praised Communism, before showing his great good sense by concluding with a speech in praise of the

---

[7] Bury, 165.

[8] Bury, 167.

[9] At least, it is not too unfair to characterize the brief statement of Stephen Usher, *The Historians of Greece and Rome* (London 1969) 100–105, and Michael Grant, *The Ancient Historians* (London 1970) 137–142 in this way.

[10] F. Jacoby, *FGrHist* 124, F 14a = Strabo 17.1.43, also F 14b = Plut., *Alex.* 27; see also L. Pearson, *The Lost Histories of Alexander the Great* (*APA* Monographs 20, Oxford 1960) 33–39.

[11] George Orwell, *Nineteen Eighty-four* (London 1962, first published 1949) 253.

Nazis.[12] Callisthenes, however, with characteristic lack of tact, walked blindly into the trap and denigrated the Macedonians only too successfully. His arrest cannot have followed too long after this incident, and he died in jail.[13] Callisthenes seems stupidly to have overestimated the sophistication of his audience. This was not a symposium of Athenian wits out for a good evening's entertainment, but a mixed assembly dominated largely by military men who would have been ill-at-ease with the casual insincerity of rhetoric. The witty display was not completely out of step with the teaching of Isocrates, except that the master would have had a better sense of appropriateness, or καιρός as the theorists called it.[14] After all, had not the master, himself, said in his *Panegyricus*: "Words enable us to tell the same story in many different ways, to make great things appear humble and to invest humble things with grandeur?" That is all right for an orator. However, when a historian tries it and takes such an approach to history, as Callisthenes seems to have done, history becomes, as Voltaire put it, ". . . but a pack of tricks we play upon the dead."[15]

So Callisthenes emerges as the rhetorical historian *par excellence*, more Isocratean than Isocrates. His aim is to pander to a megalomaniac king and his court of comrades-in-arms, sycophants and flatterers, as well as to reach and influence as broad a cross-section of the Greek reading public as possible. At best it seems to have been rhetorical history in Bury's pernicious sense, and at worst it was pure propaganda. However, even Callisthenes is difficult to adapt perfectly to Bury's neat scheme, because his reason for trying to reach a broad reading public is *not* a mere craving for popularity. It is dictated by the needs of the moment: to become a successful apologist and propagandist for the Macedonian war-machine. That the major fourth-century historians wrote with the *sole* aim of pandering to a broad public taste remains to be demonstrated.

Ephorus and Theopompus were reputed to have been pupils of Isocrates. Did Isocrates greatly influence the historical writing of the time? Thought on the subject is divided into two schools. On the one hand we have Bury's view, strongly re-inforced by Barber in his book on Ephorus, and widely accepted, according to which Isocrates' influence was all-pervasive. This idea is based on well established, widespread ancient traditions that most historians and many other important persons of the century spent some time actually studying with Isocrates. This has tended to lead historiographers to the conclusion that fourth-century history was fairly uniform, and uniformly Isocratean. The apparent differences between individual historians have tended to be overlooked or downplayed, and similarities have been assumed or hinted at, often with only slight demonstration. At the start, this view seems comfortable, because it adopts and uses in a straightforward manner the extensive testimony of antiquity. Oddly, however, it ends with a position that clashes somewhat with the same traditions. For the same ancient critics who insisted that Ephorus and Theopompus actually studied under Isocrates, often went on to observe how different the two historians were. To Theopompus, they said, Isocrates had to apply the rein, to Ephorus, the spur. The rival view was first advanced by Ed. Schwartz, and was recently revised by Truesdell Brown.[16] It is denied by these scholars that Ephorus and Theopompus were pupils of Isocrates, and stories to that effect are criticized as late biographical fictions. This approach seems to fly in the face of ancient tradition, but Brown seems to me to excel all others in bringing out the undeniable and extensive differences between Ephorus and Theopompus. However, it may be possible to have the best of both views. The ideas of the master himself were scarcely doctrines; and even he saw fit to

[12] Pearson (above, note 10), 24; Louis P. Lochner, *The Goebbels Diaries* (New York 1948) 16. Callisthenes T 7 = Plut., *Alex.* 54.

[13] Plut., *Alex.* 54–55.

[14] *DK*, Gorg. f. 13. Guthrie (above, note 2) 272. Isoc., *Against the Sophists* 12–13, 16–18, *Panegyricus* 9, *Helen* 11; G. Kennedy, *The Art of Persuasion in Greece* (Princeton 1963) 66–68.

[15] Attributed to Voltaire, at least, by Arthur Marwick, *The Nature of History* (London and Basingstoke 1970) 244.

[16] G. L. Barber, *The Historian Ephorus* (Oxford 1935) 75–84; Ed. Schwartz, *RE* "Ephorus" 1; Truesdell S. Brown, *The Greek Historians* (Lexington, Mass., Toronto, London 1973) 108.

change or jettison some of them from time to time in the course of his long life. It is perfectly reasonable to assume that Isocrates' pupils had ideas of their own, that they could have adopted the views of the master selectively, and would have made such use of his techniques as suited their personal tastes.

Did Ephorus set out to use the pernicious tricks of rhetoric simply to attract and hold the largest possible audience? The question may well be ultimately unanswerable, but it is at least worth observing that if such was his aim, his procedures come as something of a surprise. According to Polybius and Strabo he came alive in his major work, the *Hellenica*, when describing sea-battles and the foundings of colonies, or recording genealogies and geographical trivia. He was also known for a treatise *On Discoveries* (περὶ εὑρημάτων).[17] It should be admitted immediately that one can be rhetorical in dealing with any of these subjects. However, it is difficult to see how Ephorus could have maintained interest in sea-battles and trivia for a very great length of time simply by using rhetoric. For his *Hellenica* was no "quick read" for a few evenings' diversion. It was left unfinished after 29 books. At least one more had been planned, and was finished for him by Demophilus, his son.[18] These thirty books seem to have been fairly widely read and known, or at least quoted, but again our impression is that the ancients did not resort to his work for its bright intellectual flashes. He seems to have been characterized as a rather dull sort, fascinated by recondite facts; the pupil of Isocrates who needed the spur. We must, therefore, conclude that his success lies as much in his ability to select intrinsically interesting stories as to dress them in fine rhetorical garb. His infatuation with his home town of Cyme was proverbial. The allegation that Ephorus would punctuate his history by occasionally commenting, "Nothing much was happening at Cyme these days," may be a joke, but it is surely revealing.[19] On the whole it is difficult to see any concerted plan or set of doctrines around which great rhetorical flights might have been taken. We may conclude that Ephorus endeared himself to his readers with an inoffensive, if somewhat bland style, and the broad pan-Hellenic sweep of his history. That much sounds moderately Isocratean. It could indeed have been learned without ever attending the master's lectures, but who is to say?

It is tempting to group Theopompus with Callisthenes.[20] Their most famous works, the *Philippica*, and the *Exploits of Alexander* respectively, were centered on the careers of Macedonian warrior-kings. There is evidence from Theopompus' digression in book ten on the Athenian demagogues that he could invent, or at least "discover," hitherto unknown "facts" about the obscure or base parentage of politicians he wished to malign. He was famous for his merciless attacks on individuals: irresponsible vitriol, as Polybius saw it, penetrating, if somewhat judgemental character-analysis, as the more generous Dionysius of Halicarnassus saw it.[21] Whether it was analysis or assassination of character, the fragments show it as always pungent and condemning.

Callisthenes had devoted his work to flattering the Macedonian king. However, in recent articles it has been shown how unlikely it was that Theopompus had any kind words at all for Philip. The fragments and *testimonia* do indeed suggest that Theopompus was at least as rhetorical as Callisthenes. Yet it may be seriously doubted that his motive was simply to cultivate an extensive reading clientèle. He seems to have attacked Philip and his friends for their activities, and Demosthenes and his sympathizers for their inactivity, and failure. Everyone's hero comes in for some

---

[17] *FGrHist* 70 TT 1, 2, 12, 18 (= Strab., 10.3.5, Polyb., 9.1.4), 19, 20 (= Polyb., 12.25 f.).

[18] TT 9, 10.

[19] F 236 = Strab. 13.3.6. κατὰ δὲ τὸν αὐτὸν καιρὸν Κυμαῖοι τὰς ἡσυχίας ἦγον: (lit.) "At the same time the Cymaeans were enjoying peace."

[20] See especially Pearson (above, note 10), 35.

[21] W. R. Connor, *Theopompus and Fifth-Century Athens* (Cambridge, Mass. 1968) 38–41, 59, Theopompus, *FGrHist* 115, FF 91, 95.

denigration; hardly an approach for a historian seeking to curry popular favour, especially since he carried it on for 58 books![22] We need to find a better reason for the cultivation and development of rhetorical history in Theopompus, at least, and, to a lesser degree, in Ephorus. The result, I hope, will be a more accurate view of their purpose in writing history, and, therefore, of the nature of the works they produced.

The fourth century was not an age of empiricism. The old Sophistic doctrine of the primacy of the perceptual, physical world was replaced by a new view of reality according to which truth was not to be found in information from the senses, but through intellection, and the recollection of a preexistence among the "forms" or "ideas". Out went the empirical baby with the unethical bath water of sophistry. Not that sophistry was entirely dead, of course; much of the rhetorical technique of Gorgias still lived in the teaching and practice of Isocrates.[23] However, the approach of Isocrates was in one critical way different from that of Gorgias. This was in the area of the much-vexed question of the teachability of ἀρέτη, and the spiritual value of rhetoric in the life of the individual. Gorgias had disclaimed any responsibility for the quality and behaviour of his students. He gave them a tool; the use they made of it was their own responsibility.[24] Isocrates' view was different:

> I consider that the kind of art which can implant honesty and justice in depraved natures has never existed and does not now exist, and that people who profess that power will grow weary and cease from their vain pretensions before such an education is ever found. But I do hold that people can become better and worthier if they conceive an ambition to speak well, if they become possessed of the desire to be able to persuade their hearers, and, finally, if they set their hearts on seizing their advantage—I do not mean 'advantage' in the sense given to that word by the empty-minded, but advantage in the true meaning of that term; and that this is so I think I shall presently make clear.
> For, in the first place, when anyone elects to speak or write discourses which are worthy of praise and honour, it is not conceivable that he will support causes which are unjust or petty or devoted to private quarrels, and not rather those which are great and honourable, devoted to the welfare of man and our common good; for if he fails to find causes of this character, he will accomplish nothing to the purpose. In the second place, he will select from all the actions of men which bear upon his subject those examples which are the most illustrious and the most edifying; and, habituating himself to contemplate and appraise such examples, he will feel their influence not only in the preparation of a given discourse but in all the actions of his life. It follows, then, that the power to speak well and think right will reward the man who approaches the art of discourse with love of wisdom and love of honour.[25]

When we describe Isocrates' influence on the historical writing of the time we must use the word "pernicious" with caution. If there is one theme that unites the thought and life of Isocrates it is the one so clearly enunciated in the quotation above. To τὸ λέγειν εὖ (effective speaking) Isocrates has added τὸ φρονεῖν (prudent or sensible thinking). Both objectives are to be sought, and can be found by τοῖς φιλοσόφως καὶ φιλοτίμως πρὸς τοὺς λόγους διακειμένοις. This hardly

[22] W. R. Connor, "History without Heroes: Theopompus' Treatment of Philip of Macedon," *GRBS* 8 (1967) 133–154; G. Shrimpton, "Theopompus' Treatment of Philip in the *Philippica*," *Phoenix* 31 (1977) 123–144; Theopompus, T 31.
[23] Münscher, *RE* "Isokrates," 2152; Kennedy (above, note 14) 177–179.
[24] Guthrie (above, note 1), 271–272.
[25] Isoc., *Antidosis* 274–277; cf. Kennedy's translation of the last sentence (above, note 14) 179: "So that the ability to speak and think well will reward those who train themselves in a love of wisdom and honor with regard to words." The quoted translation is by George Norlin in the Loeb edition (Cambridge, Mass. 1968).

sounds like a school for historical scandal. The effect of Isocratean morality will only be pernicious if his pupils become willing to cheapen individual facts in order to make them conform to higher moral teachings. It is interesting to note that there is nothing in the teaching of Isocrates to suggest that he advocated that type of thinking.

He did not have to do so. The highly particular type of fact with which the historian (who likes to call himself scientific) must deal, and the sort of empirical observation that verifies it, were very low on the scale of priorities of most thinkers of the fourth century. The move was back to a view of reality that resembled the view of Parmenides. So the state of things described by R. G. Collingwood in our opening quotation prevailed once again. Directly stated: the fourth century failed to develop an epistemology that could be as suited to the writing of history as the one that had followed from the humanistic relativism of the Sophists. And the new ideas about the nature of reality made it such that it could be examined only by methods of intellectual activity that were unsuited to historical enquiry. On this view, it became difficult for a historian to believe he could know anything, and more difficult to believe that anything he might come to know would be worth knowing unless it could be given a more transcendental, or abiding, quality, like the Platonic "forms." It was this lack of a solid theory of knowledge that made history so vulnerable to the inroads of rhetoric.

Plato's view of reality notoriously leaves little or no room for the type of fact that interests the historian. His myth of the cave, and allegory of the line, make the events of this world, in the immediate present, distorted shadows of reality, at the very bottom of the scale of truth. The historian must work with evanescent recollections of these fleeting, ever-changing shadows that are obviously well off the scale of reality. For Plato, the only type of recollection that is trustworthy is of the changeless forms. Use can be made of recollections of the past; this can be seen in the *Timaeus* and *Critias*; but only when these recollections help the all-important conclusions of the philosopher. They are tested and verified by their conformity to philosophical truth. When in book eight of the *Republic* Plato sets out to write the "history" of the decline of the ideal state, the process is purely theoretical, and clearly detached from known historical events. No attempt is made to reflect, even remotely, the reported events from any known part of Greek history.

Aristotle's work at first seems to offer hope for the return of an intellectual climate that might foster the development of a less blatantly rhetorical and more responsible or sophisticated form of history. His later works often consist of the careful collection and classification of empirical observations, especially in the study of biology. His explanations of his own ideas are frequently introduced by reference to past attempts to answer whatever question occupies his mind; as if he is keenly conscious of the value of appreciating the history of a problem before attempting to solve it. To him or his school were attributed 158 descriptions of constitutions which included extensive historical analysis if we may judge from the surviving *Athenaion Politeia*. Despite his tendency to allow his political thinking to follow closely his own biological models of explanation, and the inclination of his historical thought to succumb to his peculiar teleological views, it is clear that his philosophical system might well be more adaptable to history than most others from antiquity.[26] But he seems to have come too late in the fourth century to have altered greatly its historical writing; and his influence on his contemporaries and their successors has been shown by Kurt von Fritz to have been negligible.[27]

[26] W. D. Ross, *OCD²* "Aristotle," 116; for an interesting look at the continuing influence of Aristotelian teleology in modern scientific models of explanation see F. J. Ayala, "Teleological Explanations in Evolutionary Biology," *Philosophy of Science* 37 (1970) 13–15; for an attempt to show how historical information may have influenced Aristotle's theories see R. A. de Laix, "Aristotle's Conception of the Spartan Constitution," *JHistPhil* 12 (1974) 21–31.

[27] Kurt von Fritz, "Die Bedeutung des Aristoteles," *Histoire et historiens dans l'antiquité, Fondation Hardt* 4 (Vandoevres-Geneve 1956) 85–145.

In the words of William Dray: "The historian is interested in *the* French Revolution or *the* execution of Charles I—individual historical events—not in revolutions and executions as such . . . . The historian's interest . . . will not be confined to those aspects or features which [events] shared with other revolutions and executions. He will want to study them in all their uniqueness and particularity."[28] The particular integrity of the historical fact, as described by Professor Dray, was noted long ago by Aristotle in a famous and highly significant comparison of history with poetry in the *Poetics*. "Poetry," he says, "is a more philosophical and higher (σπουδαιότερον) thing than history: for poetry tends to express the universal (τὰ καθόλου), history the particular (τὰ καθ' ἕκαστον). By the universal I mean how a person of a certain type will on occasion speak or act according to the law of probability or necessity (κατὰ τὸ εἰκὸς ἢ τὸ ἀναγκαῖον); and it is this universality at which poetry aims in the names she attaches to the personages. The particular is— for example—what Alcibiades did or suffered."[29] The comparison with poetry is significant, according to von Fritz. It either reflected, or led to, a sense of rivalry between the two genres. In his view, Hellenistic history addressed itself wholly to making up its "inferiority" by including generous helpings of universal or poetic truth at the expense of the particular.[30] This is a trend that began innocently in Thucydides, as I have tried to show, and must have made some advances in Ephorus and, probably, more in Theopompus.

The wider, pan-Hellenic, view of history for which Ephorus was famous makes possible the observation of parallels or patterns of human behaviour. In Ephorus, to judge from the fragments from the introductions to some of his books, this fostered a general tendency to moralize. Theopompus went further than this. His aim seems to have been to study human moral and social behaviour across as broad a spectrum as possible, with a view to exposing its underlying patterns (as I have argued elsewhere).[31] Once exposed, the patterns would make it possible for the historian to describe, or even predict, behaviour κατὰ τὸ ἀνθρώπινον ("in accordance with human nature") to use the Thucydidean term; or like the Aristotelian poet κατὰ τὸ εἰκός.

If we are to believe Dionysius of Halicarnassus, Theopompus claimed to have travelled extensively, and to have extended himself considerably to verify what he reports in his history.[32] This would certainly suggest that he had some degree of respect for individual facts. Yet the intensity of his sarcasm, his apparent willingness to invent false parenthoods for people he did not like, and his passion for exotic marvels, not the least of which being the creation of an entire fictitious world (the land of Meropis), all suggest that his respect for facts was somewhat less than Thucydidean. Either he was an utterly irresponsible liar, then, or he had a different idea of truth from what we expect of a modern historian. The evidence seems to support the second alternative.

[28] William H. Dray, *Philosophy of History* (Toronto 1964) 8; the full development of this argument is to be found in Sir Isaiah Berlin, "History and Theory: the Concept of Scientific History," *History and Theory* 1 (1960–1961) 1–31. Berlin's main idea is that the historian *qua* historian avoids theoretical generalizations. When he generalizes he approaches, or transgresses into the territory of other disciplines such as Economics or Sociology. Does this mean that the historian must forever live like one of Ihor Sevcenko's caterpillars ("Two Varieties of Historical Writing," *History and Theory* 8 [1969] 332–345), munching on one leafy fact after another and never soaring up on the wings of the butterfly to view the whole tree? According to one expert the answer would appear to be, no: Georg Iggers, *New Directions in Modern European Historiography* (Middletown, Conn. 1975) 123–174.

[29] Arist., *Poetics* 9.4 (1451b); Renate Zoepffel, *Historia und Geschichte bei Aristoteles* (Heidelberg 1974).

[30] It is interesting to note how the idea of comparing history with poetry was to recur in the nineteenth century, particularly in the works of Carlyle: "History, after all, is the true poetry . . . ." from his essay on Boswell's *Life of Samuel Johnson* (T. Carlyle, *Critical and Miscellaneous Essays* 3 [London 1899] 79; and 4 [London 1899] 26, also *History of Frederick the Great* 1 [London 1897] 17). Macauley, unlike Carlyle, did not equate poetry with history, if anything he would have separated them on the grounds of particularity *vs.* general theory, but, unlike Aristotle, he makes particularity the atribute of poetry and (implicitly, I believe) generalization the attribute of history in his essay on Milton! See, Thomas Babington Macaulay, *Critical and Historical Essays* (London and New York 1974, first published 1907) 153–154.

[31] G. Shrimpton (above, note 22), 137–144.

[32] T 20 = Dion. Hal., *Ad. Pomp.* 6.7.

Plato placed the changeless forms at the head of his scale of reality, and the phenomenal world at the very bottom. For Aristotle the universal or categorical truth of poetry was of greater value than the particular truth of history. In the fourth century the historians themselves were showing a similar lack of interest in the particular and were addressing themselves to more universal principles, repetitive or categorical truths that might be more suitable for poetry or philosophy. It would perhaps be unsafe to speak of direct influence from philosophy on historical writing, although Theopompus, at least, was aware of some of Plato's dialogues. It might be safer to speak of an intellectual world no longer able to trust in the reality of the world of becoming. In the fourth century there seems to have been a widespread search for the static and permanent: to find enduring values in a world where nearly everything seemed to be undergoing change and decay.[33]

University of Victoria   GORDON S. SHRIMPTON

[33] F 275. I am grateful to the following people for reading this paper, and offering comments: Professor Shalom Perlman, Tel Aviv, Phillip Harding, U.B.C., and my colleague in the Philosophy Department, Rodger Beehler, to whom I owe a great debt of gratitude. These scholars do not necessarily agree with all my conclusions. An early version of this essay was read by me to the Classical Association of Canada in June, 1978. It is a humble offering to a great man.

THUCYDIDES, THE *PROGNOSTIKA*, AND LUCRETIUS: A NOTE ON *DE RERUM NATURA* 6.1195.*

Of all the ancient imitators of Thucydides one is perhaps most conspicuous for being the least likely. It has long been recognized that Lucretius' account of the plague in *De Rerum Natura* 6.1138–1286 exhibits a strong dependence upon Thucydides' description of the pestilence at Athens in 2.47 ff.[1] Bailey was not the first to point out the correspondence in the two accounts of sequence of details and to note the frequent translation of Thucydides' words by the philosopher-poet.[2] He was well aware, however, as his predecessors had been, that Lucretius often deviates from the parent account on points of detail, and on occasion chooses to omit matter present in Thucydides while elsewhere he introduces new material.[3] It is the most lengthy of these non-Thucydidean passages that has aroused special interest, for here alone in his description of the pestilence Lucretius' reliance on a second Greek source may be discerned.

In 1182–1196 Lucretius sets aside Thucydides for the moment in order to list in summary fashion a number of *mortis signa* – symptoms of approaching death displayed by the victims of the plague. The commentators and others have noted the poet's dependence here upon a number of passages from various treatises of the *Corpus Hippocraticum*.[4] Some have suggested that Lucretius used an intermediate source, whether he be Epicurus, Demetrius of Laconia or a Latin, who had already brought about the amalgamation of bits and pieces of various fifth-century medical treatises with Thucydides' account of the plague.[5] Such theories are fortunately no longer tenable. In the first place, they represent a completely needless multiplication of sources. Thucydides was well known in Rome in the first century, and to assume that Lucretius had anything but a first-hand knowledge of his work is to assume far too little.[6] The poet's extensive familiarity with Greek

* I owe a considerable debt of gratitude to Carl R. Trahman of the University of Cincinnati, who criticized a number of renditions of this paper and made invaluable suggestions for their improvement. David F. Bright of Urbana read a later draft and volunteered helpful advice. Responsibility for views expressed here, however, remains my own. A special word of thanks is due to the recipient of this volume. His continuing tutelage and his friendship over the years have been a source of inspiration.

[1] H. A. J. Munro, *T. Lucreti Cari De Rerum Natura Libri Sex* 2 (4th ed., Cambridge 1886) 391; C. Giussani, *T. Lucreti Cari De Rerum Natura* 4 (Torino 1898) 297; A. Ernout-L. Robin, *Lucrèce de Rerum Natura* 3 (Paris 1928) 351.

[2] C. Bailey, *Titi Lucreti Cari De Rerum Natura Libri Sex* 3 (Oxford 1947) 1723. Also, the earlier commentators as cited in note 1 above.

[3] Bailey (above, note), *passim ad* 6.1138–1286. More recently, H. S. Commager Jr., "Lucretius' Interpretation of the Plague," *HSCP* 62 (1957) 105–118; David F. Bright, "The Plague and the Structure of *De Rerum Natura*," *Latomus* 30 (1971) 607–632.

[4] Munro (above, note 1), 394; Giussani (above, note 1), 301–302; Ernout-Robin (above, note 1), 351, 354–355; Bailey (above, note 2), 1731–1732; Commager (above, note 3), 114, note 1; Bright (above, note 3), 616.

[5] Epicurus: J. Woltjer, *Lucreti philosophia cum fontibus comparata* (Groningen 1877) 159–160. Demetrius of Laconia: Diels, followed by W. Lück, *Die Quellenfrage im 5. und 6. Buch des Lukrez* (Breslau 1932) 163 ff. A Latin source: Ernout-Robin (above, note 1), 351. It is perhaps just as well that none of these works explores fully the question of the nature and the intent of the amalgamated source for which they argue.

[6] Sallust knew Thukydides thoroughly: cf. the bibliography cited by O. Luschnat, "Thukydides," *RE Supp.* 12 (1965) 1297–1298, and by A. D. Leeman, *A Systematic Bibliography of Sallust, Mnemosyne Supp.* 4 (Leiden 1965) 37–38.

scientific and philosophical texts has been documented elsewhere.[7] It is scarcely credible that he would have drawn directly upon such thinkers as the pre-Socratics while reverting for his know-ledge of pestilence to a strange and second-hand combination of Thucydides with gobbets from assorted medical texts. What is more, Lucretius' acquaintance with both the historian and the medical writers goes beyond that in evidence in 6.1138–1286. Segal has shown that he elsewhere (3.487–509) draws upon the Hippocratic *On the Sacred Disease* and *On Breaths*, and Smith was most likely correct in discerning Thucydidean influence in 5.1440–1447.[8] Is it necessary to postu-late the poet's dependence upon an intermediate source in these instances as well? Finally, theories suggesting the presence of such a source behind 6.1182–1196 both underestimate the genius of Lucretius and misunderstand his purpose in his description of the plague.

It must not be assumed that Lucretius inserted the content of these lines simply because a learned predecessor had, or that they are little more than erudite embellishment for what he himself discovered in Thucydides 2.47 ff. Their effect is calculated and is perfectly consonant with that of other of his several deviations from the text of his historical model.[9] Their rapidity, their pattern of sound and their proliferation of gruesome detail convey a sense of the absolute relent-lessness of the disease. It afflicts the mind (1183), facial expression (1184), hearing (1185), and breathing (1186). It produces a cold sweat (1187), disturbs the colour, consistency and taste of the spittle (1188–1189), and causes the sinews to contract and limbs gradually to become cold (1190–1192). Then, at its most extreme—*ad supremum denique tempus* (1192)—it disturbs the facial features and skin (1193–1195):

> conpressae nares, nasi primoris acumen/tenue, cavati oculi, cava tempora, frigida pellis/
> duraque in ore, iacens rictum; frons tenta manebat.[10]

Death is imminent when the nostrils become pinched (*conpressae nares*), the tip of the nose pointed (*nasi primoris acumen/tenue*), the eyes sunken in their sockets (*cavati oculi*), the temples hollow (*cava tempora*), and the facial flesh cold and hard (*frigida pellis/duraque in ore*). So far, so good. It is the remainder of Lucretius' description of the face of death that has been troublesome, and this as a result of a knotty textual difficulty.

At 6.1195 the major manuscripts present the following selection of readings all prefaced by *duraque*, which is unquestionable:

O: inhoretiacetrectumfronstentamebat
O[1]:   inhorretiacetrectumfronstentameabat
QU: inoretiacetrectumfronstentamebat
AB: inhorretiacetrictusfronstentameabat
F: inhoreiacetrectumfronstentameabat
L: inhorretiacetfronstentameabat

The ninth-century manuscripts, O and Q, bear readings which border on the nonsensical. The most authoritative of the *Itali* vary amongst themselves and with the older tradition. Their

---

Cicero knew Thucydides well enough to judge him (*Brutus* 288) and to criticize his Roman imitators (*Orator* 30–32). Tacitus (*Dialogus* 25.4) and Quintilian (*Inst.* 10.1.105–116) give a whole list of late Republican "Thucydideans," in-cluding Asinius Pollio, Caelius, Calvus, and Cicero himself: cf. A. D. Leeman, *Orationis Ratio* 1 (Amsterdam 1963) 159–163.

[7] The bibliography is extensive: cf. W. Rösler, "Lukrez und die Vorsokratiker: Doxographische Probleme im 1. Buch von *De Rerum Natura*," *Hermes* 101 (1973) 48, note 1, though Rösler himself is one of the few who believe that Lucre-tius' acquaintance with the pre-Socratics is owed to a doxographical tradition.

[8] C. Segal, "Lucretius, Epilepsy, and the Hippocratic *On Breaths*," *CP* 65 (1970) 180–182; M. F. Smith, "Lucretius, *De Rerum Natura* 5.1440–1447," *Hermathena* 98 (1964) 45–52.

[9] Bright (above, note 3), 616–620.

[10] The text is that of Büchner, *T. Lucreti Cari De Rerum Natura* (Wiesbaden 1966).

renderings too, individually and collectively, convey little sense. In the face of the apparent default of the direct tradition the testimonium of Nonius (Lindsay 1.266.25), *duraque in ore iacens rictu frons tenta manebat*, has been adopted either *in toto* or with slight variation by almost all modern editors of Lucretius. Martin, following Diels, accepted it without alteration.[11] Ernout and later Büchner made the slight change to *rictum.*[12] In his monumental edition of 1947 Bailey, while opting for *rictum*, adopted Heinsius' *tumebat* in preference to the *mebat* and the *meabat* of the codices and to the *manebat* of Nonius.[13] Paratore did likewise a few years later.[14] Emendation on a somewhat larger scale has been intermittent. Yet in spite of all such machinations the essential difficulties of the line remain.

A major question concerns Lucretius' use of his source. Verses 1193–1195 are inspired by the Hippocratic *Prognostika* 2.114, a passage which describes with a scientific terseness effectively imitated by Lucretius the face of someone about to die of an unspecified illness. The symptoms of imminent death are as follows:

> ῥὶς ὀξεῖα, ὀφϑαλμοὶ κοῖλοι, κρόταφοι ξυμπεπτωκότες, ὦτα ψυχρὰ καὶ συνεσταλμένα καὶ οἱ λοβοὶ τῶν ὤτων ἀπεστραμμένοι καὶ τὸ δέρμα τὸ περὶ τὸ μέτωπον σκληρόν τε καὶ περιτεταμένον καὶ καρφαλέον ἐόν.

This description is comprised of five parts dealing in turn with the nose, eyes, brow, ears and skin. Lucretius follows the same order, though he omits any mention of the ears at this juncture and expands the picture of the nose. Furthermore, as the text now stands, he breaks down the final element of the Greek description into two quite distinct components (i.e., *pellis duraque* renders τὸ δέρμα σκληρόν, and *frons tenta* expresses τὸ μέτωπον περιτεταμένον) and interposes between them the detail of the *iacens rictum* (or *rictus* or *rictu*). Two of these alterations make good sense. Just a few lines before, in 1185, Lucretius had described the ears as *sollicitae porro plenaeque sonoribus*, and must have felt that this would suffice. The addition of *conpressae nares* is not surprising since it fits well with the picture of a gaunt, sunken face conveyed also by the phrases *cava tempora* and *cavati oculi*. What is more, *conpressae nares* implies a difficulty in breathing, and this is in complete accord with the poet's statement in 1186. *Frons* and *iacens rictum* (or *rictus* or *rictu*), on the other hand, are quite out of place.

The fact that *frons* is unprecedented as an independent component of the Greek description is not so disturbing as the consideration that the context of the Lucretian passage renders it otiose. In the preceding line the poet had just described the brow (*tempora*) as sunken (*cava*). There is no reason, short of outright carelessness, why he should have reverted to the needlessly repetitive *frons*. Furthermore, its adjective *tenta* seems accurately to reflect the participial περιτεταμένον which is used to modify τὸ δέρμα in *Prognostika* 2.114. This participle Celsus (2.6.1) chose to translate by *intenta*, using it in reference to the *cutis circa frontem* (τὸ δέρμα τὸ περὶ τὸ μέτωπον) of the diseased. While it would be rash to claim that Lucretius' manner of utilization of his source approximates to that of Celsus, this comparison is both interesting and enlightening, since it suggests the possibility that Lucretius' *tenta* refers not to the *frons* now found in the text, but to *pellis* at the end of the preceding line.

The expression *iacens rictum* (or *rictus* or *rictu*) presents a parcel of problems of its own. Lucretius found no exemplar for it in *Prognostika* 2.114, and the commentators have suggested that it renders χείλεα ἀπολυόμενα καὶ κρεμάμενα in *Prognostika* 2.118.[15] This association is not beyond

---

[11] J. Martin, *De Rerum Natura Libri Sex* (Leipzig 1934); H. Diels, *T. Lucretius Carus De Rerum Natura* 1 (Berlin 1923).

[12] A. Ernout, *Lucrèce de la Nature* 2 (Paris 1924); Büchner (above, note 10).

[13] Bailey (above, note 2), vol. 1.

[14] H. Paratore-H. Pizzani, *Lucreti De Rerum Natura* (Rome 1960).

[15] Bailey (above, note 2), 1732; Ernout-Robin (above, note 1), 1195.

doubt. In the first place, *iacens* seems to do justice to neither ἀπολυόμενα nor κρεμάμενα: *pendens* or something like it would be far more appropriate, as W. Richter pointed out.[16] Secondly, *rictum* (or *rictus*) is surely an unexpected rendering of χείλεα, for which one would rather expect *labia* or more probably *labra*.[17] *Rictum* in Lucretius means something quite different. The poet's point that outward signs are indicative of inward emotion is illustrated in 5.1063–1064 by the example of angered bloodhounds:

> irritata canum cum primum magna Molossum
> mollia ricta fremunt duros nudantia dentis/. . . .

Bailey's translation of the expression *magna . . ./mollia ricta* by "large loose lips" will not do.[18] It is better understood as referring not simply to the lips but rather to the jowl-like fleshy tissue which surrounds the mouth of such beasts.[19] *Iacens rictum* (or *rictus*) invokes a similar image: the plague would be said to cause the skin around the mouth to sag and droop, producing a jowl-like effect. We are then faced with the problem that the reading *iacens rictum* (or *rictus*) directly contradicts the picture of the afflicted face produced by *pellis/duraque in ore* and by *tenta*, which point to the hardness and tautness of the skin.[20] The same difficulty is inherent in *iacens rictu*, for here *iacens* must modify *pellis*, and *rictu* has to be explained as an ablative either of specification or of location. The phrase is an awkward one by either reckoning, and attempts to justify it by reference to *iacens mammis* in *Moretum* 34 have not been successful.[21] The contradiction still remains.

Such are the principal shortcomings of *De Rerum Natura* 6.1195. To them Nonius' *manebat* need not be added. Heinsius' preference for *tumebat* over it and the *mebat* and *meabat* of the manuscripts, though it has found favour with a host of modern editors, was unfortunate to say the least. Forms of *manere* in the imperfect and occupying the position at the end of the hexameter are reasonably common in the plague passage.[22] Lucretius was fond of such repetition for aural effect, as Deutsch took great pains to reveal.[23] Moreover, the notion of tumescence is at loggerheads with the picture that he draws in the rest of the passage. It is difficult to visualize a brow that is at one and the same time sunken (*cava tempora*) and swollen (*frons tumebat*).[24] Finally, the alteration of *manebat* to *mebat* and *meabat* is easily explained. The evolution of error, I suggest, was something as follows. The *ane* of *manebat*, contracted, as commonly, to *āe* with resultant *māebat*, was mistaken for the diphthong *ae*. Since, even in antiquity, *ae* often appeared as *e*, the peculiar but not surprising reading *mebat* found its way into our principal manuscripts. *Meabat* undoubtedly represents an attempt by an early corrector of O to impart a modicum of sense to the nonsensical *mebat* while at the same time correcting the metre. The doctored reading subsequently found its way into the *Itali*, which, as Müller has demonstrated, are the direct descendants of the corrected

---

[16] W. Richter, *Textstudien zu Lukrez, Zetemata* 60 (Munich 1974) 140–141.

[17] Cf. 4.1194: *et tenet assuctis umectans oscula labris.*

[18] Bailey (above, note 2), 1.487.

[19] This view is strengthened if, as Ludovica Rychlewska, following Lambinus, holds, Nonius' citation (Lindsay 1.327.22) of Lucretius 5.1064 (*mollia ricta tremunt duros nudantia dentis*) is indisputably correct: cf. her "De Lucretii Exemplari a Nonio Marcello Adhibito," *Eos* 54 (1964) 279–280. For in this case the *ricta* would be said to "quiver loosely." *Premunt* (OQ) is quite inadmissible, though the change from *tremunt* to it is perhaps more likely than that to *fremunt*, first suggested by Marullus and since adopted by the majority of Lucretius' editors.

[20] For the meaning of *tenta* cf. also 2.618: *tympana tenta tonant palmis et cymbala circum.*

[21] For criticism of this comparison, first suggested by Vollmer and then seconded by Diels (above, note 11), cf. F. Olivier, "En relisant Lucrèce," *MusHelv* 10 (1953) 56–57.

[22] Cf. 6.1201, 1210, and 1274.

[23] R. E. Deutsch, *The Pattern of Sound in Lucretius* (Bryn Mawr 1939) 141–142 and *passim*.

[24] Cf. the remark of Olivier (above, note 21) 56: "le *manebat* de Nonius Marcellus est excellent – sans compter qu'on aimerait savoir pourquoi, alors que toute la face s'est contractée, le front seul enflerait."

O.[25] There exist, then, strong grounds for retaining Nonius' *manebat*.[26] It is rather the centre of the line that stands in need of improvement. No emendation has dealt with its difficulties successfully while remaining within the bounds of Lucretian usage and palaeographical probability. Indeed, *frons* has gone virtually unquestioned.

Lachmann and Giussani adopted Rutgersius' *duraque, inhorrescens rictum* while leaving *frons* undisturbed and opting for the *tumebat* of Heinsius.[27] *Inhorrescens rictum* is a strange expression for which no parallel might be found in Lucretius or anywhere else. Moreover, it bears no relationship to what Lucretius found in his source. *In ore* should be retained, since with *pellis* it approximates to τὸ δέρμα τὸ περὶ τὸ μέτωπον in the *Prognostika*. Munro's *duraque, in ore trucei rictum, frons tenta manebat*, which Bailey adopted in the *OCT* with the minor alteration to *truci*, inspires no more confidence.[28] Its punctuation divorces *in ore* from its association with *pellis*, and the resulting combination of *in ore* with *rictum* is not a happy one. *Trucei* (or *truci*) represents a needless repetition, since in 1184 Lucretius has just described the facial expression (*voltus*) of the afflicted as *furiosus* and *acer*.[29]

Concerned no doubt by the absence in Nonius and the manuscripts of any detail relating to the ears (as in *Prognostika* 2.114) Merrill suggested *duraque iam auriculae tractae, frons tenta manebat*.[30] This conjecture does violence to Lucretius' close adherence in the preceding lines to the order of the components of the Greek account in which ears come before facial skin. More importantly, it is all but impossible to justify *auriculae* on palaeographical grounds. Olivier's *duraque in ore, rigens rictus* (or *rictum*), *frons tenta manebat* is more credible, but only for the fact that it retains *in ore* while attempting to dispense with the contradictory *iacens rictum* (or *rictus* or *rictu*).[31] The troublesome *frons* remains. Moreover, *rigens rictus* (or *rictum*) is not at all in accord with χεῖλεα ἀπολυόμενα καὶ κρεμάμενα in *Prognostika* 2.118. There may be doubt that Lucretius drew on this passage at all, though Olivier failed to discuss this problem and as a result his conjecture fails to convince.

Richter's suggestions for the curing of the ills of the line are more adventurous but equally questionable. In his *Textstudien zu Lukrez* he ventured *duraque in archiatri tactum; frons tenta tumebat*.[32] This proved unacceptable on many counts, as he himself came to realize. A second attempt issued in *duraque in articuli tactum; frons tenta tumebat*, which is no more compelling.[33] *Frons* and *tumebat* remain while *in ore* is absent. *Articuli* is difficult to defend on palaeographical grounds, and this Richter made no attempt to do. And whereas Lucretius does use a form of *articulus* elsewhere (3.697) he does not equate it with *digitus*. Richter must do so in order to obtain the meaning he desires, and this fact alone is sufficient to undermine his conjecture. Yet in spite of these shortcomings Richter was correct in seeing in *Georgics* 3.500ff. a possible solution for the difficulties of the line, and for this he deserves more than a modicum of credit.

Vergil's account in *Georgics* 3.478–566 of a plague which afflicts the animal kingdom is heavily influenced by Lucretius 6.1138–1286. Bailey noted that "the whole description is riddled with words and phrases derived from Lucretius," and the indefatigable Merrill found no less than nine-

---

[25] K. Müller, "De codicum Lucretii Italicorum origine," *MusHelv* 30 (1973) 166–178, 173 in particular.

[26] Müller, however, has recently rejected it in favour of Lambinus' *minebat*. Cf. Appendix below.

[27] K. Lachmann, *T. Lucreti Cari De Rerum Natura Libri Sex* (4th ed., Berlin 1871); Giussani (above, note 1).

[28] Munro (above, note 1), vol. 1; Bailey, *Lucreti De Rerum Natura Libri Sex* (1st ed., 1900; 2nd ed., 1922).

[29] In 1947 Bailey (above, note 2, 1732) withdrew *truci* and criticized Munro's *in ore trucei rictum* for being "too elaborate." Cf. also the doubt expressed by Olivier (above, note 21), 57.

[30] W. A. Merrill, "Criticism of the Text of Lucretius with Suggestions for its Improvement," *CPCP* 3 (1916) 131.

[31] Olivier (above, note 21), 56–57.

[32] Richter (above, note 16), 139–143.

[33] W. Richter, "Nachträgliches zum Lukreztext," *RhM* 119 (1976) 153–154.

teen unquestionable parallels and coincidences in the two passages.[34] Vergil, as Lucretius had done, notes a number of *signa* (503) indicative of the approaching death of the diseased. The heads of horses, he says, are afflicted as follows (500–502):

> . . . demissae aures, incertus ibidem
> sudor et ille quidem morituris frigidus; aret
> pellis et ad tactum tractanti dura resistit.

Resistit approximates to Lucretius' *manebat*, and the mention of *sudor* after Lucretius' *sudoris* (1187) and *pellis . . . dura* after his *pellis/duraque* leaves little doubt but that Vergil had Lucretius in mind when he composed these verses. In the light of such imitation here and in adjacent lines it is hardly unreasonable to seek a cure for the problems of *frigida pellis/duraque in ore iacens rictum* (or *rictus* or *rictu*) *frons tenta manebat* in *aret/pellis et ad tactum tractanti dura resistit*. The clue lies in *ad tactum tractanti*, which is blatantly redundant. Its construction with the subsequent *dura resistit* is grammatically awkward. Yet its succession of spondees rich in *a* and *t* sounds is attractive and highly evocative; by it Vergil probably intended to reproduce the sound of a drum-like tap on taut skin. In order to attain this effect he sacrificed absolute lucidity of expression, and, motivated by the spirit of *aemulatio* which so characterizes his use of all his sources, he took what he found in Lucretius one step further. There he read, I suggest:

> . . . frigida pellis
> duraque in ore iacens, tractanti tenta manebat.

"The skin was frigid," Lucretius says, "and, lying hard on the face, it remained taut to the touch." There is much to recommend this reading.

Tractanti tenta manebat, with its proliferation of *a* and *t* sounds, is attractive to the ear and simulates, much as do Vergil's *ad tactum tractanti* and Lucretius' own *tympana tenta tonant palmis* (2.618), the sound of a drum-like tap. The use of *tractare* in the sense of to touch or to stroke may be paralleled elsewhere in the poem, and so may be *manere* with the dative.[35] The rejection of *frons* makes good sense in the light of the difficulties it affords and enables *tenta* to modify *pellis* as περιτεταμένον does τὸ δέρμα in *Prognostika* 2.114. The alteration of *iacens rictum* (or *rictus* or *rictu*) to *iacens tractanti* dispenses with an unpleasant contradiction and improves the flow of the line: *iacens*, like *tenta*, may now modify *pellis* at the end of the preceding line, and the caesura, after *iacens*, is restored to a position that accords with Lucretian usage.[36] The introduction of the notion of touch accords with the Epicurean doctrine of epistemology.[37] The only way to know that the skin of the diseased is *frigida, dura* and *tenta* is to touch it. Similarly, the poet indicates earlier in the plague passage that the tongue is *aspera tactu* (1150), and that the surface of the skin affords a touch that is lukewarm: *tepidum manibus proponere tactum* (1165).

There remains the palaeographical problem. The traditional view that the archetypes of our manuscripts of the major authors were in capitals and are datable to the fourth and fifth centuries may no longer be taken for granted.[38] In the case of Lucretius, Brunhölzl has made a sound case,

[34] C. Bailey, "Vergil and Lucretius," *Proc. Class. Assoc.* 28 (1931) 27; W. A. Merrill, "Parallels and Coincidences in Lucretius and Vergil," *CPCP* 3 (1916) 216–218. Cf. also L. P. Wilkinson, *The Georgics of Vergil* (Cambridge 1969) 206, and E. Paratore, "Spunti lucreziani nelle *Georgiche*," *Atene e Roma* Ser. 3, 7 (1939) 177, 179.

[35] *Tractare*: cf. 2.399, 4.230, and 4.623. *Manere* and dative: cf. 3.1074–1075. *Remanere* appears with the dative in 3.402.

[36] The oldest of the technical studies of the Lucretian hexameter is still the most complete: cf. W. A. Merrill, "The Lucretian Hexameter," Parts 1 and 2, *CPCP* 5 (1922–1923), *passim*.

[37] U. Schoenheim, "The Place of 'Tactus' in Lucretius," *Philologus* 110 (1966) 71–87.

[38] Cf. the two articles of F. Brunhölzl: "Zu den sogenannten *codices archetypi* der römischen Literatur," *Festschrift Bernhard Bischoff* (Stuttgart 1971) 16–31; and "Zum Problem der Casinenser Klassikerüberlieferung," *Abhandlungen der Marburger Gelehrten Gesellschaft* 3 (Munich 1971) 111–143.

on the basis of certain types of error in the manuscripts explicable in no other way, for the existence of a tradition in Old Roman Cursive lying behind Lachmann's famous archetype of *De Rerum Natura*.[39] This important discovery lessens considerably the value of Nonius' citations of Lucretius as testimonia to be employed in establishing the text. For the possibility exists that they embody a perpetuation of the errors which had crept into the tradition in Old Roman Cursive at any time between Valerius Probus and Nonius himself.[40] *Frons* and *rictu*, I suggest, represent two such errors.

In the cursive exemplar *iacens tractanti tenta* would have been written something as follows:

ᴜᴢᴄᴘɴᴊᴄᴦᴠᴢᴄᴦᴺᴛʟᴛᴦɴᴄᴦ

It is readily apparent that the cluster here of nearly identical letter forms makes the possibilities for scribal error almost endless, especially if the act of transcription was performed at a time when the Majuscule Cursive was no longer in common use and had become less than familiar. Under such circumstances what began as *tractanti* could easily have issued in *rictu*. The most likely explanation for this metamorphosis seems to me to be the ensuing one. The visual effect of *iacens tractanti tenta* cluttered the mind of the copyist and caused haplography. This, combined with the misreading of the ᴛι (*ti*) of *tractanti* as ᴜ (*u*) produced ᴛᴧᴠᴄᴛᴜ (*tractu*). Then, at a subsequent stage of the transmission, but still before Nonius' day, *tractu* was in turn mistaken for *rictu* (ᴧιᴄᴛᴜ).

The case of *frons* would have been somewhat different. It probably crept into an intermediate copy containing the corrupted reading in an incomplete line, such as *duraque in ore iacens rictu* (or *tractu*) *tenta manebat*, and was meant to fill out the hexameter. It may have begun as an exegetical notation placed above the line near its beginning and intended to subsume the phrase *pellis in ore*. During the course of the transmission of the text it migrated to the right. A further possibility is that *frons* was written above *tenta* from the beginning, and was meant to explain that *tenta* (which is far removed from *pellis*, its subject) was to be construed with *pellis in ore*, with which *frons* was equated. In either case its entry into the line itself in the intermediate copy would have been easy. By the time of Nonius it had become firmly entrenched in the tradition, and there it was to remain in subsequent centuries.[41]

Appendix

I gained access to the most recent edition of Lucretius, that of Konrad Müller, only when the present paper was in its final stages. At 6.1195 Müller renders *duraque, in ore iacens rictum, frons tenta minebat*.[42] This reading is susceptible of much of the criticism that I have directed at others similar to it. It differs from those, however, in that it opts for *minebat*, originally a conjecture of Lambinus and ever since ignored. With *minebat* I should like to take issue, since it rests on the most tenuous of foundations.

[39] F. Brunhölzl, "Zur Überlieferung des Lukrez," *Hermes* 90 (1962) 97–104. Cf. also Büchner (above, note 10), *praef.* xiii–xiv. Müller (above, note 25) was apparently unconvinced: he makes no mention of the findings of Brunhölzl.

[40] W. Schmid suggests that the recension of Lucretius by Probus or one of his school had already absorbed non-Lucretian elements: cf. "Lukrez über die Mächtigen und ihre Ängste," *Symbola Coloniensia Iosepho Kroll Sexegenario . . . Oblata* (Cologne 1949) 107–108. That Probus worked on Lucretius is evident from Suetonius, *De Vir. Ill.* p. 138 (ed. Reifferscheid [Leipzig 1860]). The nature and extent of this work is uncertain, though it probably went beyond the mere insertion of critical symbols. Indeed, Lucretius' poem may very well have been one of the *exemplaria* alluded to by Suetonius (*Gram. et Rhet.* 24) as having received Probus' unrestrained attention: *multaque exemplaria contracta emendare ac distinguere et adnotare curavit.*

[41] I find it difficult to agree with Rychlewska (above, note 19, 265–266) who holds that Nonius' citation of 6.1195 was taken not from an exemplar of Lucretius but from another source, such as a glossary or a grammatical text or a marginal note in some other author. The differences between Nonius' rendition of the line and the readings of the principal manuscripts are considerable but not inexplicable.

[42] K. Müller, *T. Lucreti Cari De Rerum Natura Libri Sex* (Zürich 1975).

Minere, the simplex of *imminere, eminere,* etc., is a very rare verb. It appears in most editions of Lucretius at 6.563 (the authority being OQLA), but is attested nowhere else. 6.563 is itself a troubled verse. In describing the reeling of buildings (*extructa domorum* – cf. 561) beneath the onslaught of fierce winds the poet is held to have written that they *inclinata minent in eandem prodita partem*. OQLA, the very manuscripts on whose authority *minent* has been accepted, render *eadem* instead of *eandem* (FB) and include some sort of inexplicable gibberish after *partem*. This inspires no confidence in *minent*. Moreover, *minent* is by no means the reading of all the manuscripts. The corrected Q has *manent* which, though certainly somewhat bland, makes good sense. At any rate, it is surely a questionable methodology which bases an emendation on a single appearance of a word, especially when textual difficulties make the very existence of that word a matter for dispute.[43] These objections would be mitigated somewhat if, as Bailey thought, Lucretius shows preference for uncompounded verbal forms.[44] But this is not the case. Swanson has noted in excess of twenty-five simplexes whose compounds occur in Lucretius but which themselves are absent.[45] Finally, to return for the moment to 6.1195, it might be asked just what sort of image *frons tenta minebat* conveys and how it fits with the description of the previous lines. Though the notion of suspension inherent in *minere* is certainly an odd one to be applied to a forehead, *frons tenta minebat* must point to a swollen, pointed forehead, as does Heinsius' *frons tenta tumebat*. I find it difficult to reconcile either phrase with the *cava tempora* of the preceding line.

University of Cincinnati,   BRENT W. SINCLAIR
American Academy in Rome.

---

[43] Cf. the remark of Lachmann (above, note 27) *ad* 6.563: Ridiculi sunt qui . . .*minere* a se et hic et in versu 1195 restitutum gloriantur.

[44] Bailey (above, note 2), 1640.

[45] D. C. Swanson, *A Formal Analysis of Lucretius' Vocabulary* (Minneapolis 1962) 118. A perfect example is the simplex *vellere*, which is absent from Lucretius' poem. Yet no less than five of its compounds appear at a total of seventeen different junctures.

ATHENIAN LEADERSHIP: EXPERTISE OR CHARISMA?*

What was the key to leadership in Athenian politics? Was it the innate force of one's personality which we now call "charisma," or is Professor Andrewes closer to the truth in saying that "Kleon and his like were not simply the people's leaders on the comparatively narrow political front which Thucydides examines: a large part of the point is their mastery of finance and administration?"[1]

There can be no question that Kleon, Nikias, and Alkibiades, at least, had dominant personalities. Were they also masters of finance and administration? According to Andrewes,

> The Athenian empire was not just a moral problem about aggression . . . but a large administrative problem too. Athens needed, in numbers large relative to her size, a regular supply of reasonably competent hellenotamiai, archontes, episkopoi, and the rest. Since the first generation of democracy was not faced with such problems, the old governing class had found no difficulty in running the machine themselves, but it was different when Athens began to interfere extensively in her allies' affairs. Administrative talent could be found in the upper classes—Aristeides needed more than "justice" to assess the φόρος, and Perikles is a clear case—but their traditional habits of life and education were not geared to these new needs, and the inevitable influx of new men doubtless came, as the comic poets allege, from business families. Kleon and his like were not simply the people's leaders on the comparatively narrow political front which Thucydides examines: a large part of the point is their mastery of finance and administration.

> The bulk of the business is an important factor. It needed more than a few clear-headed experts: hence the ἑκατὸν δὲ κύκλῳ κεφαλαὶ κολάκων of *Wasps* 1033 (= *Peace* 756), and others of whom Aristophanes' plain men complain. Further, financial and administrative skill depend heavily on the capacity to master, and not to be confused by, a mass of detail which is too much for the ordinary man, who is apt to find the whole business mysterious and distasteful.[2]

Certainly, the administration of the Athenian Empire involved a million and one details, but my thesis is that these details could be, and were, attended to by functionaries while the political leaders of Athens concentrated on broader questions of policy.

---

* A lecture given at the University of British Columbia on the occasion of Professor McGregor's retirement.

[1] A. Andrews, "The Mytilene Debate: Thucydides 3.36–49," *Phoenix* 16 (1962) 83.

[2] *Ibid.* 83–84 (footnotes omitted).

So we find Demosthenes in the First Olynthiac telling the Assembly how he proposes to pay for his two-pronged campaign to rescue Olynthus and invade Macedonia:

> About provision of money, you have funds, men of Athens, you have military funds such as no one else has. But you take them as you please. If, then, you will give them to those who fight, there is no further need of provision; otherwise, there is a further need—rather, there is a total lack of provision. "What then?" someone may say, "Do you propose that this money be used for military purposes?" Not I, by Zeus. For I think that soldiers must be provided and that there must be one and the same arrangement for both taking the money and carrying out orders, but you think that somehow one must take the money without any exertion for the festivals. There remains the option, I suppose, that everyone pay property taxes, a lot if there is need of a lot, a little if there is need of a little. But there is need of money and without it nothing can happen of what must happen. Some people talk of one source of revenue, others of another. Choose whichever seems beneficial to you, and while there is the opportunity, take hold of matters.[3]

Demosthenes is a moral leader, who intends to arouse the Athenians to *action*; he does not care in the least about the details of financing that action.

Again, in the Kallias Decrees it is the political leader Kallias who decides that the time has come to repay the debts to the Other Gods, but it is fifty common citizens, chosen by lot, who must seek out receipts and other evidence of these debts, although the entire Boule of Five Hundred must attend at the physical transfer of the money.[4]

The story goes that Chief Justice John Marshall hated bibliographical drudgery so that, whenever he and his colleagues reached a decision, he would say to Associate Justice Joseph Story, "That, Story, is the law. Now you find the precedents."[5] So it was, I suggest, in Athens. Kleon and the rest of the demagogues rose to the top and stayed there, not by mastering a mass of detail, but by marking out the direction they wanted policy to take, then using the force of their own personality to convince their political allies, and finally employing their skill in debate and their prestige to win over a majority in the assembly.

It is true that some of the leaders of fourth-century Athens were the very men who administered the treasury—Androtion, Euboulos, Lykourgos. At that time a single official was in charge of a treasury and could serve for more than a single year, but in the fifth century the treasurers were mere functionaries, members of large collegiate bodies, some chosen by lot.[6] The reason for this change in financial administration is the change in Athens' own fortunes. With the vast amount of money the Athenians controlled in the fifth century, they could afford to be lenient in taxing and lax in spending while concentrating their energies on preventing outright corruption. In the difficult straits of the fourth century it was necessary to find someone who could raise funds in the first place and keep a tight rein on spending them, once raised.

Even in the fifth century some Athenian leaders combined both expertise and charisma, especially the military leaders. During the debate on the Sicilian Expedition when Nikias was asked for his estimate of the forces necessary to subdue Syracuse, he was able to answer because he had commanded an army numerous times and thus knew his business,[7] but an Athenian army commander had to have special personal characteristics before he could hope to acquire such

[3] Dem., 1.19–20.
[4] *ATL* 2. D1.9–12.
[5] Cf. Edward S. Corwin, *John Marshall and the Constitution* (New Haven 1919) 116.
[6] Cf. Fordyce W. Mitchell, "Lykourgan Athens: 338–322," *Cincinnati Classical Studies* 2 (1973) 163–214.
[7] Cf. Thuc., 6.25.

experience. If he lacked those qualities, he did not live long enough to get that experience. A general, observes Xenophon, must pay attention to details—his army will be unhappy if it is not fed. However, the general must be more than a quartermaster, according to Xenophon: he must be brave and energetic in battle and must not ask his men to do anything he would not do himself. Even so, the real key to successful leadership, as Xenophon views it, is a special gift: the power to win allegiance from other men is a gift bestowed by the gods.[8] Diodorus tells a story of Epameinondas which illustrates the point.[9] Epameinondas was once fighting as a private soldier, but when the tide of battle turned against Thebes, the men instinctively looked to him for leadership. Nikias, I suggest, had to attend to details because he was general. He did not become general by attending to details.

Again, to what did Lampon owe his influence in Athenian politics? How was he able, for instance, to win acceptance for an amendment to the Eleusinian First Fruits Decree providing for an intercalary month in the year, forbidding unauthorized erection of altars in a sacred precinct, and instructing Lampon himself to bring in a motion concerning offerings of olive oil?[10] I maintain that Lampon did not obtain his influence in these matters by his willingness to work nights in the Bouleuterion after everyone else had gone home. Rather, it was because of his divine gift of prophecy that he became a power in public affairs.

But to return to the main concern of this paper: in the realm of Athenian finance there were innumerable details which one could master. My thesis is that such mastery was not really necessary for success in the Athenian Assembly.

The outline of Athenian finance during the Peloponnesian War is clear enough.[11] Athens began the conflict with an enormous surplus, enough money in fact to man a fleet of one hundred ships for five years.[12] The Athenians naturally were compelled to draw down this money during the first years of the conflict and by 421 had used most of their reserve. After the signing of the Peace of Nikias their aim was to restore the state treasury to its former strength, and certainly great progress was made in that direction until the decision to invade Sicily. Thenceforth once more they began to drain the treasury until it was almost empty. The great victory over the Peloponnesian fleet at Kyzikos in 410 restored Athens' mastery of the sea and her ability to collect taxes from the Empire. So once again public policy was to build up a reserve military fund. This time, however, the policy was unsuccessful, for current expenditures about matched current revenues, with little left over for savings. As a result Athens was almost bankrupt when Aegospotami forced an end to the war.

The Athenian demagogues can take no credit for making the rebuilding of the strategic reserve the fundamental keystone of Athenian finance. Since the prewar reserve belonged to Athena and the Other Gods and had merely been loaned to the Athenian state, the state was religiously obligated to repay the debt. So the reestablishment of the reserve was inevitable. And religion apart, once the idea of a strategic reserve had been suggested and actually accomplished, it was simple enough to hope to re-create it. The original idea goes back to the early days of the Delian League when the old aristocracy managed affairs of state. Whether the credit for the idea of an enormous war chest belongs to Aristeides, Kimon, or even Themistokles cannot be determined. It may be that the surplus simply accumulated without any planning by Athens' leaders.

---

[8] Neal Wood, "Xenophon's Theory of Leadership," *ClMed* 25 (1964) 47–60. The key passage is *Oec.* 21.12. The lesson of *Mem.* 3.6 is that Athenian politicians normally did not have a detailed knowledge of statecraft.

[9] 15.71.5–6.

[10] *IG* 1.² 76.47–61.

[11] Cf. *ATL* 3. 326–366.

[12] Thuc., 2.13.3; six thousand talents for ships at one talent a month each, the figure Thucydides gives at 6.8.1. Actual costs varied from time to time.

Yet, if the demagogues did not determine the general course of Athenian finance during the Peloponnesian War, they certainly must have had ideas about the implementation of policy, both on keeping expenses under control and on raising additional revenues. Let us look first at how Athens collected its money.

We hear a lot nowadays about zero-based budgeting, that is, a system in which each unit of the organization must justify its entire budget and not merely the increase it hopes to receive over its allocation in the previous year. On the other hand, as the *Wall Street Journal* has noted, we do not hear anything about zero-based revenues. That is, no one seriously reexamines the various components of the revenue stream to see just how much should come from income taxes, sales taxes, and property taxes. So the property-tax take increases automatically as inflation drives up property assessments, and revenue from the income tax fluctuates in response to business conditions: the more money we make, the more taxes we pay. Athenian tax gathering was much the same. Until 425 there was apparently no serious attempt to overhaul the assessment of Aristeides under which the cities of the Empire paid tribute. When increased revenues were needed after 430, the Athenians merely increased the cities' taxes slightly without fundamentally altering the system. As for domestic taxation, revenue from the produce tax varied with the size of the harvest, and income from customs duties varied with business activity.

These facts suggest that the Athenian demagogues really needed to know very little about the details of taxation. There simply was no need for Kleon, for instance, to know the individual assessments of the various cities in the Empire and whether they were proper. According to Diodorus,[13] the Spartans after the Dekeleian War collected more than a thousand talents in tribute annually. They, of course, had no large administrative force in being, nor any native businessmen such as Athens had. Yet somehow they managed. We can see how they probably went about it. In 412 they collected thirty-two talents from the cities on Rhodes.[14] It so happens that during the Peace of Nikias Athens collected thirty-four talents a year from these same cities.[15] Thus the victorious Spartans could base their assessments on those of the Athenians. Likewise the demagogues of Athens based their taxes on the assessment of Aristeides, and it appears that he himself used Persian taxes as a model.[16]

As for domestic taxes, it was up to private tax farmers to figure out what they could collect and to bid accordingly when state officials auctioned off the contracts for tax collection.

During the 440's and 430's Athens had so much money at its disposal that there was no need to be concerned about petty details. It is only with the enormous expense of subduing Poteidaia at the beginning of the Peloponnesian War that the demagogues reacted to the need to increase revenues.[17] Their first move was to increase domestic taxes by collecting the *eisphora*.[18] Many scholars think that the burden of this tax fell primarily upon the rich. Surely that sounds familiar, but when someone says, "Soak the rich!" or "Share the wealth!" does he have to be in command of the details of the operation, or is it not simply a matter of pointing the direction public policy ought to take?

It is his connection with the exaction of the *eisphora* that underlies the view that Kleon controlled Athenian finance. As the Paphlagonian in the *Knights*, he tells the Demos of his service in the Boule: "I produced very much money in the treasury, putting some people on the rack, squeezing others, and blackmailing others, taking no thought for any private citizens, as long as I

[13] 14.10.2.
[14] Thuc., 8.44.4.
[15] Cf. *ATL* 3. 348–349, for the assessments of Brikindarioi, Diakrioi, Ialysos, Kameiros, Lindos, and Pedies.
[16] *ATL* 3. 234–235, but cf. Oswyn Murray, "Ὁ ΑΡΧΑΙΟΣ ΔΑΣΜΟΣ," *Historia* 15 (1966) 142–156.
[17] Cf. Thuc., 2.70.2 and 3.17.
[18] Thuc., 3.19.1.

might gratify you."[19] In what capacity did he do this? We know that in the fourth century Androtion served on a commission of ten to collect arrears of the *eisphora*. Demosthenes says that they went round Attica to collect the taxes and hauling citizens off to jail.[20] Perhaps Kleon headed a similar commission, but it may be that he merely took the lead in demanding that defaulters be prosecuted. If so, he would resemble modern politicians who demand stiffer sentences for convicted criminals or tougher enforcement of the antitrust laws, even though they have no actual responsibility for handling individual cases. So, Kleon was not personally the man to execute the male population of Mytilene, nor was it his job to sell off the women and children at the slave auction. And he was very free with advice to Nikias on how to capture the Spartans at Sphakteria without having the responsibility for capturing them himself. A legislative politician or an editor of a newspaper can demand more vigorous conduct of war or new initiatives in arms control without having to be very specific. It is the bureaucrats who must see to details.

The other evidence for Kleon's involvement in financial matters is his threat to enroll the Sausage Seller among the wealthy and thus subject him to payment of the *eisphora*.[21] At the same time he says that he will make him a trierarch and give him faulty equipment, so as to bankrupt him. Kleon is no longer a member of the Boule, but now one of the generals and, like Nikias, must attend to the details of the office. Kleon does not appear here as a financial expert—rather, the point of his threat is that he is in a position to abuse the power of his office and make life miserable for his enemies.

If it were possible for the demagogues to advocate general measures for increasing revenues without necessarily knowing how they would work out in detail, still surely they must have grappled with minutiae in order to keep Athenian spending in check. Or did they?

Perhaps the most elementary tool of cost control is a budget, whether the monthly household budget or the annual document of universities, corporations, and governments. There are signs that in the fourth century the Athenians began to have some sort of rudimentary budget. As Peter Rhodes puts it, "Whereas previously, so far as we can tell, every payment from the public treasury was earmarked for a particular purpose, various ἀρχαί were now given an annual allowance for their ordinary expenses, which presumably was theirs to spend without further interference...."[22] For the fifth century I have never been able to find any clear evidence that the Athenians developed a budget.[23] It is true that Kallias directs the treasurers of the Other Gods to record how much money they received and spent in any given year,[24] and it would have been no great problem for the state auditors to gather similar tabulations from each of the important treasuries in the state and compute the grand total of income and outgo. But this is retroactive and not the same as projecting *in advance* how much money will probably be received and how much will probably be spent.

One might suppose that this was possible during periods of peace, when many of the state's expenditures recurred from year to year with little change. In fact, in recent years scholars have attempted to determine just what Athens would normally spend each year.[25] But this just goes to show the difference between the ancient and the modern mentality, or perhaps I should say, the difference between the ancient and the professorial mentality. Athenian accounting methods do not seem concerned with cost control or the projection of revenues and expenses. The sheer mass

[19] *Knights* 774–776.

[20] 22.42–58 and 24.160–169.

[21] *Knights* 912–918 and 923–926.

[22] P. J. Rhodes, *The Athenian Boule* (Oxford 1972) 103.

[23] The restoration of *ATL* 2, A9.46–48 seems to me too uncertain to use as evidence.

[24] *ATL* 2, D1.24–27.

[25] E.g., Samuel K. Eddy, "Athens' Peacetime Navy in the Age of Perikles," *GRBS* 9 (1968) 141–156.

of details in the Erechtheum accounts, for instance, hampers any systematic analysis of the different cost components.[26] As de Ste. Croix says in his survey of Greek and Roman accounting, "there can be little doubt that the main reason for recording all this material in permanent form and 'publishing' it in expensive inscriptions on stone (usually . . . marble) was to prove to everyone's satisfaction that the respective treasurers, public or sacred, could account for everything which had passed through their hands, down to the very last fraction of an obol."[27]

As I say, there appears to be no evidence that the Athenians used a budget to control costs, but actually some to the contrary. We have several decrees which call for the expenditure of money, in most of which there is no estimate of the cost or any limitation thereon. The mover of a decree to build a fountain house merely says that it should be constructed for the lowest sum, [ὀ]λιγίστον χρεμάτο[ν], without being specific.[28] Likewise, in Hyperbolos' lengthy decree concerning the festival of Hephaistos we find a full array of instructions for choosing officials to manage the ceremonies and about what they are supposed to do, but no indication in some forty lines of text how much all of this would cost.[29] In the decree concerning the door of the temple of Athena Nike (or perhaps the cult statue of that temple) we learn that the Boule and overseers are to bring in a proposal about wages for the contractor, but there is no mention of the cost of building materials.[30] In another decree the supervisors of the dockyards are to negotiate wages with someone, presumably dockyard workers.[31] Thus the assembly approves two projects before learning how much the wages are to be. Another proposal simply orders the fencing of the shrine of Neleus and charges the cost to the treasury of the shrine, but again no mention of what the cost might be and no limitation.[32]

On the other hand, two decrees do impose a limit on expenses.[33] One authorizes sacrifices costing up to a certain amount—the figure is now missing from the stone—and the other permits the expenditure of public monies up to five hundred drachmai on some sort of religious construction.

One might argue that all of these various spending proposals were too insignificant in comparison with Athens' total outlay to matter. But, if we look at the other end of the scale, we can easily suppose that the construction of the Parthenon and the Propylaia was so expensive and so different from anything which Athens or any other city had attempted before that it simply was not possible to estimate in advance what the total cost would be or what would be needed from year to year. Nor could anyone have forecast how long the siege of Poteidaia would last or how much money it would cost. The point is that it had to be accomplished, no matter what the cost. If Athens had allowed Poteidaia to secede, every other city in the Empire would have done the same, and not only would Athens have lost the revenues it derived from the Empire, it would have lost its position of leadership and prestige and perhaps even its freedom.

Thus, it seems to me, it really was not possible for Athenian leaders during the second half of the fifth century to budget ahead in an effort to match expenses and income. Lacking any real control over expenditures, they resorted to pious exhortations, such as ὀλιγίστον χρεμάτον, or to total abstinence, as when Kallias calls a halt to the Periklean building program and forbids any large expenditure from Athena's treasury without a special vote of the full Assembly.[34]

[26] Cf. IG 1.² 372–374.

[27] Cf. A. C. Littleton and B. S. Yamey, Studies in the History of Accounting (Homewood, Ill. 1956) 25.

[28] ATL 2, D19.

[29] IG 1.² 84.

[30] IG 1.² 88.

[31] IG 1.² 74.11–13.

[32] IG 1.² 94; an amendment shifts the expense to the man who leases the shrine's land.

[33] IG 1.² 78 and 128.

[34] ATL 2, D2.12–19.

It is now commonly recognized that the U.S. budget is out of control. So many programs are fixed by law, so many expenditures mandatory that there is very little the president can do to pare expenses. The interest on the national debt must be paid, social security and welfare checks must be mailed, national defence must be maintained, government workers must not be laid off. The same is true, I suggest, of fifth-century Athens. The war had to be financed, hoplites had to be paid, and ships had to sail. Members of the Boule and jurors had to continue to draw their pay. In fact, pay for their government jobs enabled a large portion of the Athenians to live and to patronize Athenian farmers and merchants.

If Athenian expenses were out of control, what then did the critics of democracy and its demagogues do when they seized power? The Four Hundred resolved to spend for no purpose other than the war and to pay no one for political office, except the nine archons and the *prytaneis*, as long as the war should last.[35] Their successors, the Five Thousand, voted that no office carry a salary.[36] This alternative was not open to the demagogues. Not only was pay for offices necessary to the livelihood of their supporters, it was the thing which enabled the masses to participate in the democracy. Without that pay there would be no democracy. Demosthenes knew what lack of pay meant: "Shall we not come together and deliberate if necessary? Then shall we still be a democracy? Shall the courts not decide private and public cases? And what safety will there be for those suffering injustice? Shall the Council not come in and administer the laws? And what is left for us other than to be completely destroyed?"[37] The proposals of the oligarchs to save money meant the destruction of what many Athenians were fighting for.

Athens' greatest expenses either could not be estimated or could not be eliminated, and the raising of revenue normally did not require any financial sophistication or the mastery of complicated detail. Surely there may have been second-rate politicians who achieved some influence by gaining expertise in one area or another, but the real demagogues, Kleon, Nikias, Alkibiades, depended on their personal qualities and their oratorical skills to secure their position of leadership.

University of California, Davis   WESLEY E. THOMPSON

[35] Cf. Thuc., 8.65.3 and 8.76.3; Arist., *Ath. Pol.* 29.5.
[36] *Ath. Pol.* 33.1.
[37] 24.99.

ATHENIAN BOULEUTIC ALTERNATES

For M. F. McGregor on the occasion of his seventieth birthday

The number of Athenian bouleutic alternates or ἐπιλαχόντες has been the subject of modern scholarly controversy.[1] The ancient documentation is hardly extensive: (1) seven lines from the comic poet Platon cited as a scholion to Aristophanes' *Thesmophoriazousai*, 808; and (2) a single sentence in Aeschines' *Against Ktesiphon* 3.62.

(1) = Kock, *CAF* 166/7 = Edmunds, *Fragments of Attic Comedy* 538–539.[2]

εὐτυχεῖς, ὦ δέσποτα.

Β. τί δ' ἔστι; Α. βουλεύειν ὀλίγου ἔλαχες πάνυ.

ἀτὰρ οὐ λαχὼν ὅμως ἔλαχες, ἢν νοῦν ἔχῃς.

Β. πῶς ἢν ἔχω νοῦν; Α. ὅτι πονηρῷ καὶ ξένῳ

5 ἐπέλαχες ἀνδρί, οὐδέπω γὰρ ἐλευθέρῳ.

*   *   *   *

Β. ἄπερρ'· ἐγὼ δ' ὑμῖν τὸ πρᾶγμα δὴ φράσω·

Ὑπερβόλῳ βουλῆς γάρ, ἄνδρες, ἐπέλαχον.

Slave. You're lucky, boss.

Master. What do you mean? *Slave.* You came within an inch of being councillor. Though you weren't picked, you were picked, if you think about it.
Master. What do you mean "if I think about it?" *Slave.* Because you were picked alternate to a crook of a foreigner who hasn't yet been liberated.

. . . .

Master. Beat it. Folks, now I'll explain it all to you.
I was picked alternate to Hyperbolos on the Council.

---

* Acknowledgments. The paper was completed at the Institute for Advanced Study at Princeton with the support of a grant from the Research Board of the Office of Research Administration, University of Toronto, using funds provided by the Canada Council. To these organizations, and to S. Dow and H. J. Carroll, Jr., whose work has been fundamental to this study, I express my warm thanks. As always, I also owe a great debt to my wife, Terry-Ellen Cox Traill, for her constant help.

[1] Important items of bibliography are: P. J. Rhodes, *The Athenian Boule* (Oxford 1972) 7–8; M. Lang, *Historia* 8 (1959) 82–86; J. A. O. Larsen, *Representative Government in Greek and Roman History* Sather Classical Lectures 28 (Berkeley and Los Angeles 1955) 10–11 and 194–195, with note 23; C. Hignett, *A History of the Athenian Constitution to the End of the Fifth Century B.C.* (Oxford 1958) 150; J. W. Headlam (revised by D. C. Macgregor), *Election by Lot at Athens* (Cambridge 1933) 53–56 and 196–199; U. Kahrstedt, *Untersuchungen zur Magistratur in Athen* (Stuttgart 1936) 123, 126, 132, 134; T. Thalheim, *RE, s. v.* Ἐπιλαχών; B. Haussoullier, Daremberg-Saglio, *s. v.* Epilachon.

[2] Line 5 of Edmunds' text is emended to ⟨κ⟩ουδέπω γ' ἐλευθέρῳ.

(2) = Aeschines, *Against Ktesiphon* 3.62 (ed. Blass)[3]

μετὰ ταῦτα ἐπῄει [χρόνος] Θεμιστοκλῆς ἄρχων ἐνιαῦθ' εἰσέρχεται βουλευτὴς [εἰς τὸ βουλευτήριον] Δημοσθένης, οὔτε λαχὼν οὔτ' ἐπιλαχών,[4] ἀλλ' ἐκ παρασκευῆς πριάμενος, ἵν' εἰς ὑποδοχὴν ἅπαντα καὶ λέγοι καὶ πράττοι Φιλοκράτει, ὡς αὐτὸ ἔδειξε τὸ ἔργον.

Next came Themistokles as archon (348/7 B.C.). Then Demosthenes entered [the Bouleuterion] as councillor, not picked as a regular member, nor as an alternate, but underhandedly through bribery, so he could speak and do all he wanted on behalf of Philokrates, just as the results proved.

These two passages form the basis of the comment (3) by Harpokration, *s.v.* ἐπιλαχών, which is closely paralleled in the Suda, *Etymologicum Magnum,* and *Anecdota Graeca.*

(3) = Harpokration, *Lexicon in decem oratores atticos,* ed. Dindorf, *s.v.* Ἐπιλαχών.

Αἰσχίνης κατὰ Κτησιφῶντος "οὔτε λαχὼν οὔτ' ἐπιλαχών, ἀλλ' ἐκ παρασκευῆς πριάμενος." ἔοικε τὸ γιγνόμενον τοιοῦτον εἶναι. ἐκληροῦντο οἱ βουλεύειν ἢ ἄρχειν ἐφιέμενοι, ἔπειτα ἑκάστῳ τῶν λαχόντων ἕτερος ἐπελάγχανεν, ἵν' ἐὰν ὁ πρῶτος λαχὼν ἀποδοκιμασθῇ ἢ τελευτήσῃ, ἀντ' ἐκείνου γένηται βουλευτὴς ὁ ἐπιλαχὼν αὐτῷ. ὑποφαίνεται δὲ ταῦτα ἐν τῷ Πλάτωνος Ὑπερβόλῳ.

Alternate. Aeschines *Against Ktesiphon* "not picked as a regular member, nor as an alternate, but underhandedly through bribery." It seems to have happened something like this. Those who desired to be councillors or magistrates were chosen by lot, then another man picked by lot as alternate for each chosen man, so that if the first failed to qualify or died, his alternate would become councillor in his place. This is explained in the *Hyperbolos* of Platon.

The passage in Harpokration has been taken as evidence that every councillor had an alternate, i.e., that there were as many ἐπιλαχόντες as bouleutai. The ἔοικε and τοιοῦτον in the passage, however, make clear that the argument is speculative and should not be accepted uncritically. Indeed, because of the permitted second tenure of the office of councillor, the apparent failure of some (usually small) demes to fill their quotas,[5] and the estimated small citizen population,[6] some scholars[7] have doubted that Athens, at least in the fourth century B.C., could have provided as many as 1000 candidates annually for the Council, but these scholars had no positive evidence on which to base an accurate estimate of the number of alternates. I believe that there exists epigraphical documentation to show that at one point in Athenian history the alternates numbered half as many as the bouleutai.[8]

The seven fragments of *Agora* 15, no. 492, which were published in the *Corpus* under three numbers, *IG* 2.[2] 1697 (*a, b, c*), 1698 (*a, b, c*), 2372, have been studied by S. Dow and H. J. Car-

---

[3] The following elucidation appears in a scholion (*Scholia Graeca in Aeschinem et Isocratem,* ed. W. Dindorf [Oxford 1852]):

ἐπιλαχών] ἐλάγχανον γὰρ ἄρχοντες καὶ σὺν αὐτοῖς ἄλλοι ὥσπερ δεύτεροι αὐτῶν, ἵνα εἷς αὐτῶν εἰ ἀπέθανεν ἐν τῷ μεταξὺ τῆς ἀρχῆς ἢ ἠρρώστησεν, ὁ ἀντ' αὐτοῦ ἐγίγνετο ἄρχων. ἐκ παρασκευῆς δὲ πριάμενος, οἷον ὑποφθείρας χρήμασι τοὺς προέδρους τῆς βουλῆς, ὥστε αὐτὸν βουλευτὴν ποιῆσαι.

Cf. the citation from Harpokration (3) below.

[4] The same phrase appears in [Demosthenes] 58.29, but with respect to the office of *hieropoios.*

[5] See *Hesperia,* Suppl. 14. 14−23 and 56−58. In the Aeschines text, the awkward χρόνος was deleted by Weidner.

[6] The basis is regularly A. W. Gomme, *The Population of Athens in the Fifth and Fourth Centuries B.C.* (Oxford 1933).

[7] Notably Larsen and Rhodes (note 1 above).

[8] Preliminary discussion appears in B. D. Meritt and J. S. Traill, *Athenian Agora* 15, *The Athenian Councillors* (Princeton 1974) 341, and in *Hesperia,* Suppl. 14. 2 with note 5, and 78−79 with note 16.

roll, Jr. and associated as belonging to the same inscription.[9] The text of *Agora* 15, no. 492 is not repeated here,[10] but a schema showing the disposition of the fragments and the arrangement of the text is offered (fig. 1).

FIG. 1

Disposition of *Agora* XV, no. 492 = *IG* 2.² 1697 + 1698 + 2372

Col. I	Col. II	Col. III	Col. IV	Col. V
[ERECHTHEIS]	[PANDIONIS]	[AKAMANTIS]	[KEKROPIS]	[AIANTIS]
lacuna	*lacuna*	*lacuna*	*lacuna*	*lacuna*

[⌐Kephisia]
lacuna

fr.
a   3
[⌐]Lower Pergase
    3
⌐Anagyrous
    9
[⌐Th]emakos

fr.   [1 line *vacat*]
b   1   -[ANTIOCHIS]
[⌐]Sybridai   [Anaphlystos]
    1
⌐Agryle [Upper?]
        [Lower?]
    3 +?
lacuna   fr. [5]
                                              g

fr.   [1 line *vacat*]   [1 line *vacat*]   [4]?
c   1   -[LEONTIS] -- fr.   -[HIPPOTHONT]IS-
Phegous   f   +   [Azenia]
    1   [3] *lacuna*   [2] 1 line *vacat* [2]   11
1 line *vacat*   -OINEIS-   3
AIGEIS   [L]ousia   ⌐Keiria]dai
Otryne   1   3
    2   ⌐Ph]yle   ⌐Kopr]os
⌐Araphen   3   3
    3   ⌐Th]ria   ⌐Ana]kaia   Er[oiadai]
⌐Ankyle [Upper?]   4 +?   4 +?   1
       [Lower?]   *lacuna* *lacuna* [Demotic]
    1   *lacuna*
⌐Phegaia
    6
⌐Kydantidai
    2
[⌐]Erikeia
    1
lacuna

fr.
d   1
[⌐Kollyto]s
    4
[⌐Hal]ai .
    8
⌐Ikarion − 1   ⌐Acharnai]
    +   [16]?
    5   +
                   9   17
                 ⌐Demotic?] *vacat* *vacat*
lacuna   1
                1/2 line *vacat*
                 ⌐Demotic?] *vacat*
                 1   6¹/₂
                 ⌐Demotic?] *vacat*
                  vacat ————

---

[9] S. Dow, unpublished notes; H. J. Carroll, Jr., *Bouleutai, An Epigraphical and Prosopographical Study of the Lists of Athenian Councillors* (Harvard 1954, unpublished).

[10] The following corrections may be noted: line 33, add *v* following nu; line 43, the last preserved letter is sigma, and the name is, therefore, Phanias; line 68, add *parengraphos* above demotic; lines 86–87, the *vacat* occupies half a vertical space; lines 92–93, a full line was left uninscribed between the last name in the upper roster and the tribal heading of Oineis; line 97, a trace of omega is preserved, and the name should be restored [Σ]ωφάνης; line 154, part of the second letter, rho, is preserved; line 155, first letter is alpha with a *parengraphos* below; top stroke of a sigma appears in 151.

The text was arranged in five columns, with two phylai assigned to each: Erechtheis and Aigeis in I, Pandionis and Leontis in II, Akamantis and Oineis in III, Kekropis and Hippothontis in IV, and Aiantis and Antiochis in V. The evidence for this arrangement is as follows.

Four of the fragments preserve part of the original left side, and they all, accordingly, have been assigned to the first column. Two of them, *a* and *b,* join, and, since they have demotics of the first phyle, Erechtheis, they belong to the upper half of the column, whereas fragments *c* with the tribal heading of Aigeis and *d* with additional Aigeid demes should be assigned to positions further down in the same column. Fragment *e* preserves two columns of names above an uninscribed space, and it naturally belongs to the bottom of the inscription. The names in the right-hand column have been identified as Acharnians of the sixth phyle, Oineis. The heading for this phyle is actually preserved on fragment *f,* which, accordingly, should be assigned to a position higher up in the same (i.e., third) column. Finally, fragment *g* contains demotics (and probably part of the tribal heading) of the eighth phyle, Hippothontis, in its left column, and demesmen of Anaphlystos from Antiochis, the tenth phyle, in its right column; this fragment belongs to the middle section of the last two columns.

The lettering is stoichedon and uniform (except 1.68, second half).[11] The left margins of the columns are carefully respected: the first letters of the tribal rubrics, demotics, and names are all set in perfect vertical alignment. Only the short parengraphic lines (*ca.* 0.006 m. in length, a chisel stroke) which were inscribed above the first letter of the demotics to distinguish them from the names intrude into the left margins. The *parengraphos* in line 154 indicates that the accompanying epsilon is the first letter of a demotic.[12] Otryne in line 32, which has no distinguishing line, is the only exception; perhaps the presence of the tribal heading immediately above was felt sufficient to identify the line below as a demotic.

The names, the phyle headings, and the demotics, with one exception, each occupy a single line. Ikarion (line 68) shares a line with one of its demesmen; perhaps a name was omitted from the list and later inserted by the stonecutter (same hand, but the stoichedon order is abandoned). Although patronymics were usually inscribed along with the names, the *vacat* at the ends of lines 25 and 33 suggests that they were omitted in at least two instances. The long names in lines 127 and 130 necessitated the curtailment of the patronymics, and in line 68, of course, there would not have been room for a patronymic of normal length. The uninscribed spaces at the ends of lines 85, 87, and 89, however, probably do not signify uninscribed patronymics, but rather the presence of demotics in the lost left-hand portion of the lines.[13] The only demonstrable fully uninscribed lines in the text occur above lines 31 and 93 (correct *Agora* 15 text), each of which was occupied by a tribal heading. These spaces were surely deliberately left in order to draw attention to the beginning of the new rosters within the columns. Fragment *g* is broken immediately above the tribal heading (largely restored) of Hippothontis, but probably an uninscribed line occurred here too. The other major anomaly in the vertical disposition of this text occurs in line 87 (just mentioned in connection with restored demotics);[14] here the vertical spacing is one and a half

---

[11] Occasionally the center bar of epsilon was omitted, e.g., in lines 117 and 132.

[12] The stone is broken along a vertical stroke at the left of the second *stoichos* in this line, and there may be preserved a trace of the top horizontal stroke of a letter; the demotic is restored as Eroiadai in preference to Eiteaioi. The *parengraphos,* clearly in evidence below the alpha of line 155 (see footnote 10 above), limits the representation of this deme to one. The stone has been broken just before the first letter of the demotic in line 6 and all but a trace of the *parengraphos* lost.

[13] Leontis had an abundance of very small demes, and small demes are often found clustered at the bottom of tribal rosters, e.g., *Agora* 15, no. 62 and the Leontid roster of *Agora* 15, no. 42. The name Stratonides (cf. line 88) is attested in Oion (a possible restoration in line 87) as father of Straton who was ephebe about 324 B.C. (Ἀρχ Ἐφ [1918] 75, line 9).

[14] There is a final, slight irregularity in the vertical disposition of the text: the lettering in fragments *a* and *b* rises very slightly to the right.

times that normally allotted to a single line. Perhaps a name was crowded in below the demotic, or there was a flaw in the stone, but it seems more likely that near the bottom of the column the lettercutter simply allowed himself more than the usual vertical spacing.

Three tribal headings and twenty-one demotics have been preserved totally or in part. Four other demes, Kephisia, Acharnai, Azenia, and Anaphlystos, have been restored with much probability from the prosopographical evidence, and there are spaces for three additional demotics. If we may judge from the presence of Lower Pergase in line 6, the divided demes were listed by separate section. It is assumed that Agryle (line 24) and Ankyle (line 39), which are only partially preserved, originally designated individual sections of their respective divided demes. Since even the tiniest Attic demes, e.g., Sybridai, Phegous, Themakos (of the small Erechtheid demes only Pambotadai and Kedoi are missing), Otryne, Ankyle, Lousia, are in evidence in the extant portion of the text, it is very likely that the original inscription contained a complete roster of all 139 demes.[15] To pursue the argument further, because column II, with the rosters of Pandionis and Leontis, a total of 31 demes, terminated six lines apparently below column III which contained the rosters of Akamantis and Oineis, a total of 26 demes, the difference in the lengths of columns seems to depend very largely on the respective numbers of demotics (the discrepancy of 1 in my figures here may be due to a missing name, an additional uninscribed line, or another irregularity such as in line 68 of column I), and the numbers of demesmen in cols. II and III, I conclude, were virtually identical.[16]

If we may estimate on the basis of the number of preserved demotics, about one-sixth of the original text is now extant. There are in evidence portions of 116 names (not counting patronymics except where the first name has been lost), and the complete text, accordingly, ought to have contained upwards of seven hundred names.

The representation of the demes in *Agora* 15, no. 492 is of particular interest and immediately invites comparison with the known corresponding bouleutic quotas (fig. 2).

The tiny deme Sybridai, which went unrepresented in at least one year and may have shared a councillor with another small Erechtheid deme, Pambotadai,[17] has one representative here. Themakos, Phegous, Ankyle (Upper or Lower), Lousia, Eroiadai, and Otryne each had one bouleutes, and each has one representative in the present inscription, with the exception of Otryne, which has two. Kydantidai, with one or two bouleutai (one in the earliest list, two in two later lists; one or two in the Macedonian period),[18] has two demesmen in *Agora* 15, no. 492. The demes with quotas of two bouleutai, viz. Lower Pergase, Araphen, Phyle, Keiriadai, Kopros, and Azenia, have three representatives in the present list. Kollytos, with a bouleutic quota of three, has four demesmen here, and Phegaia, whose quota fluctuated between four and three (four on the earliest list, three on two later lists), has six. Halai, with five councillors, and Anagyrous, whose bouleutic quota was six, now have eight and nine men respectively.

The pattern seems clear. The new figures are approximately fifty percent larger than the corresponding bouleutic quotas, granted that representation in a particular instance cannot be fractional, but must be a whole-number unit.[19] The last-mentioned mathematical exigency accounts

---

[15] For the number of Attic demes see *Hesperia*, Suppl. 14. 73–103. I have not discerned any pattern of arrangement of the demes within the tribal rosters. They certainly were not grouped according to trittys.

[16] Ikarion's roster was probably complete with six demesmen.

[17] *Hesperia*, Suppl. 14. 6–7 and 14–15. Sybridai certainly was omitted from the roster of Erechtheis, *Agora* 15, no. 42, but the spacing in line 61 of *Agora* 15, no. 14 would suggest that the demotic there was Sybridai, and that Pambotadai, therefore, was omitted from that list (see *Agora* 15, no. 14, commentary, and correct *Phoenix* 30 [1976] 197).

[18] *Hesperia*, Suppl. 14. 15–16. The manner in which Ptolemais was formed suggests that Kydantidai's quota in the Macedonian period was 1 bouleutes annually (*ibid.* 59–60, with note 17); see below, p. 168.

[19] The mathematical implications are sometimes paradoxical. D. M. Lewis has drawn my attention (*per litt.*) to an extremely interesting article by M. L. Balinski and H. P. Young, "The Quota Method of Apportionment," *American Mathematical Monthly* 82 (1975) 701–730.

for the fact that Kollytos' increase is only 33 1/3 percent, whereas Halai's is 60 percent, and Otryne's and perhaps Kydantidai's are 100 percent, and explains why many of the demes with only a single bouleutes record no increase at all. It is probably owing to the mere accident of preservation that only two or three (including Kydantidai), and not precisely four, of the attested eight tiny demes show an increase of representation over their bouleutic quotas, or it may be that demes such as Halai and Phegaia made up for a slight cumulative deficiency among the tiny demes, but the numerical variation is not unreasonable for such a statistical sample. It may also be noted that none of the partially preserved rosters in this inscription contravenes this conclusion: several exceed the bouleutic quota, but none by more than 50 percent. Slight additional confirmation for

FIG. 2

Comparison of Bouleutic Quotas with Representation in *Agora* 15, no. 492.

DEME	PHYLE	BOULEUTIC QUOTA	*Agora* 15, no. 492
Sybridai	I	1/0	1
Themakos	I	1	1
Phegous	I	1	1
Ankyle [Upper?] [Lower?]	II	1	1
Lousia	VI	1	1
Eroiadai?	X	1	1
Otryne	II	1	2
Kydantidai	II	1/2	2
Lower Pergase	I	2	3
Araphen	II	2	3
Phyle	VI	2	3
Keiriadai	VIII	2	3
Kopros	VIII	2	3
Azenia	VIII	2	3
Kollytos	II	3	4
Phegaia	II	4/3	6
Halai Araphenides	II	5	8
Anagyrous	I	6	9
TOTAL 18 demes		37–38	55

Partially Preserved Representation

Erikeia	II	1	1+?
Agryle [Upper?] [Lower?]	I	2 3	3+?
Anakaia	VIII	3	4+?
Ikarion	II	4/5	6+?[16]
Kephisia	I	6	3+?
Acharnai	VI	22	17+?
Anaphlystos	X	10	11+?

the relationship just observed may be found in column V of the text.[20] If Anaphlystos had fifteen demesmen, a figure which corresponds to its bouleutic quota of ten in the 50 percent proportion outlined here, and if Anaphlystos headed its respective roster, then Antiochis began five lines above Hippothontis in the adjacent column, precisely the difference in the number of demes in Kekropis and Aiantis which respectively occupied the tops of columns IV and V. If further confirmation for the relationship of the representation in *Agora* 15, no. 492 to the bouleutic quotas is required it is offered by the figures for Kopros. In *Hesperia,* Suppl. 14, I estimated the bouleutic quota of Kopros as two on the basis of its representation of three demesmen in the present inscription.[21] A newly discovered inscription from the Athenian Agora (*Hesperia* 47 [1978] 272 no. 4) now confirms that bouleutic quota as two.

The figures for the individual demes are, of course, reflected in the totals. The eighteen demes in *Agora* 15, no. 492 for which complete figures can be given have a combined representation of 55, and a bouleutic representation of either 37 or 38,[22] i.e., the former figure (55) is approximately fifty percent higher than the latter (37/38). Each tribal roster in the present inscription should have contained approximately, if not precisely,[23] seventy-five demesmen and each column one hundred and fifty representatives. The grand total would be about 750 Athenian citizens identified by respective deme and phyle.

The conclusion is inescapable. Although *Agora* 15, no. 492 is not strictly bouleutic, it must be closely related to the bouleutic texts.[24] I submit that it is a list of bouleutai and alternates. It is, of course, unique as such, but bouleutic lists themselves were rare until the Agora excavations, and are not numerous even now. Its date also is remarkable; it is a full generation (see following section) earlier than the earliest positively identifiable bouleutic list, *Agora* 15, no. 42, which has been reasonably dated to 336/5 B.C. Finally, the present text differs in format from any of the known later bouleutic inscriptions. *Agora* 15, nos. 61 and 72 also are arranged with two rosters to a column, but with the first six phylai (these texts date from the period of the twelve phylai) on top and the last six phylai below. Because of the very narrow interlinear spaces in *Agora* 15, no. 492 (*ca.* 0.0035 m.) its total height will not be much greater than either of the two bouleutic lists just mentioned, although it contained about fifty more names per column (the letter height in all three texts is the same, *ca.* 0.006 m.). The longest column ought to be the first, with about 188 lines, not counting a heading. The total height I compute to be a little less than two meters, and the width about a meter. The thickness (0.09 m.), which appears to be original, on fragments *a* and *c* seems slight for a freestanding stele of such height and width,[25] but the dimensions are not far different from *Agora* 15, no. 43, which will have been just as tall and wide and is only fractionally thicker (0.10 m.).[25 bis]

We may return now to citation (1) (above, p. 163). Hyperbolos belonged to the deme of Perithoidai which had a bouleutic quota of three. Its corresponding quota of alternates, if we apply the

---

[20] See also, *Hesperia,* Suppl. 14. 79, note 16.

[21] P. 21, with footnote 26 *bis.*

[22] The variations in the quotas of Kydantidai and Phegaia are complementary; hence the variation in the total is due solely to Sybridai's fluctuating quota.

[23] If the figure of 25 alternates was first allotted to each phyle as a quota, and was later divided among the demes in the same proportion as the bouleutic quotas, with the restriction, of course, that the figures must be whole numbers, then it may not be unreasonable to expect the kind of precision implied in the totals here.

[24] Other possibilities are quickly excluded. The inscription is too early (see the section on dating, pp. 168 – 169, below) to be ephebic. In format and/or recorded numbers of names it differs markedly from extant lists of diaitetai, klerouchs, etc.

[25] The thickness, with respect to the height and width, bears little relationship to the proportions outlined by S. Dow for the lists of Athenian *archontes* (*Hesperia* 3 [1934] 141–144), but the latter were a specialized group of texts, and ours should more appropriately be compared with other bouleutic lists.

[25 bis] The physical description given in *Agora* 15, no. 492 should be corrected in several details. No fragment preserves the original back, and the thickness of *c* is 0.225 m. and *g,* 0.14 m.

ratio of fifty percent and judge from the parallel of Kollytos, was one. This figure gives just as much point to the remark in the comic poet Platon as the explanation proposed in Harpokration. Indeed, the solution I offer here was suggested some years ago by J. A. O. Larsen,[26] but without the positive evidence I now adduce.

The identification of *Agora* 15, no. 492 as a catalogue of bouleutai and alternates provides an explanation for the variant bouleutic quotas, which, it has already been observed,[27] generally involved the small demes. A tiny deme without an alternate, or a small deme with a single alternate, must be expected on occasion to fail to furnish its quota, whereas the larger demes with two or more alternates are unlikely to fall short of their quotas and could be depended upon to supply the deficiencies of the smaller demes.[28] More specifically, the identification of the present text offers help with respect to the variant quotas of Phegaia and Kydantidai.[29] The six demesmen listed under Phegaia in *Agora* 15, no. 492 suggest that its normal bouleutic quota, at least in the early fourth century, was four councillors, as evidenced by *Agora* 15, no. 36, and not three as recorded in the later inscriptions, *Agora* 15, nos. 38 and 42.[30] Similarly, Kydantidai's normal bouleutic quota in the same period apparently was one councillor.[31]

Evidence for Dating *Agora* 15, no. 492

The dating of *Agora* 15, no. 492 is dependent on the abundant prosopographical evidence, of which the chief items are as follows.[32]

(1) Antikleides (line 3) might be father of Leonteus who was guarantor in 343/2 (*IG* 2.^{2} 1590, line 16; *NPA*, p. 116), and also of Ἀντικλείδης Κη[- - -] who was trierarch before 356/5, etc. (*IG* 2.^{2} 1612, line 360; 1616, line 97 = *PA* 1048), but the name here might also be restored as Charikleides (*BSA* 50 [1955] 30) and the trierarch's demotic as Kettios, cf. *AthPropFam* p. 36. The dates indicated by the two proposed identifications are *ca.* 376 and *ante ca.* 389.

(2) Philonides (line 9) should be identified with Philonides, the father of Sosikedes who was councillor in 335/4 (*Agora* 15, no. 43, line 15). The date indicated, accordingly, is *ca.* 368.

(3) Euthykritos (line 18) has been identified as the father of Ekphantides on a stele found at the Heraion of Samos, dated to the period of the Athenian klerouchy, i.e., 365–322 B.C. (*AthMitt-BH* 44 [1919] 3, no. 3).

(4) Pyrgion (line 33) is probably the son of Pyrgion who was assistant secretary of the epistatai of the Erechtheion in 408/7 B.C. (*IG* 1.^{2} 374, line 258). Pyrgion in *Agora* 15, no. 492, whose gravestone, presumably, is *IG* 2.^{2} 7017, should, accordingly, be dated *ca.* 375 B.C.

(5) Nikostratos (line 42) is conveniently identified with Nikostratos of Phegaia cited in a diadikasia which Davies dates about 380 B.C. (*IG* 2.^{2} 1932, line 15 = *PA* 11055; cf. *AthPropFam* 11055).

---

[26] Above, note 1.

[27] Rhodes (above, note 1), 11; *Hesperia*, Suppl. 14, (above, note 5).

[28] This simple explanation, of course, could well be accommodated to the more elaborate arrangements I have postulated whereby the representation of the trittyes within a phyle might be deliberately varied between 16 and 17 demesmen (see *Hesperia* 47 [1978] 102).

[29] The defective lists complicate the problem (*Hesperia,* Suppl. 14. 5, 15–16). Phegaia, for instance, had 4, 3, and 2 representatives on three different inscriptions from the Macedonian period, but two of these texts are defective. The quotas, of course, may have been set in fractional terms, e.g., Kydantidai 1 1/2, Phegaia 3 1/2, Sybridai 1/2, and Pambotadai 1/2, as I have posited for the last two (see p. 167, above, with note 17), but Kydantidai's quota apparently was 1 (see p. 165, above, with note 18).

[30] The changes in the Aigeid quotas between 343/2 (?) and 341/0 might suggest a general reapportionment of quotas, but there is little support in the statistics of the other phylai for such a theory (see *Hesperia*, Suppl. 14. 16, note 20).

[31] See notes 29 and 18 above.

[32] The abbreviations and much of the information cited in this section have been taken from *Agora* 15, Prosopographical Index 349–469. Nikostratos (item 8 below), however, cannot be identified with the demarch of Halai, as suggested in that index (434), for that deme was Halai Aixonides. As in *Agora* 15, for purposes of computation a generation is taken as 33 years.

(6) Antiphanes (line 47) was father of Akestides, councillor probably in 343/2 (*Agora* 15, no. 36, line 16), and of Euthydikos, syntrierarch before 325/4 (*IG* 2.² 1629, line 773, and 1631, line 134; cf. *PA* 1248, and *AthPropFam* 5564). The respective dates for *Agora* 15, no. 492, accordingly, are *ca.* 376 and *ante ca.* 358.

(7) Leokedes (line 57) at first sight would appear to be identical to the father of Ameinias who was councillor in 343/2 (*Agora* 15, no. 36, line 42); this identification would suggest a dating about 343 B.C. for *Agora* 15, 492. The majority of the prosopographical evidence indicates a dating about a generation earlier, and Leokedes in the present inscription is more likely to have been grandfather of Ameinias.

(8) Nikostratos (line 67) might be identified with Nikostratos of Halai who was trierarch a little after 377/6 and again before 356/5 (*IG* 2.² 1605, line 38, 1622, line 266 = *PA* 11019), but cf. Nikostratos, son of Nikeratos, of Halai (*IG* 2.² 5509, with Kirchner's comments, and *AthPropFam* 11019, with stemma).

(9) Mnesikleides (line 72) may = Mnesikleides who was father of Diokleides in an inscription dated between 360 and 350 B.C. (*AthMitt-BH* 67 [1942] 168, no. 348). The date of *Agora* 15, no. 492 would, accordingly, be *ca.* 393–383. A son or grandson = Gorgiades, son of Mnesikleides, of Ikarion who was treasurer in an inscription of the phyle Aigeis dated either 340/39 or 313/2 (*IG* 2.² 2824, line 3 = *PA* 3062).

(10) Derketes of Phyle (line 97) appears as a patronymic in *IG* 2.² 75, line 7, which Kirchner dates before 378/7 on the basis of letter forms.

(11) Kleopompos (line 103) was prytanis in 360/59 (*Agora* 15, no. 17, line 31).

(12) If Euphiletos (line 107) is identified with the father of Aristoteles of Acharnai who was secretary in 378/7 (*IG* 2.² 44, lines 1–2), it suggests a dating of *ca.* 411 for *Agora* 15, no. 492. This dating is thirty to forty years earlier than that indicated by most of the other prosopographical evidence, and Euphiletos here is more likely to be brother of Aristoteles.

(13) Phanias (line 110) can conveniently be identified with the father of Autokles who was secretary in 327/6 (*IG* 2.² 356, 357, 358). The date of the present text will then be *ca.* 360 B.C.

(14) Aischron (line 126) is perhaps grandfather of Aischron, son of Aischines, of Azenia who was prytanis a little after 350 B.C. (*Hesperia* 47 [1978] 272, no. 4, lines 11–12). Aischines in the *Hesperia* prytany list, it may be noted, would nicely fit the *ca.* 8 letters which precede the patronymic in line 126 of the present text.

(15) The father of Aristophanes (line 127) was treasurer of Athena in 400/399 B.C. (*IG* 2.² 1374, line 6), an identification which would suggest a dating of *ca.* 367 for the son. Aristophanes' famous older brother Aristophon was born about 430 B.C. (*PA* 2108). The family is discussed by Davies, *AthPropFam* 2108, with stemma.

(16) The patronymic in line 129 may be identified with Smikythos, father of [- - - -]obios who was Treasurer of the Other Gods in 376/5 B.C. (*IG* 2.² 1445, line 4 = *PA* 12790).

(17) Xenotimos (line 135) is very probably father of Nikoteles who appears in *IG* 2.² 1927, lines 78–79, dated by Kirchner after the middle of the fourth century B.C.

(18) A nephew of Aristeides (line 139) apparently is Exekestos in a new prytany list of Hippothontis dated a little after the middle of the fourth century B.C. (*Hesperia* 47 [1978] 272, no. 4, lines 6–7, with comment).

In general, the prosopographical evidence indicates a dating for *Agora* 15, no. 492 between *ca.* 380 and 360 B.C. The average of the dates above, for which an approximate year has been given, is 371, and the text probably does not belong far from that year. It does not seem profitable to speculate on a suitable historical context for the setting up of this most interesting constitutional document.

University of Toronto

JOHN S. TRAILL

THE DECREE FOR LAPYRIS OF KLEONAI (*IG* 2.² 365)*

The two fragments of the decree for Lapyris of Kleonai were first associated with one another by U. Koehler;[1] subsequent editors have accepted Koehler's contention that they do not join one another.[2] In 1971 I had the opportunity to examine both fragments in the Epigraphical Museum in Athens,[3] and discovered that they do, in fact, join, and that there is no gap in the text between them. A new discussion of this document is therefore in order.

Two contiguous fragments of dark gray Hymettian marble, prominently flecked with white, now cemented together. The top, left side, and flat, rough-picked back are preserved on fragment *a*; the left and right sides, back, and bottom on fragment *b*. The stele bore originally a crowning moulding and fascia, but these have been chiselled off. The stele tapered from bottom to top in both axes, and its sides slightly undercut the inscribed face.

Fragment *a* (EM Inventory, 7179, Plate) was found on the Akropolis on July 20, 1840, in excavations east of the Parthenon, and was first published by K. S. Pittakys.[4] Height 0.438 m. Width 0.289 m. Thickness (top) 0.074 m.; (bottom) 0.089 m. Fragment *b* (EM Inventory, 7178, Plate) was also found in excavations on the Akropolis, near the Erechtheion, on October 16, 1839, and first published by Pittakys.[5] Height 0.360 m. Width 0.369 m. Thickness (top) 0.089 m; (bottom) 0.094 m.

Combined dimensions: Height 0.945 m. Width 0.369 m. Thickness (top) 0.074 m.; (bottom) 0.094 m. Letter-height 0.005–0.006 m. Lines 1–40 are *stoichedon,* with a square chequer-pattern, 0.0100 m. x 0.0100 m. Lines 41–48 are semi-*stoichedon.*

* I was initiated into the art of joining fragments of inscriptions by Professor McGregor when he, the late Professor Donald W. Bradeen, and I spent the winter of 1967–68 in Athens. I owe to these scholars an immense debt, in acknowledgement of which I dedicate this article to Professor McGregor.

[1] "Studien zu den attischen Psephismen, XI," *Hermes* 5 (1871) 328–330; see also Koehler's discussion of fragment *b* on its own, "Studien zu den attischen Psephismen, IV," *Hermes* 5 (1871) 17–19.

[2] Koehler republished this text in 1877 as *IG* 2. 181, and virtually the same text was used by Kirchner in 1915 for *IG* 2.² 365. Subsequent scholarship has concerned itself with the calendar for 323/2 B.C. (E. Schweigert, "Greek Inscriptions," *Hesperia* 9 [1940] 338–339; W. K. Pritchett and O. Neugebauer, *The Calendars of Athens* [Cambridge, Mass. 1947] 57; B. D. Meritt, *The Athenian Year* [Berkeley 1961] 105); with the role of the *boule* in preparing the decree (P. J. Rhodes, *The Athenian Boule* [Oxford 1972] *passim*, especially 262; R. A. de Laix, *Probouleusis at Athens* [Los Angeles 1973] 127 and 137); or with the *proxenia* of Lapyris and its antecedents (A. Lambrechts, *Tekst en Uitzicht van de Atheense Proxeniedecreten tot 323 v. C.* [Brussels 1958] 66; 69; 157, no. 141; M. B. Walbank, *Athenian Proxenies of the Fifth Century* B.C. [Toronto 1978] 409–410). The article of J. G. Droysen, "Die Festzeit der Nemeen," *Hermes* 14 (1879) 1–24, is concerned with the time of year at which the Nemean festival was celebrated; he discusses this inscription briefly on pages 11–12.

[3] I acknowledge with gratitude the financial assistance afforded to me by the Canada Council that enabled me to spend the summer of 1971 and the first five months of 1977 in Athens. I acknowledge here, too, the generous assistance granted to me by Mrs. Dina Peppas-Delmousou, the Director of the Epigraphical Museum in Athens, and by her assistant, Mrs. Chara Karapa-Molizani. The photograph published here is by courtesy of the Epigraphical Museum, with the permission of Mrs. Peppas-Delmousou.

[4] Ἐφημερὶς Ἀρχαιολογική, φ. 19 (1840) 335–336, no. 404.

[5] Ἐφημερὶς Ἀρχαιολογική, φ. 17 (1839) 202–203, no. 301.

Hekatombaion 11, 323/2 B.C.   ΣΤΟΙΧ. 32

a

     Ἐπὶ Κηφισοδώρου ἄρχο[ντος, ἐπὶ τῆς Ἱππο]-
     θωντίδος πρώτης πρυτα[νείας, ἧι Ἀρχίας]
     [Π]υθοδώρου ἐγραμμάτευε[ν· Ἑκατομβαιῶν]-
     [ος] ἑνδεκάτει· ⟨ἑνδεκάτει⟩ τῆς πρυτανεί[ας· των προέδ]-
5   [ρων] ἐπεψήφ[ιζ]εν Τ̣ιμόστρα[τ]ο[ς . . . ⁷ . . . · ἔ]-
     [δ]ο[ξ]εν τῶι δή[μωι]· Ἐπιτέλ[ης] Σ[ω]ιν[όμου Περ]-
     [γ]ασῆθεν εἶπεν· [π]ερὶ ὧν λέγ[ε]ι ὁ ἀ[ρκεθέωρ]-
     [ο]ς ὁ εἰς τὰ Ν[έ]μεα κ[α]ὶ Λάπυ[ρις] ὁ π[ρόξενος]
     [τ]ῆς πόλε[ω]ς [. . ⁵ . .] δεδόχ[θαι] τ[ῶι δήμωι τ.]-
10 [.] μὲν ἀρκεθ[εω]ρο[. . . . . . . ¹⁹ . . . .]
     [.]α εἰς τὸγ[. . . . . ¹² . . . . .]ν κα[ὶ . . . . ⁷ . .]
     [.] καὶ Ἀθη[ν]αῖοι[.]ω[. . . ⁸ . . .]ω[. . . . ⁹ . . .]
     [.]νον μέρος [. . . . . ²³ . . . .]
     [.]ι αὐτῶι ἀργύ[ριον . . . . . ¹⁶ . . . . . λ]-
15 αμβάνε[ι]ν ὑπὲρ [. . . . . . . ¹⁹ . . . . . . τ]-
     [ο]ὺς προξένους [. . . . . . . ²⁰ . . . .]
     [.]τρια ὅπως [.]ινα[. . . . . . ¹⁹ . . . . . .]
     [.]νουσια [αὐ]τῶι[. . . . . ¹⁷ . . . . τὸν]
     [β]ουλομεν[.]ν Ἀθη[ν . ⁴ .]ι̣[. . . . ¹³ . . . .]
20 [. ⁴ .]ν πρ[οξ]εν[.]γ [. . . . . . . ¹⁹ . . . . . .]
     [. . .]λ[.]ιγ[. ⁴ .]ομ̣[. . . . . . ¹⁹ . . . . . .]
     [. . .]ενσεσ[. .]να[. . . . . ²⁰ . . . . .]
     λη[. .]ιζηι[. . . . ¹⁰ . . . .]η[. . . . ¹³ . . . .]
     φυογ[.]ιαλ[. . . . . . . ²⁴ . . . .]
25 [.]εμ[. . . ⁶ . . .]ο[. . . . ⁷ . . .]ηγ[. . . . . ¹³ . . . . .]
     το[. . . . . ¹² . . . . .]μ̣[.]π̣[. . . . . ¹⁵ . . . . .]
     σι[. . . . . ¹³ . . . . .]ς π̣[. . . . . ¹⁵ . . . . .]
     σαι[. . ⁶ . .]λ[.]α[. .]ι̣[. . . . ¹⁶ . . . . .]
     [.]σιπ[. . . . . ²⁷ . . . .]
30 [.]αρεχ[. . ⁵ . .]λ[. .]ι̣[. . . . . ¹⁷ . . . . .]
     [.]εοις [. . .]κ[.]λ[. .]ημ̣[. . . . . ¹⁶ . . . . .]
     [.]αιγε[. .]ντα[. .] λ[. . . . . . ¹⁸ . . . . . .]
     [. ⁴ .]ειεαι[. . . ⁶ . . .]σ[. . . . . ¹⁶ . . . . .]
     [. ⁴ .]ς καὶ ὅσο [. . . . . . . ²¹ . . . .]

b

35 [. ἀρ]κεθέωρος ει[. . . . . ¹⁹ . . . .]
     τ̣ὸν θεωρὸν τοῖς προξ[ένοις . . . . ¹⁰ . . . .]
     καθὰ Λάπυρις ὁ πρόξενο[ς . . . . . ¹³ . . . . .]
     τοὺς δὲ ἀποδέκτας μερί[σαι τῶι ἀρκε]-
     θεώρωι ὃς ἂν ἀεὶ ἀρκεθεω[ρήσηι τὸ]
40 ἀργύριον.   *vacat*
                 vacat
     ἐπαινέσα[ι] δὲ Λάπυριν Καλλί[ου Κλεωναῖ]-
     ον τὸν πρόξενον καὶ καλέσαι [αὐτὸν ἐπὶ δ]-
     εῖπνον εἰς τὸ πρυτανεῖον εἰς [αὔριον]·
45 ἀναγράψαι δὲ τόδε τὸ ψήφισμα τ̣[ὸν γραμ]-
     ματέα τῆς βουλῆς εἰς τὴν στήλη[ν τὴν ἐν]
     Ἀκροπόλει ἐν ἧι γέγραπται Ἐχεν[βρότωι]

Κλεωναίωι τῶι προξένωι τῶι Λαπύ[ριος]
ἡ προξενία.   *vacat*
                vacat

Commentary

The marble is of a type often employed in public inscriptions of the later fourth century B.C. The letter-height and chequer-pattern are normal for the period, but I have not been able to find any published inscription that is by the same hand. Letters dotted in my text survive as follows: Line 5: The lower half of the vertical of tau, and the left diagonal of alpha. Line 7: The upper left corner of gamma. Line 8: The right apex of mu. Line 9: The right diagonal of the first delta, the upper curve of omicron, and the apex of the second delta. Line 10: The upper right curve of omicron. Line 11: The bottom of the left hasta of the first nu, the top of the right hasta of the second nu, and the left diagonal of alpha. Line 14: The upper left corner of gamma, and the left diagonal of upsilon. Line 15: The bottom of the left vertical of pi. Line 17: The left diagonal of alpha. Line 19: The upper part of the left diagonal of upsilon, the right diagonal of lambda, the right apex of mu, and the top of iota. Line 20: The upper left corners of pi and rho, and the lower left side and upper right side of nu. Line 21: The feet of lambda, the top of iota, the bottom of the left hasta of nu, and the left outer diagonal of mu. Line 22: The upper left corner of the first epsilon, the middle of the second (from the top) diagonal of the first sigma, the upper left corner of the second epsilon, and the bottom right tip of the second sigma (the diagonals of sigmas elsewhere in this inscription are set at roughly the same angle as those of chi and upsilon); the apex of alpha. Line 23: The bottom of the left hasta of the first eta, and the top of the right hasta of the second. Line 24: The upper left tip of upsilon, and the apex of alpha. Line 25: The upper part of the right hasta of eta, and the upper part of the left hasta of nu. Line 26: The upper left corner of pi. Line 27: The upper left corner of pi. Line 28: The apex of lambda, and the top of iota. Line 30: The right tips of the diagonals of kappa, the apex of lambda, and the bottom of iota. Line 31: The right tip of the lower diagonal of kappa, the left foot of lambda, the top of the right hasta of eta, and the left apex of mu. Line 32: The apex of the first alpha, the upper left corners of gamma and epsilon, the top of the right hasta of nu, the apex of the second alpha, and the apex of lambda. Line 33: The bottoms only of these letters survive on fragment *b*. Line 35: Previous editors printed an undotted omicron here. The marks surviving on the stone today do, indeed, suggest the lower curve of an omicron, but there are also marks that suggest the lower diagonal and part of the upper diagonal of a kappa. Line 36: The bottoms only of these letters survive. Line 39: A small part of the left side of omega survives, but without any trace of the left foot. If anything, I should be inclined to read this as the left hasta of some such letter as nu, but the text demands an omega here. Line 45: The bottom of tau survives.

Lines 2–3: Schweigert demonstrated that the secretary for this year was Archias, not Eukles, as earlier editors had thought.[6]

Line 4: The mason evidently regarded the second ἐνδεκάτει as dittography on the part of the secretary, and so omitted it.

Line 6: The orator is that Ἐπιτέλης Σωινόμου Περγασῆθεν who served as a *naopoios* at Delphoi in 327/6 B.C.,[7] and as commissioner for a festival at the Amphiareion at Oropous in 329/8 B.C.[8] He seems thus to have specialised in religious matters during the Macedonian period. An earlier Ἐπιτέλης Περγασεὺς καθύπερθεν was probably a relative, born around 400 B.C.: his son Epikrates served as a *bouleutes* of Erechtheis in 367/6 B.C.[9] A yet earlier Epiteles was the son of Soinautes: he and his brother Oinochares made a dedication to Poseidon Erechtheus, probably around the

[6] Above, note 2.   [7] *PA* 4963, *Addenda*.   [8] *PA* 4963.
[9] W. K. Pritchett, "Greek Inscriptions," *Hesperia* 11 (1942) 231–240, 43, line 32.

middle of the fifth century B.C.[10] Soinautes and Soinomos must surely be of the same family, although the name Soinautes is relatively common.[11] The family does not seem to have been wealthy enough to qualify for the liturgical class, and seems to have disappeared from public life after 323/2 B.C.

Lines 7–10: The *Arketheoros* is not named, but he is mentioned again in lines 10, 35, and 38–39;[12] in this last case the office, rather than an individual, seems to be implied. Thus, I believe, this clause and all that follows it refer to a future occasion, not to actions that have already been taken. The *Arketheoros* was the chief of the *theoroi*, the official Athenian delegation sent earlier in the summer of this year to the Nemean festival.[13] He completed his term of office, presumably, at the end of the civil year 324/3 B.C., and, together with the *Proxenos* Lapyris of Kleonai, submitted a report upon his activities,[14] as a result of which the *demos* made the decisions that are reported in this document.

Line 10: The five-letter gap before δεδόχ[θαι] is best filled by an adverb or adverbial phrase qualifying δεδόχ[θαι]: Koehler[15] reported an iota before the delta, and restored [λέγε]ι, which I find somewhat clumsy; an alternative, but one that is methodologically unsatisfactory, might be to restore [⟨ἀγαθῆι⟩τύχηι], since the phrase ἀγαθῆι τύχηι δεδόχθαι τῶι δήμωι is very common. I can see no trace of the iota reported by Koehler.

Lines 10–33: The fragmentary nature of this document and the absence of parallels make it very hard to establish the sense of these lines, let alone to restore them convincingly. From line 10 it is clear that the *demos* has made at least two decisions: of these, the first concerns the *Arketheoros*, and the second, I believe, the *Proxenoi*. Thus, Clause One, [τὸ|ν?] μὲν ἀρκεθέωρο[ν . . .], may continue down to line 14, ending with a grant of money, perhaps to the *Arketheoros* himself, at any rate, to an individual. Clause Two, beginning at line 14, involves receipt [of funds?] in behalf of someone [the *theoroi*?] by someone else, perhaps the *Proxenoi*. I suspect that lines 16–18 are an expansion, or explanation, of Clause Two. In lines 18–20 provision seems to be made for any Athenian who wishes to avail himself of the services of the *Proxenoi*. Lines 21–34 are even more obscure, but, since lines 34ff. seem to be a summary of the whole decree, these lines should probably be regarded as detailed provisions under the heading of Clause Two.

Line 34: Some such clause as ὅσο [ἄν δέηται . . .] seems to be required here; perhaps how much money is required for individual *theoroi*.

Lines 35–36: The *Arketheoros* may have to introduce, or vouch for, each *theoros*, to the *Proxenoi*, as the *Proxenos* Lapyris has advised.

Lines 38–40: A standing order is issued to the Athenian *apodektai* to disburse funds to whoever is acting as *Arketheoros*, presumably for future celebrations of the Nemean festival.

---

[10] *IG* 1.² 580. Although the script is archaic in character, Koehler (above, note 1, 329) thought that it might be an archaizing inscription, and placed it at the beginning of the Peloponnesian War. Kirchner (*PA* 13140) places it before 444 B.C. I have not seen this inscription.

[11] *PA* 13135–13140. At least five different demotics are involved.   [12] LSJ, s.v. ἀρκεθέωρος.

[13] For a summary of the evidence for the date of the festival, and of modern discussions of it, see J. G. Frazer, *Pausanias' Description of Greece* 3 (Cambridge 1897) 92–93. The festival was held on the twelfth day of the summer month Panemos, every second and fourth year of an Olympiad. Pausanias (2. 15. 3 and 6. 16. 4) mentions a winter festival; this has led some scholars to speculate that winter and summer festivals may have alternated. Since Pausanias is the only ancient writer to mention a winter celebration, it seems best to regard this as a Roman innovation, probably short-lived.

[14] Koehler (above, note 1, 329). I think that it is less likely that the *Arketheoros* is the one appointed for the Nemean festival yet to come. The archaeological evidence is that the Temple of Zeus at Nemea was completed in the late 320's B.C. (see B. H. Hill and C. K. Williams II, *The Temple of Zeus at Nemea* [Princeton 1966] 44–46): I suggest that the Nemean festival of 324/3 B.C. may have coincided with the dedication of the temple, and that the reports of the *Arketheoros* and the *Proxenos* Lapyris may have referred to this event. Indeed, the dedication of the new temple may have led the authorities at Nemea to reorganise the festival, among other things, establishing a college of *proxenoi* to deal with the official delegations of the various Greek states (see note 19, below).

[15] Note 1 above, 328.

Lines 41 ff.: After a gap of 0.020 m., a praise-clause is appended to the decree, honouring Lapyris the son of Kallias of Kleonai, the *Proxenos* named in lines 8 and 37; he is apparently present in Athens at the time of passage of the decree, since he is invited to entertainment at the Prytaneion on the morrow.[16] The secretary to the *boule* is instructed to have the decree inscribed on the Akropolis on the same stele as that on which the proxeny of Echenbrotos of Kleonai is inscribed.

The stele of Echenbrotos survives.[17] It is not that on which this decree is inscribed, and the marble is of another kind. Since its bottom is not preserved, there is no way of telling whether or not the present decree was inscribed there as well, or whether it was found impractical to do so when the stele was inspected, so that Lapyris' decree was inscribed upon a new stele.

The publication-clause of lines 44–48 is not the only peculiarity of this section: the hand seems to be different from that of lines 1–40, and the chequer breaks down towards the right side of the document. The lines vary in length, from thirty to thirty-two letters, but the restorations seem certain. In all cases but that of line 42 syllabic division is preserved at the ends of lines; this is true, too, of lines 38 and 39, the only lines of the decree proper that can be restored with confidence.

Dittenberger[18] suggested that line 47 contained a mason's error: that τῶι προξένωι should be emended to τῶι προγόνωι. Echembrotos of Kleonai, whose stele is dated in the early years of the fourth century B.C., if Dittenberger's emendation be accepted, would be the grandfather of Lapyris. Unless some such emendation be made, the Greek is very clumsy, and this minor change is surely preferable to any suggestion that the mason may have left out an entire word or phrase.

It is highly unlikely that Echembrotos was still alive at the time of passage of the decree for Lapyris. Thus, the *Proxenoi* of lines 16 ff. are not Lapyris and others of his family, I believe, but some other group. Since the decree is primarily concerned with Athenian participation in the Nemean festival, I suggest that these unnamed *Proxenoi* are religious in function and officials of the Nemean festival itself, appointed to look after the needs of citizens of the various Greek states.[19] It would thus be appropriate for the *Arketheoros* to introduce to them the members of his delegation of *theoroi*, and the context of this decree may well have been the complications arising out of the failure on the part of the Athenian delegation to take this action at the most recent celebration of the festival.

The University of Calgary   Michael B. Walbank

---

[16] The use of [δ]εῖπνον, rather than ξένια, is unusual in a decree for a foreigner, but is not unparalleled: see W. A. McDonald, "A Linguistic Examination of an Epigraphical Formula," *AJA* 59 (1955) 151–155.

[17] *IG* 2.² 63, where the name is spelled Ἐχέμβροτος, apparently the correct form.

[18] *Index Schol. Halens.* (1885–1886) x.

[19] The evidence is extremely thin for such religious *proxenoi* appointed by their home-state: Herodotos (6. 57. 2) implies that, in the fifth century at least, the Spartan kings retained the right to appoint as *Proxenoi* any citizens they wished, but there is no indication of the function of these occasional *proxenoi*. At Delphoi, ca 211 B.C., the Delphians appointed one of their own citizens to serve as *Proxenos* of Sardis, and his functions seem largely to have been religious (*SIG*³ 548 and 549). In 182 B.C. the Aitolian League instructed its members each to appoint a representative to provide hospitality for the *theoroi* of Pergamon who came to announce the festival of the Nikephoria instituted by King Eumenes II (*SIG*³ 629). The question is discussed at length, but inconclusively, by P. Monceaux (*Les Proxénies Greques* [Paris 1886] chap. 2) and F. Gschnitzer (*RE, Suppl.* 13 [1973] 629–730, sv. *Proxenos*). Kleonai had formerly controlled the Nemean Games, but at some time during the fifth century B.C. Argos acquired the right to organize (or to share in the organization of) the games (see R. A. Tomlinson, *Argos and the Argolid* [Ithaca 1972] 136–137); Kleonai, however, remained an ally rather than a vassal under whatever arrangement was made, and seems to have retained its independence. Echembrotos and his father, and his descendants down to Lapyris, all seem to be *Proxenoi* of the more familiar kind, even though Lapyris, at least, and perhaps his predecessors, too, had some connection with the celebration of the festival. Since there was no city at Nemea, the *Proxenoi* referred to in this document may thus have been citizens either of Kleonai, or of Argos, or even of the states making up the Nemean Amphiktyony (if such an organisation existed: I have not been able to find any evidence for it).

EM 7179 and 7178

THE FOUNDING FATHERS OF THE DELIAN CONFEDERACY

One of Malcolm McGregor's many virtues as scholar and teacher is that of enthusiasm for his subject coupled with a remarkable ability to communicate that enthusiasm to others. In the course of his long career it has concentrated most particularly upon the Athenian democracy of the Age of Perikles, the Athenian Empire, and the epigraphy relating to both. It is of course tempting to see that democracy at its best when that Empire was at its zenith, and to think of the one as responsible for the other—a responsibility ultimately to be derived from the naval victory at Salamis that was the triumph of the Athenian *demos* and the salvation of Hellas. Seapower and empire tended to go together in the Aegean world, as Thucydides recognised and emphasised in the opening chapters of his *History*. He took particular pains to stress that the Persian invasions were the occasion of Athenian naval power:[1] and maritime supremacy and popular rule so swiftly became interconnected in the general understanding that "the earliest preserved attack on the democracy is definitely founded on the equation seapower = democracy."[2]

The Athenians ended by reinterpreting their earlier history so as to trace both navy and democracy back to the hero-king Theseus and thus to give them an antique respectability:[3] but the claim that the ναυτικὸς ὄχλος was responsible for turning back the Mede[4] was presumably a part of that growth to self-assertiveness that culminated in the "revolution of 462 B.C." and was recorded by Aristotle in the *Ath. Pol.*[5] It may indeed have been an element turned to less successful account by Themistokles' supporters in the political conflicts of the 470s that ended with the ostracism of the great man.[6] But the important thing about the 470s is that the ἐπιεικεῖς, as Aristotle calls them, gained the ascendancy very quickly (if they had ever really lost it), and, whatever the nature of their antagonism towards Themistokles and his supporters, were able to retain it.[7] Salamis may indeed justifiably be regarded as a victory of all the people, not properly to be appropriated by the one group or the other, and more is said below on this point:[8] it was without doubt the source of that dynamic growth and unremitting effort which had the developed democracy as one of their consequences.[9] But despite the factional claims and counterclaims that

---

[1] Thuc., 1.18.

[2] F. Jacoby, *Atthis* (Oxford 1949) 294.

[3] Cf. E. Ruschenbusch, *Historia* 7 (1958) 415–418; W. den Boer, *Mnemosyne* ser. 4, 15 (1962) 229–231; also *Greece and Rome* 2nd Ser., 16 (1969) 3–6; R. Sealey, *C.S.C.A.* 6 (1973) 292.

[4] Arist., *Politics* 1304a 17–24; cf. 1274a 12–15.

[5] *Ath. Pol.* 25.1.

[6] A. J. Podlecki, *The Life of Themistocles* (Montreal 1975) 34–37, writes of a "propaganda duel" between Kimon and Themistokles, in which Kimon "set out to erase the memory of Salamis." See also P. J. Rhodes, *Liverpool Classical Monthly* 1 (1976) 147–154 (especially 147–148), and R. J. Lenardon, *The Saga of Themistocles* (London 1978) 98–100. Themistokles' influence was already waning in 479 (cf. C. Hignett, *Xerxes' Invasion of Greece* [Oxford 1963] 274–278).

[7] Cf. R. Meiggs, *The Athenian Empire* (Oxford 1972) 86–87.

[8] Cf. N. G. L. Hammond, *A History of Greece to 322 B.C.* (Oxford 1959) 263.

[9] A. G. Woodhead, *Thucydides on the Nature of Power* (Cambridge 1970) 39–43.

came to be part of the later political tradition, whether or not their origin is to be found in the immediate aftermath of the war, it is salutary to remind ourselves that the Persian Wars were won and the Confederacy of Delos was founded against a very different background of political experience, that of the still essentially aristocratic late archaic period.

One cannot of course deny the growing and continuing importance of the navy as one campaign of the new Confederacy succeeded another, and the growing importance, in consequence, of the citizens who manned it. But its *preponderating* importance was slow to mature. It belongs with the fullness of Athenian democracy, later rather than earlier, and should not be antedated. Athenian maritime effort at an earlier period had been inconsiderable,[10] in spite of the system of naukraries to provide some kind of naval force—a system that went back at least to the seventh century. A large and powerful fleet was a new thing in Athenian society. It had been created only on the eve of Salamis, and it seems unlikely that it should or could as yet be viewed in any socio-political terms or as exercising, by its existence and requirements, any effect on the origins or initial development of the new Confederacy. What comes later belongs to a different, and in many respects less commendable, period in the Confederacy's history: here we are considering the background and beginnings, and it is to be suggested that the Athenians did not possess a background of, nor were the beginnings of the Confederacy affected by, any self-consciousness on the part of what came to be called "the seafaring mob." Moreover, in spite of what Aristotle says about the increased self-confidence of the *demos* in connexion with the first use of ostracism,[11] it is not to be believed that at this stage the *thetes* in general were, so to say, flexing their muscles as a serious factor in the initiation of state policy.

The formation of the Confederacy is in itself illustrative of that spirit of which mention has already been made—the momentum of victory, the determination for revenge, the impulse to stick together for the common good, the cheerful acceptance of limitations to complete national autonomy to that end, and so forth. The initial aim of the allies, under the leadership of the Spartans, was as it were to seal off the Aegean area from further Persian attack—attack that was naturally to be expected, for no one could assume that the King would reconcile himself to the humiliation just inflicted upon him without some further attempt upon Hellas. The "liberation" of the cities of the Ionian coast kept the Persian monarch at least a little distance from the Aegean shore and denied him the bases from which he could readily undertake a trans-Aegean attack of the same character as in 490 B.C. Ten years after Marathon the King had tried the overland route, with his sea-crossing limited to the passage of the Dardanelles. To deny him a repetition of this manoeuvre it was necessary to liberate the straits there and higher up at the Bosporus: hence the care first to capture Sestos in the winter of 479/8 and later to lay siege to Byzantium. The success of these ventures would hold the King at arm's length, and the Greeks, growing bolder as a Persian response became less apparent, could develop an offensive strategy from that point onward if they so wished.

It was during the siege of Byzantium that the conduct of Pausanias, the Spartan regent, who commanded the allied forces became obnoxious to those under his command.[12] The allies made representations to the Athenians and asked them to become their leaders, their *hegemones*; and the Athenians expressed their willingness to take over. Thucydides says "the Athenians,"[13] and on the face of it this ought to mean an application to Athens itself, for the issue of general policy was a

---

[10] Thuc., 1.14. 2–3.

[11] *Ath. Pol.* 22.3.

[12] This episode has occasioned a wealth of literature in recent years; see (apart from the works of A. J. Podlecki and R. J. Lenardon cited in note 6) F. Cornelius, *Historia* 22 (1973) 502–504; J. F. Lazenby, *Hermes* 103 (1975) 235–251; A. J. Podlecki, *Riv. Fil.* 104 (1976) 293–311; H. D. Westlake, *CQ* n.s. 27 (1977) 95–110, with references to earlier discussions.

[13] 1.95. 1–2.

major one, and the attitude of the Spartan home government was unknown. Plutarch's picture is of an application by the allies at Byzantium to the Athenians at Byzantium,[14] the latter being represented by Aristeides and Kimon, who are personally responsible, on this account, for a very fundamental development of Athenian state policy. Aristotle goes so far as to say that it was Aristeides who encouraged the whole allied initiative.[15] Notwithstanding this, there must surely have been a reference back to Athens before any final arrangement was made; the Spartans certainly had time to recall Pausanias for interrogation and to send out a replacement for him before the outcome was known. When Dorkis, the replacement, arrived on the scene he found the allies unwilling to trust him with the *hegemonia,* and he returned home. Thereafter the Spartans withdrew from the joint Hellenic effort, and according to Thucydides were not sorry to be rid of it.[16] They, or the majority among them, regarded the Athenians as competent substitutes for themselves, they were on good terms with them, and they saw too much involvement with outside commitments as potentially dangerous to themselves – individually as in the case of Pausanias and, we may assume, collectively also, since Spartan control at home was jeopardized by the absence of too many Spartans and Peloponnesian allies on distant enterprises. When, after a few years, action against Athens was discussed, those who were content to let the matter stand remained in the ascendant, and the downfall of Themistokles, whose duplicity in the affair of the rebuilding of the city-walls of Athens had doubtless not been forgotten, reinforced the majority opinion that the regime there was dependable enough from the Spartan point of view.

Not enough attention has been paid, in this context, to the character of *hegemonia,* that function of leadership which is usually rendered as "hegemony." Modern connotations of hegemony, however, seem not to be apposite, or not wholly to be apposite, to the ancient world, and it is preferable to retain the Greek word. N. G. L. Hammond discussed it in relation to the Athenian military command, in which he emphasised that it had to do with leadership and not with command as such.[17] But command, or the right to command, is not absent from it. Its functions and attributes were perhaps so unlike what might casually be expected that in the use of the word it is easy to be unaware that potentially novel or unexpected aspects may lurk in it. It clearly put the Athenians in a markedly pre-eminent position vis-à-vis all the allies put together, not merely each ally individually, as the swearing of the oaths of alliance and possibly the early division of booty seem to indicate.[18] Hammond may well be correct in his suggestion that the Confederacy's requirements first called for a general chosen among all the Athenians, as distinct from the ten chosen on a basis of one per *phyle*; but at any rate the executive lay entirely with the *hegemon,* even though the allied synods took cognizance of the choice and ratified the decision as to the next object of the united endeavours; it is otherwise hard to find business for them. That nominations were the province of the *hegemon,* and that Athenians alone were nominated, is also clear in the appointment of the *Hellenotamiai.*[19]

Hegemonia, it may be judged, carried wide powers of initiative, and this would include powers of initiative against signatories to the treaty of confederacy who failed to fulfil their admitted obligations. When the allies entered into their agreement with Athens, they surely did so with their eyes open, knowing that the *hegemonia* they offered to the Athenians, and to which they were prepared to submit themselves, was comprehensive in its nature. They saw it in action at

[14] *Aristeides* 23.

[15] *Ath. Pol.* 23.4.

[16] 1.95. 7. For a different interpretation see R. Meiggs (above, note 7), 40–41.

[17] *CQ* n.s. 19 (1969) 111–144. He did not introduce it into his discussion of the origins of the Delian Confederacy (*JHS* 87 [1967] 41–61); nor was it taken up by Meiggs (note 7, above) or W. Schuller, *Die Herrschaft der Athener im ersten attischen Seebund* (Berlin and New York 1974) (see esp. 198–199). Cf. E. Badian, *Antichthon* 5 (1971) 31–32.

[18] Cf. *PCPS* n.s. 1 (1950–51) 9–12.

[19] *JHS* 79 (1959) 149–152.

once when Aristeides made his great assessment of their obligations to provide ships or money for the Confederacy's enterprises. At a much more advanced stage of the Empire they were still able to complain about the assessment made upon them, and no doubt they were at liberty to argue with Aristeides in 478; but the initiative and procedure, and indeed the fundamental distinction as to which allies should provide cash and which ships, were the prerogative of the *hegemon*. Moreover, if the contract established at the swearing of the oaths, ratified by the famous casting of the lumps of iron into the sea, was a bilateral contract between the *hegemon* and the rest, the same may be true of the arrangements for consultation, which may have been bilateral in the same way – even bi-cameral.[20] Certainly, if *hegemonia* meant anything at all, Athens could not have had merely an equal vote with the tiniest Aegean island. What has seemed fair to the United Nations, with results not nowadays universally commended, did not seem fair to the fifth-century Greeks. One suspects that the Athenians carried a decision on their part to the synod, just as the Spartans carried a decision on their part to the congress of their Peloponnesian allies, and that the synod said yea or nay: but Athenian influence, as we learn from what the Mytilenaeans said later in 428,[21] always made sure that what Athens proposed was approved. This was not a bi-cameral arrangement in any strict sense, since as far as the Confederacy's organization was concerned there was only one *camera*. The rest depended on the Athenian generals and council and assembly, from whom the initiative came. In the fourth-century Confederacy the procedure seems to have been tightened up and the role of the allies more precisely defined; but the general principle was much the same.

In the case of the Spartans we learn from Xenophon that the expression of *hegemonia* was in terms of the allies following whithersoever the Spartan *hegemones* might lead: the Achaians formulate it as ἡμεῖς ὅπως ἂν ὑμεῖς παραγγέλλητε συστρατευόμεθα καὶ ἑπόμεθα ὅποι ἂν ἡγῆσθε.[22] When the Delian Confederacy was formed, the Spartan organization was the only one that provided a clear example – and it was a good example to follow. The allies would be familiar with it. They saw themselves, thus, in a relationship with Athens comparable with that of Sparta's Peloponnesian allies with Sparta. When they took their oaths and threw the iron into the sea, the implication was that the iron would float sooner than they would break the oaths just taken. The oaths did not, we may judge, concern unremitting war against the Great King, or a simple affirmation of unending alliance. That is to say, when at the time of the Peace of Kallias the war with Persia evidently came to an end, it was not a matter of the Confederacy's raison d'être having been fulfilled, as is sometimes said. Nor is there a question of the allies having broken faith because the alliance had no fixed term. The oaths concerned following whithersoever the Athenians might lead, and the termination of the war with Persia had, in itself, nothing to do with this.

That this was so may nevertheless have surprised the allies. For Thucydides says that the πρόσχημα of the arrangement was to exact retribution for what the Greeks had suffered.[23] The meaning of πρόσχημα has been amply discussed,[24] and is here taken to imply a reason publicly alleged, which may or may not be a true or convincing reason; it is not to be regarded as the equivalent of a specious excuse, nor is it to be suggested that *ab initio* the Athenians were using the war with Persia as a pretext or cover for embarking upon a programme of domination over the Aegean Greeks. The intention was seriously and sincerely meant, and was well followed out in the Confederacy's expeditions in the 470s and early 460s. The allies evidently stomached the proposal

---

[20] N. G. L. Hammond (above, note 8), 256; *idem., CR* n.s. 8 (1958) 33, and *JHS* 87 (1967) 51–52. Cf. Meiggs (above, note 7), 460–462. On the oaths see H. Jacobson, *Philologus* 119 (1975) 256–258.

[21] Thuc., 3.10.5, 11.1. Cf. Hammond, *JHS* (note 20 above), 51.

[22] Xen., *Hell.* 4.6.2.

[23] Thuc., 1.96.1.

[24] Cf. M. Chambers, *CP* 53 (1958) 31, note 5; M. F. McGregor, *Athenian Policy, at Home and Abroad* (Lectures in Memory of Louise Taft Semple, 2nd Ser. 1967) 19.

to follow when the Athenians led them against Naxos, whatever Thucydides may say about the fate of the Naxians. They had perhaps not expected retribution against Naxos to be as severe as it was; but Thucydides' language may sound more severe than it should, and I have suggested elsewhere that Naxos may have retained its fleet, or some part of its fleet, just as Malcolm McGregor and his colleagues showed that "enslavement," which is Thucydides' word for what happened to Naxos, does not mean what at first we might think it means.[25]

In short, if we consider more carefully what the Athenians and their allies will have understood by that *hegemonia* which the one side accepted and the other acknowledged, we are likely to bring into a better perspective a whole range of events – the character and significance of the original oaths, the actions against delinquent cities, the administration of the finances of the Confederacy, and the so-called crisis of 449–47. In particular, the implications of the "Congress Decree" become more far-reaching and more liberal; more far-reaching in that the claim to a wider *hegemonia* made by Perikles on Athens' behalf was not merely a play for power but the practical adumbration of the role Perikles saw Athens as playing in her capacity as the "education of Hellas"; and more liberal in that the allies were being given an opportunity to say something about the future shape of the Confederacy irrespective of the continuing efficacy of their undertaking to follow the Athenians whithersoever they led.[26]

The early years of the Confederacy were the years in which for the most part the πρόσχημα was followed up with vigour. Kimon was the great general with whom these successes are associated. That he and Aristeides were the leading men of Athens at the time of the Confederacy's inception must have encouraged the allies to accept what Athenian *hegemonia* involved just as it comforted the Spartans when they themselves renounced further leadership. You were safe with men like that. They were men of the right sort. In the *Athenaion Politeia*, when Aristotle distinguishes the opposing leaders of the *demos* and the respectable class, the γνώριμοι, Aristeides and Kimon are on the side of the angels. Themistokles the radical had been rejected, and the seventeen years after the Persian Wars are characterized by Aristotle as years in which the Kleisthenic constitution, guaranteed by the august body of the Areiopagos, was in full and stable vigour. It was the sixth of the constitutions into which he divided the Athenian political experience.[27] We are assured that the constitution of Kleisthenes was more democratic than that of Solon. But in the time of full democracy it could clearly be seen that it stood closer to that of Solon than did the constitution of the time of Perikles, and afterwards.[28] It was the constitution to which the more moderate reformers at the end of the fifth century looked back. They wanted, as they expressed it, "a democratic government, but not of the same kind" as they had at the time.[29] It was, as Isokrates put it, "a democracy that employed aristocracy," or, in the words of Plutarch, a constitution of a mixed character of the best possible kind, which produced consensus (*homonoia*) and triumph over adversity (*soteria*) – that "good, old democracy" of the so-called centrist or middle-of-the-road tradition. In the *Life of Kimon* Plutarch went so far as to refer to it as the "aristocracy of the time of Kleisthenes,"[30] which Perikles, using the arts of the demagogue, led the people in overthrowing in the upheaval of 462/1.

[25] B. D. Meritt, H. T. Wade-Gery, M. F. McGregor, *The Athenian Tribute Lists* (*ATL*) 3 (1950) 155–157. Cf. A. G. Woodhead, in *Phoros: Tribute to Benjamin Dean Meritt* (Locust Valley, New York 1974) 176–177.

[26] Plut., *Per.* 17; cf. *ATL* 2 (1949) 61, D 12. There has been some attempt in the past decade to dismiss the "Congress Decree" as an historical forgery of the fourth century; see R. Seager, *Historia* 18 (1969) 129–141, A. B. Bosworth, *Historia* 20 (1971) 600–616. But there are no convincing grounds for this beyond the inconvenience of the decree's genuineness in the eyes of its critics. See G. T. Griffith, *Historia* 27 (1978) 218–219. Since the discovery of the "Themistokles Decree" in particular, there has been a predisposition to see in such survivals the guilt of fabrication rather than the innocence of authenticity, and to regard the latter as requiring more justification than the former.

[27] Arist., *Ath. Pol.* 41.2.   [28] *Ath. Pol.* 29.3.

[29] Thuc., 8.53. 1.   [30] Isoc., 12.131; Plut., *Cim.* 15; *Per.* 3.2.

That, under the constitution of Kleisthenes so characterized, the *boule*, with revised membership recruited on a remarkable new principle of sortition and a basis of geographical distribution, continued to exercise that executive authority it had possessed under Solon's provisions remains in my view the most reasonable hypothesis to account for the development of Athens' democracy and the manner of that development. These are days too early for the fullness of δημοκρατία, even if we could be clear what is to be understood by the δῆμος who may be held to have acquired the κράτος.[31] The currency of the term, δημοκρατία, seems initially to have responded to a wider distribution of power, in contrast with τυραννίς and in parallel with ἰσονομία.[32] Herodotos hardly uses it, and when he does he seems to mean by it a state in which power is more liberally shared than in a tyranny or oligarchy, but not necessarily a state in which power is shared totally down the line to the lowest section of society. The growth in effective power of the *plebs urbana* came to bestow on it the more particular connotation that is more familiar in our evidence and consciousness. But the *isonomia* with which in its earlier history it is equated, equality before and by means of the law, is in its origin an upper-class concept, born of opposition to tyranny rather than of championship of any popular cause. The background to the origin of the Delian Confederacy, in fact, as far as the Athenians were concerned, was what I have elsewhere referred to as the "bourgeois republic," in which the government was safely and comfortably in the hands of the upper-middle class, from the *hippeis* down to the hoplites.[33] It was a time, in Plutarch's words,[34] of καθεστὼς κόσμος and τὰ πάτρια νόμιμα – soundly established order and the ancestral laws.

This is not the occasion to defend at any length the concept of the bourgeois republic of late archaic Athens from some of the hesitation with which it has been received: but it may not be inappropriate to make a few summary points. (1) The evidence for the period of the "democracy of Kleisthenes" is so scanty that any hypothesis about it lacks the strength of evidential corroboration that one would like.[35] There has been an abundance of speculation of an armchair academic kind, and a good deal of readiness to discard, on grounds of alleged partisanship or lateness or confusion, often arbitrarily adduced, such evidential material as may be inconvenient. One must make do with what one has, not demanding of it more than it contains but equally not ignoring what has to be accommodated.

(2) Our evidence concentrates on the reformation of the *phylai* and the "mixing up" of the people. There is nowhere any suggestion of a shift of the power-base in the *polis*. Indeed, the importance of the archonship as the goal of political ambition within the framework of the aristocratic associations and as a potent political weapon worthy of intra-aristocratic contention remained undiminished until 487. Even then, since the census-groups from which election was made remained unchanged, the transition of ex-archons to the Council of the Areiopagos gave to that body a continuing significance to which Ephialtes and Perikles later felt good reason to address themselves.[36] The *ekklesia* seems at this time to have met but once a month, which does not suggest that it was overworked or burdened with the primary responsibility for the day-to-day administration of policy. The mixing up of the people, drawn (as Kleisthenes hoped) into one aristocratic *hetaireia*, makes sense only if the *boule*, where the real work was done, was the object of it. That the people possessed ratificatory rights of long standing in certain major policy decisions none would deny. Occasions when these were exercised are certainly to be discerned in archaic Athens, and their existence is apparent, in a rudimentary form, in remoter history. But the same

---

[31] A. Andrewes, *The Greek Tyrants* (London 1956) 35–36. On the nature and composition of the Kleisthenic *boule* see P. J. Rhodes, *The Athenian Boule* (Oxford 1972) 6–7 and 208–209.

[32] Cf. R. Sealey (above, note 3), 275–277.

[33] *Historia* 16 (1967) 135–140.   [34] *Cim.* 15.

[35] Cf. Sealey, *A History of the Greek City States, 700–338 B.C.* (Berkeley 1976) 160.

[36] Cf. Badian (above, note 17), 1–30.

were enjoyed by the *populus Romanus*, there too traceable to early tradition: yet in Rome the Senate managed to retain its Solonian-type prerogatives until the end of the republic, and the essentials of *de facto* power remained with the men of property.[37]

(3) It cannot be denied that the *boule* acquired additional duties as the fifth century progressed. But duties must be distinguished from power, and it is erroneous to speak of the 'powers' of the Council when duties alone, fulfilled at the behest of and under the ultimate supervision of the soverign *demos*, are in question.[38] To all intents and purposes, power came to reside wholly in the *ekklesia*: the *boule* lost, at any rate after 462, the capacity to direct its use. It was, as it had always been, a probouleutic body: but it is always assumed that it was the *ekklesia* that was the recipient of the *probouleusis*. This was so in the developed democracy: but in the earlier phase the pattern was still, in some degree, comparable with that at Rome, where the *probouleusis* of the Senate was directed to the magistrates. The formula of preamble in Athenian decrees continued to proclaim an equality of competence in decision-making between *boule* and *demos*, but the reality soon outstripped the theory, and ultimately even the substance of real advice and consent tended to elude the *bouleutai*, if the distinction between probouleutic and non-probouleutic measures is justly drawn.[39]

(4) Finally, one must have regard to the practicalities of politics, which, as Bismarck said and Lord Butler more recently reiterated, represent the art of the possible. If local aristocrats were to exert effective pressure on an assembly in which each voter voted by himself and not in any block vote, one must ask how this was done. If aristocratic landed possessions were scattered in small parcels across Attika, as was certainly the later pattern, could any such productive pressure be contemplated at all? To elaborate on the geographical bases of the great families is not of consequence unless the infrequent assemblies can be seen to have attracted men from the country for decisions that would benefit those who manipulated them. Our evidence on the other hand is concerned with the *amicitiae* of aristocrats, the hand of such friendship not (until Kleisthenes hit upon the idea to his considerable profit) being extended to the *demos*. In the ambit of this aristocratic in-fighting the aristocratic (Solonian) council was the obvious arena, and influence in it and over the magistrates the desirable object. In the 480s the changes that would move the character of Athenian political practice towards Periklean and post-Periklean democracy were just beginning. The successful defence of the state against Xerxes may temporarily have retarded them; for the tradition of the "Areopagite revival" is strong and cannot be shrugged off. At the least that tradition must be interpreted, on the evidence, as the expression of that continuing confidence in Kimon, Aristeides and men who thought as they did, which underlies the seventeen years covered by it. Salamis or no Salamis, 462/1 and not 478 was the date of the major step forward towards τὸ ἀνίεσθαι μᾶλλον τὴν πολιτείαν.[40]

If all this was the case with Athens, which seems to have been *avant-garde* in democratic development, how much the more would it have been so in the allied cities that accepted the *hegemonia* of so well balanced a state. When Herodotos tells us that, in the aftermath of the Ionian revolt, the King's commissioner Mardonios set up democracies in the cities,[41] it was, we may

---

[37] This comparison is, of course, not to be pressed too far, as Mr. G. T. Griffith reminds me. The main difference in the essence of the power of the Athenian *demos* as contrasted with its Roman counterpart lay in the reality of its judicial competence. As Aristotle rightly says, Solon's institution of the *Heliaia* contained a characteristic to be described as δημοτικόν, with a potentiality for developing political consequences; and these were greater than anything developed from the *provocatio ad populum* traditionally established in the first year of the Roman Republic. The trial of Miltiades during his term of office is a point of unlikeness that deserves emphasis.

[38] P. J. Rhodes (above, note 31), 209–215.

[39] Rhodes (above, note 31), 52–81 (esp. 66–68).

[40] Arist., *Ath. Pol.* 26.1.

[41] Hdt., 6.43. Cf. Sealey (above, note 3), 276–277.

suspect, this kind of limited, bourgeois democracy that he organized. Tyrannies in the Greek cities of Asia, which the King had previously supported, had played him false, and he sought another kind of government on which he could better depend for loyalty and effectiveness. When we read of Mardonios' action, we may be inclined, without adequate reflection, to assume that the King was allowing the pendulum to swing to the other extreme; it is easy, from knowledge of Periklean democracy and a disposition to see it as a *summum bonum*, to associate it with *demokratia* whenever we see the word. It is of course known that a number of the Athenian allies were oligarchically governed and remained so to a much later date: where there *were* democracies, these were undoubtedly of what must be seen as a general Kleisthenic type–a "limited" or "moderate" democracy if such a description will help, but one in which those whom Thucydides later called the *sophrones*, the men of restraint and self-discipline,[42] felt at home and exercised effective governmental control. When the allies and the Athenians came together and created the new organization, with men such as Aristeides and Kimon to shape it and lead it, like was speaking with like, and the world was safe for the men of sense and substance. Doubtless they could not envisage it otherwise, now that tyranny seemed a thing of the past, and they entered into their agreements with complete confidence that it would so remain.

After all, they had saved the world by their exertions. There may indeed be a temptation to dwell on the part played in the victory of Salamis by those who rowed in the fleet, the precursors of the ναυτικὸς ὄχλος. But to a later generation the grand old men of this generation were the men who fought at Marathon, the Μαραθωνομάχαι. It was these men who had first shown that a Persian army could be defeated, and that the future lay with the Greek hoplite. Indeed, a more perceptive look at the great Persian war of 480/79 enables us to recognize that, although the battle of Salamis was the turning-point of the defence of Greece, it was the battle of Plataia, a hoplite battle in its entirety, that had settled the issue. What is more, when the war was carried to the coast of Asia Minor, the great victory of Cape Mykale was a land battle also, and not a battle by sea. Not that Salamis should be accounted a "naval" battle, in the style, for example, of Phormion. The essence of the affair was that of a land battle on shipboard, with the hazards of falling overboard and drowning being added to the normal risks of hand-to-hand combat on *terra firma*. We should also note the part played even in the "naval" tradition of Salamis by the attack on the Persians stationed on the islet of Psyttaleia. Aristeides is said to have led a hoplite force against what is described as an elite Persian detachment, and to have wiped it out.[43] The action was small but memorable, wrote A. R. Burn.[44] But it has become fashionable to dismiss it as trifling,[45] and even to see in it an attempt by the γνώριμοι to claim Salamis for themselves and to devalue the triumph of the *demos*.[46] The correct view of it may in fact be the reverse of this, the attempt by a growing popular tradition to obscure and downgrade the very real hoplite contribution to what it was more desirable to see as the victory of the common man. It occupies an important place in the very earliest accounts of the battle, and cannot be seen as resurrected by some later writer interested in exaggerating it. Both Aischylos and Herodotos give it an emphasis that cannot be lightly dismissed. But be that as it may, there can be no doubt that the great triumph over Persia was in a

---

[42] Thuc., 4.28.5; cf. A. G. Woodhead (above, note 9), 209, note 5.

[43] Hdt., 8.95; cf. Aisch., *Persae* 447–467; Plut., *Aristeides* 9.

[44] *Persia and the Greeks* (New York 1962) 467.

[45] Peter M. Green, *The Year of Salamis* (London 1970) 196.

[46] C. W. Fornara, for example (*JHS* 86 [1966] 51–54), suggested that Herodotos got hold of a partisan version, not apparent in Aischylos (where the marines from the fleet do the work ascribed by the historian to Aristeides and the troops from Salamis island). Yet the marines were presumably hoplites, and Herodotos had, one assumes, no lack of testimony to the event, which involved the disembarkation of hoplites from ships on to Psyttaleia. These could have come both from the fleet and from the shore. In either case, the episode was a striking one, well-remembered. It cannot be discarded either as unimportant or as an historical fiction, to accommodate modern theory.

very large degree indeed a hoplite triumph. Although in the new Confederacy the fleet had an important role and the rowers in it acquired commensurate importance with the passage of time, at the beginning, which is the present focus of inquiry, the distribution of military consequence seemed firmly enough to lie where it always, or at least for the last couple of centuries, had lain — with the hoplite class.

It is possible to add a few straws in the wind to this assessment of the spirit in which the Delian Confederacy was founded. When the war was over and the tidying up in Athens was undertaken, there was some concern to repair or replace the monuments the Persians had damaged or stolen. Among the items high on the list, as the evidence permits us to judge, was the memorial of the battle of Marathon.[47] It has been much debated whether an epigram recording the success of Salamis was now added to it. If the addition did refer to Salamis, one observes, as W. K. Pritchett justly pointed out,[48] that the engagement of Psyttaleia must have received emphasis in it. If both epigrams refer to Marathon, the emphasis on hoplite prowess is even more marked. Another restored memorial, of which a fragment survives, is that which commemorated the great Athenian victory over the men of Boiotia and of Euboian Chalkis in the last decade of the sixth century, in a year generally agreed to be 506 B.C. A. E. Raubitschek has argued that the restoration of the earlier monument is to be connected with the battle of Oinophyta in 458.[49] But there is no reason to wait so long: the prompt replacement of the memorial fits well with the 470s. Moreover, one other memorial of the bourgeois republic was certainly replaced as soon as was practicable. This was the monument to the so-called tyrannicides, Harmodios and Aristogeiton, who died, according to the drinking-song commemorating their deed, bringing *isonomia* to Athens.[50] It may be, as has been well argued especially by H. W. Pleket,[51] that the original motivation for the original statue-group came from the more oligarchic faction of Isagoras, before Kleisthenes got the better of these opponents and, as Kleitophon said in 411, "set up the democracy."[52] But the action of the tyrant-slayers had had the effect, as things turned out, of creating the hoplite democracy, and Kleisthenes and his supporters to some extent stole the heroes and the watchword from their defeated adversaries. As they had struck down the tyrant in Athens, so, it might be said, the Athenian bourgeoisie whom they had helped to "liberate" had delivered the city from the tyranny of the Persian King.

The men who organised the Delian Confederacy, then, were inspired, not by a tradition of full participatory democracy but by the understanding that effective participation stopped with the upper-middle class. They were not riding the wave of naval supremacy or expressing the urge to wider enterprise of the *thetes* who manned the triremes, but they dwelt on the consciousness that it was the hoplite soldiers, men of their own solid and prosperous station in life, who had saved Athens from her foes. They could be relied upon to conduct the affairs and the ventures of the Confederacy in accordance with those basic premisses, and the allies knew it. The ventures that they did engage in reflected these predispositions. The first great venture was the capture of the Persian stronghold of Eion in Thrace; it is worth noting, in connexion with the monuments already discussed, that when Kimon and his men had captured Eion epigrams commemorating their success were inscribed on three herms, and the texts, now lost, were quoted by Aischines.[53]

---

[47] R. Meiggs and D. M. Lewis, *A Selection of Greek Historical Inscriptions to the End of the Fifth Century B.C.* (Oxford 1969) no. 26.

[48] *Marathon, CPCA* 4 (1960) 160–168.

[49] Meiggs and Lewis (above, note 47), no. 15, agree. See Raubitschek, *Dedications from the Athenian Akropolis* (Cambridge, Mass. 1949) no. 173; *IG* 1.² 394.

[50] Athenaios 15. 695a–b. On *isonomia* see especially G. Vlastos, *Isonomia: Studien zur Gleichheitsvorstellung im griechischen Denken*, edd. J. Mau and E. G. Schmidt (Berlin 1964) 1–35; M. Ostwald, *Nomos and the Beginnings of the Athenian Democracy* (Oxford 1969) 96–136; B. Borecky, *Eirene* 9 (1971) 5–24.

[51] *Talanta* 4 (1972) 63–81 (esp. 72–75).

[52] Arist., *Ath. Pol.* 29.3.

[53] Aischin., 3. 183–185. See A. W. Gomme, *CR* 62 (1948) 5–7.

The place where the herms stood, now overlaid by the Athens-Piraeus railway and buildings to the
north of it, attracted the subsequent dedication of comparable monuments, and became known as
the Stoa of the Herms.[54] It may be no coincidence that this was the favourite assembly-place of the
young cavalrymen, the well-to-do *hippeis,* and of the phylarchs who commanded and trained
them. It was to be the starting-point for the ceremonial ride round the Agora prescribed for the
cavalry by Xenophon in the *Hipparchikos.*[55] And Plutarch, who also quotes the Eion epigrams,
adds that permission to set them up, although they nowhere mentioned Kimon's name, seemed to
the people of the time an enormous honour. "Neither Themistokles nor Miltiades had ever met
with such distinction."[56]

From a governing bourgeoisie rooted in *isonomia,* the allies could and did expect treatment on
an equality, ἐπὶ τῷ ἴσῳ, and this is precisely, in so many words, the point made by the Mytilenaeans when they sought alliance with the Peloponnesians in 428. They recall the terms of *hegemonia* which have already been considered – "as long as the Athenians led us on a footing of equality, we followed with enthusiasm."[57] The theme of τὸ ἴσον is several times recalled in the rest of
the very significant Mytilenaean statement. It of course underlay the first assessment of obligations
carried out by Aristeides in the winter of 478/7 – an assessment so renowned for its fairness (which
as a translation often hits more exactly the meaning of ἴσον than the more generally used
rendering "equal") that it was later looked to as *the* reference for a completely just and acceptable
arrangement. We find it agreed to in the Peace of Nikias in 421 on behalf of the cities in Thrace
then still in revolt against Athens.[58] For the Athenian allies of that generation, Aristeides represented a golden age.

What upset this state of affairs, with which all participants were evidently very content, was the
Confederacy's success. This enabled trade to flourish, wealth to come in to Athens, and the people
at large to realise both how essential they were to the operation of the Confederacy's enterprises
and how much there was to be made out of them. Aristotle expresses the development in the
phrase "the city began to acquire extra confidence, and wealth was being amassed; and Aristeides
gave the Athenians repeated advice to take a firm grip on the *hegemonia.*"[59] Aristeides' role is in
fact equivocal both in Aristotle and in Plutarch. In one tradition he was a conservative statesman
and advocate of an aristocratic order, the tradition dominant in Plutarch: but he also appears as the
author of the naval empire and as the instigator of more radical democracy.[60] This duality is the
reflection of the result of the policies he initiated so successfully. The people came to require more
power and more perquisites, and a later generation of politicians came along to support their
claims. This was the fruit of the seeds that Aristeides and Kimon had planted. It was not, we may
judge, a harvest they had either intended or welcomed, but because of it the final reputation of
Aristeides had to carry the kind of question-mark that survives in our record of him.

It was left for the democracy of the Periklean period to betray the high principles of the
beginnings of the Confederacy and the just expectations of the allies. It was the democrats of the
new generation who turned the confederate arms against their fellow-Greeks. Against a city such
as Naxos that had reneged on its obligations, the forces of the organization even in the earlier
period were of course justly employed. But there is no mention of allied contingents in the purely

[54] See H. A. Thompson and R. E. Wycherley, *The Agora of Athens* (*The Athenian Agora* 14 Princeton 1972) 94–96; for the
cavalry assembly there, Athenaios, 9.402f.
[55] 3.2.
[56] Plut., *Cim.* 7.3–8.1.
[57] Thuc., 3.10.4.
[58] Thuc., 5.18.5.
[59] Arist., *Ath. Pol.* 24.
[60] Plut., *Aristeides* 25. Cf. K. von Fritz and E. Kapp, *Aristotle's Constitution of Athens* (New York 1950) 169; J. M. Moore,
Aristotle and Xenophon on Democracy and Oligarchy (Berkeley 1975) 247–248.

private war between Athens and Thasos that Kimon conducted from 465 to 463.[61] Against Aigina and against the Spartans, as soon as the new democracy was well installed, allied troops were called in.[62] The change, observable in Thucydides' brief narrative, is significant. The rest followed — Athenian magistrates in allied cities, garrisons where expedient, requisition of territory for Athenian settlers, the use of Confederacy funds for the beautification of Athens, and (with the end of the war with Persia) the maintenance of the Confederacy, not because the allies willingly and cheerfully followed where the Athenians led, but purely and simply because the Athenians said it was to be maintained and were able to enforce what they said. This was the policy of Perikles, whom many saw as the first of the demagogues: and who, on the evidence, can deny that in so seeing him they had a point?

The recipient of this volume may not find such a conclusion to his taste, and in this he may not be alone. That being so, it may be as well to point to a helpful parallel in more modern history[63] for an organisation that came to develop along democratic lines far from the wishes of its founding fathers, where nevertheless the retrojection of the democratic myth has converted the fathers themselves into fathers of the democracy. It is popularly assumed that the American democracy was born on July 4, 1776, dedicated to, and enabling the fulfilment of, life, liberty and the pursuit of happiness. It may be that the embattled farmers at Concord fifteen months earlier, and those ordinary citizens who fought and died during the following eight years, had some notion that the liberty they defended ought to comprehend government of the people and by the people as well as government for the people. But the framers of the Constitution in 1787 were quite clear that democracy was undesirable in the new republic. Roger Sherman hoped for the people to "have as little to do as may be about the government"; William Livingston remarked that "the people have ever been and ever will be unfit to retain the exercise of power in their own hands."[64] "There is no maxim, in my opinion, which is more liable to be misapplied," wrote James Madison, "than the current one that the interest of the majority is the political standard of right and wrong."[65] The founding fathers believed that government is based on property, and that men without this lack the necessary stake in an orderly society to make reliable citizens. "George Washington, Gouverneur Morris, John Dickinson and James Madison spoke of their anxieties about the urban working class that might arise some time in the future."[66] They indeed regarded "a democratical branch in the constitution" as essential, but by "the people" they intended the yeoman-farming element alone, and their partnership in affairs of state was limited. With time, American political conviction and practice deviated more and more from what we might regard as in essence an anti-democratic position on the part of the founding fathers. "Yet, curiously, their general satisfaction with the Constitution together with their growing nationalism made Americans deeply reverent of the founding generation, with the result that as it grew stronger, this deviation was increasingly overlooked."[67] For the United States, the equivalent of "the revolution of 462/1" was perhaps the

---

[61] Thuc., 1.100.2.

[62] Thuc., 1.105.2; 107.5.

[63] F. W. Walbank, in his presidential address to the Classical Association (*Proc. Class. Assn.* 67 [1970] 13–27), observed (p. 14) that it is unpopular and even thought to be slightly disreputable for a historian to point to modern analogies — an attitude which he very properly rejected and which Malcolm McGregor, together with other sensible scholars, would unhesitatingly join him in rejecting. An ancient historian, by reason of his ignorance and the obscurity of his subject (cf. E. H. Carr, *What is History?* [London 1961] 8–9), must profit from illumination wherever it is to be found. Comparisons must be drawn with due reserve, but it is both foolish and arrogant to disdain them.

[64] Quoted by Richard Hofstadter, *The American Political Tradition* (New York 1948) 4. Cf. G. S. Wood, *The Creation of the American Republic* (Chapel Hill 1970) 488–499.

[65] Madison to James Monroe, 5. October 1786. See M. Beloff, ed., *The Federalist* 17; Sir Denis Brogan, *Politics in America* (New York 1954) 26, note 2.

[66] Hofstadter (above, note 64), 13.

[67] Hofstadter, 14–15.

election to the presidency of Andrew Jackson in 1828, by which time a new generation was viewing things very differently.

There is much here that may illuminate the changing ideas in the Athens of the *pentekontaetia*. It is noteworthy that when Thucydides son of Melesias pressed his opposition to Perikles it was the rights of the allies that provided his main platform.[68] But by then, in 444/3, the change had advanced too far; habit and profit, no less than Perikles' oratory, were too strong, and the Empire had come to be regarded as a necessity. "It may have been wrong to acquire it, but it would certainly be dangerous to let it go"—Perikles was at least frank, if Thucydides the historian reports him correctly.[69] But the sentiment bears no relation to the "spirit of 478," and the Greek world was the poorer for it.[70]

Corpus Christi College,   A. GEOFFREY WOODHEAD
Cambridge

[68] Plut., *Per.* 12.

[69] Thuc., 2.63.2.

[70] It is, as always, a pleasure to record my thanks to Mr. G. T. Griffith for his willingness to read and comment on what I have set down. This paper (see especially note 37) has, like its predecessors over the years, benefited greatly from his advice.

David Joseph McCargar
July 5, 1940 – March 7, 1980

DATE DUE
